EUROPEAN HISTORY
1648-1789

EUROPEAN HISTORY.
1648-1789

By

ROBERT M. RAYNER

LONGMANS, GREEN AND CO
LONDON . NEW YORK . TORONTO

LONGMANS, GREEN AND CO LTD
6 & 7 CLIFFORD STREET LONDON W 1

ALSO AT MELBOURNE AND CAPE TOWN

LONGMANS, GREEN AND CO INC
55 FIFTH AVENUE NEW YORK 3

LONGMANS, GREEN AND CO
215 VICTORIA STREET TORONTO 1

ORIENT LONGMANS LTD
BOMBAY CALCUTTA MADRAS

First published 1949

Printed in Great Britain
SPOTTISWOODE, BALLANTYNE & CO. LTD
London & Colchester

PREFACE

WE are all familiar with Bolingbroke's aphorism that History is Philosophy teaching by Examples. It is none the less true for being trite. All knowledge has value even if its applicability to daily life is not obvious; but this study can be very practical indeed. This is as true of periods comparatively remote as for the last decade, for man has not changed his nature in the 3,000 years or so of recorded time. If some persons, nameless here, had known more history they would have been warned of follies which have cost themselves and their peoples and the rest of us so dear. History is indeed the only road to wisdom for statesmen; and in a democracy we all have to be statesmen, passive if not active.

The capacity to draw on the experience of the race is indeed one of the differences between man and lower animals. To be able to learn from the deeds of previous generations, to draw inspiration from their achievements, encouragement from their successes, and (more frequently, alas) warning from their mistakes: this is an essentially human attribute, and the question how we came to be where and what we are is what gives meaning and interest to the study.

Here then is the point of view from which this book is written. The application of past to present has been sometimes indicated, more often left to the reader's perception. And it does not overlook the vital fact that the personages it deals with were human beings with like passions to ourselves. Too often history text-books seem to deal with figures which differ from algebraical symbols only in having incalculable functions.

At the end will be found a short list of books accessible in any public or school library should the student want to learn more than this necessarily superficial treatment provides. And if he does not want to, then the writer will have failed in his desire to share with others his delight in the "unending adventure" of this most human of studies.

NOTE ON PROPER NAMES

Confusion sometimes arises from the fact that names have different forms in different languages—that Regensburg is the same place as Ratisbon, for instance, and Aachen the same place as Aix-la-Chapelle. The logical alternatives are either to use the language appropriate to the person or place—to follow Carlyle's practice of calling Frederick William "Friedrich Wilhelm" and Pomerania "Pommern"; or to translate all names into their English equivalent—to call Louis "Lewis," like Macaulay. But there is a middle course—to conform to the inconsistencies hallowed by common usage. That is the practice adopted here—with certain exceptions, such as calling Charles II of Spain "Carlos" to distinguish him from his contemporary, our own much merrier monarch.

Of the place-names that occur in this book it should be noted that Trier is the German equivalent of Trêves, Mainz of Mayence, Köln of Cologne.

CONTENTS

MAPS

DIAGRAMS

CHAPTER ONE

THE PEACE OF WESTPHALIA
1648

THE starting-point of this book is the famous set of treaties which ended
a century of wars of religion and laid down the political framework within
which European civilization was to develop for a hundred years and more.
(As late as 1791 Edmund Burke gravely indicted the Jacobins with impious
disregard of its terms.) It crystallized German disunity, it marked the decay
of Hapsburg ascendancy, and it placed France on the threshold of her *Grand
Siècle*.

THE RAMSHACKLE EMPIRE. Hapsburg greatness had begun early
in the sixteenth century with the Emperor Charles V. *Bella gerant alii,
tu felix Austria nube.* Timely marriages and fortunate deaths had
brought an agglomeration of territories under his rule: Spain with her
transoceanic possessions; Milan and Lombardy, and therewith hegemony in Italy; the Burgundian Circle of the Empire, including the
Netherlands and Franche Comté; the Archduchy of Austria with its
dependencies of Istria, Carinthia and the Tyrol; the Kingdoms of
Hungary and Bohemia. Furthermore he was Holy Roman Emperor.

This last position was one of dignity rather than of power. It
made him nominally overlord of Germany; but for historical reasons
beyond our present scope, "Germany" was little more than a geographical term. The German people had no national institutions.
The Emperor had some of the external attributes of monarchy, the
Imperial Diet some of a Parliament; but things were not what they
seemed. The Empire was not held together by any cohesive force,
sentimental or political. The Emperor was chosen, whenever the
position was vacant, by a "College" of seven ruling princes called
Electors. Three of these were dignitaries of the Catholic Church—
the Archbishops of Mainz, Trier and Cologne; the others were laymen
—the Electors of Brandenburg and Saxony, the Elector Palatine, and
the King of Bohemia. In theory the Emperor was the successor of
Charlemagne, the lay head of western Christendom; actually he was
crowned president of a loose federation of miscellaneous states, some
as large as England, others as small as a country parish; some ruled
by churchmen, others by laymen, some of them "Free Cities." Their

rulers met, or were represented, in the Imperial Diet which assembled periodically at Regensburg; but this body had little power, and its members were scarcely conscious of a duty to "Germany." Their main concern was to uphold their individual rights and sovereign status.

Just when Charles V was elected Emperor (1519) a new cause of disunity appeared—the Lutheran Reformation. It began as a revolt against the malpractices and exactions of the Catholic clergy; but princes made it an excuse to loot the vast wealth (especially in the form of land) which the Church had accumulated during long centuries of domination over men's minds and consciences. Charles himself was too much of a Spaniard to be taken with Lutheranism (Spain was the most unshakably Catholic of countries), and he wanted very much to crush it; but he was hindered by one distraction after another— attacks by the Turks, revolts by the Hungarians, above all by the fact that he could not count on the support even of the Catholic princes of the Empire, whose religious zeal was overborne by reluctance to increase the power and prestige of their suzerain. In 1555 he abdicated, a weary and disillusioned man.

His son Philip succeeded to the Spanish monarchy, his brother Ferdinand to the Austrian dominions and to the Imperial Crown. Thus two branches of the Hapsburg family were now ruling in Europe. The new Emperor accepted the fact of religious differences, and made the Peace of Augsburg (1555), the basic principle of which was *cujus regio, ejus religio*: every ruler to fix the religion of his own subjects. For it had scarcely occurred to anybody that a ruler could not claim authority over the faith of his people. Religious unity was assumed to be as essential to a state as political unity.

RELIGIOUS SCHISM. But a new form of Protestantism, as hostile to Lutheranism as to Catholicism, had just appeared. Lutheranism, though it has spread to Scandinavia and to Poland, was a specifically German movement; and after the Peasants' Revolt, when Luther supported the rulers' savage repression of a rebellion inspired by his doctrines, it had become associated with princely power. One of its main attractions in rulers' eyes was that it brought religion under their control. Moreover, even when Luther was led on from protest against Catholic practice to repudiation of Catholic doctrine, his teaching was always based on Catholic foundations. But the spirit of the age called for a more drastic purge of men's ideas—a revolution in their way of looking at life here and hereafter. This was provided by Jean Calvin.

The church of which he set up the archetype at Geneva in 1536 was quite free from state-control. It was ruled not by kings and bishops, but by ministers chosen by, and associated with, laymen; and the chief duty of the "presbytery"—the local committee of ministers and "elders"—was to enforce a rigid moral discipline. Its characteristic tenet of "predestination" made people desperately anxious to avoid sin, since evil-doing might be a sign that they were among the non-elect condemned in advance to an eternity of fire and brimstone.

Calvinism has been one of the great formative influences of our civilization. It carried further Luther's reaction against celibacy, regarding family affairs and responsibilities as part of the full Christian life. Indirectly it promoted economic prosperity, for it encouraged unremitting attention to business, that people might have no time for mischief; it repudiated the ban which the Catholic Church had put upon advancing money at interest, and so helped the growth of modern capitalism; and its cult of austerity left successful merchants and manufacturers with profits to put back into their businesses. Furthermore, its very narrowness and rigidity helped to give Calvinism a toughness of fibre and a fiery zeal which lent it immense "survival value." Its devotees were stark fighters, spiritual and physical. It added something to the Scots and the Dutch that made great nations of them; it inspired the French Huguenots with a spirit that carried them through seven Wars of Religion to win toleration in the Edict of Nantes (1598); and we know well what manner of men it made of the English Puritans and the Pilgrim Fathers.

This new driving-force came just in time to enable Protestantism to resist the Counter-Reformation which assailed it in the latter half of the sixteenth century. The Catholic Church put its house in order at the Council of Trent (1545–63), which ended the worst evils in its practice while refusing all compromise on its essential doctrines. Popes cast off the worldly interests which had corrupted their Renaissance predecessors, and devoted themselves to winning back the lost ground, with the Society of Jesus to preach and teach against heresy, and the Holy Inquisition to root it out. During the next hundred years the Catholic Church recovered its hold over southern Germany, Bohemia, France, Poland and Ireland; but Protestantism held fast in northern Germany, the Scandinavian countries and Great Britain.

THE OPENING OF THE GREAT WAR. One of the most notable results of the Jesuit training was the Emperor Ferdinand II. By his time four-fifths of Germans were Protestants, but he determined to bring them back to the Catholic Church by the exercise of secular power. Even before his accession forces were getting into alignment for the conflict which had been merely postponed by the compromise of Augsburg. The Elector Palatine had formed a Protestant Union, which the Duke of Bavaria countered with a Catholic League.

In 1618 Ferdinand became King of Bohemia. The Bohemians were Slavs who had cut adrift from the Roman Church a century before Luther, and they now responded to persecution by revolt. They denied the Emperor's authority, they "defenestrated"[1] his representatives at Prague, and they chose the Calvinist Elector Palatine (son-in-law of our James I) as King. But the other Protestant princes, being mostly Lutheran, did nothing to support him, and he was overthrown at the Battle of the White Mountain (1620) just outside Prague. Ferdinand now began a systematic Germanization and Catholicization of Bohemia by force. He succeeded in rooting out Czech Protestantism, but not Czech nationalism—which, indeed, has survived other savage blows in our own day. And the Palatinate was overrun by Maximilian of Bavaria, restoring the Rhineland to the Catholic Church.

This was the first stage of a war which devastated central Europe for a generation. It soon ceased to be a struggle between Catholicism and Protestantism; for Calvinists and Lutherans hated each other quite as much as they hated Catholics. And even among the Catholics there were deep rifts. Ferdinand of Austria (with his famous general Wallenstein) and Maximilian of Bavaria (with his famous general Tilly) were cousins, and both were products of Jesuit training; but Maximilian was determined to resist Ferdinand's centralizing policy—he aimed at being an independent ruler. And as time went on Danish, Swedish, Spanish and French troops were all thrown into the war from political rather than religious motives.

And in the north-western corner of the Empire there began almost at the same moment another struggle between Calvinism-cum-Local-Rights and Catholicism-cum-Centralization.

Philip II of Spain had anticipated his Austrian relative Ferdinand as protagonist of the Counter-Reformation. He was deeply shocked to find Calvinism spreading among his subjects in the Netherlands. These seventeen little provinces had once belonged to the Counts of Burgundy. They were practically independent of each other, and cherished charters of self-rule. The southern provinces were mostly engaged in

[1] I.e., threw them out of the window of the Council Chamber.

manufacture, especially of woollen cloth, while the northerners, beginning as fishermen who won their land as well as their living by hard labour from the sea, were now trading up the great rivers and across the ocean. Such self-reliant bourgeois were just the type to take up Calvinism and to resist political subjugation. Persecution only hardened their resistance. The Revolt of the Netherlands, covertly supported by France and England, became a running sore to Spain; and the chance to attack Spanish shipping led to a rapid growth of sea-consciousness among both English and Dutch. The Revolt was directed by a Prince of the Empire with great possessions in the Low Countries—William of Orange, known (rather oddly, for he had plenty to say for himself) as "The Silent."

After his assassination in 1584 at the instigation of Philip II, the leadership fell to his son Maurice of Nassau, who proved himself a soldier of genius. Philip died in 1598, puzzled at the inscrutable ways of Providence. Protestantism, after his lifetime of war on it, was stronger than ever in England and the Netherlands, and had gained a firm foothold in France. Worst of all, his crusades had eaten away the strength of Spain, leaving a load of debt under which, after staggering along for another half-century, she collapsed.

He left the Netherlands as a separate appanage to a distant relative; but this relative was dependent on military support from Spain, which Spain could not afford. In 1609 a twelve years' truce was made, by which the independence of the seven northern provinces was recognized de facto, the ten southern returning to their Spanish allegiance. When the truce came to an end in 1621, the seven United Provinces renewed their struggle for independence.

RICHELIEU STRIKES IN. That the Thirty Years' War ceased to be a specifically religious conflict was largely due to Cardinal Richelieu. He was one of the chief architects of the modern world, for he not only built up the centralized monarchy of France but perpetuated the religious schism of Europe. Even when he repressed the Huguenots it was not because they were Protestant but because they formed an imperium in imperio incompatible with the unity of the state; and in taking away their political privileges he left their religious privileges untouched. He took even sterner measures against the great Catholic nobles who made common cause with foreign foes in defence of their feudal independence.

These foreign foes of France were the Hapsburgs. Rivalry between the monarchies of France and Spain dated back to the French invasion of Spanish Italy in 1494. Now that Hapsburgs were Emperors as well as Kings of Spain, France was threatened with encirclement; for the Netherlands, Franche Comté and northern Italy all belonged to Spain, while Lorraine and Savoy were ruled by clients of the Emperor. It was therefore with some anxiety that Richelieu saw the Imperial forces so sweepingly successful in the opening phase of the Thirty Years' War. But he soon realized that the French army was in no shape to strike into the great melée with success; and while he was building it up he had to find allies to do his fighting for him. Gustavus Adolphus, the warrior-king of Sweden, accepted a French subsidy to march against the Imperial army advancing towards the Baltic. He fended off the Counter-Reformation from Germany by a daring incursion into Catholic Germany. His innovations in military science—in discipline, weapons, equipment, strategy and tactics—swept all before them. He pulverized the Imperialists at Breitenfeld (1631), invaded Bavaria, and overran the Palatinate. It was a dramatic reversal of fortune— Vienna complained that God had suddenly turned Lutheran. But the Swedish triumphs ended as suddenly as they had begun, with the death of Gustavus Adolphus in the following year at the battle of Lützen. The Swedish army remained in Germany, but it now lacked the magnetic personality of its great leader and was defeated at Nordlingen (1634). The Peace of Prague left the religious situation very much as it had been at the beginning of the War; but two political issues had yet to be decided—Bavaria still held the Palatinate, and Spain still refused to recognize Dutch independence. France was deeply concerned in the result of both struggles; for if the Catholic Hapsburg Powers were successful they would be established all along her eastern and north-eastern frontier, which ran dangerously close to her capital. And so the Cardinal, having by this time subdued the nobles and the Huguenots and reformed the army, declared war—on Spain in 1635 and on the Emperor three years later. But his new army, though commanded by Condé and Turenne, the famous pupils of Gustavus Adolphus, did not make good until after his death. Then, in 1643, Condé shattered at Rocroi the reputation for invincibility so long enjoyed by the Spanish infantry, and went on to master Alsace. And when, some years later, Turenne, joining forces with the Swedes under Wrangel, devastated Bavaria and threatened Vienna, the Emperor had to come to terms.

Thus ended the Counter-Reformation in Germany, and the prospect of German national unity under the Hapsburgs.

THE FIRST PEACE CONFERENCE. Discussions on terms had been going on since 1641 at two towns in Westphalia—Münster and Osnabrück. But they had been delayed by disputes about procedure; for this was the first great international conference ever held, and there were no settled conventions of diplomacy. The fact that it had to meet in two different towns, for instance, was due to the fact that Sweden would not admit the claims of France to precedence. It was, perhaps, significant that the treaty was the last to be drawn up in Latin, for it marked the end of the Church-and-Empire ideas of the Middle Ages.

Perhaps the delegates would have got down to business more urgently if they had had the same need for a quick peace as the wretched folk of central Europe. It is doubtful if people at any time—even in the war of 1939–45—have suffered more fearfully from the ravages of war. The troops mostly depended on pillage for a living; and the devastation of a countryside—the deliberate destruction of people, buildings and crops —became a regular operation of war, designed to deprive the enemy of subsistence, or to provoke him to combat, or as retaliation for some atrocity he had committed elsewhere. Before long the peasants refused to grow crops they had little hope of reaping, traders would not transport goods unlikely to reach their destination. Millions died of starvation, millions more of the pestilences which result from under-nourishment. By the end of the war the population of the Empire was reduced certainly by more than half, possibly by two-thirds—in Bohemia by three-fourths. Stains from the iron which then entered the soul of the German people have lasted right down to our own day.

Naturally, the chief gainers by the Treaty of Westphalia were France and Sweden. France acquired by legal right three bishoprics which had long been in her possession for all practical purposes—Metz, Toul and Verdun. The Emperor also ceded her "all his rights" over the ten towns of Alsace—Landau, Weissenburg, etc.—together with the territories dependent on them. The vague wording of this clause led thirty years later to further complications, as we shall see. Meanwhile it should be noted that "Alsace" was not the name of a province but of a district, like "Westphalia" or "The Black Country"; also that its most important city, Strassburg, ruled by a bishop who was ex officio "Landgrave of Lower Alsace," was not included in the cession. Sweden gained all that Gustavus Adolphus had entered the war to get—Western Pomerania, Stettin, and the Bremen-Verden Bishoprics. Of the princes of the Empire, the Duke of Bavaria retained the Upper Palatinate with the rank of Elector; the Lower Palatinate was restored to the family which had been dispossessed at the start of the war, with a newly-created Electorate; Saxony acquired Lusatia; and Brandenburg, being called on to cede Western Pomerania to Sweden, was compensated with Jülich and the Bishoprics of Minden, Halberstadt and Magdeburg. (Brandenburg owed these handsome concessions to France's desire to see a strong state set up in north Germany as a counterpoise to Hapsburg Austria.)

By the Treaty of Münster, concluded the same year between Spain and the Dutch Republic, Spain recognized, finally and unreservedly, the independence of "The United Netherlands."

One dispute remained unsettled: France and Spain were still locked in mortal strife, and so continued for another decade.

As to religion, prime cause of all the bloodshed and misery, the result was a compromise. German Protestantism was preserved in the north, but the Catholic Church recovered the south. All lands taken from the Church before 1624 were to continue in lay hands. (That is why for the next two centuries we find German bishoprics held by Protestant princes.) The Augsburg principle was extended to Calvinist rulers: there was to be religious freedom for them, but not for their subjects.

The centralizing aim of the Hapsburg Monarchy was defeated even more decisively than its Catholicizing aim. Ferdinand II had begun the war with an idea of restoring a Catholic Empire with real authority over all central Europe; but the result of the fighting was to put his son, who succeeded him as Ferdinand III in 1637, in a weaker position than ever. For thirty years of anarchy had given boundless opportunity for the staking out of claims, and subdivision was now carried to fantastic lengths. The Treaty of Westphalia splintered Germany into 343 sovereign states—158 under secular rulers, 123 under ecclesiastics, and 62 Free Cities. The Imperial Diet, which usually met at Regensburg, consisted of three Colleges, the eight electors in one, the reigning princes in another and the representatives of the Cities in the third. But it was more like a United Nations Assembly than a Parliament. It discussed such matters as the making of war and peace, the raising and billeting of troops, the contributions of each member towards expenses, but had only the clumsiest and rustiest of machinery to carry its decisions into effect. And there was a crazy contraption of Imperial Councils and Imperial Courts which clanked on year after year without producing any results worth mentioning. The Treaty left each member free to make his own arrangements for security, and to conduct his own "foreign policy"—provided only (it proved an illusory limitation) that this was not directed against the Emperor.

Henceforth the Austrian Hapsburgs gave their attention more to their hereditary domains than to their Imperial functions, and these domains were preponderantly non-German (i.e. Czech and Magyar).

The effects of the Thirty Years' War—the impoverishment and thinning out of the German people, the debasement of their minds and hearts, the multiplicity of their internal frontiers—left a clear field to be exploited by France, if she should find a ruler capable of taking advantage of it.

CHAPTER TWO

THE SEA POWERS

1648 – 1653

BRITAIN and the United Netherlands had affinities in geography, race and speech. When, forty years later, they were linked together for a time under one ruler, it was but the culmination of a century and a half of parallel development, as Protestant, parliamentary and maritime nations in a predominantly Catholic, monarchical and military Europe. In this chapter we shall see how they simultaneously threw off attempts to establish authoritarian rule, and became oligarchical republics.

THE SWORD OF GIDEON. Though England had taken practically no part in the Thirty Years' War, this was not for lack of national partizanship. Indeed the conflict was one of the very few issues of the day on which throne and people were agreed. For circumstances, varied and persistent, had made the nation aggressively Protestant; and the Elector Palatine, whose Protestantism was the immediate cause of the war, was a member by marriage of the Anglo-Scottish royal family. But almost throughout those thirty years the attention of the British had been centred on domestic conflicts which only reached their tragic *dénouement* when the Westphalian Peace was bringing the great continental war to an end.

The issues were too interwoven to be reducible to any simple formula. In a way they began with a question whether our legal system is based on Roman Law, issuing from the Prince's will, or from a Common Law with an existence independent of personal sovereignty. With this was bound up the constitutional position of Parliament, particularly its claim to control government through the power of the purse. A challenge to Monarchy had been gathering subterraneously even under the "Tudor dictatorship," with the growth of an influential class of "parliament-men." And as this class owed much of its importance to the spoliation of the old Church, it had everything to lose by a Catholic reaction. The drift towards uncompromising Protestantism was intensified in the middle classes by that association of commerce with Calvinism which we have already noticed (p. 3). James I's refusal to modify the doctrine and practice of the national Church to "comprehend" these Puritans had driven them into schism. Archbishop Laud had harried thousands of them overseas, with the unforeseen result that a vast new living-space was established for Anglo-Saxon Puritanism in North America. But the Puritan spirit throve at home in Britain, too. Charles I might have succeeded in his attempt to govern without Parliament had he not also tried to force the national Church into an Anglo-Catholic mould. The disputes with the Scots that led to the summoning of the Long Parliament are known as "The Bishops Wars," but the name would be equally appropriate for the Great Rebellion which followed. For on political issues the Parliamentary oligarchy was almost unanimous: scarcely a voice was raised against the famous Acts which ensured that Parliament should be an integral part of governmental machinery. When the split came it was over the extent to which the anti-Catholic reaction should be pushed. To some the Episcopal Church was the vessel of Apostolical sanctity which needed merely to be purified from corrupt practices, but to others it was little better than the Scarlet Woman of Rome. This was the main issue fought out in the five campaigns of the Civil War; and the deciding factor therein was the alliance of Puritanism with the London merchants who alone could provide the cost of a long war.

There followed a struggle between two types of this Puritanism. Parliament, under contract to the Scots to replace the Episcopal Church with one on a presbyterian model, was confronted by the Frankenstein monster it had created to fight its battles—the New Model Army, which wanted independent local churches, and hated a presbyterian state-church almost as much as an episcopalian.

Down to 1648 the idea of abolishing monarchy had not occurred to anybody except a few wild extremists. Cromwell and Ireton had made Proposals which would have given it a fresh lease of life; but Charles I would not accept any form of it in which he was not the sole fount of authority, both in Church and State. By the end of that year the Gordian knot had been pulled so tight by the militant fanaticism of the Army, the factious opportunism of the Parliament, and the perverse trickiness of the King, that it had to be cut by the headsman's axe (1649). As afterwards in the American, the French, and the Russian revolutions, opposition to the acts of a mode of government had developed under the stress of circumstances into an assault upon its essential principle.

The King's execution was a greater misfortune for his enemies' cause than for his own. It hallowed Anglican Kingship with the blood of a martyr, and it confronted the shedders of that blood with an insoluble problem—how to provide a workable substitute for the monarchy they had destroyed. They set up a sort of Puritan fascism—the rule of that

very narrow oligarchy, the Godly. There followed an unhappy decade
for the British people—albeit in a military sense a glorious one. For
good people are often hard to get on with, and good people wielding
absolute power are apt to be insufferable.

THE DUTCH REPUBLIC.   Across the North Sea the Dutch were
bringing a parallel struggle to a head at this time. The period of
their War of Independence had been one of sensational expansion,
economic and spiritual. Their geographical position, with a network of
waterways and the teeming hinterland of Germany, enabled their merchants to inherit the trade which had once belonged to Venice and
Genoa ; and as Portugal was under the rule of Spain, the war gave them
an excuse to conquer Portuguese possessions in Asia (Java and Sumatra),
and America (Brazil). Their East India Company, founded at the same
time as its English counterpart, was by the middle of the century twenty
times as rich. Dutch shipping carried three-fourths of the produce of
the world, and half the world's ocean-going vessels were built at
Saardam. Amsterdam became the central money-market of Europe,
with fabulous reserves of gold in its famous vaults.

And this material development was accompanied by an equally remarkable outpouring of the spirit. Lipsius and Scaliger the scholars,
Swammerdam the physicist, Arminius the theologian, Huyghens the
mathematician, Grotius the jurist, were among the famous alumni of
Leyden University in the first century of its existence. Descartes and
Spinoza, the greatest of seventeenth-century philosophers, were not
Dutchmen, but it was only among Dutchmen that they could find an
atmosphere liberal and enlightened enough for their speculations. Half-
a-dozen independent Dutch newspapers were published at a time when
no other country had more than a meagre official gazette. Cats and
Vondel were among the most distinguished poets of their age in Europe.
But it was in painting that the Dutch spirit found its fullest expression.
This was not a case of a few great artists working for wealthy patrons.
Pictures were a national passion: scores of able painters were making
pictures and selling them to cultured burghers. Vermeer, Hals,
Hobbema, Ruysdael, Van der Helst—the list is endless, apart from the
mighty Rembrandt. The "Dutch School" had its limitations, but it was
a very definite stage in the development of European art.

Equally characteristic was the energy and resource with which the
Dutch tackled the engineering problems set by their need for locks and
sluices and pumping-mills to control the seas and rivers which were
always threatening to engulf their land.

The constitution of the United Netherlands, like our own, was an organism which had grown up spontaneously, under the pressure of circumstance. Two forces worked in it, the burgher-oligarchy of merchants, and the monarchical "stadtholderate." Stadtholders had formerly been satraps appointed by the King of Spain, but since the Revolt they were appointed by the "Estates" of the several Provinces. The federation as a whole had States General which met at The Hague, the capital of Holland.

The States appointed a Captain-General to command the armed forces of the Republic. This position had always been held by a prince of the House of Orange: first William the Silent, then his son Maurice, then a much younger son, Frederick Henry; and the fact that these princes were also appointed stadtholder by Holland and most of the other Provinces enabled them to combine the civil and military administration of the Republic. Nevertheless their position was anomalous. Sovereign power was vested not in them but in the Town Councils which sent delegations to the Provincial Estates, which in turn sent delegations to the States General. These Town Councils were corporations recruited mainly from the well-to-do burgher families. Each town employed a paid official called a "pensionary" who acted as spokesman for its delegation in the estates of the Province; and the Estates of each Province employed a similar functionary for their delegation to the States General. Of the seven Provinces by far the most important was Holland, wherein were situated not only the seat of government, but ten of the twelve largest towns of the Republic. One of these, Amsterdam, had a greater population and contributed more to the federal revenue than any of the lesser Provinces. The Estates of Holland met in the same building as the States General, and their deliberations were often of greater moment. Consequently their pensionary became a sort of unofficial Prime Minister to the Republic.

The struggle with Spain, renewed in 1621 (p. 5), had so stressed the need for unity and national defence that Frederick Henry of Orange was able to build up a semi-royal status. One of his greatest achievements in this direction was the marriage of his son and heir to the Princess Royal of England (1642). To be sure, the turn of events in the Civil War made the Stuarts very "poor relations" for the time being; still, the royal blood of Stuart and Bourbon would henceforth flow in Orange veins.

OLIGARCHY TRIUMPHANT. When Frederick Henry died (1647) the Peace of Münster (1648) closed to his successor, the young Prince

William II, the fields in which his family had won power and glory. Determined not to sink back into holding a mere primacy among Dutch nobles, he entered on secret negotiations with Cardinal Mazarin (Richelieu's successor) to renew the Spanish war with the aid of French money. Then the cleavage between the factions—the burgher-oligarchs who held the purse-strings on the one hand, and on the other the nobles, clergy and populace who were jealous of them—suddenly became manifest. For the Estates of Holland decreed that, in view of the Peace, the troops which they supported should be reduced by two-thirds. This would nullify all the plans of the ambitious and impetuous young Stadtholder. He rode round from town to town at the head of his partizans, trying to bully the Councils into withdrawing their decision. When this failed he suddenly arrested the leaders of the opposition, and attempted to master Amsterdam by force. This failed too; but the Estates thought discretion the better part of valour and agreed to most of the Prince's demands. He was preparing to enjoy the fruits of this victory when he suddenly died of smallpox.

At a stroke the whole position was reversed. William II had no brothers, and his only son was born a fortnight after his death. For the next twenty years the partizans of Orange would have no leader, and a monarchical party is helpless without a monarch. The burghers of Holland exploited their good luck to the full. They invited the Provinces to send delegates to a "Great Assembly" to decide what changes in the constitution were needed in view of the virtual breakdown of the Orange succession. It was finally agreed that the post of Captain-General should lapse, the prerogatives of the Stadtholder falling back into the hands of the provincial Estates. When the Assembly broke up it had medals struck commemorating the overthrow of Orange "tyranny."

THE FIRST ANGLO-DUTCH WAR. Thus by the middle of the century each of the Sea Powers had taken a decidedly republican complexion. We should have expected the two victorious oligarchies to co-operate; yet within a year or two we find them at war. How did this come about?

This Anglo-Dutch war, and the two others that followed it at short intervals, were like quarrels between relatives who fall out through similarity of family traits. The English and the Dutch East India Companies had from the first been bitter rivals. The Dutch Company had driven its competitor from the East Indian archipelago by the ruthless "Amboyna Massacre" (1623); and as in those days merchantmen had to provide for their own safety, "incidents" were constantly occuring between English and Dutch sailors in the harbours of the world. Then again, one of the foundations of Dutch prosperity was its fishing-fleet, and the sight of Dutch smacks working in British waters was a perpetual annoyance. Lastly, England had long demanded that Dutch shipmasters should acknowledge her sea-supremacy by dipping topsails to her vessels in the Narrow Seas.

Hitherto the English government had never been in a position to take up these various grievances; but the Commonwealth was aggressively nationalist, its "New Model" was the finest army in the world, and it was now creating an equally formidable navy. Its Admiral Blake, after winning fame as a soldier in the Civil War, was now placing his name alongside those of Drake and Hawkins.

The Council of the Commonwealth, grieved to see ill-wind growing between the two Protestant republics, sent over commissioners to urge that they should join in "one state, one government, one church." But the States General feared that the Netherlands would lose their identity in that of a predominant partner, and Orange mobs pelted the "regicide" envoys in the streets with mud and cries of "Assassins!" When they returned with nothing but diplomatic rebuffs and personal affronts, Parliament clinched the commercial rivalry with a Navigation Act (1651) which forbade the importing of foreign goods in any but British ships or those of the country of origin. This was a deadly blow to the Dutch carrying-trade. Protests only led to renewed wrangling, and when naval squadrons under Blake and Tromp made contact off the Thames estuary, the guns went off of themselves.

In the terrific sea-battles which followed, the Dutch, man for man and ship for ship, fully held their own; but the lack of a central authority to co-ordinate their supply-services was a severe handicap to them, and an even greater drawback was their geographical position. For Britain lay right athwart their sea-route to the outer world. The whole eighty years of their war with Spain did them less economic harm than as many months of war with Britain. Their fisheries were obliterated, their harbours choked with idle shipping. Thousands of families were ruined. The treasury was empty and could not be replenished owing to the decline in taxable wealth.

THE GREAT PENSIONARY. It was at this nadir of the national fortunes that the most famous of Dutch statesmen emerged. John de Witt (1625–72) was a good example of the enlightened Dutch burgher. His family had for years provided his native Dordrecht with council-lors and burgomasters. A graduate in Law at Leyden, his hobbies were mathematics and philosophy, though he was not too "superior" to enjoy music and dancing. His main interest, however, was in politics. A persuasive speaker, he got on well with all sorts and conditions of men; but he staunchly upheld the supremacy of his class, on the grounds that "people who have created wealth alone know how to use it." He was no more than twenty-five years of age when his fellow-townsmen made him their pensionary; and in that position he made such a mark that within three years he was made Grand Pensionary of Holland (1653). With the stadtholderate in abeyance this office made him acting head of the federal government, especially in its relations with foreign Powers. Yet he always kept a republican simplicity of manners, walking through the streets of The Hague followed by a single servant carrying in a baize bag the documents on which the fate of nations depended.

Naturally his first task was to make peace on the best terms procurable. England was ready to listen, for Cromwell, now Lord Protector, cherished a scheme for a League of Protestant States, and feared lest a continuation of the war might rehabilitate the Orange-Stuart family. Nevertheless, his demands were severe: the Dutch were to pay for fishing rights, to give compensation for the Amboyna Massacre, and to expel the Stuart refugees. These conditions the States General accepted without demur; but the Protector went on to require an undertaking that the House of Orange should be for ever excluded from office in the Republic. Of course this would be highly agreeable to de Witt and his friends of the dominant party, but it would be very difficult to win the consent of the Provinces where the Orange interest was strong; and by the constitution unanimity was required for the ratification of treaties. When de Witt, having put the States under an oath of secrecy, gained a bare majority of votes for an "Act of Seclusion," he sent a copy to the plenipotentiaries in London, urging them to hold it back if there was any chance of getting Cromwell to make peace without it. But the secret leaked out through the dishonesty of a clerk, and the Orange faction made such an outcry that the States ordered the envoys to return the document at once. De Witt's resources were not exhausted, however. He sent the States' instruction in cypher, with a covering letter from himself *en clair*, asking the envoys to return the paper "*if still in their possession.*" The envoys, who were his personal friends, read between his lines. While the official message was being decoded they called on the Lord Protector, delivered the "Act of Seclusion," and initialed the Treaty (1654).

Thus peace between the Puritan Republics was coupled with a step designed to hinder any revival of the monarchist element in either of them.

CHAPTER THREE

THE TRIUMPHS OF MAZARIN

1648–1661

AT our opening date Louis XIV though but ten years old had been King of France for five years. His mother was nominally regent, but the government was really in the hands of Cardinal Mazarin, who had succeeded to the position and policy of Richelieu. In 1648 by the Peace of Westphalia he crippled the Empire, in 1659 by the Peace of the Pyrenees he established French ascendancy over Spain; and between these dates he completed the overthrow of internal opposition to the centralized monarchy.

CARDINAL II. The Treaty of Westphalia, by crystallizing the jumble of discordant elements in Germany, left France free to concentrate on her long struggle with Spain. But it came only just in time; for even while the Treaty was in the making a series of internal convulsions began which threatened to shake the body politic to pieces.

The prime cause of these convulsions was hatred of Mazarin, the Italian cleric who had gained high office under Richelieu by talents for diplomacy, and had succeeded to his place by the favour of the Queen-Mother, known to history as "Anne of Austria."[1] Richelieu had aimed at national unity under an all-powerful monarchy and its ministers, by suppressing the local authority of territorial *seigneurs* and of such bodies as *parlements* and Town Councils. Naturally these classes had resented the draining off of their traditional powers to swell those of a prime minister with a satellite bureaucracy. Under Richelieu this animosity had been kept in check by the hand of a great creative statesman, but Mazarin was a person of altogether inferior metal, though a very adroit politician; and whereas Richelieu had been a French aristocrat, Mazarin was an Italian adventurer.

When at last this festering hatred came to a head it was (as so often in such cases) through a financial crisis. Richelieu had had little interest or capacity in fiscal matters; Mazarin had less. The government of France was suffering, like every other in Europe, from the decreasing purchasing-power of the revenue with which it had to perform

---

[1] She was really Spanish; her title betokens the intimate connection between the two branches of the Hapsburg family. It is almost certain that she was secretly married to Mazarin, who had contrived to become a cardinal without taking the vow of celibacy.

increasing functions. It could not make ends meet even in peace
time, yet was constantly at war. So many people were exempt from
taxation, so many evaded it, so many preyed on it, that income fell far
short of expenditure, year after year. Money had to be borrowed at
10, 12, 15 per cent., and the government was at the mercy of the *rentiers*
who lent it the wherewithal to carry on from week to week. How much
of the revenue went in the service of these debts can never be known,
for there was no systematic book-keeping at the Treasury; but it was
certainly a fifth, possibly as much as a third. The Cardinal was not the
man to promote a strict audit, for he himself peculated on a princely
scale. At his death he left vast fortunes to three nieces, and still had
enough to establish two of the wealthiest educational foundations in
Paris.

THE PARLEMENTARY FRONDE. At last (April 1648) the Parlement
of Paris threw down a challenge by refusing to register one of Mazarin's
financial decrees.

Here let us note that these *Parlements* resembled the English Parliament in little more than name. Both sprang from similar medieval
origins—the King in consultation with his chief subjects; but whereas
in England the barons and knights and burgesses had maintained their
right to be consulted, in France it was the lawyers who had done so.
The Parlements (there were eleven altogether, but that of Paris was
by far the most important) were legal corporations something like our
Inns of Court. Membership was bought from the Crown, and might
become hereditary. As the Parlements had to administer the law they
had to know it: royal decrees were not valid until placed on their
register. They could protest against a decree, but if they persisted in
opposition the King could come in person to what was called a *lit de
justice* and command the registration. Thus the Parlements were in no
sense representative of the nation; but in the abeyance of the States
General (the elective assembly of nobles, clergy and bourgeois which
had not met since 1614 and did not meet again until 1789) they were as
near to an outlet for public opinion as France could get. Their resistance at this juncture was stimulated by what was going on in England;
but the struggle was but a travesty of our Civil War. For a few months
the Parlement of Paris had the support of the bourgeoisie (from which
it was mainly recruited), and of the populace, the two classes who
suffered through the fiscal malpractices of the Cardinal; but after the
first few months all trace of principle evaporated.

The four Chambers of the Parlement appointed a committee which met in the Chamber of St. Louis to draw up a scheme of reforms. One of these forbade the creation of any more offices for sale; another reduced the *taille*, the poll-tax which bore so heavily on the poor; a third required that new taxes should be sanctioned by Parlement; a fourth forbade imprisonment without trial. These "Propositions of St. Louis" were germs of constitutional liberty such as was even now being evolved in Britain; but in France they never had a chance to develop. While the Queen and the Cardinal were still hesitating whether to accept the reforms news came of a great victory of Condé over the Spaniards at Lens (August 1648), and they took advantage of the rejoicing to attempt a counter-stroke by arresting some of the Parlementary leaders. At this public indignation frothed up in revolt. At first the Queen-Mother tried to take a high hand, and when Paul de Gondi, Coadjutor-Archbishop of Paris[1] came to the Palace to plead on behalf of the prisoners, she drove him away with contumely. Thereupon this scheming, ambitious cleric took up leadership of the Paris mob. Hostile crowds clamoured outside the Palace, and the city militia refused to disperse them. News of events across the Channel did not encourage resistance. The Queen had to release the prisoners, who were fêted with hilarious enthusiasm.

But Anne was only biding her time. As soon as Condé returned from the front she invited him to bring troops and reduce Paris to obedience, while she and Mazarin took the young King to St. Germains (January 1649). But the threatened city now found allies in an unexpected quarter. The Princes of the Blood, who had long been chafing against the new régime, came flocking in with their supporters to put themselves at the head of the *frondeurs*,[2] in the hope that the disturbances would lead to a return of the good old days when they were lords of creation. Notable figures among them were the Prince de Conti, younger brother of the great Condé, with most of his egotism but none of his military talent, and their sister the flaxen-haired Duchesse de Longueville, with her passion for intrigue. These and their friends Beaufort, Bouillon, Madame de Montpensier, and La Rochefoucauld, seem to walk straight out of the pages of Dumas.

But the Parlement was ashamed of being associated with the unruly rabble of the streets, and with the self-seeking princes who were plotting

[1] A coadjutor was assistant and presumptive successor to a prelate. This Gondi afterwards became famous as the "Cardinal de Retz," one of the best-known letter-writers of the period.
[2] The word *fronde* means "sling." The allusion was probably to stone-slinging mimic combats of the *gamins* of Paris in the old moats round the city.

to get support from Spain, with whom France was at war; and it made terms with the Court by which most of the "Propositions of St. Louis" were confirmed. (Treaty of Reuil, March 1649.)

THE FRONDE OF THE PRINCES. The Court returned to Paris, and all was quiet, outwardly, for the rest of 1649. But beneath the surface there were constant intrigues and quarrels. The centre of the trouble was the ebullient personality of Condé, victor of Rocroi and Lens while still under thirty. Arrogant and egotistical, he wanted to lord it over everybody and everything, and was particularly aggrieved that "Monsieur"[1] should take precedence of him at the Court. At last the Regent could stand it no longer: she suddenly had him and his brother arrested and imprisoned at Vincennes (January 1650). It was a great mistake, for Parlements, populace and Princes now coalesced again with a twofold rallying-cry: the release of the prisoners and the dismissal of Mazarin. The Governors of several provinces raised revolts; Turenne himself led a Spanish army into France. It seemed as if France was going to suffer the fate of Germany. In February 1651 the Court gave way. The Princes were released and Mazarin retired to Brühl—where, however, he continued to conduct the government by correspondence. There was frantic rejoicing at his overthrow; his house was raided and a bonfire made of his belongings.

Still, he was not unduly depressed, for he foresaw that his enemies would not long hold together. Condé's new allies found him as insufferable as the Court had, for he despised lawyers and loathed the *canaille*. Leaving Paris in a huff, he took service under the King of Spain, whose armies he led against those of France for the next seven years. Now that Mazarin was banished, Turenne returned to his allegiance, and a civil war began between two generals who had hitherto been colleagues. For the nobles it was a comic-opera affair of waving plumes and prancing chargers; but the wretched peasantry who saw their crops ridden down, their homes burned and their goods stolen, had a taste of what the German people had suffered in the Thirty Years' War. And there could no longer be any pretence of fighting for constitutional principles: this second Fronde was undisguisedly the struggle of a territorial aristocracy to maintain prescriptive rights to misgovern.

The high light of the war came when Condé and Turenne met outside

---

[1] "Monsieur" was the Duke of Orleans. This was the title traditionally held by eldest brothers of Kings of France, just as the second sons of our own Kings are traditionally Dukes of York. The Duke of Orleans' eldest daughter was called "Mademoiselle." The King's eldest son, the Dauphin, was "Monseigneur." Condé belonged to a collateral branch of the royal family.

the walls of Paris in the Faubourg St. Antoine (July 1652). Condé's force was threatened with destruction, when the guns of the Bastille opened fire on the Royalists. The city gates were opened to admit the fugitives and closed against their pursuers. This *coup de théâtre* was the work of "Mademoiselle," who was burning to play a greater part in the government than she would be able to do under Mazarin and the Queen. For the next few months Condé was master of Paris, while high-born ladies made the Hôtel de Ville the centre of a web of intrigue. But Paris soon became disgusted with them and their kind, and a great revulsion of feeling became evident, not only there but all over France. Loyalty to the throne was deeply rooted in the soul of the nation; and the young King, who had lately been declared of age, displayed a gracious gravity that made him a fit object of royalist sentiment. Ready as most Frenchmen were to fight against the Cardinal, very few were willing to fight against their lawful king.

Mazarin had sidled back to the Court as soon as it seemed safe; but he now tactfully withdrew once more, to give Paris a chance to return to its allegiance to the King without compromising its hostility to himself. This move was immediately effective. The storms of faction and revolt abated, and a few weeks later the young King with his mother and his Court returned to Paris in triumph (October 1652).

An amnesty (with certain exceptions) was given to the *frondeurs*, but the "Propositions of St. Louis" were sunk without trace. Constitutionalism, the partition of political power, had not struck deep roots in France as in England; nobody troubled any more about it for a long time to come. Parlements ceased to interfere in politics. The young King may or may not have cut short one of their addresses with his famous aphorism about being himself the State; [1] but the words sum up the point of view which was crystallizing in his adolescent mind. He never forgot how he and his mother had fled in the night from factious nobles, nor how the people had acclaimed the restoration of royal authority as ending the troubles that were devastating the land. The nobles themselves, lacking the traditions of public service which animated their class in England, soon became reconciled to a régime which gave them unlimited pride and splendour without the cares and duties of government.

MAZARIN AND CROMWELL. Mazarin now enjoyed the prestige of having saved the monarchy, and with it the nation, from deadly peril.

---

[1] It does not ring true. Louis was too shy, too polite, and too slow-witted to have made such a remark—especially in these youthful days.

The Queen Mother slipped into the background, the King long kept the diffidence of boyhood, and the Cardinal's power was unchecked for the rest of his life. He accumulated vast wealth, splendid palaces, priceless works of art, a magnificent library. He transacted state business *en roi*, while his barber trimmed his beard and great functionaries stood obsequiously around.

His ultimate purpose in foreign affairs was to ensure the ascendancy of France over the two branches of the House of Hapsburg. So far as the Emperor was concerned, he had made a good start with the Treaty of Westphalia; but he had made one oversight therein. He had insisted on the Alsatian fiefs being granted to the French crown in full sovereignty (p. 7). If only he had let the King become a vassal of the Empire for there he would have had direct representation in the Imperial Diet; and once within that sacred circle there was no knowing what French money and influence might gain. Possibly the Imperial crown itself ! But the Emperor saw this possibility too, and took good care to keep such a disturbing influence away from Regensburg.

So by way of substitute the Cardinal encouraged the formation of a "League of the Rhine," to impose collective security on western Germany in view of the recent slackening of Imperial ties. The original members were the ecclesiastical Electors, and the League's head-quarters were at Frankfort. France and Sweden both joined it in 1658.[1] Obviously this organization would tend to rob the Emperor of what little authority he still possessed in Western Germany.

As for Spain, the Cardinal's first business of course was to win the war, a task made more difficult by the defection of Condé. It led him into a surprising alliance with the regicide Republic of Britain. The grim Puritan Cromwell and the feline Cardinal Mazarin made an odd partnership, but each had good reason for entering on it. Mazarin was even less religious in outlook than Richelieu had been; and he had no interest in promoting the principle of monarchy in any country but France. The armed forces of the Protectorate were the most formidable in Europe, and it was obvious that if he did not gain their support for France, Spain might get it. As for Cromwell, he had started with a vision of a great Protestant League to challenge the militant Catholicism which had lately been manifested in the Duke of Savoy's persecution of the Waldenses.[2] But this fell through, for de Witt clung to the tradi-

---

[1] Sweden joined because her King, Charles X, was Count of Zweibrücken. (See later, p. 28.)
[2]   "Avenge, O Lord, thy slaughter'd saints, whose bones
         Lie scatter'd on the Alpine mountains cold!"

tional Franco-Dutch alliance, and the interests of Charles X of Sweden were confined to the Baltic. So that notion faded from Oliver's mind, and his attention was directed to the Franco-Spanish struggle. Some people say that he ought to have preserved the balance of power by propping up declining Spain instead of accelerating the preponderance of France. But the decline of Spain was nothing like so visible to contemporaries as it is to modern historians; on the map she was still by far the greatest Power in the world. And Cromwell was biassed against her by the fact that she was undoubtedly the most Catholic, with an Inquisition of her own, and no Edict of Nantes. Moreover she maintained a policy of rigidly excluding foreigners—especially Protestant foreigners—from any share in the trade of her overseas dominions. The Spanish government offered to ban the Stuarts and to help Cromwell to make himself king; but when he asked for free trade with the West Indies and exemption of British subjects from the Spanish Inquisition, Philip IV's minister, Luis de Haro, replied that his master would sooner give up his two eyes.

So Oliver swung over to the idea of a French alliance. After all, France had twice saved Protestantism—in the Netherlands under Henri IV and in Germany under Richelieu. And the British fleet could help pay for its upkeep by capturing Spanish treasure-ships, and by asserting the right of Britain to a share in the exploitation of the New World. As time went on, the Protector was drawn more and more in this direction. In 1654 he made a commercial treaty with Portugal, now fighting a war of independence against Spain; and in 1655 Mazarin intervened on behalf of the Waldenses, inducing the Duke to indemnify them for the loss of their homes.

The actual *casus belli* came when Cromwell sent Admirals Penn and Venables to seize San Domingo. He seems to have supposed that he could do this without fighting Spain in Europe; but Philip IV viewed the matter otherwise, and declared war.

An alliance between France and Britain seemed obvious now that both were at war with the same enemy, but some time passed before it came into being. For a year or more Mazarin angled for a reconciliation with Spain, to be sealed by a marriage between the young King and the Infanta Maria Teresa. This idea had long been at the back of his mind. Already in 1635 he had noted that "If H.M. were married to the Infanta he could aspire to the Spanish succession, whatever renunciation she might be forced to make." There had then been a half-brother between her and the throne, but the boy had since died; and what made Mazarin particularly urgent about the match was that there was talk of her marrying the eldest son of the Emperor—a union that threatened to resurrect the two-fold empire with which Charles V had dominated Europe in the previous century. It did indeed appear to Philip IV that if his lack of a son condemned Spain to be swallowed by an outside power, the swallower had better be a member of his own family. So he rejected the French proposal, leaving the Cardinal with no alternative but to knock Spain out by force of arms.

Just at that moment Spain forced Cromwell's hand by promising full support to the Stuarts, while Condé's victory over Turenne at Valenciennes made Mazarin apprehensive of another Fronde. So the Franco-British alliance was signed at last (March 1657). France was to provide 20,000 soldiers, England 6,000 and a fleet; the immediate objective was to be the conquest of Dunkirk for Britain and Gravelines for France.

This was the most purely aggressive war that Britain ever waged. The Protector had visions of a crown—the Vasa had gained one in Sweden in similar circumstances. And if that came to pass, conquests in the Spanish Low Countries would provide commands and satrapies to appease the jealousy of former colleagues. Moreover the Stuarts found themselves supporting the enemy with whom England was at war; the Dukes of York and Gloucester served under Condé in the Spanish army that was defeated largely by English troops at the Battle of the Dunes (June 1658). ("The finest troops imaginable" Turenne called the Ironsides.) Dunkirk was duly handed over. England had regained a foothold on the Continent exactly a century after Queen Mary lost Calais. Cromwell had made her for the first and last time a military state, and the regicide had become "*mon cousin*" to the King of France. "His greatness at home was a mere shadow of his greatness abroad" wrote his enemy Clarendon. What did it all portend?

Nothing. His failure to win the consent of the British peoples to the rule of Puritanism was already breaking his heart, and on September 3rd of this same year he died.

THE PEACE OF THE PYRENEES. When Spain, now on the verge of collapse, put out feelers for peace, Mazarin let it be known that he still had the marriage project in mind. Circumstances had changed since Philip had rejected it some years before. Not only was Spain unable to continue the war, but the match with the Austrian archduchess had fallen through, and a son had been born to Philip IV. For a time Philip continued to hold aloof; but the Cardinal broke down his resistance by an elaborate piece of play-acting. He took the Court to

Lyons to meet the Duke of Savoy, as if with a view to a marriage with a princess of that House. The bluff was successful. Fearing that another campaign might lead to the loss of all that was left to Spain of the Low Countries, anxious to concentrate his waning forces on the

MAZARIN ADVANCES
THE FRONTIERS OF FRANCE

GERMANY

Dunkirk
Antwerp
Cologne
Brussels
SPANISH
Lille
Liège
Aix-la-Chapelle
NETHER-
-LANDS
Moselle
Rhine
Mainz
Luxemburg
Trier
FRANCE
Philippsburg
Landau
Weissenburg
Verdun
Metz
LORRAINE
Hage-
nau
Paris
Toul
Stras
-burg
Rosheim
Enzheim
Keissersburg
Schlettstadt
Munster
Turckheim
Kolmar
Breisach
Kolma
SUNDGAU

Frontier after Westphalia ----
    "   *Pyrenees*
Acquisitions at Westphalia
    "   *Pyrenees*
100 MILES 50   0

FRANCHE
COMTÉ

100   MILES 200

recovery of Portugal, and dreading lest France should enter into a family alliance that would give her a highway to the Milanese, Philip gave way.

The details of the settlement were thrashed out in a pavilion set up on the Isle of Pheasants in the Bidassoa, on the Pyrenean border. There was a good deal of haggling as to which of France's conquests should be restored and which retained; whether Condé was to be reinstated in all his former honours and dignities on returning to his French allegiance; and over Spain's refusal to recognize the independence of Portugal. By the terms eventually agreed upon France gained most of Artois, some parts of Flanders, and Roussillon. As to the marriage, Spain promised a dowry of 50,000 crowns to be paid in three instalments on fixed dates, "in consideration whereof" the Infanta renounced all rights she might otherwise have inherited from her parents. Those words *moyennant lesquels paiements*, adroitly inserted in the final draft by Lionne, the French plenipotentiary, turned out to be the most important in the whole document. Spain could not demur to them without admitting her own insolvency, but everybody knew that she would not be able to pay the money, and that the renunciation would therefore become void.

The marriage took place some months later in the great church at St. Jean de Luz. The new Queen of France was a plain, undersized, submissive girl, but she brought with her into France immense possibilities.

Thus ended a war which had lasted for a quarter of a century, and was itself only the last phase of a feud begun in 1494. The predominance of Spain in European affairs was now over; that of France was about to begin.

CHAPTER FOUR

THE HEGEMONY OF THE BALTIC

1648 – 1661

THE first half of the seventeenth century saw Sweden displacing Denmark as the leading country washed by the Baltic Sea; the latter half of it will see other competitors arising. A crisis in this struggle came in the sixth decade.

THE SCANDINAVIAN RIVALS. When our period opens Danish ascendancy among the Baltic states was ending; 1648 was the year in which old King Christian IV, during whose sixty years' reign the balance had shifted, died of vexation.

Denmark's paramountcy had been largely due to her geographical position astride the famous Sound that forms the narrow entrance to this "Mediterranean of the North." Like the Austrian Hapsburgs, the Kings of Denmark owed their crown mainly to great family possessions: Norway,[1] the right to tolls from ships passing through the Sound, and the Duchy of Schleswig. These resources enabled the Kings to hire foreign troops; but the fact that their position was elective made it impossible for them to crush the factious nobles who had gained hereditary offices, immunity from taxation, and local independence. In some countries the aristocracy made a return for such privileges by leading the nation in war; but in Denmark there was no nation for them to lead, inasmuch as they had crushed the peasantry into serfdom.

Christian IV, ambitious to win for his country the status of a great Power, had intervened on the Protestant side in the Thirty Years' War, but had fared very badly; and towards the end of the conflict he had been faced by an upstart rival.

The history of the Swedish state went back little more than a century and a half. The country owed its sudden advance to its King Gustavus Adolphus, who had conquered the eastern Baltic littoral (Ingria, Estonia, Livonia), and had then made a meteoric intervention in the great German war. After his death on the battlefield of Lützen (1632) his

---

[1] The days when Norway's Vikings had been the terror of every Christian coast were long past; the country had lost even its separate existence.

daughter Christina became queen at the age of eight. For the next ten years the country was ruled by a junta of nobles dominated by the most famous of Scandinavian statesmen, Axel Oxenstierna. He kept the Swedish army fighting in Germany to gain all the late king's aims; but in 1643 the King of Denmark challenged Sweden's growing importance by an increase in the Sound tolls that would have crippled her foreign trade. So Torstensson, commander of the Swedish expeditionary force in Germany, suddenly invaded Jutland; and despite a gallant defence of the islands by the old King, the Peace of Bromsbrö made Sweden free of the Sound, and gave her as security the province of Halland.

By this time Christina had grown up into a very remarkable young woman. Intrepid in spirit and highly intelligent, but whimsical and selfwilled, she was the last of the brilliant women of the Renaissance. One of her first cares on reaching her majority in 1644 was to press on the peace negotiations which had begun at Münster, despite Oxenstierna's desire to hold out for better terms. She resented the old minister's domination, which was bound to continue as long as the war continued; and even as it was, Sweden made very important gains: Bremen and Verden which gave her control of the great Elbe traderoute into central Germany, and Stettin which gave her that of the Oder.

The hand of the young Queen was much sought after, but while still in her early twenties she announced that she would never marry. This reminds us of our Queen Elizabeth; but Christina was readier than Elizabeth to face the fact that this involved providing for the succession. She selected her cousin Charles Gustavus, son of the sister of Gustavus Adolphus and of the Count Palatine of Zweibrücken.

For the next few years she continued to attract to Stockholm some of the most famous savants, artists and philosophers of the age. Unfortunately for Sweden she regarded the welfare of that somewhat primitive and impoverished country as beneath her serious attention. Her reckless expenditure she met by selling the crown lands from which the State had hitherto drawn most of its revenue, ennobling the purchasers wholesale to qualify them as landowners. Her alienation from her people increased when she became a Catholic; but she had the sense to see that such staunch Lutherans could not in the long run have a Catholic sovereign, and the heart not to try to compel them to. In 1654 she once more startled the world by abdicating and going to live in Paris.

She had a romantic vision of herself as an exiled Queen surrounded by a brilliant and admiring circle in the hub of European culture; but the reality was disappointing. People found her airs and vanities rather absurd; and she eventually retired to Rome, where she frittered away a bored and boring old age.

BRANDENBURG-PRUSSIA. We now turn to a very different personality. Frederick William, Elector of Brandenburg and Duke of Prussia, was a singularly unromantic individual—a ruler who kept his eye very steadily on the main chance, and lived so close to the earth that there was scarcely anything he would not do to get more of it. But he played a vital rôle in seventeenth-century Europe. Germany, parcelled into hundreds of little states, would have become a mere no-man's-land between French aggression and Slav barbarism had not Brandenburg grown strong enough for German nationalism to rally round; and it was Frederick William who gave the Electorate the qualities which enabled it to do so: centralization, militarism, acquisitiveness. That is why his countrymen called him "The Great Elector."

When he succeeded his father at the age of twenty his domains consisted of three widely separated segments. The central one was the Electorate of Brandenburg, the original appanage of the House of Hohenzollern, with its capital, Berlin, and its Diet of nobles and burghers claiming ill-defined powers of counsel and control. Away to the east was the Duchy of East Prussia, which had fallen to the House by a process typical of the time and place. The territory had in the Middle Ages been held by the Order of Teutonic Knights, under the suzerainty of the Kings of Poland. The knights were military missionaries who had migrated thither to save the souls of the Slavonic heathen natives. But in 1525 they had gone over to Lutheranism and had turned their domains into a Duchy held by their Grand Master, Count Albert of Hohenzollern. Later this branch of the family had been merged into that which ruled Brandenburg, and the Elector became Duke of Prussia. Here too there was a Diet, very determined to maintain Prussian independence of Brandenburg. Lastly, in the north-western corner of Germany there were Cleves, Mark and Ravensburg, three little Duchies which had been claimed by the House since the beginning of the century, had been accorded to it by treaty just before the Thirty Years' War broke out, but had ever since been a battle-ground for Spanish and Dutch. Brandenburg had fared even worse in the war. For the old Elector George William had claimed Pomerania under the will of the last Duke thereof; but the Swedes also wanted it, and when the Elector appealed to the Emperor, they harried his own precious Electorate, lying between Bohemia and the Baltic. In the end George

William had been driven out to die in despair at Königsberg (1640), leaving Brandenburg with two-fifths of its pre-war population.

His youthful successor, seeing that his battered little army would have no chance against the superb Swedes, contracted out of the war by a local armistice, and devoted himself to building up the economic and military strength of his Electorate. He centralized authority at the expense of the discredited and disunited Diets, and he created a standing army on the Swedish model, supported by a carefully-planned financial system.

Frederick William was a Calvinist ruling over Lutherans, but he never let religion affect policy. He had been educated at Leyden, and had served on the staff of the Stadtholder Frederick Henry. From the Dutch he acquired not only his religion but insight into the practical advantages of religious toleration; and also an excellent wife, Louise Henrietta of Orange, who encouraged him to bring Dutch peasants to settle in under-populated Brandenburg, offering them farms rent-free for a term of years. Soon that dreary waste was growing fruitful under diligent and intelligent Dutch husbandry.

By 1648 this building-up process had already gone far enough to give the Elector a voice at the Peace Conference. Sweden carried off the lion's share of Pomerania—the Oder mouth and the valuable ports of Stettin and Stralsund, while Brandenburg had to be content with the harbourless eastern part known as Outer Pomerania. But even this was more than had seemed possible at the death of his father; and he was also accorded the secularized bishoprics of Magdeburg and Halberstadt to round off Brandenburg, and Minden, which was contiguous with Ravensburg and commanded the middle Weser. There was one fly in the ointment—a Swedish army of occupation in Outer Pomerania demanding payment of an indemnity awarded to Sweden in the treaty. But by tact, persistence, and a certain amount of cash, he got them all out by 1653.

POLAND IN TROUBLE. A year or two later there began a confused struggle in which all the countries of northern and eastern Europe became involved, one by one.

The trouble arose through the fact that King Charles X of Sweden, the cousin and successor of Queen Christina, was by nature a fighting-man. He had learnt the art of war under Torstensson, and longed to put his lessons into practice. Moreover, war was necessary to maintain the army which was the country's main asset, and to draw off the energies of the nobles from making trouble at home. So, taking as excuse a protest against his accession by John Casimir, King of the Polish Republic, he invaded Poland.

"King" of a republic may sound odd, but it accorded with the facts. Poland was the largest and most populous Slav state in Europe; but its strength had begun to decline from 1572, when upon the extinction of Jagellon dynasty the monarchy had become elective. It was further weakened by its social constitution. The ruling class consisted of nobles, some of them great magnates but mostly what we should call "gentry" —the *schlachta*. But the needier they were the greater their pride. They had crushed burghers and peasants into serfdom, and commerce was practically monopolized by Jews. Too haughty to admit subordination to anybody or anything, they controlled their kings by their Diet, wherein they maintained such a degree of equality among themselves that a minority could not be coerced by a majority—even if it was a minority of one. They were not quite consistent in observing this *liberum veto*, but more than one session was "exploded" by the departure of a single fractious (or venal) member. When a new king was to be chosen, they came in hundreds, with armed retainers in thousands, and camped in the plains round Warsaw. The Poles (and when we say "Poles" we mean "Polish nobles," for no others mattered) were fatally lacking in "give-and-take," in discipline and in public spirit. Otherwise their country would have become the greatest in central Europe now that the great war had ruined Germany.

To explain the situation which arose in 1648 we must go back sixty years. In 1587 the Swedish heir-apparent was elected King of Poland. The fact that he was a Catholic which made him acceptable to the Poles (who after a Calvinist phase had reverted to Catholicism in the Counter-Reformation) made him unacceptable to the Swedes; and soon after his accession the latter deposed him in favour of his uncle, a member of the junior branch of the Vasa family. That uncle, Charles IX, was father of the great Gustavus Adolphus, and grandfather of the brilliant Christina and the warlike Charles X.

It was singularly ill-advised of King John Casimir of Poland to claim Sweden, for that country was now more firmly Lutheran than ever, while he was an ex-Cardinal and a Jesuit, who had half-reluctantly renounced his vows to become King of Poland and marry his brother's widow. Furthermore, his hands were already full with his turbulent subjects, and with defending his ill-defined frontiers against the Dneiper Cossacks, the Muscovite Russians and Crimean Tatars.

The Cossacks were freebooters (that is the meaning of the word) who held the Ukraine (="border-land") from Poland by a sort of collective military service in keeping Tatars and Muscovites at bay. (The Tatars were the sediment left in the Caspian and Euxine regions by the receding tide of the Mongols in the thirteenth century.) But under John Casimir's predecessor they had complained of Polish oppression—social (many of them had been reduced to the status of peasants), religious (they were of the Greek Orthodox Church) and economic (at the hands of Jewish *entrepreneurs*). Under Chmielnitsky, the national hero of the Ukraine, they joined forces with the Tatars in revolt. For four or five years the struggle went on. Two or three bloody battles were fought. For a time Chmielnitsky seemed about to establish a semi-independent principality; but in 1654, finding himself in difficulties, he offered allegiance to the Tsar Alexis of Moscow, who had the great advantage in Ukranian eyes of belonging to the Orthodox Church. With Russian aid he defeated the Poles at Smolensk and Vilna.

And now John Casimir was challenging the warrior King of Sweden!

FREDERICK WILLIAM CHANGES SIDES. From Pomeranian bases Charles X swept across Poland to Warsaw, and before the end of the year was in Cracow, the very heart of Polish nationality, the coronation-town of Polish kings. The only restraint on his movements was the presence of other invaders, Cossack, Russian and Tatar. John Casimir, betrayed and deserted, fled to Silesia. So many axes were hacking at the tree of Poland that it seemed the only question was which way it would fall. The nobility looked on at what they regarded as a family quarrel between the Vasas, and many of them did homage to Charles, on the grounds that it was more becoming to own allegiance to a warrior than to a priest.

The Elector was perturbed at the prospect of the bellicose Charles of Sweden becoming King of Poland. He went to Königsberg and began to make preparations to pounce on West Prussia. But Charles was too quick for him. Hearing what was afoot, he dashed back across Poland, seized Thorn and Elbing, the key-fortresses of West Prussia, and con-fronted the Elector with his redoubtable Swedish army. Frederick William hastily disclaimed hostile intentions, and made the Treaty of Königsberg by which he owned Charles as his overlord for East Prussia and promised aid for his Polish campaign.

For Charles X was finding it easier to overrun Poland than to master the Poles. He had offended their pride by tactlessly behaving as conqueror instead of as rightful suzerain; and his troops, on whom he had at first imposed the iron discipline of Gustavus, had now been so long unpaid and unrationed that they had broken out into rapine and plunder. Their ranks were thinned by disease and desertion. Worst of all, they wounded the deepest feelings of the Poles by derisive desecration of Catholic sanctuaries. If Charles had been able to abolish Polish serfdom, as he talked of doing, he would at least have gained the hearts of the peasantry; but he was too busy rushing about trying to keep the country quiet by force of arms.

Thus John Casimir, returning with help from the Emperor, became the centre of Polish national feeling; and thousands flocked to support Czarnieski, the able guerilla chieftain to whom he entrusted the organization of national forces. For weeks Charles scoured the snowy plains trying to bring his enemy to action. Once he penetrated to Galicia, losing half his numbers in doing so; and his retreat thence through marsh and forest to Warsaw was a masterpiece of military skill and spirit. He had to buy more support from Brandenburg by the Treaty of Labiau, which recognized Frederick William's sovereign independence as Duke of East Prussia. But he continued to flounder, and it was with a sense of relief that in the summer of 1657 he learned that King Frederick of Denmark had sought to take advantage of his difficulties by declaring war on him. For he could now abandon his hopeless Polish enterprise without loss of prestige.

Frederick III had taken this step in the hope of rehabilitating the Danish monarchy by the recovery of Scania and Halland. He sent his fleet to cut Charles off from Sweden; but that astute warrior had no design so obvious as a return thither. After a ruthless forced march recalling Torstensson's in the last war, he hurled his army into Holstein, and within a few weeks had overrun all the Danish mainland. But he could not take the islands, where the heart of Denmark lay, without command of the sea, and his fleet had been driven off. Thus Charles was already in grave difficulties when he learned that his one and only ally had gone back on him. Frederick William wanted to be on the winning side, and the events of the summer had convinced him that this would not be Sweden. So he fell in with a scheme propounded to him on behalf of the Emperor by Lisola, one of the ablest diplomats of the age. By the Treaty of Wehlau John Casimir followed the example of Charles X by releasing him from vassalage for East Prussia. Thus he had made doubly sure of his sovereignty there without using up his military strength in any serious operations. Of course, scrupulous persons might consider his conduct dishonourable; but he covered it with a smoke-screen of complaints that the King of Sweden had deserted him.

THE OLIVA SETTLEMENT. King Charles was furious, but did not let his wrath deflect him from his immediate purpose. By capturing the fortress of Fredericia he completed his mastery of the Danish mainland; and to counteract his lack of sea-power Nature came to his aid with the

coldest winter on record. Even the rapid currents of the Little Belt were frozen, and by the end of January the ice was thick enough to bear the Swedish cavalry across to Fünen, where they routed the astonished Danes. A fortnight later, the frost intensifying, Charles ventured even more boldly on the Great Belt to reach Zealand, whereon Copenhagen is situated. The combination of daring, skill and good luck make this one of the most memorable winter campaigns in history. It completely knocked out Frederick III. He agreed in the treaty of Roskilde to surrender everything on the Scandinavian mainland, and the island of Bornholm.

When Charles X had time to think things over he regretted that he had not pressed his advantage further: to be master of the Baltic he must be able to close it at will. So in August he attacked Denmark again. But the Danes now retrieved some of their military prestige by a resolute defence of Copenhagen, while a composite force of Austrians, Poles and Brandenburgers marched into Jutland against him. Worst of all, the Sea Powers decided that no single janitor should hold all the keys to the Baltic, from which they derived timber, pitch, copper and iron essential for ship-building. "The Concert of the Hague" provided for joint action against Sweden, and a Dutch squadron under Opdam drove the Swedish flag from the sea. King Charles, now in desperate straits, sent envoys to open negotiations with Poland, and talks began at the monastery of Oliva, near Danzig. Meanwhile, he struggled on with heroic obstinacy against Denmark. He had crossed to Gothenburg for a meeting of the Swedish Diet when he fell ill of a camp-fever and died at the age of thirty-seven.

There was now no obstacle to the general settlement which everyone else had long desired. By the Treaty of Oliva (May 1660) John Casimir renounced all claim to Sweden and confirmed the independent status of Frederick William in East Prussia. A month later the Treaty of Copenhagen reiterated Denmark's renunciation of Scania and Halland to Sweden, but restored Bornholm to her.

CHAPTER FIVE

GRAND MONARCHY

As Louis XIV was the dominant personality of this epoch, it behoves us to make some acquaintance with the man, the ideas which he embodied, the instruments with which he worked, and the political world with which he had to deal.

"MOI." On the morning after Mazarin's death (March 1661) the young King summoned the chief members of Council and Court, and forbade them to sign anything without his express authority. When the archbishop of Paris asked to whom in future they were to address themselves for instructions, he replied "To me, Monsieur l'Archevêque!" The moment to which he had looked forward, so eagerly but so anxiously, had come. Hitherto others had ruled in his name; now at the age of twenty-three he was to enter upon what he himself called "the most delightful of avocations—that of being king."

Time, place and nature had combined to embody in him Hereditary Monarchy—the "legitimate" monarchy that depends on birth as distinct from the heroic monarchy to which Caesar, Cromwell and Bonaparte raised themselves through capacity for leadership. Odd as it may seem, the kingly gifts with which Providence endowed such men as these seemed to Louis and his like of infinitely less validity than a claim derived from royal descent.

Inherited kingship may be irrational, but it has been of great service to mankind in giving order, unity and cohesion. Seventeenth-century France needed this centripetal force, and knew she needed it. The medieval polity had crumbled, and with it the idea of a king who was *primus inter pares* with his nobles. The Fronde had been its death-struggle. France needed welding into conscious and proud nationhood. So did Germany and Italy, but in those areas national feeling was as yet too weak to make the demand effective. The French had aspirations for glory which could only be realized in the person of a glorious king.

Louis XIV fitted the rôle to a miracle. Kingship was as natural to him as painting to Rembrandt or composing to Beethoven. His earliest memory was of sitting on a throne, with his mother standing at his side and venerable statesmen kneeling to ask his commands. His writing-master had set him to copy such sentences as *L'hommage est dû aux rois;*

36

ils font tout ce qui leur plaît. And during those distracted years of the Fronde, all parties had claimed to be his true servants: *"Vive le roi tout seul!"* the crowd had shouted. As he grew up his personality filled out the mould thus created.

He had escaped the Hapsburg degeneracy so unpleasantly manifest in many of his relatives. Physically he was healthy and active, mentally up to the average. His mind worked in an uncreative, unimaginative routine, but it was sufficiently acute to enable him to grasp quite complicated ideas when lucidly explained. Listening to such explanations, indeed, was his main occupation; and a talent for making them was a sure passport to his favour. And it is to his credit that he never allowed his appetite for pleasure to interfere with the steady work by which alone he could attain the greatness he desired for himself and for France. For hours a day, week in week out, year after year, he presided over councils, gave audience to officials, heard reports, instituted enquiries, weighed opinions, never deciding on anything until convinced that it would redound to his prestige. Of such activities he never seemed to tire. After twenty years of it he wrote for the encouragement of his dull-witted son:

You must not suppose that affairs of state are like the thorny and obscure sciences which may have bored you in your studies . . . The function of kings consists mainly in giving scope to good sense, which acts naturally and without conscious strain. Our business is sometimes less toilsome that what we do by way of pleasure.

Court etiquette gradually grew into a ritual almost blasphemous in its approximation to worship; and the scene of it became more and more magnificent, from Marly to St. Germains, and from St. Germains to Versailles. This last cathedral of Divine Monarchy accommodated ten thousand persons; but only for the bluest-blooded was attendance direct and personal. Those of the very highest rank entered the bed-chamber as soon as Majesty awoke; the second entrée were permitted to see it dress, the Hander of the Shirt and the Placer of the Peruke being posts for which peers of France contested in bitter strife. And so on all day. A hushed congregation of worshippers watched the Eating of the Dinner, persons of the Blood Royal being very occasionally allowed to participate in the repast. And when bedtime came they left the Presence in the reverse order of their appearance in the morning.

Here is another glimpse of the outlook of the cult, from the Memoirs which the King wrote for the education of the Dauphin.

About this time I learned that my brother was thinking of asking that his wife might be allowed to sit in the Queen's presence on a seat with a back to it. My friendly feelings towards him made me unwilling to refuse him anything; but seeing of what great moment this matter was, I let him know forthwith, with all possible gentleness, that I could not possibly give him satisfaction; that I should always do what I could to raise him above my other subjects, but that I did not feel able to grant this, which would seem to· be an approach to my own elevation. . . . But all I could say did not satisfy his mind, nor my sister-in-law's. Their prayers gave place to complaints, their complaints to tears, and finally to anger. . . . His passion even betrayed Monsieur into declaring that our Mother before she died had intended to speak to me on the subject; but I knew my Mother too well to believe that she, who valued Royalty so highly, would have approved a proposition which would so gravely weaken one of its principal advantages.

LOUIS AND EUROPE. As King of France Louis felt himself high above all other kings—he would not allow his name even to be coupled with theirs in diplomatic documents. In his Memoirs he laments that Burgundy, Germany and Italy should have been lost to "our House" by the unfortunate partition of the heritage of Charlemagne. The existing Holy Roman Empire could have no claim to such a position; for, being elective, it lacked the Divine sanction conferred by hereditary right. And when, later on, he quarrelled with the Pope, he reminded him that Popes owed their authority merely to the votes of cardinals.

The ascendancy which he claimed for himself and for France was favoured by the lack of possible rivals among the other states and rulers of Europe. Let us glance round at them.

Spain, whom France had just overthrown, was smitten with a creeping paralysis. Her vast Empire was no more than an immense façade on the verge of collapse from economic decay. The spoils of Peru had given Spaniards the false notion that they could be rich without labour. They had driven out their industrious Moriscoes for not being good Catholics; French workers came to gather their harvests. Without industries the country had nothing to sell to its colonies, and Dutch and English merchants shipped their goods to Cadiz for Spanish America at great profit to themselves. A quarter of the land of Spain lay in the dead hand of the Church. There were hordes of nobles, mostly impecunious, but all too proud to do anything but fight. The discipline of the Spanish army had gone to pieces when it could no longer be paid regularly; similar causes had reduced the fighting power of the navy almost to zero.

The country had never been unified. The various Provinces had separate "Cortes," and administrations in various stages of decomposition; and the natives of each preserved with burning jealousy all that differentiated it from the others. The central government was a congeries of ministries and councils, too complicated to be understood by the ministers and councils themselves. The wealth of the Indies was drained off by so many hidden channels on its way to the Treasury that little of it got there. Philip II had built up a governmental machine which depended for power on his own ant-like industry; but his grandson Philip IV lurked in slothful seclusion, hating the whole business of kingship as much as his energetic cousin of France enjoyed it.

As for Germany, circumstances and the two French cardinals had combined to prevent the growth of a national state. The formation of the League of the Rhine was the first round in the game which France was to play with great success for the next century and a half: the fomenting of resistance to the Imperial authority among the princes.

In Vienna the younger branch of the Hapsburgs ruled over an assortment of hereditary principalities—Austria, Styria, Carinthia, the Tyrol —as well as two kingdoms, Bohemia and Hungary. Their subjects included four distinct races—German, Magyar, Italian, and Slav. Each province cherished its own political régime. Bohemia had been mastered by a persecution atrocious even for the days of the Thirty Years' War. Hungary, of which the kingship was nominally elective, was more of a liability than an asset, for much of it was under Turkish rule; and the people, being Protestants, preferred the tolerant slackness of Moslem pashas to the proselytizing zeal of Austrian Jesuits.

The Austrian Hapsburgs had been elected Holy Roman Emperors for two centuries; but as we have seen, the position was august rather than powerful. It made them hereditary defenders of Christendom against the Ottoman peril, with an Imperial revenue of 14,000 florins per annum, and no Imperial army except such as could be wheedled from the Diet from time to time in each emergency as it arose. And as they shared many of the interests of their Spanish cousins, they had always to face two ways at once.

The Archduke-King-Emperor at this time was Leopold II. He had been educated for the priesthood, and hated the dignity which had been thrust upon him through the death of his brother. Religion continued to be the mainspring of his life. He exemplified every Christian virtue —including humility and chastity, which were rare among sovereigns of the period. His sense of responsibility weighed upon him so heavily that he already seemed middle-aged in his twenties. He was almost as assiduous in his duties as Louis himself, and was by no means unintelligent; but such a timid, hesitant, self-depreciating little man could not cope successfully with the robust and exultant vigour of the Sun-King.

The Baltic States had exhausted themselves in their recent struggle, and Sweden, the strongest of them, was now under a boy-king and a regency. And of the two little Sea Powers, the Netherlands were ruled by the oligarchy headed by de Witt, with a policy based on the French alliance which had carried the Republic to independence and security. In the other, Britain, a Stuart Restoration had ended the decade when militant Puritanism had given weight to the country's foreign policy.

This Restoration had been the only way for the English and Scottish nations. British republicanism withered away like the seed that fell on stony ground, having no roots in the people's hearts. Their conservative instincts made them long for a return to government by King, Lords and Commons, to the Rule of Law, and to social traditions which had grown up with the nation itself. The first Parliament of the reign was boisterously royalist, but it could not make the water that had flowed under London Bridge since 1640 flow back again. Nor did it try to. It retained all the measures taken by the Long Parliament to prevent non-Parliamentary taxation, and it contrived that the permanent revenue should fall so far below expenditure that the King would always be dependent on the House of Commons to make ends meet. Thus although the "Cavalier Parliament" disclaimed all right to interfere in the government, it continued to hold the power of the purse, and it soon began to use that power to further its views both on religion and on foreign affairs. And recent experience had given the ruling class a horror of standing armies, without which there could be no effective intervention on the Continent. This situation, coupled with the character of the King—a shrewd, epicurean cynic, with Catholic and authoritarian predilections tempered by a determination not to go on his travels again—made Britain an open field for the deployment of King Louis' diplomatic forces.

LOUIS' FIRST MINISTRY. The main machinery of the Government of France consisted of four standing Councils, three of which were presided over regularly by the King. The most important was the Council of State. It met seven mornings a fortnight for three or four hours to discuss matters of general policy, the King on his embroidered fauteuil, the ministers on backless stools. Louis would not let them sit in any fixed order, nor allow any of them to act as *rapporteur*, so anxious was he to prevent the emergence of a prime minister. The Council was merely a group of individuals whom it was his pleasure to consult upon his affairs.

There was much overlapping of function among the ministers and the secretaries of state, for apart from departmental duties each was responsible for the affairs of one or two Provinces; and this also tended to magnify the master who was the sole bond of union among them and the sole director of their activities. Their labours were both assiduous and continuous. In almost daily contact with each other and with the King, each had to be ready with his *dossiers* and memoranda, with views and suggestions, and to have at hand the machinery by which decisions could be carried into effect. Changes in personnel were so rare as to be sensational disturbances of an ordered routine that had about it a suggestion of the solar system, with planets circling in appointed orbits about the Sun which gives them life and movement.

For the first few years after Louis took control, his chief ministers were Lionne, Le Tellier, and Fouquet.

Michel le Tellier was typical of the French governing class of the period—intelligent, circumspect, observant, diligent. A scion of the lesser nobility, he had held administrative posts under the cardinals, and was now, as Secretary for War, engaged in overhauling the organisation of the army. Hitherto in France, as in most other countries, when war broke out, regiments and companies and squadrons had been raised *ad hoc*, by the private enterprise of commanding officers. By modern standards this arrangement was absurdly inefficient. It gave endless opportunities for fraud—the drawing of pay and supplies for dead men, for instance. It prevented the organized training of large units—doubly important since Gustavus Adolphus revolutionized the arts of war. It made uniformity of arms and equipment impossible. It left the country without protection in an emergency. Richelieu had begun to reform it, and Le Tellier was now building up a permanent army, assisted by his son, who carried on the work after 1666 and became famous as the Marquis of Louvois.

Hugues de Lionne, in charge of Foreign Affairs, had also made a mark under Mazarin, doing much of the spade-work in the Treaty of Westphalia, the League of the Rhine, and the Peace of the Pyrenees. Knowing the courts of Europe like the palm of his hand, he was founding French pre-eminence in diplomacy, with a network of ambassadors and agents far more highly developed than anything of the sort at the disposal of other governments.

2*

Fouquet was the Controller-General of Finances who had devised the jugglery by which Mazarin had amassed such wealth; and he had not omitted to feather his own nest in the process. Briefly, the device consisted in depressing the Funds by neglecting to pay the interest, and buying them up cheaply; then raising the price by paying good interest, and selling out at the top of the market. He contrived to lend to the King as a subject the money which he borrowed as Treasurer; and latterly he had taken to receiving the revenue and conducting Treasury business in his own house. His personal expenditure was on the same scale as the late Cardinal's. Indeed, it was his lavish hospitality that brought his downfall; for he entertained the King with a magnificence which aroused the royal jealousy. Mazarin had asked no questions so long as the money he required was forthcoming; but Louis was not the man to allow his revenues to be employed by a subject in rivalling his own magnificence. Moreover, it came to his ears that Fouquet was expecting to succeed to Mazarin's position as soon as the young King should have tired of being his own prime minister. For a year and more Louis bided his time, while he privately enquired into the falsified accounts which the Treasurer laid before him with such smiling assurance. Then he suddenly had him arrested and charged with malversation. The case dragged on for years. Fouquet defended himself with such skill that more than once it seemed that the prosecution would break down. Eventually he was sentenced merely to confiscation and banishment, but Louis intervened and sent the culprit off to spend the rest of his long life in the remote mountain fortress of Pignerolo.

The King had shown that he was not to be trifled with, and his ministers needed no further object-lesson.

COLBERT. The fall of Fouquet was largely due to the underground work of a man whose zeal may not have been altogether disinterested. Jean Baptiste Colbert succeeded him at the Treasury, and became the most remarkable controller of it in French history. Louis had the good sense to support his work for many years, but he never appreciated it at its true value; for it did not lie in the glittering achievements of war and diplomacy, but in the economic foundations that underlay that superstructure.

Colbert, like the other ministers we have mentioned, had been employed by Mazarin. His whole nature was realized in the work of administration. He once declared that a few years of idleness, or even of moderate labour, would kill him. He had a card-index mind, a passion for codification, an inexhaustible delight in pigeon-hiolng

information. Not that he was a mere routineer: he could devise
sweeping plans, and had the driving-power to carry them through.

The aim of his life was to make France supreme by making her rich.
He was in no position to abolish the traditional anomalies and leakages
at the Treasury, but he did all that was possible in the way of reform.
The exchequer no longer drifted blindly. He stopped up some of the
worst leaks; he put a check on the tax-farmers; he reduced *rentes*
(interest-payments); above all, he developed the taxable wealth of the
country by what would to-day be called "a planned economy." This was
the heyday of the Mercantile System, and Colbert provided the most
thorough-going example of it in action. He regarded its principles as
self-evident truths. Since there was but a limited amount of gold in
Europe, France's proportion of it could only be increased at the
expense of other countries. Commerce was therefore a money-war.
If France could manufacture goods hitherto imported, she would keep
more of her gold; and she could "attract" it by manufacturing goods
for sale abroad.

A townsman by birth and breeding, he thought more of industry
than of agriculture as a wealth-maker. The only crops that interested
him were those which provide raw materials, such as hemp and flax.
Of industry, on the other hand, and of French resources for developing
it, his knowledge was profound. He put fresh vigour into the manufacture of wool and silk begun under Henri IV; he started manufactures
of glass, porcelain, lace, tapestry and steel which became world-
famous; he built factories with state capital, and conducted them under
state supervision; he imported skilled workmen from abroad; he
established mass-production; he issued official handbooks prescribing
in detail the technique of industry, the quantity and quality of goods
required, and the subdivision of labour. He ignored the traditional
governments of the Provinces in favour of "Intendants" appointed by
himself. With them—and there were hundreds of them—he kept up a
constant stream of correspondence on an infinite variety of administrative details: local industries and farming; financial disputes between
local bodies; roads, bridges and canals; harbours and markets;
hospitals and schools; the relief of the poor, the collection of taxes,
the preservation of works of art. The same with the colonies: he con-
scripted emigrants, provided them with transportation, tools, arms,
seeds and instructions, and marketed their produce. To him colonies
were simply out-farms run in the interests of the proprietor.

He was specially active in ship-building. When he took office the
Dutch still led in the ocean carrying-trade, with England a poor second

and France nowhere. Determined that France should not go on parting
with the "invisible export" of freightage, he developed ship-yards and
provided a bounty on tonnage constructed in them. A merchant fleet
required a Navy to protect it, so he set to work on building warships,
with such effect that the 18 ships of the French navy in 1660 had
increased twenty years later to 276.

GOVERNMENT AND PEOPLE. We must not over-estimate the effect of
all this, however. Colbert was one of the most remarkable men of the
era, but his freedom of action was far too limited to enable him to
overthrow economic errors which had grown up through centuries,
especially when his master began to upset his arrangements by wars.
The old régime was not so easily uprooted—it took a revolution of
unprecedented violence a century later to do that; and even a cursory
examination of life in France during the reign of Louis XIV will show
what changes in ideas that revolution made. Since conditions in France
were, broadly speaking, very much those of all western Europe (always
excepting the Dutch Republic and Britain, which were a century ahead
of other countries in social and political development) it will be of
profit to us to note one or two of the outstanding features of the
régime.

The first thing that strikes us is the lack of homogeneity. The Provinces which had been added to the central core of France during the
past three centuries had never been assimilated. They retained their
own manners and customs, taxes, institutions; and their own form of
French, even among the educated classes. The *Pays d'état*, such as
Provence and Burgundy, kept at any rate the ghost of their local
Estates and Parlements; the *Pays d'élection* (a misnomer from our
point of view) such as Champagne and Bourbonnais, had none
at all.

Then as to the fiscal system. In all civilized countries to-day expenditure and revenue are worked out in advance, taxation is contrived on
a definite plan, the proceeds are paid into a general fund. But there was
nothing of this in Old France. There was no national bank through
which to anticipate revenue, and no civil service to assess and collect it.
The State had to borrow from private persons, and the collection was
largely hired out to "farmers" at ruinous cost. The proceeds of particular taxes was allocated to particular purposes in the most confusing
way. All sorts of "Extraordinary Expedients," such as the sale of
salaried offices and pensioned titles, were resorted to in the emergencies
which were constantly recurring. And the taxes themselves were

encrusted with anomalies and privileges. In no two of the Provinces was their incidence the same. And whereas the oligarchs of Britain and Holland, whatever their faults, rendered public service for their privileges, which did not include immunity from taxation, the French aristocracy, lay and clerical, did next to nothing for their keep, and regarded it as the hall-mark of a gentleman not to pay *taille*.

This *taille*, a kind of graduated poll-tax, was the most burdensome of all the taxes; but in many parts of the country the *gabelle* hit the poorer classes even harder. This was a Government monopoly of salt. Every household was forced to buy a certain quantity, the price being fantastically high, though varying enormously from Province to Province. Obviously the burden was infinitely heavier on the poor than on the rich, and the most frightful penalties, including the galleys, were inflicted for evasion.

History is full of the doings of the great, but let us not quite overlook the millions of nonentities who toiled to supply the wherewithal for these comings and goings and battles and intrigues.

In the towns industry was still largely controlled by the old guilds, which were much better preserved in France and Germany than in England. Apprenticeship, the quality of goods, prices, and the conditions of manufacture were still regulated by medieval custom, despite Colbert's efforts to push on the evolution which was beginning to replace all this with large-scale production, economically more efficient though less agreeable to the individual worker.

But the vast majority of the population of Europe still laboured on the land. In France serfdom—the attachment of the villein to the estate he worked on—had gradually disappeared. In most parts of the country systems of *métairie* had grown up, whereby the peasant paid a proportion of his crops to the landlord who supplied him with his stock. Many agricultural workers, however, were hired by the day, with no certainty of employment and no provision for old age.

As to the sort of life they led, there is a tragic unanimity among contemporary witnesses. Provincial Governors, Intendants, government agents, clergymen, literary men—all tell the same tale. We can here quote but two such accounts among many. In a description of the State of France in an Almanack of 1661, the writer, after passing in review the various classes of society, adds, almost as an afterthought:

Although he is more numerous than the others, the peasant furnishes us with little matter for discourse. We can only say that it is from him that the taxes are raised, and that he cultivates the soil for the nourishment of the towns.

And here is a passage from La Bruyère:

One sees certain wild animals, male and female, about in the countryside, black, livid, burnt with the sun, attached to the soil which they till with an invincible obstinacy. They have the gift of speech, and when they straighten their backs we see that they have human faces. . . . During the night they retire to lairs where they live on black bread, water and roots. They save others the trouble of sowing and reaping for food, and so deserve not to lack the bread they have made.

CHAPTER SIX

THE WAR OF DEVOLUTION
1663–1668

THE foreign policy of Louis XIV was polarized round two centres of ambition: to thrust back his north-eastern frontier, and to gain possession of the Spanish monarchy; and these objectives were connected by the fact that the Low Countries belonged to Spain. We shall here see how they first came into view.

"THE RIGHTS OF THE QUEEN." The great question for Europe at this juncture was, when and on whom would this ambitious young King of France make war? For war was an essential function of his kind of kingship.

As a matter of fact his goal had been marked out for him by long tradition, and imbued into his boyish mind by Mazarin. It was to extend France to her "natural frontiers"—the Rhine, Alps and Pyrenees of ancient Gaul—thus breaching the Hapsburg ring with which she was encircled. Mazarin's two treaties had been strides towards it; the next advance would involve Belgium[1] and Franche Comté which belonged to Spain, and Lorraine whose Duke was a prince of the Empire. Colbert wanted aggression postponed until he had secured French ascendancy in trade and shipping; but Louis was not impressed by his argument, nor even very interested in it. Trade, manufactures, sea-power, he regarded as useful adjuncts to a state, but ignoble objects for it to pursue. He had been accustomed from childhood to associate glory with war, and war against Spain. Even his marriage had been designed as a claim upon that monarchy.

And there were geographical facts urging him in the same direction. His north-eastern frontier ran within striking distance of Paris. Every mile that it could be pressed back, every fortress that could be held on it, would increase the margin of safety. Moreover, Lorraine and the Comté separated him inconveniently from his new Alsatian domains.

He had not to look far for a pretext. The days of Philip IV were obviously numbered. His only son had just died; and although another male child was born a few weeks later, it was such an extraordinary and distressing example of degeneracy that survival seemed impossible.

---
[1] "Belgium"="Spanish Netherlands"="The Low Countries."

47

Of his first marriage there were two daughters, the elder being married to Louis XIV of France and the younger betrothed to Emperor Leopold. When King Philip and his infant son were dead, Louis would through his Queen have a claim to the whole Spanish inheritance—a claim barred only by a renunciation conditional upon dowry-payments that had never been completed (p. 26).

Nor was that all. The French chancellery had discovered that a feudal custom had once existed in certain parts of the Low Countries by which children on the death of a parent inherited property left by that parent, the surviving spouse having only the usufruct. According to this principle of "Devolution" the Queen of France, whose mother was dead, already owned a large part of the Low Countries, and would enter in full possession of them on the death of her father. Of course the claim was bogus. The custom had been in disuse for centuries, and it had applied only to fiefs within the Provinces, never to the Provinces themselves. But such objections were not likely to deter Louis when he decided that the hour for action had come.

CLEARING THE DECKS. Louis' concern for his prestige made him careful to make assurance of success doubly sure. Before each of his wars he employed all the resources of his diplomatic machinery to isolate and weaken his opponent.

On this occasion he began by trying to induce his father-in-law to cancel the renunciation. He politely hinted that as a matter of fact it was already invalidated by the non-payment of the dowry; and he offered to help Philip suppress the Portuguese rebellion if he would put the Queen of France back in the direct line of succession. But Philip, after consulting the highest authorities, ecclesiastical as well as juridical, declared this to be impossible.

So Louis and Lionne set to work to cut Spain off from any possible outside help. Their first step was to prevent Philip's Austrian cousin from coming to his aid; and their second was to wean the Princes of Germany from their allegiance to the Emperor by professing concern for their "liberties." And when the League of the Rhine expired it was replaced by an agreement of the Bishops of Cologne, Münster and Mainz to bar Austrian or Imperial troops coming down the Rhine to succour the Spanish Netherlands.

England was easily dealt with, for the policy of Charles II, foreign as well as domestic, was governed by his perpetual shortness of money. Louis' revenue was five times as great, and was not dependent on parliamentary votes; and this fact ruled the relationship between the two kings. The first example of it was the sale of Dunkirk. The place required a garrison which Charles could not afford, and was useless except as a bridgehead for an expeditionary force which he had no prospect of possessing. It had formerly belonged to Spain, and Spain wanted badly to recover it; but Louis had what Philip had not—the money to pay for it. So the bargain was struck.

Louis also intervened to the disadvantage of Spain in the matter of the King Charles's marriage. Possible brides of the Hapsburg clientèle —"a whole litany of them" as Charles himself said—were suggested to him; but Louis contrived that he should marry a princess of the House of Braganza which had just hoisted itself into royal rank through Portugal's war of independence. The bait was Tangier, Bombay, and a dowry which paid off the bridegroom's outstanding debts and left something in hand to meet the deficits of the next year or two. But of course from Louis' point of view the important point was that Britain was now attached to the state that was in rebellion against Spain.

The people most affected by Louis' designs were the Dutch, and he spared no pains to allay their apprehensions. The traditional connection between France and the Republic was now formalized in an alliance which bound each to go to the other's aid in war, and exchanged commercial privileges. But when de Witt discovered that Louis intended to claim the Low Countries on the death of Philip IV, he was much upset. *Gallus amicus sed non vicinus:* it was good to be on friendly terms with France, but she would be a very uncomfortable neighbour. The Spanish Netherlands formed a very useful buffer. In fact, with France in possession there, Dutch independence would not be worth three years' purchase.

THE SECOND ANGLO-DUTCH WAR. The treaty with the United Provinces soon placed Louis in an embarrassing position, however. Another naval war had just broken out between the United Provinces and England. Normally a conflict between the Sea Powers would have been welcome to him; but he was now under a treaty obligation to join in it, just when he wanted to keep his powder dry for the coming conflict with Spain.

The causes of this second Anglo-Dutch War were even more purely economic than those of the first. The Dutch had made a wonderful recovery; their commerce had regained nearly all its old ascendancy and ubiquity, and they were constantly fighting with English crews in the harbours of the East Indies, West Africa, and North America. When public opinion became heated over all this, King Charles was quite ready to go to war; for a popular war would loosen parliamentary purse-strings. Moreover, a Calvinist oligarchy combined the two principles most distasteful to him, and naval affairs were always very near his heart.

At first matters went badly for the Dutch. Off Lowestoft (where the English fleet was commanded by the Duke of York) their Admiral Opdam was killed and their ships so badly mauled as to be fit for nothing for the rest of the year. And a subsidy enabled that very worldly prelate the Bishop of Münster (purely for the sake of adventure, as he admitted) to invade Overyssel with 20,000 men. The rulers of the Republic had let the army fall into decay, for they associated it with the stadtholderate which they were trying to keep in abeyance. The Pensionary had to improvise a force to check the Münsterians, and at the same time to suppress a revival of Orange sentiment. For in times of danger the nation instinctively looked to the House which had led it to victory in its War of Independence. Prince William was still a mere boy, and his position was compromised by the fact that he was half English by blood and upbringing. Nevertheless there was a strong demand that he should be given the title of Captain-General, with a grown-up cousin to control operations. De Witt managed to get this proposal set aside, but he saw that his party could not go on indefinitely ignoring the lad's existence. So they persuaded his guardian (his mother, the Princess Royal of England, had died in 1660 while on a visit to her restored brother Charles) to let him become "Child of the State," with de Witt himself as instructor in the principles and practice of government.

Just at this moment Philip of Spain died (September 1665), his last hours darkened by the decisive victory of the Portuguese at Villaviciosa. Not unnaturally he was full of bitterness against the son-in-law who had encouraged the rebels, and he vented that bitterness in his will. Therein he declared the Queen of France to be for ever excluded from all claim to any part of his dominions, and exhorted his successors to defend the Low Countries against French aggression with all their might. In the event of his infant son Carlos dying without issue the heritage was to go to his second daughter Maria Margareta, betrothed to the Emperor. That would keep it in the family, at any rate.

So now Louis had to decide whether he would declare war on England (under the Franco-Dutch treaty of Alliance) or on Spain (to enforce the rights of the Queen) or on both at once. His reflections on the subject for the edification of the Dauphin, throw a high light on his outlook.

I envisaged with pleasure the design of these two wars as a vast field on which occasions would arise for me to respond to the expectations which I had for some time excited in the public mind. . . . To be sure, the more dearly one loves glory the more careful one should be to acquire it with safety. . . . But in refusing to expose myself to the difficulties which had been surmounted by my predecessors, I was in danger of missing the eulogies which they had earned.

In the end he decided to declare war on England first, so as to be able to claim the merit of keeping his word to the Dutch; but he contrived to do so with such an apologetic air that King Charles could not take offence. The appearance of a small French force on the Yssel was sufficient to drive out the Münsterians, but his new warships kept at a discreet distance from the English fleet.

The fortunes of the war now veered in favour of the Dutch. De Witt had made prodigious efforts to refit the fleet after the Lowestoft setback, and de Ruyter had all the better of a tremendous four-days' battle in the Downs. By the winter both sides were growing tired of the war. The English government, afflicted by Plague and Fire in successive years, was paralysed by lack of funds; and the Dutch were apprehensive about the intentions of their ally. Were they to fight themselves to a standstill while he stood by, practically neutral, waiting for his chance to overrun the Low Countries? So early in 1667 negotiations were opened at Breda, though for a time the English held out for better terms than the Dutch thought reasonable. And now Louis justified Dutch apprehensions. He sent 50,000 men into the Low Countries, forwarding to Madrid at the same time a *Treatise on the Rights of the Queen*. He was not making war, he explained, but merely taking over the Queen's property. The Governor of the Spanish Netherlands was in no position to resist such an incursion; what followed was a leisurely parade-march for the French forces with the King and Court in attendance.

This made the Dutch more anxious then ever to get free from the English war, and they determined to end it by a shattering blow which had often been discussed at their councils of war. King Charles and his advisers had let their wishes beget their thoughts. Assuming that the war was now "practically over" they economized by laying up most of the fleet. De Ruyter (with John de Witt's brother Cornelius as commissar from the States General) sailed unopposed up the Thames estuary and into the Medway, to attack the naval base at Chatham. It was no mere raid. The Dutchmen were there for two days and nights. They burned several ships at their moorings, and towed others away as prizes. London was panic-stricken. The contrast between this ignominy and the power of British arms under the Protectorate was too obvious to be missed: it gave a bad shock to Restoration royalism. Dutch exultation overflowed in bonfires and banquets and medals. The statesmen who had planned the exploit and the sailors who had carried it through became national heroes.

England could no longer haggle at Breda. By the treaty signed there shortly after she restored to France Acadia (the modern Nova Scotia), and exchanged Surinam and Goree with the Dutch for the New Netherlands (renamed New Jersey and New York).

THE TRIPLE ALLIANCE. The French occupation of southern Belgium so excited the Orangist opposition in the Republic that de Witt foresaw acute danger to his party if this loyalty to the Princely House got out of hand, and decided on bolder measures to keep it in check. There would be no great harm in the Prince becoming Captain-General when he grew up, provided that this military office was not combined with the civil office of stadtholder. It was the combination of the two that had made his father so dangerous to "True Liberty." So he and his friends framed an "Eternal Edict" whereby the Province of Holland abolished the office of stadtholder for all time. Not all the lesser Provinces followed this example; still, Holland was so immensely preponderant that its edict would practically exclude the Prince from civil power throughout the Republic.

When the document was signed the old Pensionary of Dordrecht tried to cut the edge of it with his knife: "I am trying whether parchment can resist steel," he said. A few years later the experiment was tried in earnest, with results disastrous to the parchment.

King Louis was very anxious not to have the Sea Powers and the Empire united against him. At the close of the campaign of 1667 he tried to forestall this by offering a compromise on his Belgian claims: he would give up most of the places he had occupied provided that he could have either Luxemburg or Franche Comté. De Witt, delighted to see French ambitions turning away from the Low Countries, urged Spain to agree to one of the alternatives. Meanwhile Louis gagged the Emperor with a secret partition treaty. By a combination of threats and cajolery his ambassador at Vienna induced Leopold to the "Eventual Treaty" which provided that if the Spanish throne fell vacant, Louis was to annex the Netherlands, Franche Comté and the Two Sicilies, while Leopold took all the rest (January 1668).

But when King Louis turned his attention to England he was baffled by the political situation there. The royalism of Parliament had, as we have seen, lost its first fine careless rapture. Charles let his old chancellor Clarendon act as scapegoat for recent calamities, and installed in office the famous "Cabal." One member of it, Arlington, who had social connection with Holland through his Dutch wife, suggested that an alliance with the Republic to check France would do much to restore the King's popularity. To prevent any strong Power from establishing itself in the Netherlands had been an established tradition of English policy since the fifteenth century; and hatred of the French had driven hatred of the Dutch out of English hearts—the Dutch were Protestants, at any rate. King Charles was ready to go with the stream. Such an alliance would raise his price to Louis, and would envenom him against the Dutch, to the ultimate advantage of England.

The negotiations were entrusted to Sir William Temple, the ambassador at Brussels, who was a personal friend of de Witt's, and they were pushed through with such good will that the agreement was signed within three days. The two Powers undertook to support each other should either be attacked by a third party, and to insist on Spain choosing one of the alternatives proposed by Louis. In secret articles it was agreed that if the King of France refused to abide by them, both the signatories would help Spain to re-establish the frontier laid down in the Treaty of the Pyrenees. A week later the agreement became triple through a guarantee of its terms by Sweden.

THE TREATY OF AIX. The French ambassador at The Hague heard nothing of this Triple Alliance until it was an accomplished fact. Louis was highly indignant, especially when the secret clauses leaked out. It was of no avail for de Witt to point out that the terms to be enforced were those which he (Louis) had himself proposed. It was one thing for the great King to make a suggestion; but quite another for states which he despised to concert plans to compel him to abide by it. And if there was nothing offensive to France in the Alliance, why had the signatories been so secretive about it? At first he was for instant chastisement of their insolence, but wiser and cooler counsels prevailed. A coalition such as this was just what he had tried to prevent, and he did not feel in a position as yet to face it with absolute assurance of success. He must have time to divide his foes before conquering them.

In the negotiations which followed at Aix-la-Chapelle he had now a fresh asset to bargain with, for at the beginning of February he had marched into Franche Comté. The Spanish Government was weak and defenceless here as in Belgium, and the whole Province was in his hands within a fortnight.

So it was finally settled that he should keep all the towns he had taken on the Belgian frontier, twelve in number, in consideration of giving back the Comté—where he had dismantled the fortresses, and could walk in again whenever he chose.

It was not quite the solution that the Dutch would have wished, especially as Louis' acquisitions would place the vital spots of the Spanish Netherlands—Brussels, Ghent and Antwerp—at his mercy the next time he was in an aggressive mood. Still they could pride themselves on having put a spoke in the wheel of the haughty monarch.

But pride goes before a fall.

CHAPTER SEVEN

THE WRONG TURNING

1668–1673

THE Peace of Aix ended the first period in the reign of Louis XIV. So far he had been engaged on national objects designed by his predecessors; but during the next decade he allowed his policy to be deflected by personal aims and passions. In the process he led Charles II of England into a line of action which brought disaster on the House of Stuart, and provoked collective resistance of the smaller Powers (personified by the Prince of Orange) to his ascendancy.

LOUIS PREPARES FOR VENGEANCE. The traditional Franco-Dutch *entente*, which had begun when the Dutch were fighting Spain, was shaken by Münster, and extinguished altogether by Aix. Louis had laid down his arms less because of the Triple Alliance than because of the prospects opened by his secret "Eventual Treaty" with the Emperor; but he was cut to the quick by the knowledge that the Dutch *thought* they had triumphed over him. He was shocked at such ingratitude after all that he and his House had done for them, and he was furious that "a nation of cheesemongers"—themselves merely successful rebels —should dare to interfere in the affairs of kings. Moreover, though he was not a very obedient son of the Church, Protestantism of any form stank in his nostrils, and the Republic was a hotbed of it—was founded on it. His letters of this period are full of moral indignation at Dutch depravity, and of delight at the prospect of becoming the arm of the Almighty to chastise it. Hitherto in his designs on the Spanish Netherlands he had placated the Dutch, but to crush them would be a delightful alternative.

The minister most eager for this change of policy was the aggressive Louvois, who saw in an attack on Holland a chance to display his army reforms in action. But for once in a way Colbert was on the same side. France suffered, like all the rest of Europe, from the lead which the Dutch had gained in overseas trade. England had waged two wars to break it down, but France was equally concerned now that Colbert had established East and West India Companies. He had opened a tariff-war in 1664 by putting special duties on Dutch goods (especially their salted herrings), and he now increased these duties to an almost

55

prohibitive level. The Dutch protested, retaliated; but being more
dependent than the French on foreign trade they were far more vulnerable.

Hardly had the Treaty of Aix been signed when Louis began preparations for an invasion of the Dutch Republic that would warn the whole
world of his power and of the catastrophic demolishment that awaited
any state that dared to offend him. Louvois completed his reorganization of the army. Fresh regiments were raised; a new drill-book was
put into practice by such officers as Colonel Martinet, whose name
still stands for strict discipline; for the first time in military history a
special corps of engineers was raised, with pontoon equipment of
leather for crossing the numerous waterways in the theatre of war.

The King safeguarded his future communications by suddenly
pouncing on Lorraine, whose Duke Charles IV had had the temerity
to offer his services to the Triple Alliance. The Duke, spirited old
soldier as he was, could not withstand the French force which swept
into his Duchy: he fled across the Rhine and took service under the
Emperor. Louis declared that his occupation of Lorraine was only
temporary; but meanwhile it was a fact, and a very disturbing one to
Germany, Lorraine being a fief of the Empire.

Louis had now cut through the Hapsburg corridor to the Netherlands,
and had conducted a useful rehearsal for his invasion of the United
Provinces. He also took care to deprive his intended victim of any support from Germany. He won over Bavaria, not merely for his campaign
but for life, by betrothing the Dauphin to the Elector's daughter. He
could not persuade Frederick William of Brandenburg to take sides
against a Protestant state with which his personal ties were so close
(p. 30), but he intimidated him into promising not to give it active help.
The raffish old Bishop of Münster was delighted at the chance to make
another attack across the Yssel, this time as an ally of France. The
Archbishop-Elector of Cologne was a Wittelsbach, brother of the
Elector of Bavaria, and a client of Louis XIV. Himself on bad terms
with the Dutch, he was very ready to promise to let the French forces
march through his territories, including the Bishopric of Liége which
ran like a wedge into the Netherlands. Louvois surveyed the route and
collected great magazines of food and munitions along it.

As for Sweden, Louis had little difficulty in bribing her out of the
Triple Alliance. Her adhesion had been contingent on Spanish subsidies which were never forthcoming. The half-French Count de la
Gardie was now chief Minister, and the threadbare Swedish nobles
could not resist the lure of French gold. The upshot was an undertaking

to attack Pomerania, should Brandenburg show any disposition to aid the Dutch.

"THE GREAT DESIGN." But Louis' chief diplomatic preoccupation was to win over England. Of course, Charles II was as much a member of the obnoxious Alliance as de Witt, but that seemed different. Charles was a fellow-king; and if he could be rescued from his dependence on Parliament he might be useful to France, especially with his navy. So Louis sent over Colbert de Croissy, brother of the minister, on a special mission. He was to point out to the King and his ministers how advantageous it would be for England if her great commercial rival were destroyed. Surely they must see which side their advantage lay, and join him in the good work!

The envoy found a situation apt for his purpose. Charles II lacked principles, in his father's sense of the word; but he had strong predilections for monarchy, toleration and the Catholic Church. The three ideas were associated in his mind; for he could not relax the penal laws against Catholics without doing the same for Protestant Dissenters, and nothing of the sort would be possible so long as Parliament was the controlling power in the State. When he tentatively opened the subject to his brother and heir he found that York (hitherto known for a hard-and-fast Church of England man) was himself on the verge of becoming a Roman Catholic. The brothers realized that there would be serious trouble when they announced their conversion—in fact it would not be safe for the King to do so until he was assured of military help from outside. Louis was not very interested in the spiritual welfare of Charles or his subjects, but he saw in these circumstances a chance to gain the naval support he needed for his Dutch enterprise.

Secret discussions went on for a year or more. It was very much a family affair; Charles's sister, Henrietta Duchess of Orleans, the only person he really loved, took a large share in the correspondence; and their nephew the young Prince of Orange was not forgotten—he was to be ruler of what was left of the dismembered United Provinces. But there were thorny points. Which was to come first, the Dutch war or the English conversion? Louis feared that the " going over to Rome" of the Head of the Anglican Church would lead to disturbances which would make Britain useless as an ally. Again, what was to be Charles's share of the booty? He demanded certain Belgian towns and an ultimate share in Spanish America. Louis thought this too much, and for some months the discussions dropped; but the two kings had too much need of each other for the estrangement to be permanent. At last

Louis sent "Madame" to clinch matters in a family gathering at Dover (May 1670). It was agreed that Charles could announce his conversion at his own time, when Louis would provide him with 2,000,000 livres [1] and 6,000 troops. Louis was to decide on the date for the war, for which 6,000 British troops were to be provided, while thirty ships of the new French navy were to join the fleet commanded by the Duke of York. Only the Catholic ministers, Clifford and Arlington, were present at Dover; but as it would be impossible to disguise the war-preparations and the receipt of subsidies, Charles enjoyed a joke at the expense of his boon-companion Buckingham (who thought himself so clever!) by sending him to Paris to negotiate a mock-treaty consisting of the same terms without the Catholic clauses.

Incidentally, Louis showed a nice appreciation of his cousin's weaknesses by sending over the charming Louise de Querouaille (who soon became Duchess of Portsmouth) to captivate him and to carry French policy into his most intimate circles.

Charles II has been accused of selling British interests at Dover, but unjustly. He certainly wanted to weaken Parliament's financial grip on his government, but his immediate purpose in doing so was to promote religious liberty. And his ultimate aim was a sort of royal Cromwellism—a powerful executive based on military force, combined with toleration and imperialism. Most of the advantages to be gained by the destruction of the Dutch Republic would accrue to British trade and sea-power. Still, his method of bringing this into effect was unfortunate, to say the least of it. In preferring dependence on France to dependence on Parliament, he pushed his dynasty, and the cause of real monarchy in Britain, down the slippery road to destruction.

THE EMERGENCE OF WILLIAM OF ORANGE. As Louis' preparations developed he took less and less trouble to conceal their purpose, and de Witt's anxieties became more and more acute. At first he and Temple (now ambassador at The Hague) had hoped to draw other Powers into their Alliance, but they met with one disappointment after another. Hidden forces were working against them. Brandenburg had been intimidated into quiescence; the Emperor had tied his own hands by the secret Treaty (p. 52), of which he was heartily ashamed, to partition his Spanish cousin's heritage; the Rhine princes were trying to insure their own safety by seeking the favour of France. True,

---

[1] About twelve livres went to the £, but the purchasing-power of money was quite ten times what it is to-day.

Spain signed a defensive treaty with the Republic, but in the lamentable condition of Spanish arms and finances this was a liability rather than an asset. It was soon painfully obvious that the Triple Alliance itself had disintegrated—if indeed it had ever had any real existence. Sweden had never shown the least sign of implementing it; the English government seemed bent on raking up old grievances against the Republic and supplementing them with fresh ones. And when Temple was replaced as ambassador by Sir George Downing, whose truculence had provoked the last Anglo-Dutch war, the writing on the wall became only too unpleasantly legible.

The Pensionary's position in home affairs was cracking, too. Some of the leading personalities in the "True Liberty" party, men whom he had advanced to high posts in the Republic, were growing jealous of him, and were turning to the rising Orange faction. His success in suppressing the latter had been favoured by twenty years of security for the Republic and of immaturity for the Prince; but these conditions were fast disappearing.

William Henry, Prince of Orange (1650–1702) was growing up into a remarkable young man. An orphan and an only child, he had spent a joyless childhood among jarring relatives, and a repressed boyhood among men who had made a principle of thwarting his inmost nature. With the blood of William the Silent, Henri Quatre and Charles I in his veins, he was imbued with a deep-seated ambition to play a part worthy of the ancestors who had brought the Republic through terror to triumph. In keeping him under and depriving him of the military training he longed for, de Witt and his clique had driven the lad in upon himself. The constant feeling that anything he said or did might be used in evidence against him made him precociously watchful and circumspect. The grim Calvinistic faith in which he was nurtured added to this gravity, he was singularly lacking in the graces of seventeenth-century culture, and chronic asthma robbed him of the careless high spirits that are the charm of youth. But beneath this unattractive exterior there was developing an unflinching courage and a steadfast devotion to duty which were to find scope in the crisis now at hand.

The Council of State appointed two major-generals to bring some sort of order out of the chaos in the army, but they lacked the prestige which attached to the Head of the House of Orange—a House, as one might say, of hereditary dictators in such times of danger. By a recent "Project of Harmony" the Prince would not become eligible as Captain-General until his twenty-second birthday (November 1672); but after much haggling the Pensionary consented to his filling the post on probation until then. William, however, with characteristic prudence, declined to be responsible for the inevitable disasters of the first campaign with no chance to retrieve them in the second. So de Witt had to agree that at the end of the year he was to continue in office without further formality. On these terms the Prince was sworn in as Captain-General on February 25th, 1672.

Without the loss of a moment this young man of twenty-one, quite without military training, set to work to improvise an army. For it amounted to that. The land forces, so long neglected by the oligarchy, now consisted of about 30,000 men, ill equipped and worse disciplined, officered by the less capable members of burgher families who had never regarded soldiering as a serious profession. Confusion was worse confounded by the facts that each of the seven Provinces maintained and controlled its own quota, and that the Captain-General could give no orders without the approval of a committee of civilian "Field Deputies," one from each Province.

The Council insisted on dissipating its very limited strength by keeping garrisons in scores of decrepit fortresses, instead of concentrating a force, as the Prince urged, to strike at the enemy. And when after six weeks of furious activity, he reviewed his field army there was little ammunition for the infantry,[1] few horses for the cavalry, and no carriages for the guns. And at that very moment 100,000 of the best-trained troops ever seen, led by young nobles desperately anxious to win the notice of their King, and commanded by Turenne, Condé and Luxembourg, were marching down the Rhine.

THE BLOW FALLS. King Charles unmasked in mid-April with a declaration of war on the Republic and a Declaration of Indulgence allowing freedom of worship to all his subjects. His ultimate aims were summarized with admirable succinctness by his brother in a letter to the King of France.

Affairs here are in such a state that Parliament and King cannot subsist together. Nothing is to be thought of save carrying on the Dutch war boldly until victory is won, when we shall be able to gain by force what we cannot have by milder methods.

As for King Louis, he did not even condescend to declare war. He merely proclaimed that he felt it incompatible with his glory to

---

[1] Louvois had taken the precaution of buying up all the powder stored in the Dutch magazines. Then as now despotism had a huge advantage in efficient planning for war—but then as now it eventually turned out that democracy had a little something that despotism lacked.

THE FRENCH INVASION OF THE DUTCH REPUBLIC 1672

Allies of France ....

Supporters of the Dutch ..

Flooded Area ....

NORTH SEA

Haarlem

ZUIDER ZEE

Amsterdam
Muiden

OVERYSSEL

BISHOPRIC OF MUNSTER

Leyden

The Hague

Rotterdam

HOL L A N D

UTRECHT

Utrecht

Gouda

R. Lek

R. Waal

GELDERLAND

R. Yssel

Arnhem

Nymegen

Emmerik

R. Meuse

Dordrecht

s'Hertogenbosch

CLEVES

Rees

Wesel

Breda

Antwerp

SPANISH

Brussels

Vossem

NETHERLANDS

Namur

Charleroi

BISHOPRIC (to COLOGNE)

Liege

Cologne

SPANISH NETHERLANDS

ARCHBISHOPRIC OF COLOGNE

Neuss

R. Rhine

Cologne

Bonn

Maastricht

Aix-la-Chapelle

GERMANY

MILES 10   0   20   40   60   80   100 MILES dissimulate any longer his anger against the Dutch. He had an army of 60,000 already mobilized at Charleroi. On May 5th he "took command" in person and marched down the Meuse to Maastricht, where Condé joined with another 30,000 from Sedan. The States General had counted on Maastricht holding up his advance, for some time at any rate, and had filled it with their best troops; but he merely left a few regiments to mask it, and pushed on to the Rhine. The Dutch were thrown into still greater consternation by the failure of the fortresses along that river which they leased from Brandenburg; for the German townsfolk would not allow the Dutch garrisons to make trouble by trying to defend the crumbling walls.

The States had expected the French to continue down the right bank until they reached the frontier along the Yssel, so they had a trench dug along that line and stationed the Prince with his field-force to cover it. But Louis gave them yet another shock. Taking advantage of the lowness of the water in the river (there had been a drought all the summer) and of his novel pontoons, he suddenly crossed into the mesopotamia between the two main streams (the Waal and the Lek) by which the Rhine finds its way to the sea. Then by crossing the Lek at Arnhem he threatened the Prince's rear. To save his army, the only defence now left to the Republic, William retired precipitately to Utrecht; and when that city, fearful of offending the invader, refused to admit him, he continued his retreat to the borders of Holland. There he gave orders for the carrying out of a scheme which had been prepared for some time before—the flooding of a strip of low-lying land to protect the great cities of the Province. Everything really depended on the lock-gates at Muiden on the Zuider Zee. The French, who had already occupied Utrecht, overlooked the importance of the place for some days; and when at length they sent a detachment thither it was too late: the Dutch had opened the sluices, the country-side was already under a sheet of water, and the Prince had posted his little force on the causeways by which alone it could be crossed.

However, the King and his staff were not perturbed. Condé was for pressing on to complete the occupation of the country, but Louis and Louvois wanted to play with their victim as a cat with a mouse; and Turenne agreed that the Dutch could not resist any further. The States thought so too. Envoys were sent to ask what terms the conqueror would be pleased to grant.

But in the five days during which they were travelling to Utrecht and back, a political revolution changed the whole outlook.

THE DUTCH REVOLUTION. For twenty years the merchant-oligarchy had run the government, on the whole, with great success. But the corner-stone of their foreign policy had been the French alliance, which had now collapsed in frightful ruin; and they had made bitter enemies of the Orange Party, which included the bulk of the nobility, the clergy and the populace. As long as de Witt and his friends had been able to give the country peace and prosperity the opposition had been half-hearted; but in this day of disaster it surged up with irresistible fury. The Pensionary personified the policy of appeasement and disarmament which had brought these calamities upon the country. This was scarcely just, for he had striven in vain during the past year or two to induce the government to repair the neglect of the defences for which he had admittedly been responsible in the past. He was set upon by a gang of "patriotic" roughs in the streets of The Hague and left for dead, while his brother Cornelius, accused of conspiring against the Prince, was tortured [1] and imprisoned. The Estates of Holland, frightened lest it should be their turn next, and now deprived of the steadying lead of the Pensionary, rescinded their "Eternal Edict" (their eternity having lasted rather less than five years!) and appointed the Prince as Stadtholder on the same terms as his ancestors.

The effect was a remarkable manifestation of the spirit of "legitimacy." The promotion of this pale, glum, round-shouldered youth, untried in politics or war, whose only distinction thus far was his birth, was greeted as if it had been a national triumph. Wherever he appeared the mere sight of him inspired fresh hope and determination. The new spirit found its way even to the grave and reverend signiors who until recently had kept him in the background. When their messenger returned with the great King's demands—the cession of a strip of territory and several important forts, the payment of a large indemnity, the granting of unreciprocated advantages for French trade, and the annual sending of a gold medal to the King recording gratitude that he should permit the continued existence of the Republic,[2] they let his ultimatum expire without reply.

---

[1] He fortified his spirit during the ordeal by repeating the famous Ode of Horace (III. i) beginning *Justum et tenacem propositi virum.* His copy of the Elzivir Horace, found in his cell after his death and now in the South Kensington Museum, opens naturally at that place.

[2] This was the great age of commemorative medals. It is said that one of the causes of Louis' anger at the Dutch was a medal celebrating the Treaty of Aix in which the Republic was depicted as bidding the sun stand still—the sun being the emblem adopted by Louis. And to celebrate his invasion of Holland he had a medal struck in which the sun was drying up the exhalations from a marsh, with the inscription: *Evexi sed discutiam:* "I raised them up but I will scatter them."

A month later the revolution was sealed with the blood of the brothers de Witt. Not a shred of evidence could be found against Cornelius, but he was sentenced to a banishment by judges who feared to draw the fury of the populace on themselves by acquitting him. By this time panic suspicions of what would to-day be called the "Fifth Column" had risen to white heat. When John (who had by this time recovered from his wounds and had resigned his post as Pensionary) came to the prison to fetch Cornelius away, a great mob gathered, burst into the building, dragged the brothers out, almost literally tore them to pieces, and hanged their mutilated bodies by the feet to a nearby gibbet. The circumstances of this crime have never been cleared up. The Prince certainly did not instigate it, and he was far away on the water-front at the time it was committed. But he probably knew what was likely to happen, and (although as Stadtholder he was responsible for law and order) he did nothing to prevent an occurrence which fitted in with his plans and ambitions. For it frightened the "old gang" in office all over the Republic into resigning and making way for his Orange partizans. William was a man of one idea. That idea was not to arouse the admiration of posterity but to beat back the French; and this in his view could not be done so long as the country was dominated by the oligarchy which had brought it to the brink of ruin.

King Louis' failure to press on with his campaign after reaching Utrecht was the turning-point of the war—perhaps of his whole reign. For the floods, with the Dutch contingents guarding the five raised roadways, proved an insuperable obstacle; and after a month or two Louis went off home, leaving Luxembourg to take charge of the offensive that was to be resumed as soon as frost turned the waters into a means of approach. A mild winter frustrated that design, and when in December there were a few days of sharp frost, the French detachment that tried to take advantage of it was nearly cut off by a sudden thaw, and retired to its headquarters with more haste than dignity. The English naval offensive also went adrift, for de Ruyter so severely handled the fleet in Solebay (May 1672) that it was unable to make the attack on Zeeland that had been part of the Anglo-French scheme for the campaign.

Just before Christmas the Prince made a daring counter-attack. He set off to the south with the intention of cutting the French communications by capturing Charleroi. He was joined on the way by some Spanish troops, and there were plans for joining forces with an army which the Emperor and the Elector of Brandenburg (indignant with

Louis for marching through Cleves) had collected at Halberstadt. The coup failed, for the German forces retired when Turenne marched against them, and William was recalled by news of the French attack in Holland. But the mere attempt was evidence of a new spirit in the Dutch after their abject defeatism in the summer. And in the course of the following year the aspect of the war changed so completely that it became evident that the two kings had indeed taken the wrong turning.

CHAPTER EIGHT

THE EMPEROR'S GRAND ALLIANCE
1 6 7 3 – 1 6 7 9

From this point to the death of Louis XIV in 1714 Europe was constantly preoccupied with "collective security" against his ambitions. The Emperor Leopold was the central, if not the most active, personality in the first form of the Grand Alliance.

GETTING TOGETHER. The flooded water-line and the new courage inspired by the young Stadtholder had given the Republic a respite, but it would not be able to withstand the vast weight of French resources indefinitely. The only thing that could save it in the long run would be for a coalition of German states to make a diversion. William tried hard to bring such a coalition into existence, but for a time he had very little success.

A false start had been made in August 1672 when the Emperor Leopold (alarmed that a French army should march down the Rhine with the connivance of Imperial princes) and the Elector of Brandenburg (vexed that this army should go through Cleves without so much as notifying him) had joined in an armed protest. But the Electors of Mainz and Trier had been too afraid of Louis to let the allied force cross the Rhine by their bridges; and Leopold full of trouble (as usual) with Magyars and Turks, had given his General Montecuculi instructions to do nothing that might provoke an open breach with France. So it was small wonder that the contingents separated with Emperor and Elector nursing greater grievances against each other than against King Louis. And Frederick William followed up his retirement by a reconciliation with France. Why, he argued, should he be expected to stand up to Louis single-handed? There was no depending on the Emperor; Grémonville the French ambassador was still the most influential personage in Vienna. The Archbishop of Cologne and the Bishop of Münster, instead of helping to defend Germany, were complaining of him in the Diet as a "peace-breaker." And the resources of the Dutch seemed to be already drying up: they had failed to pay his promised subsidies since November, and he had never pretended to be able to keep an army in the field out of his own revenues. And now they were on the point of losing Maastricht, the fortress which lay on their main route to Germany and dominated the Spanish Netherlands.[1] So he made the Treaty of Vossem (June 1673), by which he undertook to give no further aid to the Dutch, and received back his Rhine Provinces (recently occupied by Turenne) together with a *pourboire* of 800,000 livres.

Prince William was very hurt at his uncle's defection; but it was not his way to cry over spilt milk, and it was largely due to his pertinacious diplomacy that within three months the Republic had formed a definite alliance with the two branches of the House of Hapsburg, pledged to maintain the settlement of the Pyrenees, including the restoration of Lorraine to its Duke.

For Spain this was a mere act of self-defence, inasmuch as Louis' ultimate purpose in this "War of Holland," as in his earlier "War of Devolution," was to rectify his frontiers at the expense of the Spanish Netherlands. But why should Leopold, usually so timid, have suddenly nerved himself to take this stand? Partly it was the influence of his minister Lisola, the tireless advocate of collective action to curb French aggression. But mainly it was due to William's warning that without speedy help the Republic would have to capitulate, and to the plain fact that if Louis was established on the Lower Rhine nothing could save the Spanish Netherlands, or western Germany either, from falling into his hands. The sense of duty which was Leopold's most admirable trait was touched—both his family duty to other Hapsburgs, and his Imperial duty to the Reich. It helps to an understanding of his disposition to learn that, having decided on this alliance he made a pilgrimage to a sacred shrine, and there, crucifix in hand, prayed as follows:

O Lord, whose image I hold in my hands, I declare before Thee, Thou searcher of men's hearts, that I am assembling my army not from greed for more territory, being fully content with that which Thou hast already given me, and for which I thank Thy holy goodness. I hope that my righteous intentions are not displeasing to Thee, and protest that I am being forced into this war. And therefore Thou wilt not in the Day of Judgment, demand of me the blood that will be shed in this war. In Thee, O Lord, is my trust.

The decision he had taken was indeed momentous. It gave direction to Austrian policy for a century and a half.

---

[1] This siege of Maastricht was the occasion for a great display of warlike apparatus, and Louis cast himself for the chief rôle in the drama. "Vauban suggested what I thought best," he remarks in his Memoirs.

It was always difficult for such disparate forces to co-operate effectively, but the Alliance opened with an encouraging achievement. William and Montecuculi (an experienced commander who had made a name in the Turkish wars) joined in an attack on Bonn, in the Electorate of Cologne. They carried through the plan with such precision that the place fell almost at once (November 1673). Then they wanted to go on and attack Cologne itself, but the Emperor would not tempt Providence further and recalled his troops. The Prince went home in disgust, but on the way he was greeted with great news. The French were evacuating the Republic. Their army had swept the country bare, and the loss of Bonn emphasized the danger of relying on such elongated communications. After all, the annihilation of the Republic was not a pressing necessity. Louis proposed to draw them into a separate peace while he concentrated on the overthrow of the two Hapsburg states which were obstructing his expansion to the Rhine.

ENGLAND DROPS OUT. Meanwhile Charles II was getting into a very tight place indeed. He had reckoned on a quick victory that would turn aside Parliament's wrath at his French alliance and his Declaration of Indulgence by enabling him to claim that he had avenged a defeat and destroyed a rival. But that programme had become sadly deranged. The Dutch had held off the French onslaught, and the Battle of Solebay—though technically a British victory, inasmuch as the Dutch declined to renew the conflict—was tantamount to a defeat, since it left the enemy with a "fleet in being" to lurk behind their islands and protect their shores.

By this time all his French money was spent, and in February 1673 he had to face Parliament. When it met, King Louis began a new political method—the bribing of English M.P.s. He wanted to focus the opposition on the Declaration rather than the alliance, for he cared a great deal more for England's support in his war than for the convenience of English Catholics. His manœuvre was successful: Charles had to cancel the Indulgence to get a vote of money for the war. And the Opposition pressed home their victory with a Test Act which required all persons in the public service to take an oath abjuring Popery. An alarming number of men resigned rather than take the oath, including Clifford the Lord Treasurer, and the Duke of York who was heir to the throne. This seemed to confirm the suspicions of alarmists that a conspiracy was afoot against Protestantism.

The King's surrender had gained him no more than a respite. In October he had to call Parliament again, after a summer during which the war had gone worse than ever. The French were now evacuating the United Provinces, and the navy had suffered another "technical victory" off the Texel. The French ships which formed the van of the allied fleet had sailed on out of the battle; and it was commonly said that, having paid the English to fight, they had merely come to see that they earned their pay. Prince Rupert, who had succeeded York in the command of the British fleet, was so disgusted that he swore he would never again fight with the French for allies. This was the last combat in the great Anglo-Dutch naval epic which had begun twenty years earlier.

Naturally Parliament's Francophobia was hotter than ever, while its "No Popery" passions were inflamed by York's marriage to the Princess Mary of Modena. Shaftesbury (the Ashley of the Cabal) who had advocated the war by applying to Holland Cato's famous phrase *Delenda est Carthago*, now guessed the truth about the Dover Treaty, and threw himself furiously into organizing opposition. When Parliament met again in February 1674 the King was in desperate straits. Parliament would not, and Louis could not, provide him with any more money for the war; so he had to make peace. The Dutch were ready to buy him off with an undertaking to salute the British flag on the Narrow Seas "not merely from courtesy but as a right," together with a gratifying little indemnity. (Treaty of Westminster, February 1674.)

Too MANY COOKS. The treaty of mutual support between the Hapsburg states and the Dutch in the autumn of 1673 grew in the course of the following spring into the first "Grand Alliance." The example of successful resistance set by the Republic, and the lead given by the Emperor, put new heart into the princes of Germany, and they seemed more disposed to make common cause to meet the common danger than for a long time past. In January the rulers of Mainz, Trier and the Palatinate formed a little anti-French League of their own, and next month the two Brunswicks and Hesse joined it. Denmark became a member of the Hague coalition in March. In April the Bishops of Cologne and Münster, threatened with submergence by the rising tide, and feeling that Louis XIV could no longer protect them, made peace with the Republic. In May the Diet of the Empire declared war on France. Most important of all, William of Orange won back his Hohenzollern uncle to the cause. Frederick William's conscience had pricked him for leaving his Dutch friends in the lurch, while his loyalty to the Emperor was second only to his loyalty to himself. He had left a loophole in the Treaty of Vossem, which made his non-belligerence conditional on the Empire not being involved in the War; and he now took advantage of this to send a contingent to co-operate with the Allies on the Rhine—to be maintained by Dutch subsidies, of course.

Thus King Louis' plans for a triumphal progress had got badly out of gear. It was now he who was isolated, while the despised Republic which he had been about to tread beneath his feet had become the pivot of a coalition formed to curb his ambitions.

It is of interest to note in parenthesis how the political alignment of Europe had been reversed by this war. When the Dutch under the first Prince of Orange had taken arms against Hapsburg Spain, they had looked for support to France and England; now it was France and England who had threatened their independence, and this later Prince of Orange was looking for support to Hapsburgs. Again, whereas Catholic France had formerly for political reasons set up this Dutch pillar of Protestantism, it was now the Emperor, even more Catholic, who was for political reasons propping it up.

But Louis had one asset which outweighed everything that his enemies could claim: there was only one of him. He was absolute master of his war-machine; whereas the Allies had no supreme command, and were never able to integrate their efforts. The Prince of Orange could not give orders to the Dutch army without the approval of a whole hierarchy of civilians, and he was always afraid of seeming to dictate to the Allies. More than once in the close season he drew some of them together to plan joint action for the coming campaign, but the proceedings usually opened with fierce recriminations about unpaid subsidies or undelivered supplies; and while the pandemonium was at its height a French army would sweep into the Low Countries and mop up two or three valuable fortresses before the Allies could put a regiment in the field. On one occasion the Prince induced the commanders of the Spanish and Imperial forces to join in an incursion into France; but when they tried to slip past a French army posted in a fortified camp at Seneffe (just north of Charleroi), Condé pounced out on them (August 1674). The result was in itself indecisive, but the invasion had to be abandoned, and the three generals were soon at loggerheads again.

But usually it was Louis who took the initiative. He had always coveted Franche Comté, which was indeed part of France by geography and ethnography. Now that he was at war with Spain he had a better excuse for overrunning it than in 1668; and this time he intended to keep it. In the summer of 1674, after careful preparation by Louvois, the operation was carried through with such efficiency that by July the province was as French as Touraine.

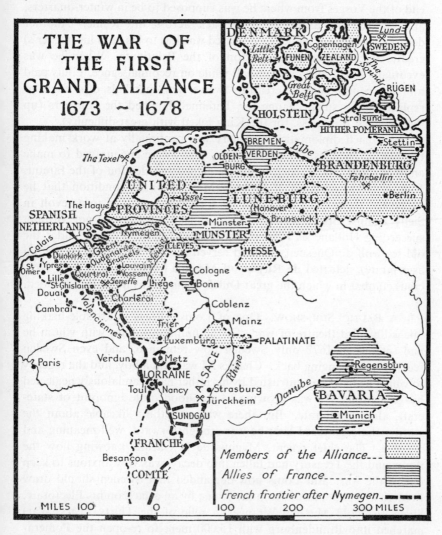

THE WAR OF
THE FIRST
GRAND ALLIANCE
1673 ~ 1678

Members of the Alliance_ _ _
Allies of France_ _ _ _ _ _ _ _
French frontier after Nymegen_ ▬ ▬ ▬
MILES 100   0   100   200   300 MILES

On the middle Rhine, Marshal Turenne (1611–75), the greatest soldier of the age, had little trouble in frustrating the disjointed movements of the Germans. Unlike Condé, whose penchant was for terrific blows improvised on the spot, and Vauban, the master of siegecraft, Turenne was pre-eminently a strategist: he won his battles by moving his forces to the right place at the right time. Perhaps his most famous exploit was Türckheim (January 1675), where after seventeen days of forced marching in atrocious weather he suddenly debouched at the opposite end of the Vosges from where he was supposed to be in winter-quarters, and bundled the Brandenburgers back across the Rhine. Another deed with which his name is associated was less to his (and his master's) credit: the systematic devastation of the Palatinate. When he was eventually killed by a cannon-ball while on reconnaissance, Louis paid him the compliment of creating twelve new marshals of France to replace him—"small change for Turenne" laughed the courtiers (up their sleeves, doubtless, for the King joked with great difficulty).

The French diplomatic machinery was continually at work making trouble for enemies. The Hungarian rebels were encouraged to make another stand, and French influence helped the election of the famous John Sobieski as King of Poland (May 1674) on condition that he supported them. The aid given by a French squadron to a revolt in Sicily against Spain seemed likely to lead to France, not Britain, succeeding Holland as ruler of the waves; for the French, under the old sea-wolf du Quesne (who had served his apprenticeship to the sea as a pirate), defeated de Ruyter off Messina (April 1676) after a ferocious combat in which the great Dutch admiral was mortally wounded.

A BALTIC SIDE-SHOW. One of Louis' efforts at trouble-making opened a third theatre of war. Of the numerous allies with whom he had set out in 1672 only Sweden now remained, and even Sweden seemed to be hanging back. Charles XI was still a boy, and the regency to which he had been entrusted by his father had scandalously neglected his education. He was growing to manhood quite ignorant of statecraft, almost illiterate. But there was something likeable about the sturdy, sharp-featured lad: he was straightforward, well-meaning and sensible. The chief regent, Magnus de la Gardie, knowing how the Army and the Treasury had fallen into decay, was very anxious to keep out of the war. But Louis now demanded that Sweden should draw Frederick William away from the Rhine by an attack on his Electorate. So in 1675 old Marshal Wrangel (a relic of the Thirty Years' War) marched into Brandenburg with 15,000 men, to re-open the Pomeranian question which had been slumbering since the Peace of Oliva. The Elector was in Franconia reorganizing his forces after Türckheim; but he set off at once across Germany, defeated the Swedes at Fehrbellin (June 1675), and drove them headlong out of his lands.

Fehrbellin was a mere skirmish in which the total casualties were less than 600, but it was a severe blow to the prestige of the Swedes, it gave Brandenburg a new standing in Europe, and it caused Frederick William to be known as "The Great Elector."

He had indeed earned some such title, if not by his military exploits, by his political achievements. Intelligent despotism was particularly applicable to heterogeneous domains like his. The peoples of Germany were not ripe for parliamentary government—it is questionable if they ever have been; and with hundreds of miles of open frontier, to lack defences was to lack the means of survival. So Frederick William had built up a régime in which all classes contributed to maintain a large army, while the Estates, though not abolished, were side-tracked. Twice the Estates of East Prussia had tried to assert themselves, and had even appealed to their former overlord the King of Poland; but a combination of firmness and tact had kept these discontents under control. He had also nursed the country's economic strength. Not only were immigrant Dutchmen draining marshes, but refugee Huguenots were setting up industries, and internal transport was expedited by a canal between Elbe and Oder.

His failure on the Rhine and his success on the Spree disposed him to concentrate on his own interests—to keep the Swedes on the run until he had wrested Hither Pomerania from them. In this he was supported by Christian V of Denmark. Christian, too, had set up an absolutist régime, by his famous *Kongelov* (King's Law), to the great advantage of his people as a whole. And he, too, though nominally a member of the Alliance, had devoted himself to a private war—against the Duke of Holstein, uncle and ally of the King of Sweden.

So the two rulers joined forces to partition the Swedish Empire. Denmark was to have the island of Rügen, and to recover Scania and Halland lost in the last war; while the Elector was to get long-coveted Hither Pomerania. This roused the spirit of the Swedes; they swept aside the feckless regents, and young Charles XI defeated the invaders at Lund.[1] But in Germany the confederates carried all before them. They overran Bremen and Wismar, while a Dutch-Danish fleet destroyed the Swedish navy off Oland, cutting Sweden off from Pomerania. Christian began to dream of gaining permanent control of the commerce of the Elbe. For a time the Swedish army held out in Stralsund and Stettin, but at last these too fell, and it seemed that Swedish power was banned from Germany for good and all.

---

[1] They were doughty fighters, these Scandinavians. At the battle of Lund more than half the combatants were killed.

3*

THE TREATY OF NYMEGEN. The Prince of Orange was very keen to gain England for the Alliance, and in urging this on the English ministers he had a good deal of support from Parliament. King Charles, of course, disliked the idea of an open breach with his wealthy patron, and wanted the war to end before he was dragged into it. He had therefore promoted a peace conference at Nymegen; but the Dutch, anxious for the Spanish Netherlands to be a strong barrier against future French aggression, would not agree to the demands which Louis made on Spain. Charles and Louis tried to suborn the Prince of Orange with a promise to set him up as sovereign Duke of Gelderland. But he was not interested: he had set his heart on a peace that would both safeguard the Republic and satisfy its allies.

In March 1677 Louis marched into the Netherlands before anybody expected him and captured Valenciennes, Cambrai and St. Omer in quick succession. Then, instead of following up his advantage he broke off the campaign, having done just enough to alarm the Allies without heating English vexation to the point where Charles would be obliged to declare war on him. The loss of these fortresses, each of which would be a valuable bargaining counter at the Conference, made William think that Spain might be well-advised to make terms before she lost any more. England being the mediating Power, his first step was to ingratiate himself with his Uncle Charles.

There had already been some talk of his marrying his cousin Mary of York. At the time he had been too busy with the war, but he now reverted to the idea. It would not only bring the Sea Powers together in this conflict—it might make their co-operation permanent by a personal union. The Princess had been born before her parents became Catholics, and as heir to the throne she had been brought up an Anglican. It was questionable whether her father and uncle, with their Catholic and Francophile predilections, would consent; but the King would do much to win William's support for a quick peace, and the opposition would no longer be able to complain of his favouring the Catholics if he promoted a marriage which would probably ensure a Protestant succession.

So in the autumn William got himself invited over to England. He approved of the Princess—a simple, kind-hearted, pious, empty-headed girl of fifteen. Danby, an old-fashioned cavalier whom Charles had taken as chief minister when the Dover scheme broke down, eagerly promoted the match as a snub for the pro-French party at Court and in Council, while the King was glad of a chance to raise his price with Louis by showing that he could act independently on occasion. The Duke of York gave his unwilling consent, as an example to the nation of obedience to the Royal will. The wedding took place a fortnight later, and the Prince at once returned home, bringing not only a bride but an agreement as to the general terms on which France and Spain were to be asked to make peace.

He found the States General veering strongly in favour of an immediate peace without waiting to win the consent of their allies. He made frantic efforts to counteract this, pointing out that the Republic might want allies again later on. But the "True Liberty" party, crushed in 1672, was raising its head again, encouraged by French money and intrigues. It urged that the war was ruining trade, and it whispered that the Prince's royal marriage forboded a revival of his father's attempt to set up a monarchy.

The Dutch envoys at Nymegen were on the very point of coming to terms when Louis suddenly announced that he would not evacuate any of his conquests until Brandenburg and Denmark had restored their conquests to Sweden. No doubt he felt, like William, that to leave an ally in the lurch was to forfeit his support in future need; but his new demands revived the war-spirit both in Holland and in England. Charles declared that if they were not withdrawn by August 11th, he would join the Alliance, and he actually sent some troops over to the Low Countries.

A compromise was reached and an agreement initialled, one hour before England's ultimatum expired. Spain and the Empire, bereft of the Dutch guilders which alone kept their armies in the field, had to accept it, with many protests and loud cries of indignation. France restored Sicily, certain places which she had acquired after the last war (Charleroi, Oudenarde, Courtrai), and also certain of her recent conquests (Ghent, Louvain, St. Ghislain); but she kept Franche Comté, Valenciennes, St. Omer and Ypres. Thus Louis had done pretty well out of the war, and had some reason to boast, on the medal struck to celebrate the Peace, that he was *nec pluribus impar*; while the Dutch Republic, which at the outset had been threatened with extinction, retired without loss, leaving its allies to foot the bill.

The Great Elector wrote to his nephew more in sorrow than in anger:

Who would have believed that a republic which owes its very existence to constancy and fidelity in the execution of engagements would have abandoned faithful allies who had only taken arms to protect it from ruin?

William begged his uncle not to blame him, or even the Republic, for what was the act of a party. But for the time being that party had recovered much of its hold over the government. The States General would not even delay ratification long enough to allow the Elector to make his own terms with France; and though he tried to hold out, the occupation of Cleves by a French army soon made him surrender. It was the same with Denmark: Louis would not let King Christian keep a square yard of Bremen and Verden, and invaded Oldenburg to make him give them up. As for the Emperor, the only concessions he could extort was that the Duke of Lorraine should get his Duchy back minus Longwy and Nancy; but Duke Charles would not accept such a mangled heritage, so Louis kept it for himself.

CHAPTER NINE

THE SULTAN'S LAST SALLY

1648 – 1683

WE now turn to see the Ottoman Empire making its last attempt to master Europe. That it came so near to success was mainly due to the disunity of Christendom; that it ultimately failed was largely due to one of the most remarkable men of the age.

THE OTTOMAN EMPIRE. For some centuries past the dominant race in south-eastern Europe had been the Ottoman Turks, the rearguard of the great westward migration that peopled the continent. A kindred race, the Seljuk Turks, had preceded them in Syria and had provoked the Crusades, only to be themselves overrun by these Osmanlis at the end of the thirteenth century. The Osmanlis, spreading across Asia Minor and Thrace, had gradually subjugated the Balkan peoples —Serbs, Bulgars, Rumans and Greeks. These amalgams of various strains of Slavonic immigrants with various indigenous races had once been subject to the Eastern Roman Empire. They were Christians of the Greek Orthodox Church which had been separated (1054) from the Roman Catholic over one of those subtle theological points[1] about which men fought so stubbornly and ferociously in those days of faith.

The tide of Turkish conquest washed all round the walls of Constantinople, the capital of that Empire, but did not actually submerge it until 1453. That event is often taken as the starting-point of modern times owing to the stimulus it gave to the Renaissance which was already transforming western Europe. And it destroyed the source from which the Turks drew their own slender stores of culture. They had never developed much talent for the arts, or for political organization, or even for commerce; they now ceased to be anything but conquerors unable to assimilate the races they lorded over.

In 1517 their Sultan assumed the Caliphate—the position of Head of the Muslim faith and spiritual heir of the Prophet. Then came the greatest of all the conquering Sultans, Suliman the Magnificent, who

---

[1] The "Orthodox Eastern Church" is based on Greek culture as the Roman Catholic Church is based on Latin. Greek having been the language of the New Testament and the Early Church, it claims to be the original and only genuine form of Christianity.

overwhelmed the Hungarians (another race of Turanian origin which had settled in the Danubian plain and become Christianized about 1000 A.D.) at the Battle of Mohacs (1526). Thereafter barely a third of the Magyar (Hungarian) people remained under the rule of their Hapsburg kings.

The Turks owed much of their military success to the famous Janissaries, then the only whole-time professional soldiers in Europe; but a good deal also to the fact that the crusading spirit had long since faded out of Europe. Clerics were busy with secular interests, princes with dynastic ambitions. Francis I of France showed how little he cared for the interests of Christendom when he entered into an alliance with the Sultan against the Emperor. He thereby established a tradition which was inherited by Louis XIV, despite the latter's claim to be "eldest son of the Church." The Hapsburgs were elected Emperors largely because their hereditary dominions were not only large enough to enable them to keep the Turks at bay, but so situated geographically as to compel them to do so.

Fortunately there were traits in the Turks' national character which brought their career of conquest to an end before it had reached the vital centres of western culture. Firstly, they had no taste and no talent for the hard work of administration, which they mostly left in the hands of native officials. Secondly, they were far more tolerant than Christians to people of other faiths. They liked to dominate and tax subject peoples, but did not systematically suppress their racial customs and ideas. All the same, the cultural backwardness of these Balkan peoples to-day is due mainly to the Turkish incubus which for centuries lay so heavy on them.

When the Turks ceased to conquer they ceased to prosper. After Suliman a decline set in, symbolized by the annhilation of their sea-power by the Spaniards at the battle of Lepanto (1571). Too many of the Sultans were sottish degenerates; their government was honeycombed with harem intrigues; the Janissaries, like their prototypes the Pretorian Guards, were constantly involved in palace revolutions; local pashas oppressed the subject races with corruption and misrule.

THE TURKISH REVIVAL. Turkish despotism was tempered by assassination, and it was by this means that the Ottoman Empire made a fresh start in the very year that our epoch begins. The heir was a child, but the Sultana-Mother took charge, and in 1656 she appointed as Grand Vizier a septuagenarian from Albania named Mohammed Kiuprili,

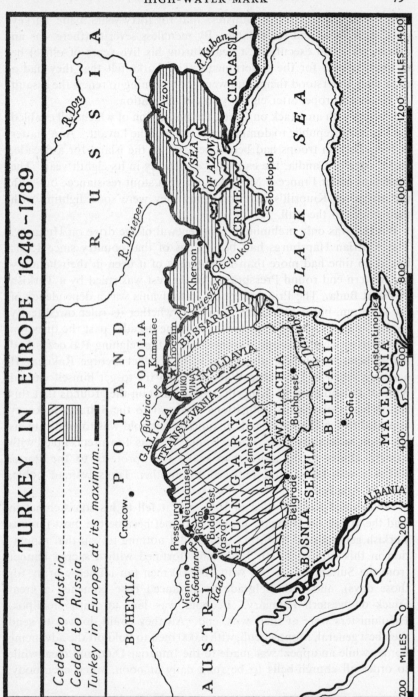

TURKEY IN EUROPE 1648-1789

Ceded to Austria............
Ceded to Russia.............
Turkey in Europe at its maximum..

RUSSIA

CIRCASSIA

R. Kuban

R. Don

R. Dnieper

AZOV

SEA OF AZOV

CRIMEA

Sebastopol

BLACK SEA

Kherson

Otchakov

R. Dniester

BESSARABIA

Kamieniec

Khoczim

PODOLIA

POLAND

Cracow

GALICIA

BUKO-VINA

MOLDAVIA

R. Danube

Constantinople

BULGARIA

Sofia

MACEDONIA

Budziac

TRANSYLVANIA

WALLACHIA

Bucharest

Temesvar

BANAT

Belgrade

SERVIA

BOSNIA

ALBANIA

HUNGARY

Neuhausel

Raab

Buda Pest

Vasvar

Pressburg

Vienna

St. Gotthard

Raab

AUSTRIA

BOHEMIA

MILES 1400

1200

1000

800

600

400

200

0

MILES 200

who founded a dynasty of ministers that for forty years made Turkey once more great and formidable. By merciless severity (there was an average of 5,000 executions a year during his five years of office) he restored respect for the government. The Turks felt that they had a ruler who understood them, and were soon burning to renew the assault on western Europe, after eighty years of stagnation.

It began with an attack on Crete, the possession of which still enabled the Venetian Republic to dominate the trade of the Levant. As a matter of fact, Turkish troops had been operating in the island for a decade, and a siege of Candia, the capital, was already in its eighth year. The Venetians under Franceso Morosini put up a stout resistance; but with the arrival of Kiuprili's reinforcements they were soon fighting with their backs to the wall.

But this was only preliminary to a renewal of the drive on Hungary. The Austrian Hapsburgs had been kings of that country since 1526; but at no time had more than three-tenths of it been in their hands—the western end round Pressburg. All the rest was ruled by a Turkish Pasha at Buda. The Principality of Transylvania was a dependency of the kingdom, but it had never been clear whether its ruler owed fealty to the Sultan or to the Emperor. For some decades past the question had been an academic one, however, since the reigning Rakoczys had made themselves practically independent; in fact George Rakoczy II had intervened in the Baltic War (p. 31) to try to get himself elected King of Poland as well. Kiuprili deposed him on the grounds that this action had violated his obligations as vassal to the Sultan. Rakoczy appealed to the Emperor; but, anxious as Leopold was to vindicate his claim on suzerainty over Transylvania, he was too preoccupied with western affairs to do more than make vain protests to the Porte. Rakoczy was killed, and replaced by another Transylvanian noble, Michael Apaffy.

Mohammed Kiuprili died in 1661, and it fell to his son Achmet to lead the attack on Hungary proper. Achmet became the most famous Turkish general of the century, but he did nothing to win that reputation in this campaign. In June 1663, fortified with a sacred banner from the Sultan, he set out with 120,000 men (an immense army for those days), and with Belgrade as advanced base launched a great attack on western Hungary. Leopold was laid up with smallpox. His ministers were at their wits' end. All they could do was to send their best general, Montecuculi, with 6,000 men to hold off the advancing hordes while an appeal was made to the Imperial Diet, and meanwhile to order all church-bells to be rung daily at noon, when everybody, indoors or outdoors, was to kneel and say a Paternoster for the deliverance of the land. Montecuculi handled his gallant few with such skill, and the forts along the Danube held out with such obstinacy, that the Vizier decided to postpone further operations till the following spring.

But during the winter the situation changed. The Turkish advance aroused a spark of the old crusading spirit even in cynical seventeenth-century Europe. The nobles of western Hungary, who were as usual in rebellion against the Emperor, romantically came forward to offer him their swords. The Imperial Diet, before whom Leopold appeared in person, voted a force of 20,000 men. Even Louis XIV, though he did not want his hereditary enemy the Emperor to defeat his hereditary ally the Sultan, felt he must do something to vindicate his title of "Most Christian King." Moreover he wanted to patronize the League of the Rhine, whose princes were much alarmed at the Turkish advance. So he sent 6,000 men, not as King of France but as member of the League, on condition that the League's contingent was kept separate from the other troops.

Kiuprili had missed his opportunity. Even when spring came he was so slow to open his campaign that Montecuculi had plenty of time to assemble his composite force, and even to take the initiative. When the Turks tried to cross the river Raab, Montecuculi, who had been moving along the other bank, attacked them while their forces were divided. The Imperial centre made a poor showing, but the Austrian and French horsemen on the wings covered themselves with glory. The Turkish army was broken to pieces, all their artillery was taken, and the Vizier drew off his shattered remnant (Battle of St. Gotthard, August 1664).

The Emperor, who in the expectation of a defeat was preparing to leave Vienna, threw away the fruits of the victory by his anxiety to rid himself of any further obligations to France. Ten days after the battle he made the Treaty of Vasvar, which recognized the suzerainty of the Sultan over Transylvania, and left in his hands vital fortresses along the Danube, including Neuhaüsel. Kiuprili was immensely relieved by this moderation, for Constantinople was not a healthy place for defeated Viziers; and he made the most of his good fortune by subjugating Crete—the last Turkish conquest in Europe.

POLES AND MAGYARS. One of the main threads in the tangled skein of the history of eastern Europe throughout modern times has been France's policy of encircling Germany by alliance with the latter's hostile eastern neighbours: Poles, Hungarians, Turks, Czechs, Russians. We have seen how for some years the Emperor Leopold remained in alliance with France. His chief minister Lobkowitz was hypnotized by Grémonville, whom Louvois praised as "the most overbearing ambassador in His Majesty's service." Appeasement, as expressed in the "Eventual Treaty" (p. 52) was the outcome of this line of policy. But Louis never abandoned the tradition of fomenting trouble for Austria in the east. He made repeated efforts—sometimes open, sometimes latent—to gain control of Poland. King John Casimir was a French nominee, his wife (his brother's widow, be it remembered) being a daughter of the Duc de Nevers. He was the last of the Polish Vasas; on his death all dynastic continuity in Poland would be broken; a free fight was in prospect. Louis tried to get Condé elected in advance; whereupon Austrian influences stirred up opposition to such an "unconstitutional" proposal, and put forward Philip William of Neuburg. Much would depend on the Polish army, and the French party gained an advantage when it procured the appointment as Commander-in-Chief ("Grand Hetman") of John Sobieski, a noble with French connections.

In 1668 the critical moment came. John Casimir insisted upon vacating his uncomfortable throne and returning to the career of clerical preferment for which he was more suited. (His wife had most opportunely died.) There followed a wild and confused scramble. Philip William was now nominally the candidate of France, Leopold having transferred his support to a young prince of the House of Lorraine; but Louis was still soliciting votes, underhand, for Condé. In the end the Poles sought the obvious way out of the clash: they chose one of themselves, a *piast* (descendant of the primitive Kings) named Michael Wisniewieski, who had no wealth, no ambitions, no brains— nothing to excite jealousy in anyone.

But the poor man came in for plenty of trouble all the same. For the Cossacks of the Ukraine saw trouble ahead for them, inasmuch as his father had taken a leading part in savagely suppressing their last revolt (p. 32). Once more they rushed to arms, once more they were checked, this time by Sobieski. Thereupon they turned to the Sultan, offering him suzerainty for his support. Achmet Kiuprili was delighted to find a new direction for the expansionist aims which had been checked at St. Gotthard. So having now completed the subjection of Crete he collected a great army, and taking the Sultan along as a mascot, he invaded Podolia in the interests of oppressed nationalities. Poland was torn by internal dissension. Sobieski was soon to show himself possessed of a marvellous natural genius for war, but as a politician he was restless, unscrupulous and incapable, and was subject to his ambitious, and devoutly adored, French wife. He had supported Condé in the late election for a substantial bribe, and he was now conspiring against King Michael in the hope of a continuance of Louis' favour—which might well culminate in his own election, later on. His disaffection left Poland defenceless before the Turkish onslaught. Within a month Podolia was overrun, the fortress of Kameniec, reputed impregnable, had fallen, and King Michael had been intimidated into the Treaty of Budziac (October 1672) by which he ceded Podolia (including Kameniec), and agreed to pay an annual tribute.

In any country but Poland a commander-in-chief who had so neglected his duties would have received short shrift; but King Michael was too weak and Sobieski too irreplaceable for strong measures; and it was well for the country that this was so. For Sobieski now burst forth in his full glory as rescuer of the fatherland. In a brilliant raid against the Tatars, who were trying to take advantage of Poland's discomfiture, he defeated them four times in less than a fortnight. The Diet now repudiated the shameful treaty of Budziac, a fresh national army was organized, and in November 1673 Sobieski advanced against Khoczim, where the Sultan's forces were concentrated. The Polish army was a disorderly and half-insubordinate rabble, but Sobieski contrived by sheer energy of character and native capacity for war to win a great victory, which drove the Turks into the flooded Dniester, made casualties of nine-tenths of their personnel and cost them the whole of their baggage and guns.

That was not the end of Sobieski's good fortune; for at the very moment when the churches of Poland were ringing with Te Deums King Michael died. There could be little doubt about the result of the election, when the Grand Hetman appeared as a candidate with an army of veterans and the trophies, spoils and captives of the most sensational victory in Polish history. He became John III, and Louis XIV had a supporter on the throne of Poland who wielded more real power than any occupant of it for a century.

Louis lost no time in sending a special envoy to make a treaty of alliance, by which France was to help King John to recover Polish suzerainty over East Prussia (the Elector of Brandenburg having just gone over to the Grand Alliance, p. 70), and Poland was to support the Hungarian rebels against the Emperor.

For the Hungarians had recently renewed their revolt against the Emperor. Any good feeling that might have been aroused by the battle of St. Gotthard was more than wiped out by the treaty of Vasvar. They protested against it as a breach of the coronation oath by which the King-Emperor undertook not to make war or peace without consulting their Diet. They strongly suspected that he had made it in order to free his hands to reduce them to subjection, and that the fortresses he was building to replace those surrendered in the Treaty were intended for this end. They noticed that he kept Imperial troops in their country, and suspected that the Jesuit clique at Vienna intended a great drive against Magyar Protestantism (which in truth was largely an expression of resistance to the Hapsburg). So the nobles once more put their conspiratorial heads together, among the foremost being Francis Vesselényi the Palatine (= Viceroy chosen by the Diet) of Hungary, and Nicholas Zrinyi, the Ban (= Viceroy chosen by the Emperor) of Croatia. The conspiracy took shape in romantic fashion at the wedding festivities when Zrinyi's beauteous daughter married George Rakoczy, who inherited a famous name from his father and vast wealth from his mother. Support was sought in all quarters likely to be disaffected to the Emperor. Michael Apaffy, the Prince of Transylvania, was the channel of communication with the Sultan; overtures were made to King John of Poland; above all Grémonville now had the card of Hungarian revolt up his sleeve in the game he was playing for control of Imperial policy. But a conspiracy is not an affair in which there is safety in numbers. There were rifts among those in the secret, for Apaffy was jealous of possible claims by young Rakoczy. Inept as the government at Vienna was, the conspirators were inepter. Prince Lobkowitz, the most capable of Leopold's ministers, collected evidence till he had sufficient, and then shattered the whole affair by arrests and executions (1670). The Emperor followed up the consternation thus caused by an attempt to end Hungarian resistance once and for all by a wholesale persecution which recalled his father's treatment of Bohemia, and cast a shadow on his otherwise blameless name. He abolished the office of Palatine and ruled Hungary through Austrian officials, and handed over the direction of religious affairs there to Jesuits, who treated Protestantism as high treason.

But the Hungarian revolt was scotched, not killed; and it could still rely on the money and influence of France. For the aversion of Louis XIV to aristocratic independence and religious liberty was not due to political theory. It was merely an expression of his determination to be master in his own house; and he naturally wanted his enemies

to suffer from the weaknesses which the Crown of France had overcome.

THE OTTOMAN PERIL. Achmet Kiuprili, who had carried Turkish
power to what proved to be its furthest bounds, died just after the
Treaty of Zarevno (1676) had restored the Ukraine to Poland: Kara
Mustafa, his son-in-law and successor, inherited all his haughty contempt for the giaour, and had visions of vast conquests. In the fifteenth
century St. Sophia in Constantinople had become a Mohammedan
mosque; in the seventeenth St. Peter's at Rome should become a stable
for the Sultan's horses. With western Europe pre-occupied with the
ambitions of Louis XIV, and the Holy Roman Empire in an advanced
stage of decrepitude, such things might well have come to pass but for
one nation—the Poles. For Poland had what the Empire lacked, a man
to lead it. John Sobieski, like Kara Mustafa, had a dream: to turn the
Turk bag and baggage out of Europe, and set up a Balkan Republic
with Athens as its capital. The last half of his vision proved but a
mirage, but he came very close to achieving the first.

The chief obstacle in his way was, oddly enough, his patron the
King of France. To Louis XIV the safety of the rest of Christendom
mattered little compared with his own *raison d'état*, which included
anything that would weaken the Emperor. He not only entered into
close relations with the Sultan, but encouraged the Hungarians to do
so. As matters turned out, Vizier Kara was in no position to start his
great offensive at the moment, for the Cossacks had now drawn him
into a war against Russia, the one Christian power for whom he felt
any respect. This was the more annoying to Louis as Poland had also
backed out of helping the Magyars. For Sobieski realised the gravity
of the Turkish menace, and in any case he found it impossible to
induce his staunchly Catholic nobles to take up arms on behalf of a
rebellion tainted with heresy.

Then the Emperor Leopold rather took the wind out of his sails by
a new policy towards the rebels. When the Treaty of Nymegen was
made in 1678 people expected that he would resume forthwith the
persecution of the Magyars which had been suspended by his entrance
into the western war; especially now that they no longer had Turkish
or Polish support. But he had begun to suspect that Louis XIV still
meant mischief (a suspicion that was soon confirmed), and to feel that
the best preparation for a renewal of the struggle with France would
be peace and order in his own dominions. So in 1680 he made a truce
with Tökölyi, the Hungarian leader; and at the Diet of Oedenburg

(1681) he restored the office of Palatine in the person of the popular Esterházy, offered a complete amnesty, and promised that no Hungarian should be disturbed on account of religion. These seemed substantial concessions, but Tökölyi rejected them as insincere, and offered the suzerainty of Hungary to the Sultan. Whether this action was due to French influence (and money), or whether Tökölyi was justified in his distrust of the Emperor, is a matter of doubt. Possibly he could not forgive the judicial murder of his father after the last rebellion.

By this time Kara Mustapha was nearly ready for the long-projected offensive. Leopold had plenty of warning about it, and sent a special embassy to ask the Sultan for a renewal of the truce (now about to expire) made at Vasvar; but all the time he was more concerned with Louis' new aggressions on the Rhine than with the mortal peril that was threatening from the east. Even when Tökölyi raised the standard of revolt and made himself master of upper Hungary, Leopold could not bring himself to take matters seriously, and he made a truce which left the rebels in possession (September 1682).

Kara Mustapha kept the Imperial envoy dangling on with well-spaced interviews until the end of the year. Then he suddenly announced that before the Treaty could be renewed the Sultan would require the cession of more territory on the Danube and the recognition of Tökölyi as King of all Hungary under Turkish suzerainty. This was tantamount to a declaration of war, and as such the Emperor was forced to take it.

THE SIEGE OF VIENNA. All through the early months of 1683 Kara Mustapha was assembling at Adrianople a motley array of warriors from the races of Anatolia and Turkestan and the Balkans; and at the end of March he set out for the conquest of the west, complete with the banner of the Prophet, a numerous harem, and a well-equipped execution-squad. When at Essek he was joined by Tökölyi and his Hungarians, the host numbered a quarter of a million.

At last Leopold's eyes were opened to the magnitude and imminence of the danger. The Diet responded loyally to his call, and among the princes who brought contingents were the Electors of Bavaria and Saxony, and Prince George of Brunswick-Lüneburg, later to become our George I. But the Great Elector hung back owing to a quarrel with Sobieski over Silesia; Spain was too busy watching France to have time to attend to other people's troubles; and the Prince of Orange could not induce the States General to take up arms for the Emperor, despite the obvious fact that his overthrow would be as disastrous for the Netherlands as for Germany. As to Louis XIV he scoffed at crusades as out of fashion. His hope was that when the Turks had spent their strength in destroying the Emperor, he would be able to assume the proud rôle of Champion of Christendom—when presumably crusades would be in fashion again.

But this was John Sobieski's hour. He at once began to collect an army at Cracow. It was doubtful whether he would be able to mobilize in time, for the German forces were slow to arrive, and by the beginning of July the Turkish host was bearing down on Vienna. On July 7th the Emperor and his court left for Passau. "Nothing was heard," writes a chronicler, "but execrations against a sovereign who after drawing on them the enmity of the Turks had left them without protection." And while Emperor and court were moving out, refugees were crowding in. The streets were filled with confusion and lamentation. Duke Charles of Lorraine marched out with 20,000 men to hold back a Turkish army of ten times that number; Count Starhemberg the Governor organized students and burghers to rebuild the crumbling walls and destroy the suburbs. About the middle of the month Mustapha appeared with his miles of baggage-train. He could have taken the city by storm but was anxious not to lessen the value of his prospective booty.

The Emperor sent frantic messages urging Sobieski not to wait for a full muster, but to come at once. Sobieski came, but a three-hundred-mile march through roadless, bridgeless central Europe, picking up German contingents on the way, took the whole of August. When he approached the capital it was not a moment too soon, for the defenders were at the last gasp, and the Turkish sappers had already mined right under the walls. Fortunately disease and disaffection were already taking toll of the besiegers.

Sobieski decided to approach not by the obvious route over the plains, but across the precipitous Kahlenberg mountains. This meant several days of severe climbing, in which every man had to carry his own rations and the horses had nothing but dry oak-leaves for fodder. Dreadful rumours about the power of the enemy began to demoralize the troops, and nothing but the King's personal magnetism could have overcome incipient mutiny. At last on the morning of September 12th the citizens of Vienna were overjoyed to see the banners of the relieving force topping the summit of the hills.

Even then there might have been a slip 'twixt cup and lip, for despite all Kara Mustapha's losses his forces outnumbered King John's by three to one. But moral ascendancy and tactical skill overcame the odds. Sobieski allowed the Turks to exhaust themselves by a long advance under deadly artillery-fire, and then broke them by a perfectly-timed cavalry charge. That night the Turks drew off from Vienna, leaving behind them booty of bewildering richness; and by the next evening they had gone as far in retreat as they had covered in a week during their advance. When the King passed through the streets of the city he had saved, says our eye-witness, "he was surrounded by inhabitants who hailed him as father and deliverer, struggling to kiss his feet, or even to touch his horse." In the Cathedral the archbishop took as his text "There came a man sent from God, and his name was John."

The ten years of life that remained to Sobieski were a sad anti-climax. The Turkish peril had united the Poles, but when it was beaten off they fell apart again. The King was desperately anxious to recover Kameniec. At one time he traded Smolensk and Kiev to the Tsar of Muscovy for help against the Sultan, but the expedition came to nothing, and the fortress remained in Turkish hands until after his death. His attempts to develop commerce *via* the Black Sea and by a trade-pact with Holland were also ineffective: the Poles were not a commercial-minded people. Greatest disappointment of all, he failed to persuade the Diet to turn the Republic into an hereditary constitutional monarchy. This would have been quite the best thing that could have happened to it, and might have saved it from the submergence that was its doom in the next century. He had great hopes of putting some such scheme through in the Diet, but the party of the Hetman of Lithuania, always a jealous rival, assembled in strength and threw it out, and Poland remained a prey to anarchy, intrigue and corruption, where "anybody could always raise a party for anything."

So the great warrior-king withered out his last years, disillusioned but not embittered, reading and gardening, and somewhat henpecked by the self-willed French wife to whom he was so devoted.

CHAPTER TEN

THE ENGLISH REVOLUTION
1 6 7 9 – 1 6 8 9

NYMEGEN was the zenith of the fortunes of Louis XIV. "Spoilt" by his successes, he pressed on to fresh aggressions which in the long run enabled William of Orange to build up a new and stronger coalition. The decisive question was which side England would take; and this was settled through the perverse unwisdom of James II, which not only led to the overthrow of the causes for which he stood, but placed all the resources of Britain, including the throne itself, at the disposal of William.

KING LOUIS MARCHES ON. *L'appétit vient en mangeant*—especially the appetite for power and glory. Like the dictators of our own day, Louis XIV could never rest and be thankful. Each settlement led to fresh demands. And the fact that he had kept his army in being when his neighbours had disbanded theirs enabled him to go on for years getting his way without fighting—especially as he contrived by neat timing to preclude his victims from common defence. Each hoped until the blow fell that it would fall elsewhere.

We have already seen Louis' experts in political jurisprudence at work over Devolution; and the dust had scarcely died down after Nymegen when they were again called to action. The treaty of Westphalia had given France a number of places "with their dependencies" or "saving their feudal obligations" (p. 7). The King now set up judicial committees to interpret these phrases. "Chambers of Reunion" (suggestive title!) met at Metz, at Breisach (for Alsace), at Besançon (for the Franche Comté) and at Tournai (for Flanders). So successful were their researches into local history that each of the places in question was found to extend up to the boundary of the next, while Imperial fiefs were declared forfeit because the holders had failed to do homage for them to the King. In this way Saarbrücken was taken over from the Elector of Trier, Zweibrücken from the King of Sweden, and Wildenz from the Elector Palatine. Of course as a judicial process this was farcical—a party to the case was acting as judge, advocate and jury. But it was very serviceable: by the end of 1681 Louis had thus acquired an eighth—by one computation a sixth— part of the Empire.

But the most important of his gains was not adjudged to him by any legal proceedings at all—he merely took it. Strassburg, a Free Imperial City, was the most important bridgehead on the Rhine; possession of it gave access into the very vitals of Germany. When the Reunions had carried his territory right up to its gates Louis threatened it with dire penalties if it presumed to admit an Imperial garrison or to repair its defences. Then his forces marched in (October 1681). So foregone was the result that he set out from Fontainebleau some days earlier to be on the spot for a triumphal entry.

On the very same day he made another most important acquisition, hundreds of miles away. The fortress of Casale, in the Duchy of Mantua, dominated the Milanese, the most valuable and cherished of the Italian provinces of Spain. Possession of it would give Louis the means of applying severe pressure to the Spanish monarchy. Through an agent named Matteoli he approached the Duke of Mantua, who had ruined his fortunes as well as his health by his vices.[1] The Duke at first refused, but Louis had a convincing argument in the form of an army corps assembled on the Alpine frontier. So an agreement was reached by which the Duke received a lump sum and a pension, and put himself under the protection of the great King, handing over Casale to him that the protection might be the more effective. Thereupon the French corps marched through Piedmont as if it had been a French province, and occupied the fortress (October 1681). Louis could boast that he had outdone Caesar in that he had conquered Rhine and Po on the same day.

We have become familiar with this sort of action in our own day; but there is this to be said for Louis as compared with our modern aggressors: he made no attempt to denationalize his new subjects. They kept their own languages, customs, institutions, and local government. National feeling had not then taken such violent possession of men's souls, especially in the historical No Man's Land of the Rhine valley. People pursued their avocations without troubling themselves much about who ruled them, apart from a general feeling that "whate'er is best administered is best." But among other rulers alarm and apprehension grew. There was no reason why Louis should stop at the Rhine—or for that matter at the Elbe. No repose was in prospect for Europe until this spirit of aggression should be checked. But who was to take the lead? The Great Elector, to vent his annoyance with

---

[1] Matteoli tried to "double cross" Louis by betraying the negotiation to the Spanish Governor of Milan; but he was caught, and it is sometimes thought that he was "The Man in the Iron Mask."

the Dutch for leaving him in the lurch at Nymegen, had made an alliance with France; the Emperor had his hands very full of Magyars and Turks; the Prince of Orange had to cope with the isolationist States General. And Britain?

Charles II was now back on Louis' pay-roll. The two kings had fallen out at the time of the William-and-Mary marriage, but the Whigs under the furious, factious Shaftesbury had overreached themselves in their struggle to disinherit the Duke of York. Charles tried to meet them half-way. He offered an agreement by which someone else—say the Prince of Orange—should carry on the government during his brother's reign, but he would not consent to an interruption of the succession. He did not concern himself much with principles, but if he and his family did not stand for "legitimacy," what did they stand for? He would far rather revert to dependence on France. So after one last attempt to make the opposition see reason (the "Oxford Parliament," 1681) he accepted Louis' offer of a subvention for three years in return for an undertaking to call no more Parliaments and to evade fulfilment of a guarantee which William had recently persuaded him to give to Spain. The Whigs were "dished." Shaftesbury took refuge in Holland —the Carthage whose destruction he had called for a decade earlier (p. 69); and the discomfiture of the party was completed by the Rye House Plot, only one degree less fictitious than the Popish Plot which was its prototype. Thereafter Charles II could sit back and take things easy for the rest of his reign.

In 1683 Louis rounded off this phase of his aggressions by a siege of Luxemburg; and when this alarmed the threatened Powers to the point of renewing the coalition he offered to raise the siege and forego further demands in return for a guarantee that he should he left for twenty years in undisputed possession of his recent acquisitions. It was pretty obvious that a potentate with so much force and so much guile at his disposal would be certain to find some excuse for making good his hold on them long before the term was up, and William fought hard to prevent the States General from agreeing to the proposal. But the oligarchy had now fairly got the bit between its teeth, and it put through a resolution urging the Government of Spain to acquiesce. So Louis got his way. (Truce of Regensburg, August 1684).

THE REVOCATION. Louis XIV, like modern dictators, required religion to subserve political unity; and since *l'état c'était lui* it became a form of treason for any of his subjects to differ from him on the subject. Nor could even the Pope be allowed to interfere with the French Church.

The last issue became critical over the *régale*. French kings had long cherished a customary right to appropriate the revenues of vacant bishoprics. This applied only to the fifty-odd bishoprics in old France; the fifty-odd in the newer provinces knew nothing of the right. But in 1673, as part of Louis' general policy of unification, he and Louvois began to apply it to all dioceses without discrimination.

Innocent XI, a high-minded and courageous Pope, took up the challenge by supporting French bishops in refusing the King's demand for arrears of *régale*. The quarrel developed, most of the clergy taking the King's side, most of the populace the Pope's. The climax came when in 1682 the Assembly of the Clergy drew up the famous "Four Articles." These were carefully guarded in expression, but amounted to a denial of the Pope's power to interfere in temporal affairs, particularly between the King and his subjects. If the wording of the Articles was ambiguous, the Pope's response was very much the reverse: "We disapprove, we break, we tear up, everything that has been done in the matter of the *régale*."

The dispute went through various stages during the next twenty years, but King and Pope had the example of Henry VIII and Clement VII to warn them not to let it develop into schism. Innocent would not consecrate French bishops, but they became "spiritual administrators" of their sees, and the difference was not obvious. New Popes let bygones be bygones, and in 1701 Louis, on the eve of the last and greatest war of his reign, withdrew the Articles.

As if to emphasize that this quarrel with the Holy See did not imply religious laxity, the King was at this very time pressing on with measures for the suppression of the Huguenot heresy.

The Edict of Nantes (1598) had been issued by Henri IV to end the Wars of Religion which had torn France for forty years. It guaranteed freedom of worship to French Calvinists, together with the right to manage their own affairs in certain cities and to hold offices under the State. Like their co-religionists elsewhere, the Huguenots had prospered in trade and industry, becoming a flourishing, intelligent and vigorous part of the nation, centred mainly in the towns of the southwest. Richelieu had withdrawn their political privileges but made no attempt to curtail their religious liberties. They remained quiet during the Fronde, when their support to the malcontents might well have turned the balance against the Court. They supplied excellent officers to the King's forces, including Turenne and Schomberg.

But as the urge for unification grew upon Louis and his ministers, this spiritual island in the Catholic ocean of France became more and more irritating. As early as 1665 the King had acted upon a request from the clergy that a commission would be appointed to "interpret" the terms of the Edict—the heretics should have the letter of it and not a jot more. For instance, it said nothing about new places of worship, so all those built since 1598 were pulled down. It guaranteed freedom of worship without mentioning future generations, so the children of Huguenots were brought up as Catholics until the age of seven, after which their relapse was visited on the parents with severe penalties. Protestants continued to be eligible for public office, but none were appointed. Funds were started to reward apostasy (at 12s. 6d. a head) and many persons contributed to them as an investment on which they hoped to draw dividends in the next world. But the most celebrated of the missionary methods were the *dragonnades*. Recalcitrant Huguenots were forced to billet soldiers who were instructed to make themselves as objectionable as possible, especially towards the womenfolk of the household. This proved the most effective argument of all—more convincing than thumbscrew or galleys.

About 1680 the King experienced the libertine's revulsion against libertinage. His poor neglected little Queen had died some years before, and as an expression of his new-found virtue he married Madame de Maintenon, the devout and highly-respectable governess of some of his illegitimate daughters. Another expression of it was the final step of withdrawing the Edict altogether, "so that the undisturbed reign of Jesus Christ may be re-established in France." Louis was convinced that it was only a negligible minority that still clung to the *Religion Prétendue Reformée*, and his action was regarded by the great majority of Frenchmen as the grandest and noblest of all his grand and noble achievements.[1] But it proved one of the most disastrous miscalculations ever made by a ruler. It did not in the long run stamp out Protestantism from France; it gave Frenchmen an impulse towards the scepticism which became one of the prime causes of the Revolution; and it struck a deadly blow at the economic structure which Colbert had been at such pains to build up. For although emigration was punishable with slavery in the galleys—a life as near to hell as man can contrive—tens of thousands did succeed in getting out of France.

[1] Mme. de Sevigné wrote that it was *la plus grande et la plus belle chose qui ait jamais été imaginéé et executée.*

Into the Netherlands, Switzerland, Brandenburg, England, they took their sterling qualities of mind and character—and their trade secrets. And in the foreign land that mattered most to Louis XIV the sight of these refugees was a warning of what Protestants must expect from a Catholic king bent on converting them.

QUEM DEUS VULT PERDERE . . . James II had begun his reign as the idol of the dominant High Anglican party which took "Non-resistance" as its watchword. All might have gone well with him if he could have taken life and duty as easily as his brother did; but he had adopted the Dover project very seriously and had never outgrown it. He was Catholic with the zeal of the convert and authoritarian by deeply-rooted instinct; and whereas Charles had after one or two tentative moves accepted the very evident fact that the country simply would not have either Popery or absolutism, James could not jettison his principles so readily. But his programme could not be carried through with the active support of France, and his *amour propre*, national and personal, revolted at the idea of dependence on a foreigner. The conflict was too much for his wooden head and limited vision, and it ultimately brought him to ruin. He started out with good resolutions of moderation urged on him by the Pope and the old Catholic families of Britain, but fell more and more under the influence of an ill-chosen little clique of confidants, some of whom were in the pay of France. He determined to make Parliament repeal the Test Act; and meanwhile he "dispensed" with that Act by appointing Catholics wholesale to key-positions in army and government.

These developments were watched with opposite reactions by Louis of France and William of Orange. Each was very anxious to have the naval and economic power of Britain on his side in the coming struggle; and an exciting contest ensued between them for the soul of James II and the support of Britain. William wanted to see his uncle on good terms with Parliament, knowing that British public opinion was stoutly anti-Catholic and anti-French. Louis, on the other hand, worked to keep Parliament at loggerheads with James by inciting him to extreme measures of Catholicisation.

James wavered. Family and patriotic feeling both made him favourable to William—if only William would support the repeal of the Test. For the Prince would dominate the country when (as seemed inevitable) his wife became Queen; and he had a wide circle of friends in England who believed in Anglo-Dutch co-operation against France. But William declared that though entirely favourable to freedom of worship he felt that to admit Catholics to high office, including Parliament, would undermine the national church, which was a bulwark of stability.

James's evil genius was Lord Sunderland. This most cunning, crooked and corrupt of English ministers in an age when nearly all English politicians were cunning, crooked and corrupt, earned a French pension by urging the King to accelerate the pace of his efforts to make Britain Catholic. James was convinced that there was little theological difference between High Anglicans and Roman Catholics, and that they could be brought across the line by patronage. He dismissed the brothers Hyde (Lords Clarendon and Rochester), who had carried complaisance to his illegalities to shameful lengths but could not turn Catholic themselves; then Lord Halifax—the man who had stood between him and Exclusion in the critical days of 1680. And he forced Catholic Heads on Oxford Colleges, thus destroying the stoutest pillar of Legitimacy and Non-resistance.

. . . *PRIUS DEMENTAT.* James II was an unlucky man—even events which seemed the happiest of his life brought disaster on him. In the last days of 1687 he joyfully announced that the Queen was likely to become a mother. If a son was born (and everybody assumed that it would be a son) he would take precedence over the Princess of Orange, and a new situation would arise. Hitherto the British peoples (and William himself) had comforted themselves with the reflection that when the King, already well on in middle life, passed away, the heir would be his Protestant daughter; but now there was a prospect of a succession of Catholic sovereigns. James, on the other hand, feared that if he died within the next few years a Protestant regency would bring the boy up as a member of the Church of England. The only way to prevent this would be by legislation; so he must call a Parliament and "pack" it well with supporters. He courted the Dissenters with another Declaration of Indulgence, and ordered the clergy to read it aloud to their congregations. Seven bishops presented a petition asking that they and their brethren might be excused from breaking the law, to which James replied by having them indicted for sedition. Their trial and acquittal (June 1688) gave an opportunity for overwhelming demonstrations of hostility to the Court, in which Dissenters were as vociferous as Churchmen. The most insulting form which this hostility took was a rumour that the little Prince of Wales (born on June 10th) was not really the child of the King and Queen, but a changeling brought into the Queen's room in a warming-pan. But

James stopped his ears and hardened his heart and went on his foolish way.

The very night of the bishops' acquittal a letter signed by seven representative men in public life of both political parties, was sent to the Prince of Orange, asking him to come over with an armed force to save the religious and political constitution of the realm.

That was an important step towards William's design; but was it likely that the States General would let him take their army and navy away on such an errand at a time when the King of France was showing every sign of going on the war-path again? For trouble was manifestly brewing on the Rhine. Louis had thoroughly alarmed the princes of western Germany by the way he was nibbling at the Reich year after year. (He was now claiming the Palatinate for "Madame" the Duchess of Orleans, sister of the late Elector.) In July 1686 they had sent representatives to Augsburg to form a league to maintain existing settlements from further one-sided revision. Historians used to regard this as the beginning of the Grand Alliance which the Prince of Orange formed a few years later, but the Grand Alliance was an international coalition, whereas this was merely an agreement between certain members of the Empire. England of course, did not join it, nor did the Dutch Republic, for William felt that it would only annoy Louis without providing any effective check on him. And the need for some such check became more obvious than ever in the following year, when he tried to get his satellite Fürstenberg made Archbishop-Elector of Cologne; for this would give him a representative in the Electoral College of the Empire. The Emperor, the Pope (already at odds with Louis over the *Régale* and over the extra-territoriality of the French embassy at Rome[1]), the Rhine princes and the States General—all were made angry and apprehensive by this new stroke. When William received the invitation from England he hinted to the States that an expedition thither might be the best form of defence, but for the moment they could not see so far ahead. Louis was gathering an army near the Rhine; he might at any moment send it down the river again as in 1672—that year of dreadful memories for all Dutchmen.

Then the Prince had a stroke of luck. Louis warned the States General not to allow their forces to be used against his friend and ally James II; but this only stung James's patriotic pride. He denied any alliance with France, and declared that he was quite able to take care

[1] The custom by which an embassy is considered to be under the jurisdiction of the sovereign whom it represents.

of himself. Louis was annoyed, and in September he launched an attack on the Palatinate which for the moment quite precluded his sending help to England or attacking the Dutch.

He opened this new venture with a manifesto, a *Mémoire des raisons qui ont obligé le Roi à reprendre des armes.* The gist of it was that though he had refrained from attacking Germany when Vienna was in danger, the Emperor had requited his magnanimity by forming a league against France. It has a painfully familiar ring to us, this lament of the poor wolf compelled in self-defence to devour lambs. Simultaneously with the manifesto, a French army crossed the Rhine, and the capture of Philippsburg, Mannheim and Kaiserslautern put the Palatinate into French hands almost without resistance. To create a zone of wilderness between France and Germany one of the loveliest countrysides in Europe was systematically laid waste. At once the princes began to arm, and the Great Elector sent a force to cover his possessions on the Lower Rhine.

Now that the French army was engaged in Germany there was no reason why the States General should hesitate any longer: to get England on their side would be well worth the risk involved. The Prince sailed with the forces he had gathered from all the Protestant peoples of Europe—Dutch, Danish, Swedish, German, Huguenot. He landed at Torbay on November 5th, an anniversary of ill omen for English Catholics. King James advanced with his army as far as Salisbury, then lost his nerve and returned to London. That was the turning-point. Many waverers now decided that his cause was lost. Among those who went over to William was John Churchill, Earl of Marlborough, whose wife had great influence over the Princess Anne. James, fearing that his life was in danger, fled to France, whither he had already sent the Queen and the infant Prince. This relieved William of an embarrassing situation; and indeed, the whole affair had gone better for him than he could have anticipated. His father-in-law, whatever his faults, had always been a man of mettle; who could have supposed that he would turn tail at the first brush and leave a clear field? He had thereby forfeited the last shred of his people's affection. The truest of true-blue Tories did not want him back as King except under restrictions which even they could not trust him to observe. His heir (assuming, as nearly everyone did, the truth of the story of the warming-pan) was the Princess of Orange. But William refused to remain as the subject of his wife ("much as he esteemed and loved her"), and he alone could give the country order and good government. So

4

Parliament offered the throne to them conjointly, on terms laid down in a Bill of Rights (October 1689).

Thus was born "constitutional monarchy," a polity since imitated in many other countries with varying success. It embodied two very English traits: the love of historical precedent and the spirit of compromise that contrives to make the best of two worlds. William and Mary and their successors reigned *Dei Gratia*, but also by sanction of Parliament. It was a position very different from the Stuart claim to authority flowing from a mystic Right Divine.

THE RE-BIRTH OF THE GRAND ALLIANCE. This was well enough as far as it went; but by accepting the irksome duties of a constitutional King of England William had merely ensured that British power should not be used against his cause: he wanted it on his side, which was quite another matter. For the British people, then as now, had a poor opinion of foreigners and their wars. Their new King had got them out of a dangerous situation at home, but they found this grim laconic little Dutchman singularly unattractive, and had no intention of letting him drag them into an incomprehensible scheme for a preventive war against France.

But matters were developing apace on the Continent, and William now put the finishing touches on a treaty between the Emperor and the United Provinces which was to be the foundation of a renewed Grand Alliance.

The repulse of the Turks from Vienna in 1683 had made Leopold face the question which was never quite out of his mind: East or west? Should he follow up the retiring Turks and win back all the other Christian lands over which they ruled, or should he now concentrate on checking Louis XIV, who was continually disturbing the peace of the Empire? Long were the debates and deep the intrigues at the Imperial Court. The upshot was a Holy League consisting of the Pope, the Emperor, the King of Poland, and the Republic of Venice, for the chastisement of the Turk. Each member was to keep his own conquests, and they varied greatly in the extent of their contributions to the cause. The Pope had little to offer but apostolical blessings. Sobieski was not the man he had been, and was hampered by French intrigues operating through his wife and the venal Polish nobles to hinder active measures against Louis' old ally the Sultan. But Venice made dashing onslaughts on Dalmatia and Greece under Morosini, the hero of the defence of Candia. The most famous campaign was in 1687 when Athens was captured after the guns of the besiegers had tragically battered the Parthenon. But it was Austria that bore the brunt. Duke Charles of Lorraine captured Buda, the ancient capital of Hungary, and Neuhaüsel the great prize of Achmet Kiuprili; and at Mohacs in 1687 the Turkish régime in Hungary was decisively overthrown on the spot where it had been established 161 years before. All this time Austrian forces had been hampered by guerilla attacks from Hungarian rebels instigated by Louis XIV, and Leopold determined to make an end of this combination of heresy and treason once and for all. He instituted a reign of terror centred at Eperies, where a military tribunal with scarcely a show of justice or equity destroyed the remnants of the Hungarian nationalist party by executions at the rate of thousand a week for weeks on end. When Leopold shortly afterwards summoned the Hungarian Diet to Pressburg, the members were sufficiently impressed by these events to acquiesce in two measures which they had so far evaded. They formally repealed the famous clause in the Golden Bull of 1222 which was supposed to give Hungarians the right of rebellion; and they declared the Crown of St. Stephen no longer elective but hereditary in the male line of the House of Hapsburg.

Thus, although Austrian forces were still following up the Turks into the Balkans (about which we shall have more to say in a later chapter) the crisis of 1688–9 in the west found Leopold with his hands comparatively free, and with a feeling of indignation against Louis XIV, who had been so false to his position as a Catholic sovereign as to support rebels, heretics and unbelievers against the Holy Roman Empire. William III urged him to cut his eastern entanglements altogether by a peace with the Sultan. He would not go so far as that; but he entered into a firm alliance with the Dutch Republic (May 1689) for the defence of Germany and the Low Countries. The parties agreed to re-establish the settlement of Westphalia as amended by the Treaty of the Pyrenees, and to restore Lorraine to its Duke. By articles kept secret from Spain, the Dutch undertook to help the Emperor to get possession of the Spanish monarchy, should Carlos II die without issue.

By this time the ranks of the Alliance were filling up fast. Louis had himself declared war on the States General. In December (1689) the Imperial Diet broke off relations with him. The Great Elector had just died, and his successor Frederick I, who was anxious to ingratiate himself with the Emperor in the hope of becoming "King of Prussia," threw aside all caution, sent troops to protect his Rhenish possessions and declared war on the aggressor. To cover his army on the Rhine Louis now ravaged the Palatinate once more. Without the smallest provocation, his troops destroyed every vestige of human life over hundreds of square miles. Thousands died of cold and hunger, tens of thousands carried into other parts of Germany a hatred of France which still bears bitter fruit to-day. In March the glorious castle of Heidelberg was blown up, in April Mannheim was devastated and Spires battered. These atrocities drove the Elector of Bavaria into the coalition.

The King of Spain (whose French wife, Marie Louis of Orleans had died, and had been succeeded by a princess of Neuburg nominated by Leopold) gave passage to German troops through his Netherlands; whereupon Louis declared war on him, too.

The Empire, Spain and the United Provinces were once more standing together as in 1672. Suppose England, then the ally of France, now joined them!

This question, too, Louis decided against himself by his own un-wisdom. He realized now that he had been precipitate in launching his attack on Germany before waiting to see what happened across the Channel. He had anticipated that James with a large professional army would beat William off, after a tough struggle which would eliminate the latter and teach the former to appreciate French help. But within a few weeks James was a fugitive living on his charity at St. Germains, and William was in a stronger position than ever, while the forces of France were engaged up to the hilt in Germany. What was he to do? Policy and generosity towards a friend in distress combined to make him lend James forces to recover his throne. He sent him over to Ireland (fervently Jacobite because fervently Catholic) with the nucleus of an army, hoping to give a religious aspect to the war. But the Pope repudiated this idea; he joined the Alliance, and recognized William and Mary as rightful sovereigns of England. And Englishmen who could not be interested in continental politics were outraged at a Catholic despot's design to provide them with a King after his own kind, to be supported, presumably, by a French army of occupation. Great Britain declared war on France on May 17th.

Thus the Stadtholder-King saw his dream come true—the Sea Powers were to fight France side by side.

CHAPTER ELEVEN

KING WILLIAM'S GRAND ALLIANCE
1689–1697

THE struggle which went on in the Low Countries and on the Rhine between 1689 and 1697 is often called "the War of the League of Augsburg." But, apart from the exasperation of Louis XIV at the creation of the League, this is misleading. The League never had more than a shadowy existence, and it did not include the Stadtholder-King who—as we shall now see— was the life and soul of this war.

KING WILLIAM AND HIS WAR. Now began the struggle which William of Orange had worked for, hoped for, prayed for, ever since the Peace of Nymegen. He held together the disparate forces of the coalition with patient and persistent statesmanship unexcelled in history; and he commanded its armies, though in this field he was not so talented or successful.

He enjoyed those summers campaigning in the Low Countries he knew so well. He was never in such good health and spirits as when fighting. It was the autumn that he dreaded, when he had to go back and attend to his duties as King of England, amid Thames fogs which made his asthma unendurable, dealing with intriguing politicians. There was scarcely a man in English public life who did not at some time correspond with the ex-King at St. Germains, trying to insure against the restoration which for years seemed likely. Their treachery to William made them dislike him more than ever; but truth to tell he was not a very likeable person. He had a cold heart and no manners. In Britain he was merely doing his duty by people whom he disliked; and he was too preoccupied to pretend that it was otherwise.

His best gift as a statesman, apart from the steadfastness which was the foundation of his character, was his capacity to let well alone. He never tried to do too much. He was as authoritarian by instinct as any of his contemporaries (was he not half Stuart?), and he hated to see the prerogative of the English monarchy whittled away by the Revolution. But acquiescence was the price for something he wanted much more—British help in the war. And whatever his faults he was a payer of debts and a keeper of promises.

101

As the Revolution was largely a reaction against French entanglements we might have expected it to make Britain more insular than ever. But in the long run the effect was to carry her into the main stream of continental affairs, from which after five great wars with France she emerged in 1815 as the financial and economic hub of the world, with great fighting traditions, military as well as naval.

William III certainly did not foresee all this. His vision was intense rather than wide. Like Nelson a century later, all he really cared for was beating the French. But the process involved tasks which would have tried the patience of Job: arguing with half-hearted allies, coping with factious States General and fractious Parliaments, managing two sets of ministers who were jealous of his authority. And he was pitted against an Olympian power commanding the whole resources of a country which outweighed in population and wealth all the Allies combined, in a position to say to one "come" and to another "go" without demur or cavil, served by an adoring nation and an aristocracy emulous only to win his favour.

Fortunately for the Alliance, Louis was not quite the man he had been. Otherwise he would not have blundered into war with England at all; for like aggressors of later centuries, he realized in calmer moments that war with England would be fatal to his main policy. In 1688 his real objective was Germany, in 1701 it was Spain; on each occasion he gratuitously brought in England against him by an act of quixotic generosity towards the House of Stuart. It was magnificent (and so he felt it to be) but it was not statecraft. But (again like later despots) he had fallen victim to megalomania—he no longer saw things in their true proportions. Moreover he had outlived the ministers who had created his régime. Colbert was no longer at hand to provide ways and means, there was now no Lionne to direct foreign relations, and Louvois, the superlative organizer of victory, died soon after the beginning of this war.

THE IRISH ADVENTURE. One sign of Louis' lack of counsel was his support of James II; he did just enough to harden Britain's will to resist and not enough to beat it down.

There was much to be said from a military point of view for his decision to send James to Ireland with officers, money, arms and equipment. Ireland would be an admirable base for an attack on Britain which might knock the keystone out of the Alliance; and James represented deliverance to the Irish people, burning with indignation under alien masters imposed successively by Elizabeth, James I and

Cromwell. But the ex-King found himself in a difficult position there. The nation was terribly backward, economically and culturally; and he could not satisfy their claims for restitution without aggravating the distrust which was already felt for him by the ruling classes in England.

At first William wanted to ignore this complication, and save Ireland by beating the French in the Low Countries; but his English advisers did not see matters in that light. So in the summer of 1690 he went over with 40,000 of his veterans and beat James at the Battle of the Boyne. The anniversary of that battle is still kept up with bonfires and broken heads in Northern Ireland, for it ensured the establishment of a Protestant ascendancy which lasted for two centuries. James, his nerve by now completely gone, rushed back to France leaving his supporters in the lurch. Yet up to this point his cause was by no means lost, for William failed to make the most of the great odds in his favour both in the battle and after it.

When he was called away he left the mess to be cleaned up by Ginkel, one of his Dutch generals. The Irish were eventually rounded up at Limerick (October 1691), where they surrendered on a promise that Catholics should enjoy the same privileges as in the time of Charles II. These terms were broken by the passing of a series of laws known as the Penal Code. It placed Irish Catholics in much the same position as Nazi Germany placed the Jews—with this difference, that Nazi Germany at least broke no promise, and that in eighteenth-century Ireland it was an alien minority persecuting a native majority. For this national crime England paid national retribution for two and a quarter centuries.

Louis' blindest spot in the conduct of war was his neglect of sea-power. Colbert had built up a navy which on the day when the Battle of the Boyne was fought in Ireland, inflicted on the Anglo-Dutch fleet "the completest defeat in the history of naval warfare" (July 1690) off Beachy Head. In this, the first round of the great conflict which ended at Trafalgar, the English did not even maintain their reputation as good fighters. For nearly two years to come Tourville, the French admiral, was master of the British seas. But he did not know how to take full advantage of it. If he had done so William would never have been able to transport the flower of his forces to the continental theatre of war. James, who had an almost professional understanding of naval matters, constantly urged his host to fit him out for a large-scale invasion of England while the Channel was clear. But Louis, still under the influence of Louvois, had changed his mind about the order of events in his programme. He was now confident of quick success in the Low Countries. For Waldeck, whom William had left in command of the allied forces there, had been marching to meet the Elector of Brandenburg coming with his contingent from Cleves, when he had been pulverized by Marshal Luxembourg on the plain of Fleurus. That battle too had been fought on the day of the Boyne, and the news of it brought William hurrying back from Ireland.

SIEGE WARFARE. This was the height of the period when the aim of generals was not so much to destroy the enemy's forces as to overrun his territory, capturing the fortresses that guarded it.[1]

In those days of bad roads and primitive smooth-bore artillery, attacks usually consisted of sieges conducted with an established ritual, in which lines of circumvallation, siege-trains and the opening of trenches all had their prescribed place. Two forces were usually employed, one to carry on the actual siege-operations, the other to hold off attempts at relief. The exact point when the governor of a beleaguered fortress ought to surrender involved nice questions of honour. He was expected to resist one main assault, possibly two, but to do more (unless relief was at hand) was to give an ungentlemanly amount of trouble. If he surrendered at the right moment, the garrison would be allowed to march out "with the honours of war," banners flying, drums beating, matches lighted, bullet in cheek. That night the commanders would probably sup together, and on the morrow the besiegers occupied the place without more ado. But if the fortress had to be taken by assault the garrison might be slaughtered and the city sacked. It was thus a matter in which the civic authorities took a lively interest, but over which they had very little control.

France was fortunate in possessing the greatest master of the art of fortification that ever lived—Vauban (1633–1707). Louis had set him to work making the places ceded at Nymegen into a screen along the north-eastern frontier of France, and he was kept busy on this sort of work all his life. He developed his system of starry bastions and ravelins, with crossing fields of fire, into a special branch of geometry. He was equally skilful on devising methods of attack, based on those employed by the Turks at Candia; and his system of parallels, the first out of the defenders' range and the last right under their walls, with zig-zag

---

[1] Sieges were Louis' favourite form of warfare. He had a genuine grasp of the elaborate staff-work involved, and the chief risks were starvation, exposure and disease, from which he was protected by his exalted position.

communication-trenches, still remains the basis of attack on fortresses. It was said of Vauban that he never attacked a place without taking it, nor defended one without holding it. Incidentally he was much more

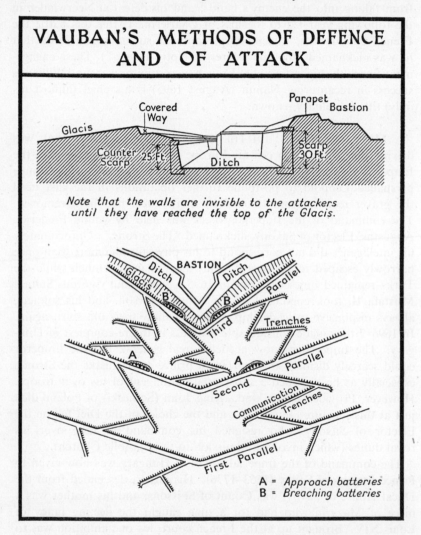

VAUBAN'S METHODS OF DEFENCE
AND OF ATTACK

Glacis — Covered Way — Parapet — Bastion

Counter Scarp — 25 Ft. — Ditch — Scarp 30 Ft.

Note that the walls are invisible to the attackers until they have reached the top of the Glacis.

Glacis — Ditch — BASTION — Ditch — Parallel

B — B

Third — Trenches

A — A — Second Parallel

Communication Trenches

First Parallel

A = Approach batteries
B = Breaching batteries

than a soldier. He was indeed, one of the choice spirits of the age, modest, humane, patriotic and high-minded; we shall catch another glimpse of him later on, when he tried in vain to make Louis deal sensibly with the economic problems of France.

Using their own fortresses as bases the French generals advanced each

4*

spring to attack some enemy stronghold, and in the autumn retired for the "close season" to prepare for the next campaign. The battle of Steenkirk (August 1692) was William's vain attempt to save Namur from falling into the enemy's hands, and his defeat at Neerwinden in the following year led to the loss of Charleroi. (After this battle the French commander, Luxembourg, captured so many standards that he was nicknamed "the upholsterer of Notre Dame.") These engagements mark the highest point of French success in the war; and William's success in recapturing Namur (August 1695) is his chief (almost his only) title to military renown.

MORE SIDE-SHOWS: (a) THE DANUBE. The pressure that was driving the Turks from central Europe (p. 98) was relaxed when the Emperor was drawn into the Grand Alliance, for William of Orange persuaded Leopold to postpone further operations in the east until the graver menace from Louis XIV in the west had been removed. The command of the Imperial forces was held by young Frederick Augustus, Elector of Saxony, nicknamed "The Strong." Unfortunately his intelligence did not correspond to his physique; he more than once narrowly escaped total disaster. This did not matter much while the Turks remained quiescent; but in 1695 a young and vigorous Sultan, Mustafa II, took command of the army in person, and his soldiers, always responsive to leadership, began to show their old spirit again. In 1696–7 they made considerable progress in the re-conquest of Hungary. The Imperialists now needed a real general, but the Emperor could scarcely dismiss so important a prince as Augustus the Strong, especially as he provided a substantial contingent of his own troops. However, Providence was kind. King John (Sobieski) of Poland died just at this juncture (June 1696), and the choice of the Diet fell on the Elector of Saxony, who resigned his command to take over his royal duties (which involved admission to the Catholic Church).

The command of the Imperial forces in Hungary was now given to Prince Eugene of Savoy (1663–1736). His father, descended from the Ducal House of Savoy, was Count of Soissons, and his mother was a niece of Mazarin who had for a time caught the fleeting fancy of Louis XIV. Brought up at the French court, his one ambition was to hold the Great King's commission, but Louis thought him better fitted for a clerical career, and called him his "little abbé." Mortally offended, the young Prince went off and took service with the Emperor. He learned the art of war under Charles of Lorraine and Ludwig of Baden, and took part in the relief of Vienna. Then he did some useful work in the diplomatic field, bringing his relative the Duke Victor Amadeus of Savoy into the Grand Alliance. And now in September 1697 at the age of thirty-four he was a Marshal of the Empire. He lost no time in proving his capacity. At Zenta (August 1697) he won an overwhelming victory in which the Janissaries were utterly destroyed, and the whole of the Turkish apparatus of war was captured. By the Treaty of Karlowitz (January 1699) the Sultan surrendered to the Emperor all claim to Hungary and Transylvania, and ceded Podolia and the western Ukraine to Poland, while Venice retained the Peloponnese and Dalmatia. This was the first stage in a gradual shrinkage of the Ottoman Empire which went on at intervals right down to the war of 1914–18.

(b) THE SEA AFFAIR. In 1692 King Louis reverted to the idea of an invasion of England. He collected 30,000 men in Normandy, but before they could be transported the convoying fleet was destroyed off Cape La Hogue (May 1692). The unfortunate ex-King, who had come to see the embarkation of the troops who were to win back his throne, watched from the cliffs his hopes going up in smoke from fires kindled by the navy he had done so much to create. La Hogue, like Quiberon and Trafalgar in later centuries, made Britain safe from invasion for the rest of the war. But the Admiralty had much to learn about the use of the sea-power it had recovered. Faulty staff-work allowed a great merchant convoy sailing for Smyrna with merchandise valued at a million sterling to be destroyed by a French war-fleet off Lagos (September 1693). And after La Hogue French privateers took heavier toll of Anglo-Dutch shipping than before; for Louis XIV, unable to raise a grand fleet, lent his warships as "cruisers" to serve under such commanders as the famous Jean Bart who (like our own Drake) was half naval commodore, half pirate.

Spain, though too decrepit to be dangerous to France, was in a position to make herself a nuisance, and Louis decided to knock her out by a sharp blow. He sent an army to invade Catalonia under the Duc de Noailles, with the support of the fleet under Tourville which had done the damage to the Smyrna convoy. Several coast-towns fell to the French, and Barcelona was in danger. To check this the Sea Powers decided to challenge the supremacy in the Mediterranean which had been held by France since the death of de Ruyter. Admiral Russell sailed in through the Straits with a combined fleet so strong that Tourville retired to Toulon and fortified himself there. King William showed a remarkable grasp of the importance of sea-power, and it was almost entirely due to him that Russell retained it by wintering at Cadiz instead of coming home (1694–5). And when, two years later, the Anglo-Dutch fleet had to be withdrawn, the immediate result was a serious gap in the encircling grip in which the Alliance held King Louis.

(c) THE SAVOY AUCTION. The chief factor in the Italian theatre of the war was Duke Victor Amadeus of Savoy. His domains included, besides the Alpine province of his title, Piedmont in northern Italy. ("Italy," it must always be remembered was not a country but a peninsula.) The geographical situation of his duchy, astride the Alpine passes between France and Italy, made him the object of bribes and threats from King Louis and the Emperor. Prince Eugene once remarked that Dukes of Savoy could not afford to be honourable; but it is to be feared that they did not try very hard. Their foreign policy consisted mainly in timing the transfer of their support from one belligerent to another.

Victor Amadeus had been cajoled into the Grand Alliance, but he had a great respect for French armies, which was soon confirmed by experience. An incursion which he made into Dauphiné came to nothing, whereas a French army under Marshal Catinat defeated Austrian-cum-Savoyard forces at Staffarda (1690) and Marsaglia (1693), and overran Piedmont. This convinced the Duke that he had backed the wrong horse. He opened secret negotiations with Louis, offering his neutrality in return for the evacuation of Piedmont and a marriage for his daughter to the Duke of Burgundy (heir to the French throne). Louis did not bite, so Victor Amadeus revealed the negotiations to Leopold, enquiring the price for remaining faithful to the Alliance. The Milanese, and a marriage to the Archduke Joseph? But the Emperor was equally cool, so the Duke went back to Louis, and this time he put through the Treaty of Turin. It was agreed that a French army should make a great show of attacking the unoccupied part of Piedmont; that Victor Amadeus should make an appeal to the Allies for troops which he knew they could not send, and should then surrender (on pre-arranged terms) to Louis. This comedy was duly performed in August 1696, and a month later the Duke's troops were attacking the Milanese alongside the French. To save his Italian heritage from total destruction, Leopold agreed to "demilitarize" it for the rest of the war.

THE TREATY OF RYSWICK. By this time peace was in the air. Louis had let it be known as early as 1694 that he did not attach any great importance to retaining his conquests. But in 1696 the defection of Savoy and the neutralization of Italy enabled him to bring Marshal

Catinat and his army into the Low Countries, where they swung the balance heavily in favour of France. Spain too was at the last gasp. The withdrawal of Russell from the Mediterranean enabled Tourville to come out of Toulon and blockade Barcelona, and that important place now fell to Noailles; and another French squadron took Cartagena, the chief entrepôt of Spanish-American trade, with vast booty of gold and silver and jewels (1697).

The war-will even of the Sea Powers was weakening. William's position in England got worse instead of better. After the death of Queen Mary (December 1694) he was merely an unpopular foreign ruler waging an unpopular foreign war with good British money and good British lives, and stuffing his Dutch friends with peerages and estates and sinecures. As for the United Provinces, the pro-French "republican" Party was always clamouring against the Stadtholder-King, and they now had the excuse that French privateers were crippling Dutch foreign trade, while the herring-barrelling which was still, as in the Middle Ages, the sheet-anchor of Dutch prosperity, was practically at a standstill.

The war was, indeed, putting severer financial strain on the belligerents than any previous war in history. Louis had expected to get it over quickly. The economic system of Colbert, undermined by the war of 1672-8, was quite unable to stand up to the strain now imposed upon it. Trade was ruined; debasement of the coinage raised prices; new taxes squeezed the life out of the poor. "The nation was perishing to the sound of the Te Deum," and its cry penetrated even the walls of Versailles. The expenditure of the Sea Powers was even higher, especially as they had to finance the German members of the Alliance. But they had the great advantage of a modern banking system. Amsterdam's development of "instruments of credit," by which paper promises to pay do the work of metal currency, had been one of the foundations of Dutch greatness. England had done something similar in the course of this very war. Her kings had often had to anticipate revenue by borrowing from wealthy citizens, but the need had never been so great and long-continued as now. So in 1694 a number of moneyed men had clubbed together to finance the coming campaign in return for banking privileges. Thus began the National Debt and the Bank of England; and within a couple of years the Debt had reached the breath-taking total of £16,000,000! But the landed classes, still the most influential in Parliament, were showing signs of revolt against the control which Big Business was beginning to gain over the national policy.

So it was with relief that King William learned in the summer of

1697 that Louis was throwing out feelers for a settlement based on the *status quo ante bellum* and a recognition of the new régime in Britain. Negotiations were conducted under Swedish mediation in a castle belonging to the Orange family at Ryswick near The Hague. King Louis would not expel ex-King James and his family from France, where he had now been living for ten years, but he promised not to assist "directly or indirectly" any plots to restore him. Lorraine was restored to its ducal House after twenty years in French hands. France retired to the left bank of the Rhine, restoring Philippsburg, Freiburg and Breisach to the Emperor, but retaining Strassburg and all the rest of Alsace. Spain recovered Catalonia and half a dozen places which the French had captured during the war. The Dutch were to keep garrisons in certain fortresses on the French frontier of the Spanish Netherlands, as a barrier against any future aggression.

The Emperor would not at first agree to these arrangements. He was on very good terms with himself at the moment, for he was just on the point of making the triumphant Peace of Karlowitz with the Sultan, and he had got his candidate the Elector of Saxony elected King of Poland. He particularly demurred at the loss of Strassburg. But when he saw that the other Allies were not going to continue the war to gain it for him, he gave way.

It had been a very great war—as far as numbers went the greatest in European history. France, for instance, put into the field twice as many men as in the War of Devolution, which at the time had been of an unheard-of scale. Louis had once more made a wonderful show against his ring of foes. He had the best of matters in every theatre of war; but the obstinate persistence of William III robbed him of the fruits of victory by reducing France to such economic straits that he had to make peace on what terms he could get. The Allies had not fulfilled their declared purpose of thrusting him back to the frontiers of 1659, but they had got him back to those of 1678, and had forced him to abandon the bold design which he had formed with Louvois and Vauban of carrying his territory solidly up to the middle Rhine. Indeed, for the first time since Richelieu France came out of a war smaller than when she entered it. And the champion of legitimacy had been obliged to recognize a usurper (and his declared enemy) as King of England, to the exclusion of the rightful King who was his client.

As for William, he could congratulate himself that, after losing practically every battle in the war, he had won practically every clause in the peace.

CHAPTER TWELVE

THE GREAT NORTHERN WAR

1697–1709

THOUGH the régime and policy of Louis XIV formed the high-light of a picture of this period, there were changes of great moment going on in the background—no less than the fading out of Sweden as a great Power and the emergence of Russia. And each of these changes was associated with a personage of heroic dimensions. In considering these phenomena we shall have to go a little way backward and forward from the point of time which we have reached in western affairs.

RUSSIA AND PETER. Russia came into existence during the later Middle Ages as an agglomeration of Slav tribes absorbed by the greatest of them into the Tsardom of Muscovy. Such culture as they acquired was imported by the Greek clergy who converted them to Orthodox Christianity; and this Byzantine influence is still visible in their architecture and their alphabet. The Tsars were despots, but their state was too inorganic for their authority to make itself felt continuously. A kind of feudal system grew up with local power exercised by landowners. Land being useless without labour to till it, the nobles succeeded during the first half of the seventeenth century in transforming the peasantry into serfs tied to the soil.

Such a people was bound to remain primitive and backward. Having no seaboard except in the Arctic north, its intercourse with the outer world was scanty and intermittent. To the north there was nothing but barren wastes; pressure eastward or southward merely brought contact with Tatars and Turks; and on the west the wide expanse of Lithuania and Poland divided Muscovy from the centres of European culture.

These barriers were broken down by a scion of the ruling House of Romanov known to history as Peter the Great (reigned 1689–1725).

His family history was typical of the time and place. His half-brother Theodore, though deformed by disease, had spent his short reign trying to grapple with the family pride which prevented people from serving under persons of lower status in a complicated system of precedence, to the ruin of efficiency in the military and civil services. As a child Peter shared the throne with his half-brother Ivan, the government being in the hands of his half-sister Sophia, an energetic and ambitious woman who burst the bonds of the *terem*, the Russian equivalent of purdah. When Peter approached manhood she resolved to dethrone him with the aid of the *Stryletsi* (a privileged corps of musketeers, several thousands strong). But the *Stryletsi* were divided in loyalty, the tables were turned, Sophia was banished to a nunnery, and young Peter took over the government himself.

His education had been deliberately neglected—he had had no tutor since the age of eight; but he was not the type to profit much by book-learning. His dominant trait was the enjoyment of life, and the volcanic ardour with which he threw himself into the pursuits that took his fancy. He early developed a keen delight in technical and mechanical arts, including an interest in ship-design which was to have great results for Russia.

His bosom friend in these early days was a Swiss named Lefort, a disreputable, hard-drinking, devil-may-care fellow, who nevertheless had the sense to recognize the genius that underlay Peter's self-willed follies. He encouraged his interest in ship-building and sailing, at first on the river and lake near his residence at Preobashensk, later at Archangel, where the young Tsar fraternized with foreign seamen and qualified as a coasting skipper. But the White Sea, frozen for three-fourths of the year, was too restricted a field for Peter's nautical ambitions. The Baltic had been closed to Russia by the expansion of Sweden; Turkish and Tatar hordes cut him off from the Caspian. So he decided to fight his way out to the Euxine through the Sea of Azov, approachable by water from Moscow. This meant war with the Tatar Khan of the Crimea, who could look for support from his overlord the Sultan; but counsels of prudence were thrown away on Peter. Such folk can only learn by experience, and the failure of this first attack on Azov (1695) was so complete as to be ridiculous. His re-actions were characteristic. He sent to Germany for engineers and ship-wrights, and to Holland for a model ship; he made his soldiers cut and haul timber; he grappled with frost, snowstorms and forest-fires, living in a hut with his workmen. By the following April he had a flotilla on the river, in May he sailed down to Azov, and by July the place was in his hands. Equally characteristic was the triumphal march through Moscow (September 1696), his chief officers riding in gilded sledges, while Captain Tsar Peter Alexeivitch—six feet four and massive of build—marched behind them, pike on shoulder.

He had got to the Black Sea now, but it did not long satisfy that yearning for a maritime outlet that had become a sort of claustrophobia. To prepare for the next step—as yet only vaguely outlined in his mind—he sent a party of fifty young men to learn the practical arts of the West in Holland and England—and at the last moment joined it himself, hewing timber and rigging derricks at Saardam and Deptford. On the way back he learned that the *Stryletsi* had revolted. By the time he reached Moscow the revolt had been suppressed, but he now evinced another side of his nature—ferocious and relentless cruelty. He wiped out the whole corps, having the ringleaders broken on the wheel, and beheading scores with his own hands, during an orgy of bloodshed and drunkenness (October 1698).

This frightful savagery was not quite pointless. The revolt had been symptomatic of resistance to his determination to initiate his people into the ways of the West. He had made the year begin on January 1st instead of on September 1st; he had ordered his nobles to cut short the long beards and flowing robes that were traditional with them; and when they disregarded his ukase he went round their ranks in his throne-room with a pair of shears and showed them what he meant. And his liquidation of the *Stryletsi* symbolized a break with the past.

Theodore Golovin, his first foreign minister, made a good peace with the Sultan by which Muscovy annexed the whole district of Azov; but by this time the young Tsar's interests had shifted. He now had hopes of a sea-base that would give him far more direct contact with the West; for Sweden, the Power which had a couple of generations earlier thrust the Tsars back from the Baltic, had now come under the rule of a lad of fifteen. It was now or never!

FATHER AND SON. We must now note what had been going on in Sweden since the Treaty of Nymegen. Louis XIV had supposed himself to be behaving with rare magnanimity in insisting on satisfaction for Sweden in that settlement; but his lofty manner of doing it, as if conferring a benefit on a humble but deserving client, made a very unpleasant impression on the young King Charles XI. Since then five years of fighting had made a man of him, but he never outgrew his prejudice against all things French—including the pro-French politician de la Gardie. He took as chief counsellor a hundred-per-cent Swede named Gryllenstierna, who convinced him that the country was being ruined by the overstrain of its natural resources. Gustavus, Christina, and Charles X, had been picturesque but expensive sovereigns; Charles XI undertook the more homespun tasks of national recovery.

The chief work of his reign was the "Reduction"—the return to the Crown of the estates which had been alienated by reckless predecessors (p. 28). The process ruined hundreds of new Counts and Barons; but Charles softened the blow by representing it as their sacrifice for the fatherland. After a good deal of opposition and some compromise, the measure was carried through and state bankruptcy averted. Charles won the hearts of the gentry and the peasantry, and it was at their urgent petition that he made himself an absolute ruler on the model of Louis XIV. For, odd as it may seem to us whose ancestors wrested "liberty" from kings by the co-operation of Lords and Commons, in most countries it was the nobles who had to be checked, by kings acting on behalf of ordinary folk.

For the rest of his reign Charles XI devoted himself to reforms of the navy, of commerce and of education; and he refused to be dragged into wars that would interrupt the good work. But his early death in 1697 left the throne to his fifteen-year old son, and a very different story opened.

Charles XII had been assiduously trained for kingship by his father, but for the first two years he did not seem to take to the position very kindly. He was polite, straight-forward, punctual, but singularly taciturn and unresponsive. Only during the visits of his kinsman the young Duke of Holstein did he relax—and then it was into the crude buffoonery of one to whom relaxation does not come naturally. The Duke's marriage to Charles's sister made closer a connection which had been originally based on the fact that Holstein, like Sweden, was an hereditary enemy of Denmark. Sweden's possession of Hither Pomerania had made the Duchy an obvious route for attacking the common enemy—it had already been so employed by Torstensson and Charles X.

COALITION AGAINST SWEDEN. Our attention now falls on one Johan Rembald Patkul, a Livonian noble who ten years before had come from Riga to Stockholm to complain of the "reductions." Charles XI had been impressed by the magnetic personality of the man, but had not satisfied his claims, and had replied to a later demand by condemning him *in absentia* for treason. Patkul had fled to Switzerland, and planned vengeance. He found plenty to listen to him, for all the Baltic states had accounts to settle with Sweden. As long as Charles XI was alive they had been kept quiet by fear of the Swedish army, still reputed second only to the French. But now that the centralized monarchy of Sweden and its military command had fallen to a child, Patkul's hour had come.

He began with Poland. When John Sobieski died in 1696 there were eighteen candidates for the succession, including the late king's son James, and the Prince of Conti who had the backing of Louis XIV. But the prize fell to Augustus the Strong, Elector of Saxony, who arrived with money to spend at the last moment, when the agents of his rivals had spent all theirs. He cheerfully abandoned his Lutheranism in order to qualify, and took the title Augustus II. His reign began auspiciously with the reaping of a harvest he had not sown: the Peace of Karlowitz by which Poland recovered Podolia and the Ukraine.

But the first interest of Augustus was still his Electorate, and he lent a ready ear to the persuasive Patkul in the hope of gaining territory for it. The two of them thrashed out a great scheme by which all the Baltic states were to join in tearing off bits of the Swedish empire. Tsar Peter was to have Ingria and Carelia—just what he wanted for his "window to the West." Bremen and Verden would be very acceptable to the King of Denmark, being adjacent to his Duchy of Schleswig; and no doubt Frederick, Elector of Brandenburg and King of Prussia, would be very glad to get Hither Pomerania, which his father had been forced to give back to Sweden in 1678 (p. 75). As for Augustus himself, he was to have Livonia, nominally for Poland, really for Saxony.

Patkul was unable to make much impression on old King Christian V of Denmark; but Christian died in 1699, and his son, Frederick IV fell in with the scheme at once. An agreement was made by which Augustus was to invade Livonia in the ensuing February, while Frederick attacked Sweden directly, from Schleswig and from Norway. Then Patkul rushed off to Moscow, where Peter needed very little persuading to undertake an invasion of Ingria, as soon as his Treaty with Turkey should be ratified. But Frederick of Prussia, with a full share of the family caution, decided to wait a little to see how the cat was going to jump.

He was wise. For these bandit-kings, seeking to take advantage of a hapless child, were about to have the shock of their lives.

CHARLES THE CONQUEROR. The plotters' zero hour was in February 1700. Danish troops overran Holstein, while a Saxon army invaded Livonia and besieged Riga.

The crisis tore the veil from the spirit of young Charles. He found out what he was meant to be—a warrior-king. Wine, woman and song meant nothing to him; nor was he at all interested in government or diplomacy, or in any form of culture. His métier was fighting, and for its sake he exulted in hardship and privation. His military methods were of the simplest: to attack with cold, intelligent ferocity until the enemy was destroyed; but this sufficed to make him arbiter of Europe at the age of twenty-five. The Swedish army still maintained the traditions which had been given it by Gustavus Adolphus, and it only needed Charles's inspiring leadership to make it as formidable as ever. On April 20th he left Stockholm never to return.

First he proceeded to Denmark, where he had the help of the Sea Powers. They were guarantors of the settlement of Oliva, and William III had special reason for wanting to keep Baltic quarrels in abeyance at this juncture, when he was rounding (as he hoped) the dangerous corner of the Spanish Succession by means of Partition (see later, p. 124). So an Anglo-Dutch squadron came to bring the Danish king to reason on the subject of Holstein; and when Charles made his own little navy force the "impossible" passage of the Narrows to join it, the Danes lost command of their own home waters. By bold and resourceful tactics he landed his army in Zealand, laid siege to Copenhagen, and intimidated Frederick into the Treaty of Travendal, all in the course of a fortnight (August 1700).

At this juncture Peter of Muscovy, having concluded his treaty with the Sultan, marched into Swedish Ingria with 35,000 men and beleaguered Narva. This was his first attempt at soldiering and he found that he had a good deal to learn about it. His men were half-trained, his guns inefficient, his victualling arrangements inadequate: his one comfort was that the only possible relieving force was hundreds of miles away fighting the Danes. Then he suddenly learned that Charles had landed at Pernau, had stormed his way through two formidable defiles, and was only two days' march from Narva. Peter remembered an important engagement elsewhere, and his army, thus deserted by its commander, became a demoralized rabble. Charles, with barely 7,000 men who had marched almost continuously for 48 hours, in the course of which they had fought two sharp engagements, went straight at them and wiped them out of existence as a fighting force.

It would have paid him to keep the Tsar on the run, but he was choking with wrath against Augustus, whom he regarded as the moving spirit in the coalition. Livonia had been so harried by the Saxons that it took him some time to get his forces into trim for a prolonged

campaign, and it was not until the beginning of 1702 that he was ready
to invade Poland. Having crashed his way into Warsaw he proclaimed
that he had come to aid the Republic to free itself from the yoke of a
perjurer. He backed this up by smashing a Saxo-Polish army at Klissov,
then, after chasing Augustus out of Cracow, smote him hip and thigh
at Pultusk (April 1703). Later in the year he assured his communica-

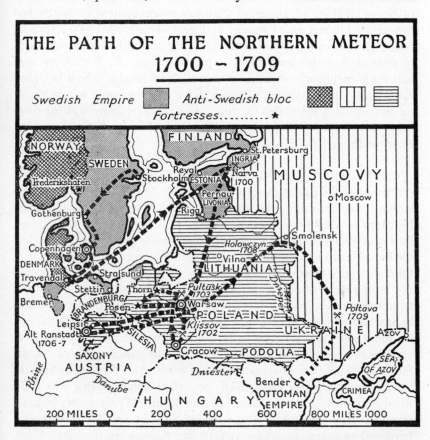

tions with Sweden by the capture of Posen and Thorn. The Polish
Diet declared Augustus dethroned, and asked Charles to take his
place; but this Protestant autocrat would have felt out of place trying
to rule a Catholic republic. Remarking that he preferred giving
crowns to receiving them he nominated a Polish noble named Stanislas
Lesczinski for the post (July 1704). The Poles did not take very kindly to
this arrangement until Charles had driven the Saxons helter-skelter out
of Poland and over the Oder. Then Stanislas was crowned at Warsaw,

with the Kingmaker (who cared for none of these things) present in the Cathedral *incognito* (September 1705).

During the four years that King Charles was campaigning in Poland, Peter was reorganizing his army. One of his best gifts was an open mind. He could learn from experience, and he did not waste the lesson of Narva. Taking advantage of Charles's preoccupation he established himself in Livonia and Estonia; and near the mouth of the Neva he found the site for the city of his dreams. He established his government in a street of timber-built shacks which he named St. Petersburg, and had some earthworks thrown up on an island nearby, which he called Kronstadt. It was typical of his audacity, thus to found a capital city on territory not yet under his rule. And his new army was far from ready for battle—it was repeatedly beaten by the Swedish general Levenhaupt in 1704–5.

Charles could not feel that he had finished with Augustus until he had put it out of his power to disturb Stanislas. Marching through Silesia without even informing the Emperor, he invaded Saxony and pitched his camp at Alt Ranstadt, near Leipsic. Here he remained for the best part of a year (1706-7), keeping a rough military court which became the hub of European diplomacy. Hitherto his career had been so active, filled with such dazzling deeds in such remote regions, that Europe had not been able to discover much about him, especially as he would not trouble himself to receive foreign diplomats or authorize his ministers at Stockholm to do so. But the Spartan simplicity of his headquarters, his plain attire and cropped head, contrasting with the silks and laces and perukes of his visitors, and the unsmiling taciturnity of his demeanour, caught the imagination of the West. The War of the Spanish Succession was, as we shall shortly see, at its height in this year 1707. Blenheim, Ramillies and Turin had put Louis XIV in a very difficult position. The support of the King of Sweden and his 60,000 war-hardened veterans, to whom victory had become an ingrained habit, could save him from disaster in the course of a fortnight. And there was just a chance that he might get that support, for Charles was disputing fiercely with the Emperor about the rights of the Silesian Protestants; and Leopold's frontier was temptingly close to Alt Ranstadt. But much as Charles disliked the Emperor and his Jesuit camarilla, he disliked the persecutor of the Huguenots much more. Indeed, he had some idea of forming a league of Protestant Princes (which would have shattered the Grand Alliance) to attack France. The Allies, realizing that this inscrutable personality (aged 25!) was as threatening to their world as to their enemy's, sent their great Duke himself to Alt Ranstadt. Marlborough began with the extravagant compliment of declaring that it was his ambition some day to complete his study of the arts of war under the King's command. This thawed even Charles for a few hours, but he showed no inclination to commit himself as to his future intentions. However, the Duke departed in good spirits, for he noticed on the table a large-scale map of Russia, which he took as an indication that the trend of the King's thoughts was eastward. And so it proved. Charles was incapable of carrying through any long-range policy. "A hare-brained Hotspur, governed by a spleen," he could not rise for long above the pursuit of personal grievances. As he had chastised Augustus, so he would chastise Peter. He came to terms with Saxony and the Emperor, requiring Augustus to recognize Stanislas as King of Poland and to extradite Patkul to be executed as a traitor; and insisting that Leopold should re-open the Lutheran churches in Silesia (September 1707).

POLTAVA. By this time the winter was approaching, and there was a further delay for guns to arrive from Stralsund. It was November before the Swedish army was able to set out; but Charles said that as they had spent the summer in camp they could spend the winter in the field—the nearest that this grim young man ever got to a joke. He chased Peter out of Warsaw (where he had been trying to reinstate Augustus) to Vilna. There the Swedes caught up with the Russians, but their horses were so exhausted that a halt had to be made until the morrow—by which time the Tsar had made good his escape. The Swedish officers assumed that Charles would turn north to win back the Baltic provinces and destroy the infant St. Petersburg; but he was bent on dictating peace at Moscow, and pushed on across the desolate plains of eastern Poland. The Russians obliterated every vestige of cultivation as they went, and the Swedes had to march over charred earth towards an horizon of blazing villages. Only one engagement enlivened those dreary weeks, at Holowczyn (August 1708), where Charles's handling of his cavalry was a brilliant example of his use of that arm, quoted in military textbooks ever since. The Russians were defeated, but the Swedes noticed a new toughness in them; and after marching on for a few weeks more Charles was forced to accept the stark fact that by the time he reached Moscow he would have little left of his army. For once in a way he consulted his staff. They suggested going back to the Dnieper to wait for Levenhaupt, who was bringing reinforcements; but this was too much like retreat for the King, and eventually it was decided to turn southwards and join the Cossacks of the Ukraine, whose hetman Mazeppa had promised to join them with 35,000 wild horsemen from the Steppes. Moreover there were said to be plentiful supplies of corn in that region, and the army would be able to resume the advance on Moscow in the spring with fresh strength.

But everything went wrong. Mazeppa's estimate proved a trifle optimistic—the number of Cossacks that he actually brought was 1500, and Levenhaupt's convoy was ambushed and cut to pieces by the Russians. Then followed a march whose hardships surpass anything that can be described or imagined. It was one of the severest winters on record—even the lagoons of Venice were frozen over, and birds fell dead on the wing. Of the Swedish army, stumbling on mile after a mile, scarcely a man had the full complement of fingers and toes. Hundreds died every night, and still the indomitable King slogged on, sharing every hardship. By the spring he had lost two-thirds of his army. He decided to attack Poltava, a minor fortress where there was a good stock of provisions. His exhausted men used up the last reserves of their strength in carrying the siege to the point of success, when Tsar Peter arrived with a relieving force, fresh and vigorous and five times as numerous. On the first of three days of fighting Charles had most of his right foot shot away, but he commanded first from a carriage, and when that was destroyed by a cannon-ball he was carried about on crossed pikes. He might have surmounted even these odds—he had done such things before; but the fever of his wound clouded his judgment, his army was destroyed, and he was carried off in a state of collapse (June 1709).

Peter was exultant as a schoolboy. "At last the foundations of St. Petersburg are firmly laid" he exclaimed. They were indeed. Poltava was the end of Sweden's greatness as a European power, and the beginning of Russia's.

Although the issue of the Great Northern War was now settled, it dragged on for twelve more weary years. During five of them Charles remained a not very welcome guest of the Sultan at Bender. At one time he managed to drag his host into a war on Russia. The Tsar was defeated and forced to give back Azov, but with the King of Sweden in helpless exile, Peter had matters his own way on the Baltic. He conquered Estonia and Livonia, and possession of Riga and Reval gave him two first-rate ports. Then he mastered southern Finland, and transformed St. Petersburg into a stone-built town on the western model. He re-established his crony Augustus in Poland and made a fresh alliance with him; and in 1713, to his extravagant delight, some ships he had built at St. Petersburg got the better of a Swedish flotilla in the Gulf of Finland.

All Charles's shortcomings were painfully apparent during his exile. He quite lacked the statesmanlike capacity to cut one's coat according to one's cloth. The Kings of Prussia and Poland, alarmed at the rapid growth of Russian power, offered to help him win back his Baltic provinces if he would give up trying to restore Lesczinski. The ex-King himself, now a penniless fugitive, begged him to agree; but Charles's reply was, in effect, "What I have said I have said." And later he refused Prussian support because King Frederick wanted Stralsund as its price. He seemed unconscious of any duties towards his country beyond fighting battles. He has been well compared with our Richard Cœur-de-Lion; for he spent all his reign abroad, treating his kingdom as a mere base for military supplies.

CHAPTER THIRTEEN

A TREATY VERSUS A TESTAMENT

1698–1701

THE Peace of Ryswick proved to be only a truce. Hardly had it been signed when a question which had long been hanging over Europe had to be settled. Louis XIV and William III tried to solve it peacefully; but circumstances —some fortuitous and some inherent in Louis' character—brought these efforts to nought, and the War of the Spanish Succession began.

THE HERITAGE. The exhaustion of France was not the only reason why Louis XIV was in such a hurry to make the Treaty of Ryswick. The question of the succession to the throne of Spain, which had seldom been out of his mind since it was put there by Mazarin in his boyhood (p. 23), was about to become acute. With a Hapsburg mother and a Hapsburg wife, he had already made a good claim to part of the inheritance; at any moment now the rest of it would be going begging. As long before as 1668 he had arranged to share it with the Emperor Leopold by the "Eventual Treaty," but events had made that so much waste paper. He wanted to have his hands free for the scrummage he saw coming; and in any case it would be unbecoming for the crisis to find him at war with the Crown in question.

Carlos II had had one foot in the grave ever since he was born (1661). He was the tragic outcome of in-breeding, and of the sins of the fathers that are visited on the children. So backward that he was still at the breast at the age of six, inheriting half-a-dozen chronic illnesses, having the "Hapsburg jaw" so developed that he could neither masticate nor articulate, so deficient mentally that he could scarcely concentrate his attention long enough to make his mark on documents of state, he was a poor advertisement for the Divine Right of hereditary Kingship. He had more reason than his namesake of England to apologize for being such an unconscionable time dying; but now, at the age of 38 in years (but 83 in decrepitude) his demise was really at hand.

All his life the Powers had been concerned about the succession to his vast domains. He had made one marriage in the French interest (to Marie Louise of Orleans), and a second in the Austrian (to Marie of Neuberg). The Government of Spain was as decayed as its master:

122

the navy consisted of worm-eaten hulks, the army of threadbare scare-crows; with vast wealth coming in every year from the Indies the treasury was bankrupt; the most powerful institution in the country was the Inquisition, with its secret police and secret tribunals; the streets of the towns were crowded with beggars, the countryside infested with brigands. So long as this paralysis continued Spain could not take an active part in European affairs; but if her potential resources fell into the grasp of Louis XIV there was no knowing what might be achieved with them. It was this possibility that riveted the attention of Europe, and of Louis himself, as the crisis approached.

THE THREE CLAIMANTS : 1698-1700

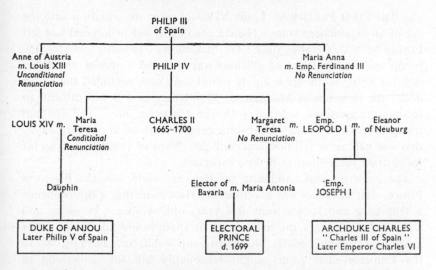

In default of a direct heir or of a younger brother, the inheritance would normally pass to one of the King's half-sisters, the daughters of his father Philip IV by his first wife. Of these the elder, Maria Teresa, had married Louis XIV, and her heir was the Dauphin. She had on her marriage renounced all claim to the Spanish heritage *provided that* her dowry was duly paid—which it never was. The younger, Margaret, had married the Emperor Leopold, their only child being a daughter, Maria Antonia, who had married the Elector of Bavaria and had borne an only son, the Electoral Prince Joseph Ferdinand. Maria Antonia had been induced by her father the Emperor to transfer all her Spanish claims to himself; but this was of doubtful legality, and certainly could not affect the rights of her son. Going back a generation to the direct offspring of Philip III, there were again two sisters married to a Bourbon and to Hapsburg, respectively. Of these the former had renounced, while the younger had not. That seemed to debar the rights of Louis XIV in favour of those of Leopold. But Louis did not admit that there was any need to go beyond the rights of his Queen, and denied that Leopold had any right to profit by a renunciation which he had imposed on his young daughter.

There were also political considerations. France would not permit the union of Spain with the Austrian family, Austria would not permit its union with the French family, while the Sea Powers would not permit the vast commercial possibilities of the Spanish Empire to be monopolized by either.

THE FIRST PARTITION. Louis XIV looked at the situation with the eye of an experienced ruler. The decade of the war just ended had left France in a deplorable state. He himself was growing elderly—the pomp and circumstance of glorious war had lost some of its attraction for him. Moreover a highly moral tone now pervaded the Court under the influence of Madame de Maintenon, and it was difficult to reconcile acquisitive warfare with the Christian life. And he had learned from experience—what some people overlook in our own day— that one can never tell how wars will go. None of those he had so far fought had turned out as he had expected.

The most obvious candidate for the succession was the Electoral Prince. His weakness was his strength. He was neither a Bourbon nor a Hapsburg and he was only five years old. Under a boy-king and a regency of grandees, the government of Spain would not be a cause of anxiety to any other State. No doubt a sop would have been thrown to the Emperor, and Louis might reasonably ask for something to counter-balance this; but these adjustments would not upset the balance of power.

So early in 1698 Louis sent a special envoy over to London to open the subject. At first William was suspicious of any suggestion coming from his old enemy; but he soon saw that he had nothing to lose by the proposed arrangement. If Louis were to come into possession of the whole heritage his own life's work would be undone. And he could do nothing to stop him, for both Britain and the Netherlands were rapidly disarming. Nothing would induce either Parliament or the States General to undertake another war to check France—they had had enough of that sort of thing to last them a very long time.

But throughout the negotiations it was Louis who took the initiative, while William and Heinsius (the Grand Pensionary) interposed objections and criticisms. To England the vital matter was to detach Louis from the Stuarts, and so maintain the Revolution Settlement; to the Republic it was to secure a barrier between them and France; and both wanted a share of South American commerce, and feared for the future of Protestantism if the Power that revoked the Edict and the Power that maintained an Inquisition came into one efficient and vigorous hand. The treaty eventually signed provided that the Emperor's son the Archduke Charles should have the Milanese, the Dauphin the two Sicilies and the Tuscan Ports, and the Electoral Prince all the rest (October 1698).

When the terms became known, there were loud protests from three directions. The Duke of Savoy wanted part of the Milanese for himself. and felt that his geographical position gave him sufficient bargaining-power to enable him to demand it. Spain was indignant at the proposal to carve up her Empire, and King Carlos made a will bequeathing it all to the Electoral Prince. The Emperor with wooden obstinacy insisted on his claim to the whole heritage, despite the fact that he had made thirty years before the Eventual Treaty which gave him much less. Still, none of these objectors would be able to resist a settlement backed by the united force of France and the Sea Powers.

Then an unpredictable mishap upset the whole thing. In February 1699 the little Electoral Prince died of smallpox, and the labours of five months were wasted.

THE SECOND ATTEMPT. Louis lost no time in vain regrets—there was indeed no time to lose, for alarming tales were coming daily about the Spanish king's health. The Archduke was now the only candidate acceptable to the Sea Powers for the bulk of the Spanish possessions; so Louis bent all his energies on winning such concessions for his House as would neutralize the increased power of Austria. This second partition gave Spain, the Indies, and the Netherlands to the Archduke, while the Dauphin was to receive, in addition to the territory allotted to him by the first treaty, the Milanese which he was to exchange with the Duke of Lorraine for his Duchy (May 1699). Once again the Emperor protested: the Italian provinces were precisely those which he coveted most for his son.

Perhaps Louis was only half in earnest about this second partition, for he now saw a chance of getting the whole heritage for his own family. In Madrid a tragic farce was going on round the dying King. His Queen was sister-in-law of Leopold, and she set herself to see that Spain and its Empire should not pass from the Hapsburgs. With this in view she made remorseless use of her position as the King's spouse, playing on his weaknesses and terrors, with the aid of the confessor she had appointed for him. But Louis organized a party of his own at the Court, headed by his ambassador Harcourt and Cardinal Porto-carrero. They bribed and intrigued busily, but for a long time the Queen managed to prevent their gaining access to the dying King. The efforts of both parties intensified as his infirmities increased, for it was obvious that those who were "in at the death" would carry off the brush. The wretched King, suspecting poison in his food and in dread of his wife, sank into depths of melancholy from which he could scarcely be roused to feed himself. As the year 1700 went on he became too weak to rise from his bed, save when the Queen dragged him to totter and mumble through some ceremony. His room was so filled with sacred relics that one could scarcely move across it. Doctors plied him with nauseous drugs, and priests with spells against witchcraft.

Meanwhile the state of the Spanish people became desperate. Famished but ferocious crowds round the palace blamed the Queen and her Austrian clique for their miseries. At last she was intimidated into flight; and this was the Cardinal's opportunity. He drummed into the terror-stricken King that his conscience would not be clear nor his soul safe until he had bequeathed his possessions, whole and entire, to his rightful heir the Duke of Anjou, second son of the Dauphin. In this the Cardinal was expressing the mind and soul of the whole Spanish people. Amid all their degradation they clung to their pride in their great Empire. Divided and nerveless about all else, on this subject they were united and determined. Apart from man-made renunciations and partitions, the true heir of Philip IV was his eldest daughter, whose rights descended to the children of Louis XIV. Of course, it was no use leaving the heritage to the future King of France— the other Powers of Europe would unite in determination not to allow two such crowns to be on one head. But if it passed to a younger scion of the House their resistance would be weaker, and the great resources of the King Louis would be sufficient to overcome it. So at the beginning of October King Carlos was cajoled into signing a will which made Philip Duke of Anjou his "universal heir." Failing him his domains, still whole and entire, were to pass to Anjou's younger brother, the Duke of Berry, and failing him to the Archduke Charles.

A fortnight later (November 1, 1700) Carlos was relieved of his unhappy existence, and his will became known to the world.

"*Il n'y a Plus de Pyrénées.*" The news reached Louis at Fontaine-bleau on the morning of November 9th. In the afternoon he summoned his inner cabinet to Madame de Maintenon's room, where affairs of state were commonly transacted. After some hours the discussion was adjourned until the morrow to give time for individual weighing of the points at issue.

Of course, the King was not compelled to accept the will—one can always decline a legacy. He could stand by the Treaty which he had signed so recently, the Treaty which was his political masterpiece, created with so much trouble and advertised with such insistence. To repudiate it would impugn a reputation as a man of honour which meant a great deal to him, and would strike a blow at international ethics of which he professed himself the champion.

But there was much to be said on the other side. He did not want a war; that was why he had been so active to promote partition. But the English and Dutch oligarchies were in no mood to fight for anything short of national existence. They would certainly not support him if he were to try to force partition on an unwilling Spain. They had had no part in the making of the Treaties, and much resented William's having agreed to them on his own authority. Was it reasonable to expect Louis to fight for that settlement by himself, in order to thwart the interests of his own grandson? Whereas if he accepted the will, even if by some chance he had to take the field against a resuscitated Grand Alliance, it would be much less Grand this time than last; for Spain and her possessions would now be on his side instead of against him. That meant that the western Mediterranean would be a Franco-Spanish lake, and that instead of having to conquer the fortresses of the Low Countries piecemeal they would be in his hands from the start. Savoy, whose defection had been such a blow to the Allies in the last war, was still faithful to him, and he had also won over old King Pedro of Portugal. The navies of Britain and the Netherlands might still command the sea, but what use would that be to them if no ports were open to them around the theatres of war? Furthermore, he was in the process of suborning two Electors of the Empire. If he could win over Maximilian of Bavaria, he would have an advanced base in Germany within striking distance of Vienna; and Max's brother the Archbishop of Cologne had already promised a free road for French troops by the route which they had taken to attack the United Provinces in 1672.

So the die was cast. On the morning after the "great consult," when the doors of the royal cabinet were thrown open, Louis advanced into the Great Hall with his hand on the shoulder of the seventeen-year-old Duke of Anjou. "Gentlemen," he said to the assembled court, "I present to you the King of Spain"; and the Spanish ambassador made a famous epigram about there being no longer any Pyrenees. It was an indiscreet remark, for of course, Louis did not want the foreign Powers to think that the two countries would henceforth be one. On the contrary, in announcing his decision to them he gave the most explicit assurances that the crowns would never be united.

THE GRAND ALLIANCE RECONSTRUCTED. It was just as William had feared, "I am troubled to the bottom of my soul," he wrote to Heinsius, "to find that nearly everybody prefers the will to the treaty, insisting that it is much better for England and for the whole of Europe." And in the United Provinces the Republican party rejoiced to see the Stadtholder discomfited. Amsterdam scoffed at the danger of Antwerp taking away its trade, and professed unconcern even at the danger to the new "Barrier." Of course, the Emperor was extremely disgruntled. In fact he was already trying to induce some of the chief German states to join him in resisting the treaty without waiting for the cumbrous machinery of the Reich. But without active help from the Sea Powers no German confederacy could make much headway. Spaniards everywhere acclaimed the accession of "King Philip V" who personified the unity of their Empire; and Louis pressed this home with a well-timed *coup*. The fortress-towns of the Low Countries had been as vital to the Dutch as to the Spaniards, and troops of the two armies had co-operated in guarding them. But Spain was now the close ally of France, and when French troops suddenly appeared there the Spanish part of the garrisons made way for them without demur, while the Dutch were too dumbfounded to resist being disarmed and taken prisoner. King Louis would not release them until the States General had formally recognized his grandson as King Philip V of Spain. After that William could no longer hold out against his peace-at-any-price English ministers, and England followed suit.

Louis XIV had every reason to congratulate himself on the accuracy of his political forecast: he had placed his grandson on the throne of Spain without firing a shot. One would have thought that he was too old a hand at politics to let his head be turned by his success; but ingrained habits of mind had become a second nature. He could not resist the temptation to strut once more on the world-stage as a giant among the pigmies. Common sense might have warned him to go slow and speak fair until the doubts and fears aroused by the Succession had died down. But he did just the opposite. The seizure of the Barrier fortresses would not have shaken the determined pacificism of the ruling parties in England and Holland, had he not followed it up by a *crescendo* of aggression which brought home forcibly to everybody what Europe had to expect if he were left unchecked. Despite the solemn assurance which he had volunteered only a few months before, he now made a formal announcement that King Philip had not impaired his rights to the throne of France—he was to come before his younger brother in the succession. He refused even to discuss suggestions from the British and Dutch Governments for some trifling "compensation" to appease the Emperor, or for a reconstitution of the fortress-barrier. It was particularly important for him to allay the suspicion that he was himself going to act as master of Spain; yet he sent his troops into the Low Countries and the Milanese with hardly a pretence of consulting Madrid; he obtained the *Asiento* which gave France the exclusive right to supply the Spanish colonies with negro slaves; he made decrees which seemed to identify French and Spanish commercial interests. If the unrealized resources of Spanish America were exploited by the efficient commercial organization bequeathed by Colbert, British and Dutch merchants would suffer a severe setback.

With a swelling wave of public feeling beneath them, William and Heinsius negotiated an agreement with the Emperor which revived in modified form the Grand Alliance of 1689. They would not support the Archduke's claim to the whole of the Spanish domains, for they still hoped to avoid war, and they had tied their own hands by their recognition of Philip V. Their main purpose was to prevent France getting control of the western Mediterranean and of the Low Countries. So the Treaty of the Hague, assigning the Italian Provinces and the Low Countries to the Archduke Charles, was signed on September 1st. Nothing was said in it about Spain and the Indies, for the Emperor could not be expected to make an open renunciation of the Archduke's claim to the whole inheritance; but silence gave consent to Philip V retaining them. It was really a new and improved edition of the Second Partition, and Louis was given two months to act upon it by evacuating Belgium and the Milanese.

His reply was an act which upset the apple-cart altogether. Later in that same month of September 1701 ex-King James died at St. Germains, and Louis greeted his son James Edward (of the warming-pan legend) as rightful King of Great Britain. In announcing this, he laid

5

stress on the word "rightful," implying that he had no intention of following it up by an overt attempt to make "James III" an *actual* king. To himself his action seemed little more than a gesture of adherence to "legitimacy" and of generosity to friends fallen on evil days; but to the British peoples it was not only a flagrant breach of the Treaty of Ryswick, but a public affront to their national pride by nominating a future king for them—and a Catholic, too. The effect was catastrophic. All the combustible material lying about in Europe, which might have evaporated with time, was set ablaze. Louis had done for William what William had never been able to do for himself—brought English Tories and Dutch Republicans over to whole-hearted support of his aims.

The winter of 1701–2 was spent in settling the military details of the Alliance. It was some time before the Circles of the Empire could make up their minds whether to support the Emperor. Adherents of Louis pointed out that this was a dynastic quarrel about the Hapsburg heritage, and asked why they should fight to give Austria still greater possessions with which to dominate them. But the general impression was that it was their duty to stand by the Emperor. The Elector of Hanover—Britain's future George I—who had made a mark as a general in the last war, gave a strong lead in this direction; and the insolence of French diplomatists and soldiers did the rest. In the autumn of 1701 the Grand Alliance was formally reconstituted, and by the spring of the following year the Electors of Mainz and Trier, the Landgraves of Hesse-Darmstadt and Hesse-Cassel, the Margrave of Baden, and the Elector Palatine had all joined it.

There was a certain amount of friction between the Emperor and the Sea Powers as to how the military objects of the Alliance should be defined. Leopold wanted the whole Spanish empire for his son; but William and Heinsius were bound by their recognition of Philip V as King of Spain, and aimed merely at enforcing the partition treaty. Marlborough pointed out that British interests demanded the exclusion of the Bourbons from Naples and Sicily, so these were added to the Archduke's portion; but that was as far as the Sea Powers would go, and with that Leopold had to be satisfied.

French and Imperial troops were already fighting in northern Italy. Louis, foreseeing that the Milanese would be Leopold's first objective, had sent powerful reinforcements to the Spanish garrisons there, and had forced the Duke of Savoy to give them passage. But Catinat, the commander of the French troops, was completely outmanœuvred by

Prince Eugene, who came through the Brenner and drove the French back over the Mincio and Oglio. Villeroi, replacing Catinat, fared even worse. Though a very gallant gentleman, he was more of a courtier than a soldier; he fell into a trap and was taken prisoner at Cremona. So this preliminary round of the conflict went all against France.

William did not live to direct the coalition in the field. He had used up the last reserves of his strength in creating it, and the fall from his horse which broke his collar-bone merely hastened the end. For a moment Louis hoped that this would enable him to acquire the domination at which he aimed without fighting. But this was to undervalue the issues at stake, and the forces which had been unleashed.

CHAPTER FOURTEEN

MARLBOROUGH'S GRAND ALLIANCE

1702–1704

In this, the third attempt of the rest of Europe to check the aggression of Louis XIV, the lead was taken by the greatest military genius the British race has produced. The war bore some resemblance to that of 1914-18, in that two Powers, one dominating the other, fought a coalition held together by the sea-power and economic resources of Britain; and that in each conflict the Dual Powers, though more or less blockaded, had the advantage of interior lines.

THE HOUR AND THE MAN. We have noted how much stronger was King Louis' position when this war began than when the last one ended; and his enemies were further weakened by the death of William III. The Stadtholder-King had been a personal link between British and Dutch, but now there was no King in Britain and no Stadtholder in Holland. For in the Dutch Republic William's death, like his father's, led to a revival of the old oligarchical party in which the stadtholderate was abolished; and in Britain his successor was a woman—and not a very wise or clever one. True, Queen Anne had at her command the able husband of her life-long confidant Sarah Churchill, and this Earl of Marlborough (1650–1722) was an experienced officer who had been employed by the late King in getting the Alliance together. But could the son of a Dorsetshire squire, whose sister had been a prince's mistress, who had betrayed James to William and William to James, and who had made his way largely by the hold which his "brimstone of a wife" had gained over the Princess Anne: could a man in such a position hold together a European coalition? And, in particular, would he be able to unite the self-seeking German princes, each fanatically jealous of his rank and dignity?

When Marlborough crossed to The Hague in May 1702 it was still by no means certain that the Dutch would give him command of their army. William's old comrade Ginkel, Earl of Athlone, claimed the place. He argued that whereas William had been a Dutchman with English support, Marlborough would be an Englishman with Dutch support, and the Republic would thus become the junior partner in the firm. Yet to separate the Anglo-Dutch commands would cleave

132

the very heart of the coalition. Marlborough had a firm supporter in Heinsius, who as Grand Pensionary was now virtually Chancellor of the Republic; and his own personality and tact did the rest.

Marlborough's chance had come, and he seized it with both hands. It was to bring him great toils and vexations, but also military fame comparable with that of Hannibal or Napoleon.

There was never a man better fitted in body, mind and spirit for success in war. Handsome in person, serene in demeanour, sagacious in counsel, resolute in action, he inspired confidence in all who came in contact with him. As a strategist his conceptions were bold and sweeping, yet never unpractical; and when battle was joined he had an unerring instinct for the critical point and the critical moment, and the nerve to make the most of it. Above all he had a grasp of every detail of military organization. This not only enabled him to see that his army had all it needed, but to employ it to the best advantage in the field. For in those days there were no complete units like divisions; the commander issued orders which were carried personally to subordinate generals appointed more or less *ad hoc*; and he often rode in person to place batteries and battalions. Lastly, in days when men mattered more and machinery less than in later wars, Marlborough's care for his men's health and fitness, and the kindly consideration with which he treated everybody, were assets of incalculable value.

Incidentally, he made the British army what it remained for the next century, one of the main military factors of Europe. It was he who developed infantry from being mere defensive blocks, letting off their muskets every few minutes and meanwhile defended by pikemen, into an arm as aggressive as cavalry. He did this partly by use of the flintlock at a time when the French, owing to the conservatism of Louvois, were still armed with the matchlock; partly by the fire-discipline which he built up by assiduous practice in winter cantonments; and partly by the adoption of the ring-bayonet which could be affixed without obstructing the use of the musket as a firearm.

Most wars are muddles in which the side that muddles least muddles through. Only now and again does a genius appear who makes his operations seem inevitable, like a movement by Mozart or a picture by Raphael. Marlborough was such a one. That he did not achieve even more than he did was due to the fact that he had not a free hand such as Gustavus or Napoleon or Frederick enjoyed. Like Turenne or Wellington, he had to take orders from a civil government which could only partly be brought to understand his problems and aims. On the Dutch side these restrictions were exercised by "Field Deputies" sent by the States General to see that he did not squander their precious troops. But he had a remarkable gift for suffering fools gladly. Seldom did he allow any sign of vexation to break through the unruffled equanimity with which he treated all men and all circumstances.

THE OPENING CAMPAIGNS. By the time the question of the Anglo-Dutch command was settled half the campaigning season was gone, but Marlborough made good use of what was left of it. Louis had not only taken possession of the Spanish Netherlands in his grandson's name, but had sent an army under Marshal Boufflers down the Rhine to Cleves. The Dutch were still haunted by nightmare memories of 1672, when the French had entered by this same back-door to strike them down. Marlborough compelled the invaders to withdraw by the simple expedient of threatening their communications. A safe route to a supply base was vital to an army in the field; for these were disciplined troops, not the marauding ruffians of the Thirty Years' War. Marlborough had much ado to win permission to move so far; but when he did so the manœuvre was instantly successful. The French retired with such disorderly haste that a prompt attack would have driven them right out of the Low Countries, now in 1702 instead of after three more costly campaigns. But he was twice thwarted by Dutch deputies and once by a Dutch general, and the chance was lost. Still, much had been done. Boufflers was thrust back to Cologne, and the Lower Rhine was freed from the enemy for the rest of the war. Ginkel made the *amende honorable*: "The success of the campaign is solely due to this incomparable chief, since I confess that serving as second in command I opposed all his opinions and proposals."

Having made good the ground gained by taking some fortresses on the Meuse, Marlborough returned to England and was made Duke by his delighted Queen.

Yet the following year (1703) the Dutch were more obstructive than ever. The Duke wanted to "turn" the fortified lines which the French had drawn from Antwerp to Namur. His idea was for the Dutch to threaten Antwerp and Ostend while he drew the main French army under Villeroi down towards Namur. If Villeroi weakened his army to help the threatened ports he would smash him; if not, the Dutch would have a walk-over. But he would have needed unquestioned authority to carry through a scheme which depended on prompt and exact obedience in the subordinate commands. The Dutch did not want the British to have Ostend as a base—they wanted British supplies to continue to come through their own ports. So the whole thing was a wretched failure. The campaign closed with the capture of three more fortified towns, and the Dutch struck a medal to celebrate this "Victory without Slaughter". But the Duke knew that this was not the way to win the war. A precious year had been lost, and time was not on the side of the Allies.

His difficulties were increased by the state of English politics. It was a time when all were for the party and none was for the state. The ebb and flow of political tides at Westminster, with which Marlborough like William before him had to grapple between his campaigns, had during this war important reactions on the affairs of Europe. The Whigs were still the anti-French party, the "City" party that made money out of the war, and wanted it waged on a large scale. The Tories were the squires who had to pay the land-tax which, they complained, went into the pockets of Whig profiteers; they were for a war of limited objectives—naval and colonial as far as possible.

The Queen was high Tory, being High Church. The Duke, too, was Tory by tradition, but was drifting away from the main body of the party owing to its attitude to the war. He contrived to get Godolphin, his relative by marriage, appointed Lord Treasurer, so as to be able to rely on supplies for the forces. But he was subject to relentless attacks in Parliament—the Whigs hated him for being a Tory, the Tories hated him for not being Tory enough. At the beginning of 1704 he was so disgusted at the obstruction of Dutch and British politicians that he wanted to throw up his command; but the Queen persuaded him to stand by her and the country.

NEW FRIENDS, NEW FOES. The war spread, as such wars do. Bavaria and Portugal joined in, and Savoy changed sides.

The first addition to the original combatants was Bavaria. The Elector Maximilian was a Wittelsbach, brother of the Archbishop-Elector of Cologne who had long been a client of Louis XIV. In the summer of 1702 he negotiated with the Allies, but they could not offer him the bribe promised him by Louis XIV: nothing less than a reconstruction of the Holy Roman Empire with Wittelsbach replacing Hapsburg on the Imperial throne. His alliance with France in the autumn of that year was a serious setback to the Allies, for his territories gave Louis access to central Germany.

And the Emperor already had his hands full with another rising in Hungary. Francis Rakoczy, the fourth of his family to lead Magyar nationalists, had been brought up in Vienna. But his mind perpetually brooded over the lost splendours of his Transylvanian heritage (p. 80), and at the outbreak of this war secret agents from France lured him on with the prospect of a restoration, to lead a revolt of the Hungarian nobles who still resented the loss of their semi-independence in 1671. With the Emperor thus preoccupied one swift and well-directed blow from the west might knock him out of the war altogether.

In 1703 this nearly happened. Louis had sent Villars, the only one of his later marshals fit to compare with Turenne, through the Black Forest to join the Elector for a thrust at Vienna. But the two commanders soon fell out. Max insisted on going off to Tyrol, to get control of the passes into Italy so necessary for a future "Roman Emperor". His idea was to proceed to the Brenner, join up with Vendôme coming with another French army from Italy, and return for a combined attack on Vienna in greater strength than ever. But the Tyrolese, nobles and peasants alike, fought loyally in the cause of their Hapsburg oppressors; and the Elector returned to Munich with half the summer gone, leaving the only corridor between Germany and Italy completely blocked.

It was now too late to attack Vienna that year, but preparations were made to do so with greater effect in 1704. The Emperor and his court again, as in 1683 (p. 87), gave up their capital for lost and prepared to retire to some safer spot.

That year 1703 also brought fresh support to the Allies.

We have already noticed Victor Amadeus of Savoy selling his geographical advantages to the highest bidder (p. 108). His transit to the French side in the last war had raised him considerably in the scale of near-royalties, for he had married one of his daughters to the Duke of Burgundy, ultimate heir to the throne of France; and he now married another to the Duke of Anjou, claimant to the throne of Spain. But recent events had made him reconsider his position. The immediate danger was lest Eugene, after his brilliant campaign against the French in Lombardy, might go on to attack Victor Amadeus's Piedmont; but in general the Duke's policy was to back the side that seemed to be losing the war, lest the winner should become strong enough to discard him. And, as we have seen, the Allies' outlook in 1703 was black indeed. Moreover French paramountcy in Italy would be most irksome to all the lesser rulers in that peninsula. Vendôme, commanding the French forces in Piedmont as ally of Victor Amadeus, became suspicious that he was intriguing with the other side, and in September suddenly disarmed all the Savoyard troops within reach. This merely hardened the Duke's resolve to join the Alliance. Louis angrily vowed that chastisement of the turncoat should be his first care in the ensuing campaign. But things went differently, as we shall see.

A PENINSULAR WAR. There was nothing in the terms of the Grand Alliance that committed its members to a conflict in Spain. They had realized from the first that it would be a colossal task to substitute the Archduke Charles for the Duke of Anjou there against the will of the people, and the Emperor regretfully acquiesced in this view. But circumstances committed them beyond their cooler judgment.

William III had latterly become keenly aware of the importance of sea-power, especially in the Mediterranean. In making the Partitions he had never lost sight of the fact that Spain controlled the entrance to that Sea; and when war broke out in 1702 he immediately sent Rooke to seize Cadiz as a base for the control of the Straits. That enterprise miscarried, but on the way home the admiral looked in at Vigo and demolished the fleet which had just brought forty million "pieces-of-eight" across from America. He did not capture the whole of that specie, for some of it had been landed, but his action made a vital change in the conduct of the war, and affected British policy for a century to come. For it brought us the alliance of Portugal.

The Allies had angled for King Pedro's support from the first, especially with a view to the use of his ports. He was between the Bourbon devil and the deep sea Powers; but he did not want his great transoceanic possessions to become the latter's spoil, and Rooke's exploit at Vigo came as a very timely warning of that possibility. The result was the Methuen Treaties of 1703—so-named after the two diplomatists (father and son) who carried through the negotiations. By the first of them, signed in May, Portugal became a member of the Grand Alliance. The second, which followed in December, was a commercial agreement by which Portugal admitted English woollen goods in return for Britain making her duty on Portuguese port one-third of that on French claret. This ruined the textile industries of Portugal and afflicted the British upper classes with gout for a century. But the earlier treaty was more important, by reason of the conditions which King Pedro exacted. As a guarantee that the Allies would not leave him in the lurch he required that the Archduke should be brought to Spain, proclaimed King, and supported by 12,000 "veteran troops," English, Dutch and Austrian. The result was that the Allies were led into a dangerous extension of their war-aims. Those aims as laid down in the agreement constituting the Alliance had been limited to expelling

France from Italy and the Netherlands. The vain attempt to force an unacceptable king on the proudest people in Europe prolonged the conflict by four or five years, and greatly damaged the fruits of victory from the Allied point of view.

So the Archduke set out for Lisbon *viâ* Holland and England, being received with royal honours in each country. But the Spanish people had quite made up their minds that they were not going to have him as their king. Philip V was not a strong or able or attractive character, but his vivacious little Savoyard wife made up for this; and Maria Luisa herself was under the influence of her extremely energetic *camerara-mayor* (= chief lady-in-waiting). This was the Princess d'Orsino, better known by the French form of her name Madame des Ursins. A Frenchwoman married to an Italian noble, she had been nominated by Louis XIV to guide his young grand-daughter-in-law; but, arrived in Madrid, she took up the cause of "Spain for the Spaniards"; and under her influence the King and Queen fell out with the French ambassador, who acted as if he had been sent to govern the country. The Spaniards were gratified that the new régime not only kept together their Empire on which the sun never set, but rejected foreign interference, even from France. Still, the quarrel was not good for national defence. The Duke of Berwick (an illegitimate son of James II,[1] and now a very capable general in the service of Louis XIV) had been sent to cope with the threatened invasion from Lisbon. He had little difficulty in thrusting back the "veteran troops," who were very indifferently supported by the Portuguese; but his counter-invasion into Portugal was held up by lack of military supplies.

Marlborough, more and more dominant in Queen Anne's government, fully acquiesced in the late King's belief in the importance of the Mediterranean. When France (having now abandoned the hope of commanding the narrow seas) sent the Brest half of her fleet round to join the other half at Toulon, Rooke set out to intercept it, and then to threaten the Spanish coasts, so as to draw Berwick away from Portugal. He was thereafter to make contact with Savoy, to see if an attack could be made on Toulon in conjunction with the "Camisards"—Huguenots of the Cevennes who had resisted the *dragonnades* and were now in open rebellion under a remarkable young leader named Cavalier.

All these projects fell through. The Brest squadron got safely to Toulon, the Duke of Savoy was much too busy in defence to be able

---

[1] His mother was Marlborough's sister Arabella.

to undertake an invasion of France, and the Camisards could do nothing unaided. But at the end of all these disappointments Rooke brought off an exploit which outweighed them all. An assault on Gibraltar had often been discussed in naval circles: he decided to attempt it. The place was under-manned and under-gunned, and offered little resistance (July 1704). Rooke's fleet was half Dutch, but he took care that the force left as a garrison should be wholly British.

Gibraltar provided only a roadstead: it did not become a base for a war-fleet until the moles were built a generation later. But Louis fully realized the importance of its geographical position and gave orders that it should be re-taken without delay. That was easier said than done, however. His Toulon fleet met the British off Malaga (August 1704). Rooke had been long at sea, his ships were foul, and he had shot off most of his ammunition at Gibraltar. Neither side could claim a victory; but the French fleet went home and left the Mediterranean to the British for the rest of the war. Louis then ordered a land attack, but Berwick did not believe in the success of it, especially in view of the state of the Spanish arsenals. It failed; and the Union Jack still flies from the Rock.

"IT WAS A FAMOUS VICTORY." Nobody knows who first thought of a march from the Low Countries to the Danube. The plan took shape gradually in the course of secret discussions during that anxious winter of 1703–4 in London. In any case there was no special merit in thinking of it—the merit lay in carrying it through. Marlborough only adopted it as an alternative to what was always his favourite scheme—to strike at Paris up the Moselle. The capture of Paris would more than outweigh the loss of Vienna; but the Danube scheme had the advantage that it would take him out of the reach of his Dutch masters for the time being—provided he could hoodwink them into letting him off the chain. He began by imparting the Moselle idea to them in great secrecy. As he expected, they hated the thought of denuding the Republic of its best troops and of himself, but Heinsius at last contrived to wring from them a hesitating acquiescence. The Duke was thus able to open preparations for a march as far as Coblenz, at any rate.

To go on to the Danube would be a stupendous gamble. It could not be half successful. Anything short of an overwhelming victory at the end of it would be ruin for himself and for the Alliance. But another negative campaign like the last would be equally, though not quite so immediately, disastrous; for it would lead to the disintegration of the Alliance through a war-wearied sense of futility, and at the same time to the loss of Vienna. So after long deliberation he decided that the prize was worth the risk.

Of all his preparations for the momentous campaign the most important was to procure the right commander for the Imperial forces. Ludwig of Baden the Emperor's commander-in-chief was a wooden soldier of the old school. Harnessed to him Marlborough would have got rid of one incubus only to saddle himself with another. The best mitigation was to contrive the presence of Prince Eugene as a third member of the High Command, with secret authority to supersede Baden should the latter prove too obstructive.

Marlborough set out from his headquarters in the Netherlands during the first week in May. Less than half of his 40,000 troops were British, for the English (especially the Tory) dread of standing armies had led to drastic cuts after Ryswick. But the backbone of the British regiments were re-enlisted men who had fought under William III, and they were "the finest troops imaginable." German contingents joined *en route*, one of the best being sent by the new King of Prussia. The troops did not know where they were going, but there was a feeling in the air that they were bound on a great adventure under a great leader, and all hearts beat high. They were well-found, well-shod, well-fed, for their general had taken endless trouble over these matters; they even had —luxurious novelty—a hospital train. With their heavy baggage and artillery on barges, they marched up the Rhine to Coblenz, then took a short cut across to Mainz, then on beyond Heidelberg, where they turned left-handed in the direction of the Danube. Half way between the two rivers Prince Eugene rode into the Duke's camp, and a comradeship in arms began which through seven campaigns was never clouded by a shadow of jealousy. Now the great secret was out; friend and foe rose on tiptoe of expectation.

Villars' quarrel with Elector Max had a great bearing on the results of the campaign—and therefore of the war as a whole; for he was replaced by Marsin and Tallard, who were but courtier-generals with little experience of war. Eugene went to hold off French reinforcements coming through the Black Forest under Tallard, while Marlborough and Baden marched on to the Danube. They commanded on alternate days, like the early Roman consuls—a fatuous arrangement, but one which in this case prevented complete paralysis. It was, one need hardly say, on one of Marlborough's days that the great fortress of Donauwörth was stormed by a daring feat of arms. The heavy casualties which it cost the Allies were well invested, for it gave them a bridgehead on the Danube, a starting-point for the invasion of Bavaria, and an advanced base for supplies. In the hope of goading Max to fight without waiting for Tallard, the Allies laid waste his Electorate. But Marlborough hated the job too much to do it effectively, and the Bavarians duly made their junction with the French. The Allies were now between the enemy and Vienna, but they were still in a critical position. The Franco-Bavarians had only to refuse to fight and they would be left in the air. But Marlborough and Eugene need not have troubled. Tallard and Max were eager for the glory of destroying the upstart Englishman and the renegade Frenchman. The Anglo-Dutch-German troops might be pretty good, but they had marched hundreds of miles—and who ever heard of a French army being beaten in the field?

Well, people heard of it soon. By this time Marlborough and Eugene had contrived to get rid of Baden by persuading him to go and occupy Ingolstadt and so keep open the road to Vienna. The 15,000 men he took could ill be spared, but his absence was worth all that and more. The story of the Battle of Blenheim is so full of tactical detail that it is impossible to tell it here even in outline. It must suffice that the Franco-Bavarian army was annihilated as a fighting force.

The news of Blenheim sent England wild with delight. On his return the Duke had a quasi-Roman triumph through the streets of London, and was given a great estate and money to build a palace on it. For it was indeed a famous victory. It not only saved Vienna and the Grand Alliance, but cracked the graven image of French military power, and put Louis XIV on the defensive for the rest of the war.

CHAPTER FIFTEEN

THE WAR OF THE SPANISH SUCCESSION
1704–1711

MARLBOROUGH became less and less successful in the war as he progressively lost control over the issues and direction of it. The error of making it a "war of the Spanish Succession," which it had not been at the outset, put fresh vigour into the exhausted frame of France, and disintegrated the Alliance.

RAMILLIES AND TURIN. The tide of success in the war seemed to ebb and flow over periods of two years. In the "even" years 1702, 1704, 1706 and 1708 the Allies won resounding successes; the "odd" years 1703, 1705, 1707 were disappointing for them. Marlborough started hopefully in these odd years on the strength of last year's success, but each time the States General and the Imperial Court felt that as the war had been "practically" won thereby, it would be foolish to run risks. In the "even" years, on the other hand, he started in gloom, but found the Allied governments, realizing their mistake, gave him scope for another victory.

In 1705, for instance, he hoped to press home the ascendancy won at Blenheim by his favourite scheme of a march on Paris up the Moselle; but the Dutch were determined that he should not give them the slip again. So he had to content himself with turning the "Lines of Brabant" to edge the French away from the Belgian coast. And the one small success that the Allies gained in other theatres did them more harm than good. They carried "Charles III" round to Catalonia, where he was warmly welcomed by the people. For the Catalans were always, like the Irish, "agin the government" which ignored their claim to belong to a separate, and not inferior, race. The commander of the expedition was the reckless, picturesque, bragging Earl of Peterborough. In October he stormed Monjuich, the rock-citadel of Barcelona, by an audacious *coup de main*. This gave Charles III a solid base in Spain and confirmed the Allies in the disastrous extension of their war-aims to "No Peace without Spain."

The only other important event of 1705 was the death of old Emperor Leopold; and this was not very important to anyone except his immediate *entourage*, for Joseph, his heir, was a chip of the same block.

And so Marlborough took the field in 1706 in a depressed mood. The war seemed to be hanging fire. During 1705 the French had

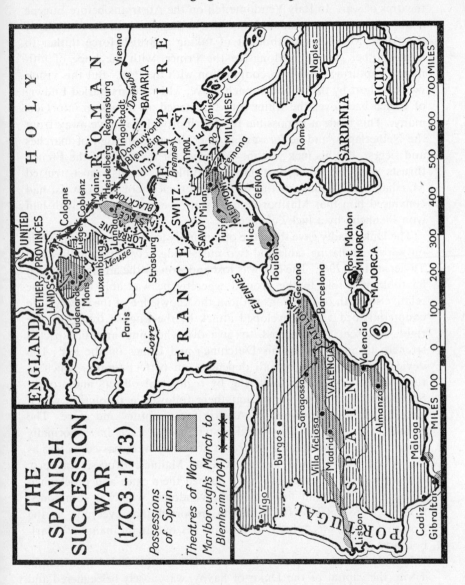

recovered much of the prestige they had lost at Blenheim, and the Allies had made no real progress towards their original aims. As a matter of fact, France was feeling the strain of the war acutely; but this only made Louis more aggressive, in the hope of bluffing the Allies into a quick peace. He made a strong move in each of the three theatres of war. In Italy Vendôme fell on the Austrians before Eugene could arrive to take command, and drove them up into the foothills of the Alps. Marlborough thought of taking a British force thither to fight another campaign alongside the Prince, with the hope of ultimately capturing Toulon in conjunction with the fleet. But this vision was cut short by the second French move, when Villars hurled Ludwig of Baden back over the Rhine and threatened an incursion into Germany. This made it impossible for Marlborough to move away from the Netherlands, and he foresaw another dreary campaign of marches and sieges. But his luck was in, this time, for the third of the French thrusts was directed against himself. Villeroi, Louis' most trusted Marshal, and Chamillart, the very inferior successor to Louvois, had convinced him that Marlborough was an overrated general who had won Blenheim by a lucky chance.

The Duke gladly gave them the opportunity to prove it, offering battle on a low undulating tableland two miles wide between Ramillies and Taviers (May 1706). The day was lost and won by the advantage which he took of a fold in the ground whereby he was able to alter the relative strength of his wings without the knowledge of the enemy. He countermanded a well-developed attack by the English troops on the right, and sent them across to give overwhelming and unexpected strength to an attack by his Dutchmen and Danes on the left. The device sounds simple, but all depended on perfect timing, which in turn required first-class soldiering by regimental officers and troops. So complete was the victory that there followed a revolution which gave Belgium to the House of Austria for a century and more. The Scheldt, the Lys and the Canal system would each have normally taken a year's campaigning to cross: now they were passed as fast as the Allied troops could march. Ghent, Malines, Bruges, Antwerp, did not wait to be besieged; they opened their gates and proclaimed "Charles III" without firing a shot. Vendôme, who was summoned from Italy to retrieve the situation, reported that everyone at the French G.H.Q. was "ready to take off his hat at the name of Marlborough."

In Italy, too, a campaign that opened in gloom ended in triumph. Turin, the capital of the Duke of Savoy, was closely beleaguered and at the point of surrender. The Emperor Joseph seemed to expect his Allies to win Italy as well as Belgium for him, while he devoted his attention to the more congenial task of crushing the Hungarians. All that he would supply towards the campaign in Italy was his general Eugene. But that was a great deal. With German troops supplied by Marlborough's diplomacy and Anglo-Dutch cash, the Prince made a wonderful march through hostile territory, over rivers and marshes, up the valley of the Po. When he joined Duke Victor Amadeus on the hills overlooking Turin, the two Savoyards could muster but 35,000 against 60,000 besiegers; but by crossing the river and unexpectedly attacking from the west in conjunction with a sortie of the garrison, they gained a victory which loosened the hold of the French on Italy as effectively as Ramillies had loosened their hold on Belgium; and Austria succeeded Spain as the dominant power there until Napoleon Buonaparte appeared on the scene some ninety years later.

RIFTS IN THE ALLIANCE. Victory brings trouble from which defeat is immune. What were the Allies to do with Belgium, now that they had won it? Nominally they had been fighting on behalf of the Archduke Charles; but the Dutch who had supplied half the cost and more than half the troops naturally claimed their guerdon—a strong barrier of fortresses along its southern frontier as an advanced defence against future French attack on the Republic. And Pensionary Heinsius pointed out that isolated towns had been useless as a safeguard in 1701; the Republic must control the intervening land and the sea-ports. They did not want to annex the territory; that would have given them a Catholic population to rule, and would have made it difficult to close the port of Antwerp—another condition they intended to impose. All they wanted was the right to instal garrisons, and to raise the cost by local taxation. The Austrians did not see the justice of this. "The Netherlands," they argued, "are part of the Spanish empire which the Dutch admit belongs to the House of Hapsburg. If they want a Barrier, let them (after they have quite finished winning the Low Countries for us) win one in France for themselves." The Archduke-King could not very well talk like this while the war was in progress, lest the Dutch should sulkily retire from the fray; so he cunningly offered the Governor-Generalship to the Duke of Marlborough at a salary of £60,000 a year. It was a magnificent position—the last Governor-General had been an Elector of the Empire; and for the commander-in-chief to hold it would have facilitated military operations. But the Dutch realized that the Duke would cut their Barrier down to a minimum, and they. opposed the plan so vigorously that he had to re-decline. The incident had done permanent injury to the Alliance, for the Imperialists resented his refusing, while the Dutch resented his wanting to accept (and feared he might do so at a later date). In the upshot the government of the Low Countries was left to a joint Anglo-Dutch Commission until the end of the war.

Policy in Spain was a difficulty to France as well as to the Allies. Louis had known from the first that the administration of the country needed drastic overhaul, and was quite prepared to carry through the process on his grandson's behalf even while the war was on. He sent a very capable finance-minister, Orry by name, to make a preliminary audit of the exchequer and gave special authority to his ambassador, Cardinal d'Estrées, to intervene in the government. But, as we have seen (p. 138), these measures were angrily obstructed by the Queen and her dominating Lady-in-Waiting. Louis, surprised and hurt, recalled Madame des Ursins, who had been his own nominee; but this only made the high-spirited young Queen more resentful than ever. Berwick's life became impossible; he retired from the country and took up the repression of the Camisards. Poor King Philip, with very little will of his own, was torn between awe of his formidable old grandfather and devotion to his charming young wife; and with the new régime thus paralysed by dissension, it is not surprising that the movement in favour of the Austrian candidate which had begun in Catalonia spread to Valencia and Aragon.

But in 1706 events took a fresh course. King Louis relented, sent the Princess des Ursins back to Spain, and provided another French army to besiege Barcelona. Both the claimants were present at the operations; but whereas Philip was little more than a piece of camp furniture, Charles was the life and soul of the defence. The French were in such strength that the fall of the town seemed imminent, when the arrival of a British fleet and the landing of some British troops reversed the position and drove the besiegers back to the Pyrenees (May 1706).

This was the critical moment for Charles. If he had gone straight to Madrid (where Lord Galway was now in possession with an Anglo-Portuguese force) he might have established himself as king; for many of the grandees were now coming over to what looked like the winning side. But he dallied in Catalonia, and he could not agree with Peterborough even as to the best route to the capital. Eventually Peterborough went off in a huff to seek fresh adventures in Italy, while Galway, finding himself isolated in Madrid and cut off by guerrilla bands from Lisbon, marched to the east coast and joined Charles there. These delays had given the Queen and des Ursins time to put fresh life into the French cause. From Burgos, where the Court was living in dire poverty, she appealed to the chivalry of the Spaniards, and not in vain. They disliked the French, but they hated the English and the Dutch, who to the offence of being foreigners added the sin of being heretics. Berwick returned with reinforcements, and the Queen had the sense to learn from the misfortunes which had followed on her quarrel with him.

For 1707 Marlborough reverted to the idea of a combined attack on Toulon which, if successful, would deprive the French of their only naval base on the Mediterranean. The scheme was to be undertaken by German troops from northern Italy under Eugene, with the support of Savoy, of the Camisards, of the Allied troops from Catalonia, and of the Anglo-Dutch fleet. But nothing went right. Eugene never cared about the undertaking, and the Emperor felt that his men were being used to pull a chestnut out of the fire for the Sea Powers. The fleet could do nothing beyond covering the coast, for the French prevented it from approaching Toulon by sinking their own fleet at the harbour mouth. The Huguenot rebels failed to appear—Berwick had done his work of repression with some success. And Victor Amadeus, who shared the command with Eugene, was disgusted at the latter's lack of enthusiasm. The result was that the French were able to throw reinforcements into the place which made the siege hopeless, and the project was adandoned.

If Toulon had fallen, the Allied forces were to have gone on to Spain, but of course there was no question of that now; and as a matter of fact the Hapsburg cause there had already been ruined as the result of a difference of opinion between the Archduke and Galway. The debate was whether they and their little polyglot army should remain on the coast or go to Madrid; and the decision "a little of each" was the worst that could have been made. If all had gone Almanza might have been won; if all had remained it would never have been fought. As it was Berwick gained a victory which extinguished the chances of "Charles III" for good (April 1707). But the British did not know they were beaten, and for four more weary years they went on with the ruinous, fruitless struggle to make good their pledge not to make peace until they had won Spain for the Archduke.

KING LOUIS BROUGHT TO HIS KNEES. The Allies were due for a good year in 1708. They had it; but each good year seemed less good than the last.

The general plan was for a threefold advance into France: from the Netherlands by the Duke, up the Moselle by Eugene, and from Alsace by the Elector of Hanover (afterwards our George I: he had succeeded Baden in the command of the main Imperial army). But this was thrown out of gear by the failure of Saxony and Prussia to send their contingents in time, and by an insurrection in Belgian towns against Dutch taxation. The French, commanded by Vendôme, taking advantage of this disaffection, had re-captured Ghent and were trying to get to Mons, when Marlborough and Eugene (who, not having men enough to act independently, had now joined the Duke) waylaid them just outside Oudenarde (July 1708). This was what soldiers call an "encounter battle": the regiments were not deployed for it formally, like football teams before the kick-off, but were thrown in one after another as they arrived on the scene. Such an engagement calls for a firm and rapid grasp of rapidly changing conditions, and Marlborough showed himself as supreme in this as in every other kind of battle.

There were now only three fortresses between the Allies and Paris: Mons, Namur and Lille, held by armies under Berwick, Vendôme and Boufflers respectively. Marlborough was for masking them and making a dash for the French capital; but Eugene, bold as he was, refused to advance into an enemy country without an assured supply-line behind him; and as usual Marlborough gave way. The two commanders co-operated in the siege of Lille. This developed into one of the biggest operations of the war. It cost the Allies five times as many casualties as the Battle of Oudenarde; and when it was accomplished winter brought the campaign to an end.

The naval success of 1708 was the capture of Minorca as a substitute for Toulon. It had a deep land-locked harbour at Port Mahon, the fact that it was an island made it secure against any Power not in command of the sea, and its central position enabled a fleet based on it to watch the Mediterranean coasts of Italy, Spain, France and Africa. "Charles III" asked England to occupy it on his behalf for the duration, but the political wiseacres of Europe forecast that we should not readily give it up at the end of the war, and they were not far wrong. One effect of the occupation was the immediate extinction of French influence in Italy. .

France was now at the last gasp of economic exhaustion. The war had begun when she had scarcely begun to recover from the last one, and it had now continued for seven dreadful years. The climax of the nation's suffering came with the appalling winter of 1708–9, when all the rivers of Europe were frozen over and the seed-corn died in the earth. Louis faced the hard fact: he must have peace. So in the spring he sent Torcy, his foreign minister, grandson of Colbert, to get into touch with the States General. (How were the mighty fallen since 1672!) He offered the Dutch a handsome barrier, and Marlborough a tremendous bribe (graduated according to the terms he could procure for France), to win their support in imposing peace on the other Allies; but news of the offer brought them all clamouring for concessions—the Emperor, the Imperial Diet, the Duke of Savoy; even old Pedro of Portugal thought he ought to get something while there were things to be got. Louis had inflicted such terrors and humiliations on them all in his days of prosperity that it was but natural that they should yap round him now that he had fallen into adversity. But having decided that he must have peace, Louis accepted every demand— even to the return of Strassburg to the Empire and Nice to Savoy; and as earnest of his good faith he withdrew his forces from Spain. Yet there was just one of these 42 "Preliminaries of The Hague" at which he stopped short. Article XXXVIII ran:

In case the King of France executes all that is above mentioned, and that the whole monarchy of Spain is yielded to King Charles III within the limited time (two months), 'tis agreed that the cessation of arms . . . shall continue.

That looked innocent enough, and the Allies had not meant any harm by it, for they assumed that Philip V would immediately leave Spain at his grandfather's behest. But Louis knew that he and his spirited young wife were determined not to give up their throne, and that the Spanish people (except those of the north-east) were equally determined that they should not be forced to. Thus the condition would not be fulfilled, and Louis would be faced with a renewal of the war in two months' time with the Allies in possession of the Barrier, and other posts of vantage which he was to hand over as "cautionary towns." Perhaps if the Allies had offered Philip Naples and Sicily as a second-best kingdom, he might have agreed; but it was now they who raised the cry of "no partition." So with mingled sorrow and anger Louis rejected the terms and gave orders for another campaign.

Marlborough is often accused of continuing the war for his own honour and profit; but he was very disappointed that Louis broke off the negotiations without putting forward any counter-proposals. Where he did wrong was in not insisting on the Allies being more reasonable in their demands. But he knew that he was losing his grip on the government at home. The Whigs had won a substantial majority at the election of 1708; they had got rid of Harley, the last remaining Tory minister (unless we consider the Duke and Godolphin to be still

MARLBOROUGH IN THE NETHERLANDS

Barrier towns given to Dutch at Utrecht................MONS
Places captured by Marlborough................O
Fortresses...★   Battlefields...✕

Tories); and nothing could be done without the approval of the "Junta" of their leaders, who were all for pushing the war à outrance. Moreover making the best of a situation created by the folly of his associates had become a second nature to the Duke. And his great object was to keep the Allies together for just one more campaign,

after which he felt they would be able to get what terms they wanted.
It was a natural mistake for a man in his position, but it was to cost
him and the Alliance very dear.

In 1709 the Allies raised a bigger force than ever for an advance on
Paris from the plain of Lille. But Villars had barred the way with a line
of earthworks forty miles long—the *Ne Plus Ultra*, as he called them.
These would have to be assaulted or turned. After careful reconnaissance Marlborough and Eugene decided to take Tournai, which
flanked the eastern end. It was second only to Lille as an example of
Vauban's defensive art, and it held out for two months. By this time
the season was too advanced for extensive operations in France, so
the twin Dioscuri decided to reduce Mons. Then at any rate they would
be in a position for an early start next year (always next year!); and an
advance on Mons might entice Villars out from behind his lines. It
did; and the result was the Battle of Malplaquet (September 1709).
The veterans of the Allied armies overran field entrenchments constructed with great skill by Villars, and defended with the utmost
valour by the raw young French troops. The casualties were on an
appalling scale—the Dutch in particular lost a third of their numbers,
and the victorious Allies lost more than the defeated French. It was
the Allies who remained on the scene of action, and Mons fell to
them in due course; but they were too hard hit to follow up, and a
French army, battered, but with its self-confidence restored, still lay
across the road to Paris.

FRANCE'S BACK TO THE WALL. After the "Preliminaries of The
Hague" were drawn up the changed character of the war became
apparent to all. What had begun as the effort of a group of small
nations to preserve their vital interests against an overbearing tyrant,
had become the struggle of a beleaguered ruler and his devoted people
against a circle of insolent and rapacious foes.

Louis was advised to call a National Assembly to meet the emergency.
He would not humiliate himself as far as that, but for the first time in his
reign he appealed to his subjects instead of commanding them. He
issued a manifesto (June 1710) to the governors of provinces and cities,
declaring that although his tenderness for his people was not less than
for his own children, he was persuaded that they would themselves
oppose conditions contrary alike to justice and to the honour of the
French name.

He was right. His people did not exactly love him—nobody could;

but they reverenced him as primitive folk reverence a tribal god. He set the nobles an example by sending his gold plate to be melted down for the public service. A fresh army was sent to the Flanders front—greater in numbers, if inferior in equipment and training. The Allies had supposed that the famine consequent on the great frost would open the road to Paris for them, but it had the opposite effect. All the corn in the land was taken for the army, and the young peasants joined it to save themselves from starvation.

But it was the last army of France, and Louis wisely gave the command of it to the one general who could make use of it. Marshal Villars seems like a forerunner of the generals of the Revolution—rough and ready with his tongue, insistent with supply-departments, full of self-assurance and good-humour, and in touch with his men, making them feel that he knew their sufferings, appreciated their cheerfulness and counted on their courage. And his master had the good judgment to support him through thick and thin.

By this time the tidal movement of success and failure had got out of order. Malplaquet (only a very qualified success, anyway) was in an "odd" year; and 1710 was the most weary, flat and unprofitable of the campaigns. A stream of reinforcements, and some well-directed digging in the Ne Plus Ultra lines, enabled Villars to prevent the Duke from doing more than take Douai. And this year saw the shutters put up on the Allied establishment in Spain. " Charles III" now held nothing but Catalonia, and there his two generals could not agree about anything. The enterprising Stanhope overrode the cautious Starhemberg to bring off two little victories; and this enabled him to insist on an attempt to recover Madrid, which resulted in the destruction of the British contingent at Brihuega (December 1710) by a newly-arrived French force under Vendôme.

A few months later an event occurred which seemed to offer the Allies a good excuse to abandon their wretched Peninsular war: the Emperor Joseph died of smallpox (April 1711). He was childless, and his brother Charles now became ruler of Austria, Bohemia, Silesia and Hungary; Italy and Belgium had been won for him in the war; and he was certain to be elected Emperor. Were the Allies to go on fighting to add to his dominions Spain and half America? Would that not upset the "Balance of Power" which statesmen were all talking about? Surely a return must be made to William III's original policy of partition. Circumstances had made this later plan of "All for the Archduke" an absurdity. But contemporaries did not see matters in that light. They felt as strongly as ever that it would be dangerous to let Spain and the Indies fall under French control. Madrid and Vienna, weak separately, would be weaker still in combination; but the Spanish empire vitalized by the master-hand of Louis XIV would give France dominion of the world.

LAME AND IMPOTENT CONCLUSION. English party politics were now becoming a vital issue for the future of Europe. For the war had become a Whig war. Though Marlborough and Godolphin were still nominally Tories they had to work with Whig colleagues and were dependent on a Whig majority in Parliament, for the Tories were bent on making peace at almost any price if they could get back into power.

This fact was behind the "Barrier Treaty" with the Dutch which the Government put through at the end of 1709. The Republic was in sore need of peace. It was contributing quite as much as Britain to the common cause without the same agricultural and industrial strength to draw on; and its prosperity depended on overseas trade, which was severely restricted by the war. Lest it should be tempted by French offers of a separate peace the Whig ministers made a secret agreement whereby the South American trade was to be shared after the war, and the Dutch were to have a barrier of twelve fortresses in the Low Countries. In return the Dutch were to support the Hanoverian Succession in England by force of arms if necessary. It was a bad bargain for the English, inasmuch as the Dutch would have had to resist a Jacobite restoration in their own interest. Marlborough refused to endorse it; but once again he failed to put his foot down firmly against a course he knew to be unwise.

The fact was that he felt his political strength slipping from him. The Whigs merely used his prestige in their party interests, the Tories hated him. And the tide of public feeling was running against the war. Godolphin found it harder every year to meet the cost, which had quadrupled since 1702. His main resource was a Land Tax of 4s. in the £, and he dared not increase it in view of the furious opposition of the Tory squires. So he had to rely on heavier indirect taxes, which raised the cost of living for the poor. And the Whigs seemed to be deliberately obstructing peace. At Gertruidenberg, where negotiations were still dragging on, Louis offered all manner of concessions—even to pay for a force to turn Philip out of Spain. But when the Allies interpreted Article XXXVIII of the Preliminaries as requiring him to use French troops for the purpose, he drew the line. If he had to make war, he said, it should be on his enemies, not on his own family. And there was much sympathy with his point of view in England.

Another factor in the Tory trend was a revival of national distrust of "standing armies"; and when the Duke indiscreetly asked the Queen to make him Captain-General for life (September 1709) he gave his opponents a chance to denounce him as aiming at a military dictatorship. Above all, the Queen was reverting to the whole-hearted Toryism of her younger days. She parted in anger from her life-long Whiggish friend the Duchess, and adopted a Tory substitute as her confidant. Under the influence of Harley and this Mrs. Masham she replaced the Whig ministers with Tories in the course of the summer of 1710. She did it very gradually, for the Directors of the Bank of England (Whigs to a man) warned her that a change of ministry might cause a panic in the City and so cripple the Government's credit—the first attempt of "High Finance" to interfere in the government of the country. But the process went on quietly, until it culminated in the dismissal of Godolphin. The changes were endorsed by a General Election in November, which returned 320 Tories to 150 Whigs.

The Queen and her new Tory ministers could not as yet dispense with Marlborough—they needed him for one more campaign while they were negotiating their Peace. But he was deprived of all authority to act as the Queen's representative in dealing with the Alliance; in the campaign of 1711 he was merely a general. In the course of that year he showed that he could still carry through a brilliantly timed and executed stratagem. He made Villars think he was going to attack at one end of the Ne Plus Ultra, and so gained four invaluable hours to carry him through them elsewhere; and he deceived his adversary not merely by movements of troops but by a demeanour of dismay and anxiety which he knew would be reported by spies. Staff Colleges consider this his greatest feat of arms, but he himself in after years looked back with more pleasure on what followed—the capture of Bouchain, in which greater forces were involved than had ever before been used in such an operation. It was the last episode in a career during which he had won every battle he fought, taken every place he besieged, lost no place he defended, and scarcely suffered the loss of a foraging party—a record unique in the history of warfare.

CHAPTER SIXTEEN

THE PEACE OF UTRECHT

1711–1713

THE peace that ended the Spanish Succession War was made by Tory politicians for party ends, and the Whigs were furiously angry with it; but is was as fair a settlement as could be made in the circumstances. The Emperor, despite his indignation, became the dominant power in Italy; Louis survived overwhelming defeats with frontiers practically intact and put his grandson on the throne of Spain; England gained control of the Mediterranean, predominance in North America, and the eclipse of her trade-rival.

THE FIGHT FOR PEACE. While Marlborough had been engaged in the operations which he regarded as the crown of his career, Queen Anne's Tory ministers had been making terms with the enemy behind his back and behind the backs of the Allies. They did it mainly for party ends, but their opponents were only one degree less responsible. For the Whigs by their headstrong rejection of the concessions offered by Louis XIV in 1709 (p. 149) had led the Allies into further commitments, and no reasonable peace could be made without betraying some of these. But the British electorate which had now sent a Tory majority to Parliament was weary of the war, and wanted it ended as soon as possible. The nation was satiated even with victories, after so many years of them, and the Tory squires, now the prevailing element in the House of Commons, were in revolt against the Land Tax.

So early in 1711 Harley sent over to Versailles a confidential agent, an obscure French priest who by the easy-going practice of the time had lingered in London after the war began, to drop a hint to the French foreign minister Torcy. We can guess how welcome was the ray of light which fell upon the old King as he sat in Council (with Madame de Maintenon at her needlework in an armchair by the fire) when Torcy first brought word of this dove from the ark.

The upshot was an agreement that the two countries should treat on the basis of Spain for Philip, a (not *the*) barrier for the Dutch, and commercial concessions for Britain. In March Harley (now become Earl of Oxford) was severely wounded by an assassin, and the negotiations were taken over by Henry St. John, a more enterprising type of politician—a man quite without moral sense in public or in private

155

life. He planned to drive a private bargain with France, and then to bring the Allies to the conference-table and compel them to accept this Anglo-French agreement by threatening to leave them in the lurch. England would thus get the first pick of the spoils of the common victory, and leave her associates to scramble for the oddments that remained.

All through the summer of 1711 St. John and Torcy bargained away, each trying to trade on the other's need of peace. St. John stuck pertinaciously to his trade-demands, for he calculated that these would be too advantageous to "The City" for the Whigs to be able to oppose the peace. He demanded the *Asiento* (the monopoly of supplying negro slaves to Spanish America), the surrender of the Hudson Bay forts (for the valuable fur-trade) by the French Canadians, the cession of Acadia and Newfoundland to command the great water-way into the heart of North America, and of Gibraltar and Minorca as bases for British sea-power in the Mediterranean. Of course these proposals ignored the Anglo-Dutch agreement of 1709 by which each party was to have an equal share in any trade-concessions won from Spain; but the Tories had always disliked the Dutch, and St. John trusted that the profits which his betrayal of the Allies would bring to British trade would silence the scruples even of the pro-Dutch Whigs. He boasted to the Queen of the concessions as the greatest ever attained, but forbore to remind her that they had been won by a general whom he and his friends were about to drive into exile by malicious slanders.

The terms were initialed on October 11th, 1711. Up to this point the negotiations had been kept secret, but it was impossible to proceed further without the sanction of Parliament. Still, St. John was expert in the verbal jugglery by which the worse can be made to seem the better cause, and the Government did not anticipate prolonged resistance. Much would depend on the attitude of Marlborough, and they hoped to blackmail him by threatening to charge him with peculation and corruption. But avid as he was of fame and money, he was a man of honour, and his honour was bound up with the Grand Alliance which had been his creation. He spoke and voted against the proposals, and his lead caused the House of Lords to reject them. The Ministry retaliated by suspending him from his command, while charges of converting Army funds to his own use were being investigated; the hostile majority in the Lords was voted down by the creation of twelve new Tory peers; and a barrage of propaganda for the Peace was opened with Swift's *Conduct of the Allies*, perhaps the most famous political pamphlet ever produced.

THE GREAT BETRAYAL. Naturally there was consternation among the Allies. Berlin, Hanover, Vienna, Turin, could not admit that England's pledge not to make a separate peace could be cancelled by a change of Ministers. The Emperor Charles sent Prince Eugene to try to stop the English Government from surrendering his claim to Spain, after he had been England's nominee there for ten years. London was crowded with sightseers hoping to catch a glimpse of the famous general, and the Tories tried (in vain) to play him off against Marlborough, but there was no reversing the vote which had just been wrung from Parliament.

There was only one member of the Alliance whose objections perturbed the Tories. This was the Elector of Hanover, who had been one of its most active members—and who was constitutional heir to the throne of England. Many of the Tories were concealed Jacobites (as he well knew), and the fact that their Peace was bound to give him offence moved them further in this direction, since they would certainly be out of favour, to say the least of it, if he became king.

When the recriminations at Utrecht (where the plenipotentiaries met at the end of January 1712) were at their height, France suddenly brought forward a new proposal: that the Low Countries should go to Bavaria, minus certain fortresses that were to be restored to France. Bolingbroke (to give St. John his new title) had all along dreaded lest the dissensions among the Allies should encourage King Louis to raise his demands; and he pointed out to the French ambassador that this was talking as if France had won the battle of Ramillies instead losing it. And the Dutch were outraged that, after their contributions in blood and money to the defeat of Louis, they should be asked to let him instal one of his clients in a Province which would facilitate further aggression against them. So for the next few months the Congress was suspended while Bolingbroke and Torcy argued behind the scenes.

Meanwhile the campaign of 1712 opened. Another victory for the Allies would have greatly strengthened Bolingbroke's hand in dealing with Torcy; but it would also have encouraged the Dutch to demand a stronger barrier and a fairer share of trade with Spanish America—boons which he was most anxious not to have to grant. Then unforeseen events made it more necessary than ever for him to keep in hand the means of putting pressure on King Louis. There was a catastrophic series of deaths in the Bourbon family. The Dauphin had died of small-pox in 1690; in February 1712 his heir the Duke of Burgundy, and a month later the latter's elder son, fell victims to it. There was now only Burgundy's younger son, an ailing infant of two, before Philip V of

Spain in the succession; and French lawyers were proclaiming that no renunciation could debar the rights of a natural King of France.

The Allies began to hope that England would put her heart back into the war; for it seemed that Philip could not forgo France and would not forgo Spain, and it was certain that even the Tory peace-mongers would not be able to sanction the union of the two crowns. But Bolingbroke's resourceful brain found a way out of the dilemma. He gained the support of the Allies for requiring Philip, as the price of retaining his contingent rights to France, to exchange Spain for Savoy plus Sicily; if he actually became King of France, he was to hand over Sicily to Austria.

However, Philip and his Queen decided to stay where they were. An attachment had sprung up between them and the land of their adoption during these ten troubled years. Not even the bait of her native Duchy could make Maria Luisa give up Spain, with or without the prospect of also gaining the throne of France. And as matters turned out the sickly infant at Versailles clung on to life, and the throne of France never became vacant after all.

While this crisis lasted Bolingbroke needed to be able to put pressure on both French and Dutch. He could neither use the British army in the Netherlands nor withdraw it, and the middle course which he took involved an act of almost unparalleled treachery. He sent the following instructions to the Duke of Ormonde, who now shared the command with Prince Eugene.

It is the Queen's positive command to your Grace that you avoid engaging in any operations till you have further orders from Her Majesty. I am at the same time to let your Grace know that the Queen would have you disguise the receipt of this order; and Her Majesty thinks you cannot want pretences for conducting yourself so as to answer her ends without owning that which might have an ill effect if it were publicly known.

P.S. I had almost forgot to tell your Grace that communication is given of this order to the Court of France, so that if the Mareschall de Villars takes, in any private way, notice of it to you, your Grace will answer accordingly.

Ormonde was also instructed to warn Villars of an intended attack by Eugene on Nieuport, with the result that the Allied force was shattered. A month or two later a Franco-British armistice was concluded, and the British contingent marched off, averting their eyes in shame from the comrades-in-arms with whom they had shared such toils and triumphs.

The man-power thus withdrawn was not very great. Only the 12,000 men of the British regiments actually left the Allied camp. The 38,000 Germans in British pay refused to follow Ormonde and were taken over by the Dutch. The loss was mainly financial: a burden was thrown on the Republic which it could not long sustain. Still, the forces of Eugene and Villars were now approximately equal, and there was no reason why Eugene should not win a victory which would open the way to Paris. He took Quesnoy, and only Landrecies now remained of the border-fortresses. King Louis trembled every time he heard a courier gallop into the courtyard at Versailles for fear that he brought news of disaster to the last army of France. But Villars achieved his master-piece. He out-manœuvred and outwitted Eugene with a feint towards Landrecies and a sudden attack on Denain; and the fact that Ormonde had gone off with the pontoons completed the Allies' discomfiture. And as it was the first defeat which they had suffered in the Low Countries in the eleven campaigns of the war it silenced those detractors of the great Duke who had argued that his victories had mainly been due to Eugene.

THE PEACE OF UTRECHT. Thus France was able to resume the dis-cussions at Utrecht with the prestige of having "lost every battle but the last."

The Peace of Utrecht was not a single instrument. It was a bundle of treaties: between France and each of the members of the Grand Alliance except the Emperor; between Spain and England; between the Dutch Republic and England. Much, but not all, of the negotiation was carried on at Utrecht; most, but not all, of the treaties were signed there in April 1713. The Congress had been formally opened in January 1712, but little progress was made until April, and after the end of that month there were no further plenary sessions until February 1713.

There was long haggling between France and Great Britain over the British demand for the dismantling of Dunkirk, the base of the French privateers which had played such havoc with the British and Dutch merchant shipping; and the armistice of August 1712 left many open questions, such as the domicile of the Stuart Pretender and the future of the American colonies. Discussions went on behind the scenes throughout the winter of 1712–13. But Louis and Bolingbroke both realized that there was a time-limit. Queen Anne's health was breaking up, and her death would bring to the throne a German Prince who was a determined opponent of the peace; while Louis himself was now an old man, his heir was an infant, and he dreaded the prospect of a regency taking over the government before France had made a sound and firm peace. In the end he gave satisfaction over the Stuarts: James Edward left French territory and settled in Lorraine. The various renunciations required to ensure that the crowns of France and Spain should not be united were solemnly and publicly registered by the Parlement of Paris; the exact frontiers of Acadia (Nova Scotia) were to be settled by a Joint Commission.

In January a new Barrier Treaty replaced the Whigs' treaty of 1709. The Republic was to garrison eight fortresses, some Belgian, some taken from the French by Marlborough, as against the nineteen which had been promised in 1709. The Dutch again bound themselves to send troops, if called upon, to maintain the Protestant Succession in Britain. They were very sore that the victories, due as much to their blue-coats as to the British red-coats, and as much to their guilders as to British guineas, should have put Britain in a position to impose such terms upon them; but so it was. Bolingbroke bludgeoned them into acceptance by threatening to leave them without even naval and diplomatic support.

Bolingbroke contrived that the Emperor and not Max of Bavaria should have Belgium; but the Barrier ate away so much of it, and it was so remote from Vienna that Charles was not very excited about adding it to his possessions.

Victor Amadeus, always a favourite of the Tories as a possible alternative to George of Hanover for the throne, came quite well out of the business. He recovered Savoy and Nice and got a good frontier along the Piedmontese Alps; he was to have Spain if Philip V died without issue; above all he joined the sacred circle of crowned heads by becoming "King of Sicily." Louis had wanted this desirable island for his client Max; but Bolingbroke was determined that it should go to a friend of Britain's who would not let it become a naval base for France. For the same reason he saw to it that Sardinia, seized by the British fleet in 1708 in the name of "King Charles III of Spain," should remain in possession of that prince now that he was "Emperor Charles VI."

Nevertheless, Charles was extremely hurt and indignant that Britain should force through a settlement that deprived him of his Spanish "birthright." Lacking the support of a naval Power he could not hope to win Spain or the Indies, but he claimed all the outlying Spanish possessions in Europe. If he had to forgo one of the Italian islands he would have preferred that it should be Sardinia rather than Sicily; for the province of Naples was of little use without its neighbouring island. When the treaties were signed in April (1713) his envoys had already shaken the dust of Utrecht from their feet and gone back to

Vienna. The other delegates waited until June for them to return; then they too went home, and the Congress was formally closed with the Emperor still at war with France.

Spain and Britain signed a commercial treaty by which Spain accorded to the South Seas Company the *Asiento* (= agreement), the granting of which to the French Guinea Company in 1702 had caused such heart-burning in the City of London (p. 129). The political treaty between Britain and Spain was not signed until July; but it was the first of the instruments to mention the prime cause of the war. It declared that the Kings of France and Spain had taken all possible steps to prevent their kingdoms from ever being united; and King Philip undertook not to transfer any part of his overseas dominions to France. He ceded Gibraltar and Minorca, but Britain promised that if she at any time wanted to dispose of the Rock, Spain should have the first refusal. Finally, he guaranteed to the Catalans a complete amnesty and the same rights of Provincial self-government as were enjoyed by Castile. This was the blackest spot in the Utrecht settlement. The Allies, having for their own ends encouraged the Catalans to revolt against Philip, now left them at his mercy; for the "Liberties of Castile" were very shadowy. The Catalans long refused to submit; even when Louis XIV sent a French army under Berwick they continued to defend Barcelona for months with the same tenacity that their descendants showed in the Civil War of 1936-9.

The Emperor struggled on single-handed for one more campaign, but that was enough to make it evident even to him that the Imperial forces which had failed to overcome the French on the Rhine with the aid (especially the financial aid) of England and Holland were quite unable to do so without it. After losing Landau and Freiburg he authorized Eugene to enter into negotiations with Villars. The result was the Treaty of Rastatt (1714) which practically confirmed the settlement of Utrecht. The only parts of the Spanish Empire that remained to Emperor Charles were Naples, Sardinia, and the Milanese; but these acquisitions practically substituted Austria for Spain as the dominant power in the Italian peninsula.

CHAPTER SEVENTEEN

THE SPIRIT OF THE AGE

"Man doth not live by bread alone" but also by his ideas about Religion and the Universe in which he finds himself, and by the Arts through which he expresses his glimpses of truth and beauty. But the spirit of his ideas does not blow altogether where it lists; its general direction shows in any particular age the influence of social and political conditions.

The Spirit of Monarchy. Political systems usually grow out of circumstances; it is only when they are already in existence that people try to explain them. The monarchism of which Louis XIV was the supreme exemplar grew up from the ruins of the "feudal system." With the gradual decay of feudalism men groped for some political structure that would give them security; and legitimacy supplied the need.

England's insularity had put her a little ahead of continental countries in breaking the feudal mould and in the substitution of unified national monarchy. She outgrew the need for despotic monarchy at the end of her Tudor century, just when the Stuarts began to make their claim to "Divine Right." The Great Rebellion, which was the nation's rejection of that claim fell just outside the period we are now studying; but the political questions which it involved were examined in the *Leviathan* of Thomas Hobbes, which appeared in 1651. This book was the first classic of modern political theory, and influenced all later thinkers on the subject. Hobbes's basic tenets were (1) that in every form of government there must be some power, whether a person or an assembly, which is absolute, and against which no other person or assemblies have any rights; and (2) that this sovereignty came into existence as the result of a contract which primitive men made with each other, when finding their free lives "solitary, poore, nasty, brutish and short," they agreed to set up a political authority which thenceforth it should be their duty to obey without question.

The British people, having given the Stuart conception of government a second chance at the Restoration, finally rejected it by the Revolution, and for their so doing they were provided with justification by John Locke (1632–1704) in his two *Treatises on Government* (1690). He followed Hobbes in basing government on a contract voluntarily made in past stages of society; but unlike Hobbes he regarded rulers as parties to the contract, and bound by the restrictions it implies. If the sovereign ignores these restrictions, subjects have a right and a duty to resist and discard him. The instances which Locke adduces were all drawn from the actions of James II: the packing of parliaments and juries, betrayal to a foreign Power, and so on. Absolute government, he argues, is no government at all, since it proceeds by caprice and not by reason. Locke was, indeed, the apostle of "reason." In his *Essay Concerning Human Understanding* he maintains that man gets all his knowledge of the universe (except perhaps his conceptions of logic and mathematics) from the experience of his senses. Even religious truth and the moral virtues must be judged by man's reasoning power. These ideas were accepted by the most vigorous and influential politicians and philosophers of Europe during the greater part of the eighteenth century.

But Limited Monarchy was a line which the British took for themselves. Over nearly all the rest of Europe this period was the golden age of hereditary absolutism. Louis XIV and his like did not condescend to justify their claims by argument, even in their own minds. Those claims they felt to be a manifest right, emanating from God, who revealed His will by having them born to their parents, taking care to remove by death any persons who might have a prior claim. If we ask why men acquiesced in this fantastic pretension (and we do so nominally even to-day in Great Britain, where we claim that our sovereigns rule "by the Grace of God") the answer must be that it was the result of a half-conscious instinct for self-preservation. For the principle of hereditary monarchy has done, and in some countries is still doing, good service to the average man, by giving to sovereignty a visible form which calls forth personal loyalty, and evades the dangerous problem of finding a successor when a ruler dies. It was this instinct which led to strong monarchies (in more or less conscious imitation of France) being set up during the period we are now studying, in Scandinavia, in central Europe and in Russia. And we have seen the chaos (with worse to follow) that resulted from the failure to establish it in Poland.

In the Middle Ages strong kings had been the only protection of common folk from the tyranny of feudal barons, and it is arguable that in the seventeenth century they were needed to protect nations from the tyranny of financiers. Louis succeeded (to a large extent) in France, but the Stuarts, even with his support, failed in Britain; for in Britain this political issue was combined with a religious issue, which at two critical moments united the landed classes with the moneyed classes; and that union produced the Revolution, the National Debt, and a Parliament which was long dominant over both Crown and People.

THE SPIRIT OF SCIENCE. During this epoch, when monarchs considered themselves masters over all things, a revolution was going on in men's minds which in the long run undermined their claim to "Divine Right."

When the seventeenth century began people still (in spite of a few prophets in the wilderness like Copernicus) sought knowledge in Authority rather than in Nature. For the Renaissance had widened the scope of Art and Literature long before it opened their minds to scientific enquiry. Aristotle's dictum that bodies fall faster or slower according to their weight was still accepted almost universally; if the evidence of the senses contradicted it, there must be something wrong with the evidence! As late as 1616 the Inquisition pronounced, once for all, that it was unscriptural, and therefore untrue, to say that the earth was not the centre of the Solar System.

But a new spirit was now stirring. Kepler and Galileo continued to observe, without obtrusively challenging the authority of the Church; and the Ptolemaic conception of the relationship between earth, sun and stars gradually faded from men's minds. Our English Francis Bacon worked out the principles of inductive reasoning (i.e., forming conclusions from examples); but the thinker who did most to give men confidence in the sovereign power of Mind was René Descartes, a Frenchman who found it advisable to live in tolerant Holland. He maintained the right and duty of doubting everything that can be doubted—and the only thing that cannot be doubted is our own existence: *cogito, ergo sum.* He set out to reconstruct the process of thought by reasoning; and this helped him to a better understanding of the nature of God by enlarging his ideas of the perfect and the infinite. But it also led to a conception of the world as a vast and intricate mechanism, and helped to set science free from theology—to confine men's enquiries to ascertainable facts about this present world.

Descartes died at the start of our period, but as it progressed the effects of his teaching upon the minds of all thinking men became more and more evident. The great philosopher of the age (though very few heard of him in his lifetime) was Baruch Spinoza (1632–77). He was by descent a Portuguese Jew, and like Descartes he lived in Holland, where he earned a scanty living polishing lenses—and thought about thought. Ejected from his own people as an atheist, he was nevertheless "the most God-intoxicated being alive." He saw manifestations of the

Deity everywhere and in all things, and declared that no one could truly love God who looked for God to love him in return. But he followed Descartes in refusing to mix science and theology, nor would he admit that religion is concerned with right conduct. He applied the critical spirit to social and political institutions, and like Descartes he looked on the universe as a mechanism ordered by coherent laws. Miracles seemed to him to contradict the idea of God.

This point of view gave a new impulse to the study of Natural Law; and the greatest manifestation of that impulse was the *Philosophiae Naturalis Principia Mathematica* of Sir Isaac Newton (1642–1727), Professor of Mathematics at Cambridge. The Principia is the greatest landmark in the whole history of Applied Mathematics. Its first part created the science of Dynamics, dealing with the motion of bodies in free space; Part II treated of motion in a resisting medium, as exemplified in waves and tides; and Part III applied these theorems to the movement of the heavenly bodies, developing the theory of gravitation.

Another great name among the thinkers of the era is Leibniz—the only first-class German mind of his day, and the first sign of intellectual recovery in central Europe after the annihilation of German culture in the Thirty Years' War. His versatility reminds us of the men of the Renaissance. A lawyer by academic training, he was a philosopher by habit of mind, and a statesman by vocation, with mathematics as a pastime. His ideas were to some extent a reaction from Cartesianism, for he tried to reconcile the new philosophy with the old; but he could never have taken the line he did but for the teaching of Descartes. He was employed for years in historical research (e.g., in the service of the Duke of Hanover, to prove that the Dukedom ought to be made an Electorate); he devised a calculating machine which could work out square roots; he undertook a number of diplomatic missions; and he invented the infinitesimal calculus.

The fact that all the thinkers of the era were mathematicians, at any rate as a side-line, resulted from the fact that science in its new form depended on the idea of immutable natural law, valid for all times and places. Even change is subject to law; hence the coincidence that Leibniz and Newton independently and simultaneously invented the calculus which provides the apparatus for analysing it. And the calculus was the climax to a century of remarkable developments in mathematical technique—co-ordinate geometry (in which Descartes was the pioneer), logarithms, the binomial theorem, and the interdependence of algebra and geometry.

Apart from the mathematical branches of science, the study which owed most to the new inductive, observing habit of mind was medicine. Earlier in the century Harvey had applied it to Physiology, proving by its means the circulation of the blood. Others—especially Malpighi—investigated the interrelated functions of the organs; and fresh opportunities of observation were opened by the development of the microscope.

England showed the way in establishing scientific research as a recognized part of cultural life. The Royal Society, which began as a club holding informal meetings at Oxford and in London to hear members report on their studies, received a Royal Charter from Charles II, who himself dabbled in chemistry. One of its founders was Robert Boyle, an Irish aristocrat who studied the effect of pressure on gases; and among its earliest Fellows were Newton and Leibniz. No other country had any such institution until 1700, when an Academy of Sciences was started in Berlin under the patronage of the King of Prussia, with Leibniz as its first President.

Such matters did not interest Louis XIV, and without his interest they could not flourish in France. Colbert started something of the sort in 1666, but it did not acquire even a regular meeting-place until 1709. And when the body of Descartes was brought back from Sweden, the King forbade any formal honour to the memory of the great Frenchman whose spirit was working in every thinker in the civilized world. For Cartesian ideas were banned by the Church; and perhaps Louis dimly realized that the doctrine of the Open Mind was inimical to all that he stood for, and would in the fullness of time overthrow it.

THE SPIRIT OF RELIGION. As we have noted before, this was not a religious age. The Protestant Reformation and the Catholic Counter-Reformation, after being locked in deadly strife for a century, settled down after the Treaty of Westphalia in a territorial partition of Europe. Persecution still went on here and there—in Hungary of Lutherans, in Scotland of Presbyterians, in Ireland of Catholics, in France of Huguenots—but religion was no longer the mainspring of policy. Authoritarian régimes tended to make it formal. Louis XIV was typical of his age in this as in so much else. Madame de Maintenon told Cardinal de Noailles that although he would never miss daily attendance at Mass or observance of the Church's festivals and sacraments, it was impossible to make him understand what was meant by reverence or humility.

But personal religion never dies, and in this age it was kept alive in France by the movement known as Jansenism, This began as a reaction against the Jesuits. The Society of Jesus had ever since its formation in 1539 devoted itself to propaganda for the Catholic Church. Its members were the "shock-troops" of the Counter-Reformation, and in concentrating their energies on gaining and keeping converts they laid themselves open to the charge of being too easy-going in the standards of conduct and piety which they demanded from their flocks. The Society issued instructions, through its semi-military organization, that confessors were not to probe into a penitent's spiritual condition, but to deal with each sin on its merits, and to interpret divine law in its most "benign" spirit. But their opponents within the Catholic Church felt that this was underestimating the importance of personal religion. One Jansen, Professor of Divinity at Louvain, attacked them in a book on St. Augustine, in the course of which he maintained that salvation depends not on outward conformity or on sacraments but on the possession of "Grace"—the consciousness of God and the Atonement. A group of men who felt the call of this personal faith went to live together (some were clerics, some laymen—they took no vows) in meditation and spiritual converse in the disused monastic buildings of Port Royal aux Champs, not far from Versailles. They revived the study of Greek literature, and their text-book on Logic was in general use for two centuries. One of them, Blaise Pascal, wrote his famous *Lettres Provinciales* (1656), which grew out of their original purpose, as a defence against Jansenism, into a devastating attack on the Jesuits and on formal religion of every kind. Like most of the active minds of the age, Pascal was a distinguished mathematician: he wrote a treatise on Conic Sections at the age of sixteen; and in these Letters he showed himself a supreme master of French prose.

THE SPIRIT OF LITERATURE. The Renaissance had liberated two broad streams of literary energy, Christian and classical. But in literature as in politics, religion had lost most of its motive force by the middle of the seventeenth century. Milton brought his *Paradise Lost* (1667) into a world that seemed to have outgrown all that he stood for; Bunyan's *Pilgrim's Progress* (1678) was the voice of outcast Puritanism. But the classical spirit survived in full vigour, especially in the France of Louis XIV—the core of European culture.

As we should expect, the literature of the age was governed by self-conscious laws of correctitude. The *Académie française*, established by Richelieu to decide upon uniform standards of lingual usage, was now taken up by Colbert and lodged in the Louvre. There it occupied itself with the preparation of an authoritative dictionary. The poise, stability and authority that we associate with the political régime of Louis XIV was equally characteristic of the literature to which he accorded his patronage. Its ideals were set forth by Boileau, whose *Art Poétique* (based on Aristotle and Horace) tells us what qualities we ought to admire in poetry: clarity, sequence, good sense and good taste: qualities that reflect the spirit of the French people.

Nothing that Louis did was more to his credit than his recognition of the greatness of Molière, who might otherwise have dragged out an obscure existence in the provinces as playwright, actor and producer of a travelling "fit-up." In his touring days Molière had come into contact with all sorts of people, and he amused the French court from 1660 to 1673 (and the civilized world ever since) by satirizing their foibles in a series of comedies which are in their own line supreme. But two types are missing from his gallery: rulers and workers; for the former were sacrosanct to such an audience, and the latter beneath its interest. That same audience also saw the tragedies of Racine straight from the mint. Racine brought into play a knowledge of Greek tragedy which he had acquired as a student at Port Royal, to create works based on the classic interplay of fate and passion constructed within the classic "unities" of time and place. These two writers alone would have sufficed to make the court of Louis XIV the centre of culture and the French language part of the equipment of educated classes all over Europe.

But it would be a mistake to attribute the great literary output in France at this time entirely to Court patronage. Some of the greatest writers of the age—Pascal, for instance, and La Fontaine, and Madame de Sévigné—owed nothing to it. The King could not of himself have evoked the efflorescence. In this field as in war and diplomacy he exploited and personified a burgeoning of the national spirit.

THE SPIRIT OF THE FINE ARTS. The domination of French ideas in Europe was as active in architecture and sculpture as in literature. Among Colbert's many offices was that of "Superintendent of Buildings, Arts and Manufactures." He controlled this department in the same spirit as he used in economic and commercial matters. He brought Art into the King's service, thereby "exalting" it to a definite place in society. Hitherto house-painters and picture-painters had been members of the same trade-guild. And by the King's order he compiled a list of artists (including some foreigners), and sent them pensions accompanied by instructions as to how they were to show their appreciation. The glories of the reign were celebrated not only by adulatory histories and poems, but in pictures, sculptures, tapestries and medals. Classical models were the final authority in matters of taste. Colbert founded an Academy of Arts, under the energetic direction of Le Brun (who also took charge of the interior decorations at Versailles); and it was the chief function of this institution to consider the works of antiquity and deduce therefrom the rules of good taste.

The spirit of an age is often revealed more by its architecture than by any other of the arts; and just as the Parthenon typifies Athens and the Empire State Building New York, so the palace at Versailles typifies the age of Louis XIV. Its dimensions were vast, its decorations gorgeous; it was built over a marsh, because such was His Majesty's pleasure, by the labour of tens of thousands of workers at the cost of tens of millions of livres; its park extended over 20,000 acres, and it had gardens designed by Le Nôtre—this was the great age of geometrical gardening. But our admiration is moderated when we find that there were no baths and no drains; that the only sleeping accommodation of its ten thousand inhabitants (except for the royal family) consisted of noisome unventilated little dens; and that the aristocratic ladies and gentlemen who spent their lives in it were profuse in the use of perfume for the most obvious purpose.

The glories of medieval architecture with which western Europe abounded were regarded as uncouth monstrosities. The influence of the Italian Renaissance was still potent. Versailles and the Louvre were provided with terraces and flat roofs suitable only for the sunny climate of the Mediterranean; churches were built with colonnades and triangular pediments, round-topped Roman arches, and domes. Sculptors depicted the gods and goddesses of classical mythology; and when they made statues of the King (which they did quite often), they gave him bare arms and legs and put him in the garb of a Roman general—surmounted by a vast peruke. For this was an age of wigs, and of the class-distinctions which they implied.

The French painters of the age had to a lesser degree the merits of the writers: skill in arrangement, grace, dignity, a sense of style. But great art needs something more, and that something was not native to the Age of Louis XIV. It is significant that the greatest French painters, Poussin (died 1665) and Claude Lorraine (died 1682), lived and worked in Italy. The last glories of the Renaissance faded out of the sky of Spain with Velasquez (died 1660) and Murillo (died 1682); and though a few great Dutch painters still lingered on the scene (Rembrandt died in 1669 and Ruysdael in 1682) the spirit of art was fading out in the Netherlands, too.

6*

The art of music was as yet scarcely adolescent. Louis XIV had a genuine liking for it, and imported an Italian musician named Lully to superintend the music of the Court. Lully, like Le Brun, was more of an organizer than a creator. No expense was spared in mounting his ballets and operas; but as entertainments we should, if we could be transported back to that age and scene, find them very stilted and formal; while the music would seem thin to ears accustomed to the tremendous developments, harmonic, contrapuntal and instrumental, which have taken place since. But this age saw the birth of modern instrumental music. The violin had now ousted the viol; this was the lifetime of its greatest maker, Stradivari, and of the founder of its technique Corelli. And keyboard music was also beginning to acquire its distinctive style under the hands of Couperin in France and Scarlatti in Italy. Henry Purcell (the last great English musician for two centuries), besides his achievements in opera and cantata, was a pioneer in what is now called Chamber Music. German music was only on the threshold of its greatness. Its first giants, Bach and Handel, grew to manhood during this era, but their work and influence lies mainly in the next.

CHAPTER EIGHTEEN

TRANSITION

THE death of Louis XIV, following closely on the Utrecht settlement of Europe and the Hanoverian Succession in Britain, was the central point in the period of European history covered by this book. In this chapter we shall take stock of the situation and make a brief survey of the historical setting through which we are now about to travel.

THE HANOVERIAN SUCCESSION. The accession of George Lewis, Elector of Hanover, to the throne of Great Britain (August 1714) was important for Europe in two ways. Firstly it confirmed the Revolution of 1688, thereby announcing that Britain intended to continue along a line of constitutional development which contrasted with continental absolutism. Secondly it brought a new complication into European affairs—the personal union of insular Britain with a state on the European mainland.

The Bill of Rights (1689) had scheduled the conditions on which British sovereigns were to reign; and the Act of Settlement (1701), passed on the death of Princess Anne's last surviving child, offered the succession to the Dowager Electress Sophia of Hanover, granddaughter of the Princess Royal of England who had married the Elector Palatine in 1613. Most British people would have preferred a return to the direct Stuart line; but the three years of James II's reign had burnt into the minds of the ruling classes the conviction that their privileges, religious and parliamentary, would always be in danger under a Catholic king; and there was no likelihood of the Stuarts turning Protestant. Thus the Hanoverian Succession was merely the lesser of two evils, and Parliament took care to limit the power of a foreign king to involve Britain in continental conflicts. The Act of Settlement declared, *inter alia*, that Britain was not to be obliged to defend the sovereign's foreign possessions, and that British affairs were to be conducted exclusively by the British Government, in which no foreigner could hold office.

Sophia died in June 1714, leaving her claims to her son, who was already Elector; but when, two months later, Queen Anne died, his succession was by no means certain. The party spirit was already strongly developed in England. The Whigs naturally supported George, for they had always stood for parliamentary rule and for war against pro-Stuart France; but the Tories were now in office, and had made the Peace of Utrecht. When the critical moment came, the ministers were paralysed by the refusal of the Stuart claimant to give more than luke-warm guarantees for the privileges of the Church of England, and the Whigs seized their chance to proclaim King George I.

The new King was fifty-four years old. In the late war he had shown himself a capable commander, and he was already an experienced ruler. But his political ideas were set in the mould of patriarchal despotism. A solid, stolid, coarse-grained German, he never tried to ingratiate himself with his new subjects, even to the extent of learning their language. Nor did he relish his position as a constitutional monarch. He accepted the crown mainly for the sake of his Electorate.

The circumstances of his accession made him feel that the Whigs alone were to be trusted, since they had everything to lose by a Stuart restoration. So he put them in office, and they contrived to monopolize it for half a century. Hence the development of constitutional devices such as Responsible Government and Cabinet Solidarity which had great influence on democratic government all over the world. But eighteenth-century Britain was not a democracy. It was an oligarchy, something like the later Roman Empire, in which patrician families had a monopoly of office. Great landowners formed the House of Lords and put clients into the Commons by their control of the constituencies, where only a small minority of the population had votes; while ministers bought parliamentary support with Government places and pensions.

SUNSET OVER VERSAILLES. King Louis was now seventy-five years old. He had outlived nearly all the great men who had made his court and realm so glorious; but his zest for his *métier de roi* seemed to grow with the years. Though his will had always prevailed, Colbert and Louvois had been men with whom he had to reckon; but since their time his ministers had been mere civil servants. He now worked all the afternoon as well as all the morning, and most evenings too. Hunting, dancing and love-making lose some of their charm when one gets past fifty; and Molière, Racine and Lully, who had ministered to pleasures of the mind, had all passed away. There was now a subdued, subfusc atmosphere at Versailles. Louis had married Madame de Maintenon, but she was not treated as Queen, and seemed like a highly respected governess or lady's companion. The younger generation of the royal family had been almost wiped out by death; the old King especially felt the loss of the gay, inconsequent young Duchess of Burgundy.

And the piety to which it was Maintenon's pride to have converted him had nothing of happy serenity about it. Louis became convinced that the defeats of his arms and the deaths of his children were hints from God that he had been remiss in purging his realm of heresy. So he revived the decrees against the Huguenots which had been allowed to lapse into disuse; he demolished Port Royal, the Mecca of Jansenism; and egged on Pope Clement XI to issue the Bull Unigenitus, which condemned as heretical Quesnoy's *Réflexions*, a widely-read manual of personal piety.

Another of the King's preoccupations during this twilight of his reign was the spectre of bankruptcy. His incessant wars had put France in debt to the extent of milliards of livres; in 1711 the revenue was only 74 millions for an expenditure of 120 millions. One obvious reason for the deficits was the absurd way the taxes were assessed and collected. The nobles and higher clergy, who consumed so much of the country's wealth and did so little in return, were exempt altogether from the most burdensome taxes. Indeed, this exemption was regarded as the hall-mark of social standing. Louis had not the moral courage for drastic reform. When Racine, touched by the sufferings of the poor, sent a memorandum on the subject to the Council, Louis was annoyed that a mere poet should have views on social and economic matters, and Racine was banished from the Court. Much the same fate befell Fénélon when it was realized that in *Télémaque* he was warning his pupil the young Duke of Burgundy against some of the shortcomings of the régime behind a veil of allegory. A little later Vauban, who had long reflected on the causes of the misery which he saw as he went about the country on military business, brought forward a scheme for merging all taxation in a *Dîme Royale*, from which there were to be no exemptions. This would have rejuvenated France and might have saved the monarchy from the Revolution. For years he urged it vainly on ministers; and when at last he published it his book was publicly burnt, and the man who had done more than any other for the military glories of the reign died in disgrace.

The King's other anxiety was over the succession to the throne. His only son was dead; of his three grandsons, two were dead, and the third had renounced the throne of France on becoming King of Spain; everything now depended on the life of one frail great-grandson aged five. He issued a decree legitimizing his children by Madame de Montespan—"the offspring of his person and not of his rank," as St. Simon puts it; and in 1714 a further decree placed them in the line of succession after his descendants born in wedlock. During the last few years he had fallen under the influence of the eldest of these legitimated sons, the Duc de Maine. This suggests senile decay; for in his prime Louis had been a good judge of men, and Maine was a weak, worthless, petulant person, dominated by his frivolous and intriguing wife.

The prospect of a long minority caused anxious discussion in this unattractive royal circle. For the position of regent belonged by tradition to the King's oldest legitimate male relative, and it was evident

THE BOURBON KINGS OF FRANCE

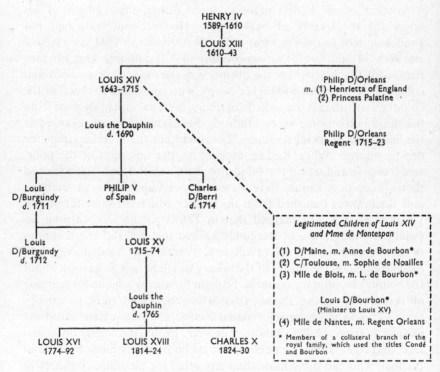

that no one would accept at its face value the legitimization of Maine and Toulouse. This would let in Philip Duke of Orleans. Orleans was a dissolute rake; but even if his character had been of seraphic purity Maine and his Duchess would have tried to supplant him, and the fond old King would have tried to gratify them. There was some talk of summoning the States General, to give its almost legendary authority to the appointment of Maine; but the King felt that such a resurrection (it was nearly a century since it had last met) would impair the sacred absolutism of the monarchy. Ultimately, at the suggestion of

Maintenon, he made a will subjecting Orleans' authority to a nominated Council, while Maine was to become the young King's guardian and commandant of the Household Troops.

When his call came, Louis met it with dignity. "Did you think I was immortal?" he asked a weeping servant. But as a matter of fact, there was little weeping. Madame de Maintenon had to take refuge in a nunnery some time before the end, utterly worn out by thirty years of perpetual attendance on egotism so lacking in the resources of inward happiness.

POWERS IN DECLINE. Nations sometimes rise quickly to the maximum strength possible to their circumstances, and then go into a slow decline—due generally to some defect in economic stability. When our period opens no fewer than five states which had played leading rôles on the European stage were manifestly receding into the background.

Spain was a classic example of this. Her golden age had ended with the sixteenth century. The spirit of adventure which had led her *conquistadors* to ransack East and West for wealth seemed incompatible with the capacity for hard work which is the only lasting source of prosperity. Much of the country's economic vitality had come from the Moorish elements which had been expelled by the Inquisition. Moreover, the success of her Hapsburg Kings in nullifying the constitutional rights of the Cortes (perhaps the oldest parliamentary institution in Europe) had made government depend on royal ability and industry, which since the death of Philip II (1598) had been conspicuously lacking. And it is from this succeeding age that we get our conception of Spaniards as either lounging peasants or haughty hidalgos.

Peace, retrenchment and reform might even now have restored a nation which has always shown high mettle when roused to some great cause; but its new Bourbon king was incapable of anything of the kind. For Philip V had been brought up to dynastic politics in the court of Louis XIV, and his manhood was enervated by uxoriousness and superstition. He was dominated by his wife and his confessor. For the first years of his reign the Government was controlled by the King of France, who provided him with a Queen (Maria Luisa of Savoy), and the Queen with a Lady of the Bedchamber (Madame des Ursins), who acted as agents for Versailles. But in the spring of 1714 Maria Luisa died. Another wife had to be provided for Philip without delay. Giulio Alberoni, an Italian cleric who represented the Duke of Parma at the Spanish Court, suggested to Madame des Ursins that his master's daughter, Elizabeth Farnese, would be a suitable candidate, being a placid, good-humoured girl who would be wax in her hands. The lady fell into his well-baited trap. The wedding took place by proxy, and the new Queen set out at once for Spain. Alberoni met her on the frontier, and Madame des Ursins also came half-way to the frontier, so as to establish control before she met the King. But in the interview between the two women it was the elder who was crushed: she emerged in tears, while the young Queen called to the guards to "take this mad woman away!" Presumably Alberoni had persuaded Elizabeth to rid herself of French influence by a bold stroke at the outset. Madame was hustled across the Pyrenees, while the Queen travelled on to Madrid where she speedily captivated the King and extorted his approval of her action. And the new Queen's Italian interests had greatly intensified Philip's determination to upset the Utrecht settlement, regardless of the real and abiding interests of Spain.

The Dutch Republic was another state which too, had by this time shot its bolt. The last century had been its zenith, in commerce and industry, in colonization and seafaring, in the arts and sciences, in the struggle for political and religious liberty. But its area was too restricted to support a large population; and its constitution hampered all vigorous action. It had played a leading part in checking the ambitions of Louis XIV, and in 1688 its Stadtholder (hereditary president) had become King of England to win support for that cause. But when William III had died childless (1702), the merchant oligarchy which had founded the Republic recovered control of the government. It continued to support the anti-French coalition, but by the end of the Spanish Succession War it had overtaxed its strength. For some time to come people continued to speak of the Republic and Britain as "The Sea Powers," but after Utrecht the disparity between them went on growing, and in the middle of the century Frederick the Great likened them to a ship of the line towing a small boat in its wake.

Sweden was another country whose habitable area could support only a small nation. Its warrior-kings had conquered most of the Baltic lands, but had thereby made enemies of all the other states of the region: Denmark, Brandenburg, Poland, Russia, and latterly Hanover. Charles XII, the Meteor of the North, had won a David-and-Goliath victory over Peter of Russia at Narva but was undone by insensate over-confidence; and his constant wars drained away the last lees of Swedish vitality.

The fourth decadent state was Poland; but here the weakness was mainly political. The country still had a population nearly as great as that of Russia; and though the Poles were of Slavonic blood, their Catholicism should have brought them into contact with western culture. But at every demise of the crown their elective kingship led to orgies of intrigue, sometimes ending in bloodshed. Votes could be bought by foreign potentates; the Diet of nobles could impose conditions as the price of their support which deprived the King of all real power; and the *liberum veto*, which required all decisions to be unanimous, paralysed it as a legislative or executive body. At the last election (1697) Augustus the Strong, Elector of Saxony, had secured the crown; but though he renounced Lutheranism for it he made no attempt to grapple with the problems of government which it entailed. Thus Poland was already threatened with disaster. A monarch with no power to rule, and owing his elevation to foreign patronage; a Diet with no political capacity and no public spirit; an aristocracy who paid no taxes and did not even serve in the rudimentary army; a middle class consisting of Germans and Jews, and a lower class of half-starved serfs—such a country would be a helpless prey to predatory neighbours with strong governments.

Lastly, the Ottoman Empire, though still sprawling all over south-eastern Europe, had manifestly passed its climacteric. The Turks were good fighters but could not govern, or assimilate, or even exploit, the peoples they subjugated. And the tide of their conquests, beaten back from Vienna in 1683, never flowed again. During the eighteenth century Austria and Russia were drawn together by the hope of aggrandisement at the expense of what seemed to be a moribund Power. But the Turk was not so easily disposed of, and the "Eastern Question" about his expulsion from Europe continued to cause wars and rumours of war for two centuries to come.

POWERS IN THE ASCENDANT. While these states were dropping out of the circle of "Great Powers," others were rising from obscurity to take their places.

In the early part of the seventeenth century the Russian monarchy had been in danger of the fate which had overtaken the Polish; but a national instinct for autocracy (which in our time takes the form of a Supreme Soviet) impelled the people to rally round a new dynasty, the Romanovs. And in Peter the Great that stock had produced a scion who gave the Russian state fresh direction and energy. He built a new capital, named after his patron saint, as a window on Europe; he approached the West by conquering eastern Poland and the Estonian and Livonian provinces of Sweden; and at this half-way mark in our period he was still engaged in making good the precarious footing as a European Power which he had thus won for Russia.

A similar phenomenon was observable in north Germany. Frederick William the "Great Elector" (reigned 1640–88) had failed to keep his grip on Pomerania, which he had snatched from the Swedes when they were in alliance with Louis XIV. But he had so husbanded the resources of his poverty-stricken, scattered and sparsely-populated heritage that his successor Frederick was able to name his own price for supporting the Emperor in the Spanish Succession War. That price was the crown of kingship (1701). This advancement of the House of Hohenzollern was to cost the Hapsburgs dear, for it led to a century of rivalry which ended (after the Seven Weeks War of 1866) in Prussia ousting Austria from the hegemony of central Europe. There was a significance, perhaps only half-realized at the time, in the fact that Frederick became King not of Brandenburg but of Prussia, a province outside the Empire. He spent money so lavishly in setting up his royal state that when he died (1713) he had brought his realm to the verge of bankruptcy. But his son Frederick William I set to work to complete the work of the Great Elector. A plain, simple-minded, duty-doing ruler, his great aim was to build up Prussian military strength.

The third of the states in the ascendant owed its growing strength partly to its geographical position, partly to the astute egoism of its ruling dynasty. Savoy was perched astride the western Alps, in the no-man's-land between France and Austria. The situation was full of peril for an unwary ruler, but offered great opportunities to one who could get the two Powers to bid against each other for his support. Duke Victor Amadeus (reigned 1675–1730) had already added Piedmont to his patrimony, and a well-timed entry into the Spanish Succession War had been rewarded, as part of the settlement at Utrecht, with the kingdom of Sicily. And he already espied a chance of further advancement in the fact that the Emperor wanted to get hold of that island in exchange for Sardinia. What if Charles could be induced to offer as makeweight a part of the Duchy of Milan adjacent to Piedmont? For the finger of destiny was beckoning him in the direction which his family was to tread until, a century and a half later, his descendant was to become the first King of Italy.

THE OLD RÉGIME. This was the culmination of the age of privilege that was to be shattered by the French Revolution. It was the last fling of dynastic kingship—of countries being treated as hereditary property. Royal marriages still settled the fate of nations, and behind the gilded wedding-coaches trooped the shades of thousands who had perished in wars waged to make good the claims they involved. Territories were carved up with no more concern for the inhabitants than a grocer cutting up cheese feels for the mites in it. We shall see glaring examples of this in the partition of Poland, and in the treatment of Italy as a reservoir of appanages to serve as makeweights in chaffering between dynasties. (Naples changed hands thrice and Parma four times in the course of twenty years.) Except in insular Britain national feeling was as yet only half-developed. German Princes hired out their regiments to fight and die for anybody who would pay. Adventurers of war and politics sought employment wherever they could find it; Alberoni, a Parmesan, and Ripperda, a Dutchman, were prime ministers of Spain; Eugene of Savoy commanded Austrian armies; Maurice de Saxe was a Marshal of France; Irishmen, Poles, Germans and Frenchmen helped to build up Russia. Travellers on the Continent —and it was a great age of travel—were scarcely conscious of being foreigners; Oliver Goldsmith, who wandered over Europe with his flute, had not the word nation in his vocabulary. Half the states of Europe had foreign rulers—a Hessian was King of Sweden, a Lorrainer was Grand Duke of Tuscany, a German was Empress of Russia, a Saxon was King of Spain, a Spaniard was King of Naples, a Savoyard was King of Sardinia.

But these last dynastic wars were overlapped by wars of a different kind, fought for economic supremacy. In the previous century England had fought such wars with the Dutch; she was now to be engaged in contests of far greater range and significance with France and Spain. The British, being the only nation (apart from the Dutch, now past their meridian) sufficiently developed, politically, to appreciate what was at stake, won a great trans-oceanic empire, and then lost half of it through misconceived attempts to exploit it, all in the course of the next three-quarters of a century.

Another characteristic of the new age was the "enlightenment" which became fashionable, even among rulers, as the period went on. Educated people now prided themselves on belonging to an Age of Reason. In place of religious enthusiasts like Luther and Calvin, Loyola and Philip II, Bossuet and Pascal, Milton and Cromwell, its representative figures were Voltaire and Diderot, Frederick and Catherine, David Hume and Edward Gibbon. But scepticism about Christianity did not imply cynicism about humanity. On the contrary, there never was an age so optimistic about the possibilities latent in human nature. All that was needed to bring out the best in humanity, it was generally felt, was wise government.

This faith led to another characteristic phenomenon: the Enlightened Despot, exemplified in Frederick of Prussia, Catherine of Russia, Charles III of Spain, Leopold of Tuscany, Joseph II of Austria. We are reminded of Plato's dictum that states would not be well governed until philosophers were kings. Many of the kings of this epoch were, or at any rate thought they were, and tried to be, philosophers.

CHAPTER NINETEEN

AN ENTENTE CORDIALE

1715–1717

GREAT BRITAIN and France, the states most concerned to preserve the peace of Europe, drew together to enforce the maintenance of the recent settlement on the Emperor Charles VI and King Philip of Spain, who would have started another great war to enforce their claims against each other.

THE NEW RÉGIME IN FRANCE. The Great King's will survived him by less than a day. Philip of Orleans was not the man to be set aside by a dead King Louis or a live Duke of Maine. He was a man of brilliant gifts, ready of speech, winning in manners, and he had shown exceptional courage and capacity in the war. But his character had decayed through self-indulgence, and by 1715 he was sunk in vice. His own mother said of him that he had all the talents except that of knowing how to use them. In general he was too good-humouredly indolent to be ambitious, but he had always detested Maine, and love of power is the last frailty that cynics can discard. To the Council on the morrow of the King's death he announced that he intended to take full control of the government himself. Maine and his friends protested, but he outfaced them at the meeting, and out-manœuvred them next day by gaining the approval of the Parlement of Paris. The Parlement was delighted at this recognition of its authority, in abeyance since 1673; and it was the only voice of the middle classes. He went on to gratify the nobles of the Court, also long excluded from power, by making them members of the Council Boards which he substituted for the individual councillors of the late King. Above all, he scoffed away the drab decorum which had weighed so heavily on Versailles for the past thirty years. There was a reaction like that after the Restoration of 1660 in England. Everybody (or nearly everybody) gave a sigh of relief and began to make up for lost time.

But even when Orleans had established his authority his position was by no means secure. France seemed on the verge of fiscal collapse. The country had scarcely begun to recover from exhaustion after the two great wars. The State so heavily in debt that it could only keep up an appearance of solvency by fresh borrowing, and the blood-tax—the maiming and slaughter in battle of tens of thousands of peasants whose labour was its only source of wealth—made recovery seem impossible. And it was these humbler classes, thus decimated and ruined by war, who had to take the strain; for in France as in nearly every other continental country, the nobles and higher clergy were not only exempt from direct taxation but had to be maintained by feudal dues which were a first charge on the produce of the soil.

A government embarrassed for revenue is always in peril. The internal danger to the Regent came from Maine and his clique; an external threat from Philip V of Spain, who on the death of the old King had actually set out to demand the Regency and the Guardianship as his natural right. His heart had failed before he reached the Pyrenees; but there was no knowing when he might pluck up courage to try again, or what the attitude of the French people would be towards his claim.

Thus Orleans' foreign policy was necessarily to let sleeping dogs lie. Any disturbance of the equilibrium set up at Utrecht would be an opportunity for his cousin to oust him.

THE NEW RÉGIME IN BRITAIN. Across the Channel King George found himself in an equally precarious position. His accession had gone off with unexpected ease; but few people thought it would be permanent. He himself seemed to live (in the two rooms which he occupied in St. James' Palace) with his trunks only half unpacked. The shortcomings of the Stuarts soon began to fade from people's minds when they saw the alternative at close quarters. For one thing, George having shown himself a Party king, the Whig politicians were making the most of it; and this at once alienated some of the soundest elements of the nation. Moreover, there were already signs that despite all safeguards (p. 171) he would drag the country into trouble for the sake of Hanover. Lastly, he had made no attempt to tone down his un-Englishness. William III had also been a foreigner, but at least he spoke our tongue, and was close to the throne by birth and marriage. But George I rarely met any of his new subjects except his ministers—with whom he conversed in bad French; and quite fifty persons had better hereditary claims to the throne. His main qualification was his Protestantism, and even this did not seem to be of the right brand. For he was a Lutheran; and although he attended public worship as in duty bound he never made even a show of following the service.

Thus Jacobite sentiment revived in some parts of the country and in some classes of society. Was it more than sentiment? Events were now to answer that question in the negative.

The Jacobite exiles in France had planned simultaneous risings in

England and Scotland, and had induced old King Louis to promise secret help—a shipload of arms from France and a contribution in cash from Spain. But everything went wrong for them. The story that James Edward was supposititious was amply disproved by his conduct in this crisis of his career: he was a true son of James II. Having issued a proclamation in which he stressed all that he should have glossed over, and omitted the assurances that everybody wanted, he gave premature instructions for the rising without even informing Bolingbroke, who had become his "Secretary of State," and was the only statesman among his adherents. Moreover King Louis died just as the expedition was about to start, and the Regent, though he did not actually stop it, would not offend King George by giving it active support. The English side of it sputtered out altogether; and although in Scotland the Jacobites managed to make a draw of the Battle of Sheriffmuir, that result was equivalent to a defeat for Highlanders who had neither the resources nor the temperament for a long campaign. It became clear that the great majority of the British people, however distasteful they might find the Hanoverian régime, had no mind to risk taking as king a Catholic pretender, who had grown up abroad and was nearly as foreign as George himself. The collapse of the rebellion showed Europe that Jacobitism was dead, at any rate for the time being; and before the end of 1715 the other rulers were already beginning to take a more respectful tone to George I. Evidently he would have to be reckoned with.

BRITAIN AND EUROPE. Britain's foreign affairs were throughout most of the eighteenth century conducted by two Secretaries of State, one of whom dealt with the northern countries of Europe, the other with the southern; and they also shared responsibility for most of the other departments of government, except the Treasury. It seems an odd system, but it worked well enough so long as one of the Secretaries acquiesced in the predominance of the other. During the first years of the new régime the Northern Department was conducted by Lord Townshend, a Whig nobleman of high principles but of no commanding ability, while the Southern was under General (afterwards Earl) Stanhope, who had served with distinction in the recent war (though ultimately defeated and taken prisoner at Brihuega), and who was not only a clever linguist but a man of exceptional vitality, intelligence and force of character.

These qualities were urgently needed in the Government, for its foreign relations were in a hazardous state. King George was on the verge of war with Sweden over Hanoverian claims to Bremen and Verden, and although the Act of Settlement forbade the dragging in of Britain there was no knowing how far the restrictions would be effective. The King's Hanoverian ministers, Bernstorff and Bothmar were very active at the Court of St. James, and they had the advantage over the English ministers that they were professional experts in European politics. And what was worse, the Utrecht settlement had left Great Britain without a friend in Europe. Of the other leading members of the Grand Alliance, the Dutch were disappointed over the Barrier, and the Emperor was indignant at England's recognition of Philip V as King of Spain. So the first care of the new Government was to restore the Alliance which had been long the core of Whig foreign policy, and Stanhope visited The Hague and Vienna to try to bring this about. It was unusual for a Minister to go in person on such missions, but Stanhope had won the respect of the Dutch and the friendship of the Emperor in the recent war, and it was hoped that his direct, unconventional approach would be more effective than the formalities of routine diplomacy. But it was not until the frustration of the Jacobite rebellion that Stanhope's activities had any success.

Signs of the change were first visible at Vienna. Charles VI began to reflect that George I had been a loyal member of the Alliance, and that his Whig ministers had furiously opposed the Treaty which gave Spain to the Bourbon. Furthermore his hope of exchanging Sardinia for Sicily (p. 160) could never be carried out without the benevolent neutrality, at least, of the British fleet. The trouble was that the British would insist on dragging the Dutch into any renewal of the old alliance, and this involved the thorny question of the Barrier. To have Dutch garrisons in these fortresses, maintained by taxes levied on the inhabitants, impaired Austrian sovereignty; and as a safeguard against French aggression they had proved useless. But to the British and Hanoverian as well as the Dutch Governments the Barrier had become a fetish. During 1715 the Whig ministry crowded on all sail to bring about an agreement between the Emperor and the States General on the subject, for the Emperor talked of ridding himself of trouble by exchanging Belgium for Bavaria; and to have the Wittelsbach clients of France established in the Low Countries would be a disaster both for Britain and the United Provinces. At last a new Barrier agreement was made by which the Dutch were to provide two-fifths and the Emperor three-fifths of the garrisons. Wrangling continued over paying for them; but the way now seemed to be cleared for a revival of the old Alliance.

But the scope of the Anglo-Austrian pact (Treaty of Westminster, 1716) was very limited. The Emperor evaded any guarantee of the "Protestant Succession" in Britain; while the British and Hanoverian ministers would not promise to maintain him in anything more than his existing possessions—i.e., they would not undertake another war to establish him in Spain.

ANOTHER TRIPLE ALLIANCE. Thus George I and his ministers were still far from any assurance that they would be able to keep the Emperor from upsetting the European equilibrium; and their anxiety about Charles VI was paralleled by that of the Regent Orleans about Philip V. The hope of preserving the settlement would be doubled by Anglo-French co-operation; but for the moment this seemed out of the question, seeing that France and Britain had been fighting tooth and nail for a quarter of a century, and that France was still harbouring the Pretender. However, the breakdown of the Jacobite Rebellion cleared the air somewhat, and Orleans gave an attentive ear to suggestions from his familiar spirit the Abbé Dubois. Dubois was a type which was by this time dying out—the ambitious politician who, being of humble birth and having to make his way by his wits, finds it expedient to take Holy Orders for which he has no vocation. Alberoni was another; but Dubois had even less moral sense than the Italian. As tutor to the young Duke of Chartres he had pandered to his pupil's vices, and had become his boon companion. When Chartres became Duke of Orleans he acted as his private secretary, and now that he was Regent he slipped into the position of confidential adviser. Perhaps his moral reputation has suffered from the fact that the most readable memoirs of the time are those of St. Simon, who was his rival for the Regent's favour. In any case there can be no doubt that he had a genuine talent for international politics. He looked at the situation with a keen eye, free from the prejudices of the survivors from the old régime who formed the Council for Foreign Affairs, and he saw that the time had come for a revolution in French policy.

In July 1716 King George went home to Hanover for the first time since his accession to the English throne. For the next six months it was difficult (as on such occasions in the future) to say whether the seat of the British Government was in Westminster or in Herrenhausen. The King left the Prince of Wales (whom, by a recurrent trait in his Guelf family, he hated) not as Regent, but as Guardian and Lieutenant, fettered by as many restrictions as he could devise. One Secretary of State (Stanhope) he took with him; the other (Townshend) he left behind; similarly with his Hanoverian ministers—Bernstorff went, Bothmar stayed.

He travelled via The Hague, still the diplomatic clearing-house of Europe; and there Stanhope was visited by a mysterious French nobleman who invited him to inspect his collection of bric-à-brac. The "nobleman" turned out to be Dubois. Contact once made, the abbé disclosed his real object—an Anglo-French-Dutch alliance to maintain the Utrecht treaty. But King George and Stanhope were stiff: friendship with France was impossible until the French government gave guarantees of good faith by driving the Pretender across its frontiers and by demolishing the harbour works at Mardyke, which had been started by Louis XIV as a substitute for those at Dunkirk (demolished under the Treaty of Utrecht).

Dubois went back to Paris, but some weeks later he appeared at Herrenhausen, and this visit was at express invitation. For events in Germany had strengthened the desire of King George and his minister to keep a hold over French policy. Peter of Russia had brought an army into Mecklenburg, ostensibly to support his nephew the Duke who was having trouble with vassal cities, but with an obvious intention of getting a foothold in Germany. Nothing but the river Elbe divided Mecklenburg from Hanover, and rumours of an alliance between the Tsar and the Regent were in the air. The danger to Hanover of such a combination assured Dubois of a much warmer reception than at The Hague. There followed much huckstering as to how much demolition would put Mardyke permanently out of action as a port, what treatment of the Pretender would give George security without affronting French public feeling and how far Utrecht could be guaranteed without offending the Emperor. At length Stanhope, always resourceful in such matters, drafted the formula:

Great Britain, France, and the United Netherlands guarantee all and every the articles of the Treaty of Utrecht so far forth as they concern the interests of each of the three Powers, and the succession to the thrones of France and Great Britain.

The document was signed at The Hague in November 1716. It was spoken of as "The Triple Alliance," but the Dutch only joined it half-heartedly some months later; for they were too keen on trade to accept any commitment which might lead them into war.

THE WHIG SPLIT. Those who had prophesied that a German king would drag Britain into continental affairs could soon say "We told you so!" Just before his accession King George had become involved in the long-standing Northern War, through his claims to Bremen and Verden. These Duchies, lying at the mouths of Elbe and Weser, would provide an outlet to the sea of the utmost value to Hanover. The Treaty of Westphalia (1648) had assigned them to Sweden, until Frederick IV of Denmark took advantage of the absence of Charles XII to seize them (1712). When Charles reappeared on the Baltic (November 1714) Frederick, fearing that he might buy the support of George I with the Duchies, hastened to forestall the bargain by one of his own. He bartered them to Hanover in return for a sum in cash and a guarantee of his claim to Schleswig.

Just before his accession George had entered into alliance with Frederick William of Prussia, partly through family feeling (Frederick William had married George's only daughter), but chiefly by the need for common action against Charles XII, with whom (Frederick William having lately seized Swedish Stettin) they were both now at war. This was awkward for the British Government, who had an alliance with Sweden dating from 1702. They could not resist the King's demand that the British fleet should be sent into the Baltic, but they assured Parliament that it had gone there merely to protect British trade. This trade was very important, British shipyards being dependent on Baltic timber and tar; and it was true that Swedish warships tried to stop it, now that Reval and Riga had been conquered by Russia. But a Gilbertian situation now arose: the King of England was bound by treaty to require the Elector of Hanover to restore Bremen, and to compel Hanover's Prussian ally to evacuate Stettin. And while Stanhope was explaining to Parliament that the fleet's objects in the Baltic were purely British, Bernstorff was boasting to Prussia of the services of the British fleet in protecting Prussian interests there.

It was this situation, coupled with the presence of Peter and his Russians in Mecklenburg and of Charles and his Swedes in Pomerania, that made George and Stanhope so eager to come to terms with France. But a breach now opened in the British Government. Stanhope, after six months in Hanover, had come to realize that there was far more community of interest between Britain and Hanover than stay-at-homes could see. There could be no doubt, for instance, that Hanover's possession of Bremen gave a valuable port of entry into Germany for British trade. Townshend, on the other hand, like most Englishmen, felt that British interests were being subordinated to Hanoverian, and he was averse to an alliance being made with France until the Dutch were ready to join it. Lord Sunderland, going over to Hanover to try to close the breach, was drawn into the Hanoverian point of view by the compelling personality of Stanhope. He put that view forcibly in writing to Townshend:

This notion of yours is nothing but the old Tory one that England can subsist by itself, whatever becomes of the rest of Europe, which has been so justly exploded since the Revolution.

The Prince of Wales was delighted to widen the cleavage. He was a person of even less moral worth than his father, but he could speak English and for his own ends could assume a graciousness which had been lacking at the English court since the days of Charles II. And his wife, Caroline of Anspach, was one of the cleverest and most attractive women of the century. They ingratiated themselves by lavish hospitality, especially to people out of favour with the King; and they took especial care to be amiable to Townshend and his brother-in-law Walpole who was Chancellor of the Exchequer. Bothmar reported all this to Hanover, and it made King George grit his teeth.

It is not surprising that in "the tryall between the Councils," as a contemporary pamphlet calls it, the Hanoverian section won. On December 15th Townshend was dismissed; and when the King returned to England to open Parliament (January 1717) most of the other members of the ministry resigned, including Walpole. This "Whig Schism" resulted in a reconstruction of the ministry, with Stanhope and Sunderland in office and Townshend and Walpole in opposition. In the long run it turned out a good thing for the party, and perhaps for the country. For the British parliamentary system requires an opposition capable of forming an alternative government; and such an opposition was now to hand without the King being compelled to have recourse to crypto-Jacobite Tories.

CHAPTER TWENTY

ENGLAND ARBITER OF EUROPE
1716–1720

CIRCUMSTANCES now enabled Stanhope to impose an exchange of territory upon the rival potentates of Madrid and Vienna which assuaged, at any rate for a time, their dynastic animosities.

STANHOPE'S SCHEME. Stanhope was now in control of the British Government, and within three years he made himself the dominant figure in Europe. He conceived a far-reaching plan to amend the Utrecht treaty in such a way as to reconcile Charles VI and Philip V, and so remove the chief danger to peace. It was based on the fact that King Victor Amadeus of Sicily, in his eager bargain-hunting, was ready to take Sardinia in exchange for the island he had acquired at Utrecht, provided that a makeweight was thrown in—say the Duchy of Milan, so conveniently adjacent to Piedmont. The Emperor, too, was anxious for a settlement, as he had just been obliged to go to war, in the tradition of his family, to keep back the Turks. The Sultan, having conquered the Morea, had gone on to attack the Venetian province of Dalmatia, which the Holy Roman Empire was bound to defend under the Treaty of Karlowitz. Some members of the Imperial Council urged that the Emperor's first duty was to deal with the intrusion of Russians and Swedes into Germany, but Prince Eugene stressed the danger to Vienna of allowing the infidel to master the Venetian Empire, and this argument carried the day (March 1716).

The Emperor did not want to leave his Italian lands exposed to the designs of Alberoni; and just before George I and Stanhope returned to London an Austrian envoy named Pentenriedter arrived at Hanover. Of course, the recent Anglo-French alliance was a sore point with Charles, but he instructed Pentenriedter to show more sorrow than anger over this, and to find out exactly what Stanhope had in mind for an all-round settlement.

Stanhope in his breezy way urged that H.I.M. ought to stop chasing phantoms, and accept the plain fact that Spain was lost to him. The argument grew warm, but both men knew the importance of coming to terms. Stanhope formulated the following proposals: the Emperor

189

to renounce Spain and the Indies; Victor Amadeus to exchange Sicily for Sardinia, receiving in addition a strip of the Milanese; Spain and France to guarantee the other possessions of the House of Austria; the Duchy of Parma, instead of lapsing to the Emperor as overlord on

ITALY IN THE 18TH CENTURY

the death of the reigning Duke, was to be at the disposal of the old Duke's daughter, the Queen of Spain, as an appanage for her baby son Carlos. Philip V was also to guarantee the Orleans family's rights to the throne of France if Louis XV died without issue. It was an ingenious scheme, but none of the interested parties rushed into accepting it. Charles VI would go no further than a promise not to interfere with "the Duke of Anjou"; but he dared not break off the negotiation altogether, with this Turkish war on his hands. Fortunately for him Eugene had justified his own counsel by routing the Turkish host at Peterwardein, the Grand Vizier himself being among the slain (August 1716); but it then became necessary to reduce the Turkish fortress of Belgrade, and this took up most of 1717. And when Stanhope laid the Scheme before France (arguing that the more firmly Philip was settled in Spain the less he would want to interfere in France) Dubois lamented that the "old gang" Torcy and Villeroi stood by Philip as the direct heir to the young King—as did nine Frenchmen out of ten.

Then in August 1717 came a thunderclap which made agreement urgently necessary. Philip V re-opened the war.

THE QUADRUPLE ALLIANCE. Alberoni had made the most of his achievement in putting on the throne to which he was accredited a princess from his native Parma. He soon became confidential minister of King Philip and Queen Elizabeth, and persuaded them to aim at recovering the former Italian provinces in Italy which had been given to the Emperor at Utrecht. In this he was acting as a good Italian; for Austrian rule was something new and strange there, whereas Spaniards were at least of the Latin race and had ruled in Italy for 150 years. He needed great patience, night after night, explaining his plans to his employers; but he made great play with the circumstance that Philip had two sons by his first Queen to inherit the throne of Spain, and Elizabeth took fire at the thought of recovering her native Duchy for her little Carlos.

Meanwhile Alberoni had been working with tremendous enthusiasm to set Spain on her economic feet. To check the drain of her wealth into foreign pockets he improved agriculture and nursed industries— in particular the woollen mills at Guadalajara which he placed under the charge of an energetic young Dutchman named Ripperda. He reorganized the Treasury and the collection of taxes. He put shipbuilding, naval and mercantile, under the inspiring direction of José Patiño, and he remodelled the army from top to bottom. He was careful to disguise the real purpose of his naval and military preparations, alleging that they were for a crusade against the Turks; and the Pope was induced on the strength of this to make him a Cardinal.

If longer preparation had been possible there is no knowing what this rebirth of Spain might not have accomplished, but the Emperor's preoccupation in the Balkans seemed an opportunity not to be missed.

A trifle sufficed as *casus belli*. A Spanish Grand Inquisitor, passing through the Italian states of the Emperor, was arrested by the latter's officers as a rebellious subject; and it was as an alleged retaliation for this that a Spanish expeditionary force sailed from Barcelona and occupied Sardinia, the most vulnerable of Charles's Italian provinces.

By the Treaty of Westminster Britain was bound to go to the Emperor's support; but the British Government was very reluctant to make war on Spain unless Holland did so too, lest the Dutch should get a monopoly of the trade with Spanish America. Stanhope made capital of the situation by intimating to the Emperor that he could expect no British help until he had come into the Scheme. A conference at Hampton Court was attended by Pentenriedter and Dubois; but Alberoni merely sent a message that Spain wanted the reversion of Tuscany as well as of Parma for the Queen. By February 1718 Britain, Austria and France had agreed upon a programme based on Stanhope's Scheme. It was called "The Quadruple Alliance," though the Dutch still contrived to avoid committing themselves.

Britain had no longer any excuse to delay the promised succour to the Emperor, and in June (1718) Admiral Byng set sail for the Mediterranean. Stanhope hoped that the mere presence of a British fleet there would suffice—his whole aim was to prevent war. But the Cardinal was no man of peace. A few days after Byng reached Gibraltar a second Spanish task-force put out from Barcelona. King Philip had wanted it to attack Naples, but Alberoni had persuaded him to send it to Sicily instead, pointing out that Britain was under no treaty-obligation to defend what was still the territory of Victor Amadeus, and that with Sicily as well as Sardinia in Spanish hands the whole Stanhope compromise would collapse. The Spanish forces met with little resistance. A century and a half of Spanish rule had made the Sicilians half Spanish—the effects can be seen to this day in everything from the churches to the donkeys. After Utrecht they had been rather proud of having a "King of Sicily"; but when they found that this was a mere phrase, that Victor Amadeus intended to rule them from Turin, their enthusiasm had evaporated. And they hated the thought of being handed over to the Emperor to be ruled from Vienna.

King Philip announced that he was merely maintaining the rights of Victor Amadeus against the threatened seizure by the Emperor; but Stanhope was not deceived. He immediately sent orders to Byng to resist the invasion, and he put his own head into the lion's mouth by rushing off to Madrid to see what his personal touch would do to bring Alberoni and his employers to reason. The little Cardinal was in his most insinuating mood: "but for the positive orders of King Philip he would have liked nothing better than to continue his peaceful activities." But he evaded the question of coming into Stanhope's Scheme; and the King maintained that he had a sacred right, which it would be sacrilege to relinquish, to both Sardinia and Sicily. If the Emperor wanted to solace Victor Amadeus let him do so with some territory of his own. He and the Queen and the Cardinal all scoffed at a hinted offer of Gibraltar as the price of their acceptance of the Scheme: nothing less than the whole pre-war heritage of the Spanish crown would satisfy them. So Stanhope had to go home empty-handed, and Alberoni wrote to his correspondent in Parma that if England could not produce a better offer there would be "a good war" in the spring.

As matters turned out, he got his *buona guerra* sooner than he expected. Byng had acted in the spirit of Stanhope's order even before it reached him, by destroying the entire Spanish fleet in the course of a few hours off Cape Passaro (August 11th, 1718). Indeed, he destroyed it so thoroughly that news of the event did not reach Spain for a month —which was perhaps fortunate for Stanhope, as he did not leave that country until the end of August.

QUADRUPLE BECOMES QUINTUPLE. The so-called Quadruple Alliance had gone a long way towards realizing Stanhope's plan, but the adhesion of Spain was still required, and this seemed less likely than ever. For Elizabeth had now set her heart on a second Italian duchy as a dower-estate for her own prospective widowhood, and Alberoni was immersed in a fresh set of warlike schemes. These centred round a Jacobite rebellion to be supported by a Spanish expedition under the Duke of Ormonde and a Swedish invasion under Charles XII, while he distracted France with a plot contrived by the Spanish ambassador, the Marquis Cellamare, to kidnap Orleans and establish Philip V as Regent and Guardian.

It turned out that Charles XII was already engaged on a line of policy, sponsored by his minister Goertz, which fitted in admirably with Alberoni's plans. Sweden and Russia were to end their long feud, to share supremacy in the Baltic, and to drive the intrusive British from its waters. Sweden was to relinquish Livonia and Estonia to Russia, taking in lieu Pomerania and Mecklenburg. The Duke of Mecklenburg was to be compensated at the expense of Prussia, and a Russian army was to hold off any interference by the Emperor. Then King Charles, after conquering Norway (an outlying province of his old

7

enemy the King of Denmark) was to land an army in Scotland and restore the Stuarts. This last seemed a big undertaking, but Charles had succeeded in military feats quite as startling, and the whole scheme now took fresh vigour under the fostering care of Alberoni.

But in December 1718 the lynch-pin fell out of the hub: Charles XII was killed by a chance bullet from an obscure Norwegian fortress that he was besieging. His successor on the throne was his sister Ulrica Eleanora, under whom the nobles recovered the power and privileges they had lost during the last two reigns; and this revolution was signalized by the execution of Goertz, whose ambitious schemes died with him.

This was only one of a whole series of setbacks which now befell the little Cardinal. The Peace of Passarowitz (July 1718) between Emperor and Sultan had left Charles VI free to resist any attack on Austrian or Imperial interests; and the fact that the mediating Power in making the Peace was Great Britain raised the prestige of George I and Stanhope higher than ever. A month later the Cellamare conspiracy collapsed. The Regent had the ambassador's house searched, discovered incriminating documents, and lodged the leading conspirators in the Bastille. It was impossible to take extreme measures against such highly-placed personages as the Duke and Duchess of Maine, Cardinal Polignac and the Duke of Richelieu; but Cellamare was expelled from France and war was declared on Spain. In March (1719) a French army crossed the Pyrenees. The best Spanish troops were shut up in Sicily by British sea-power, but Philip and Elizabeth joined such forces as could be raised in Catalonia. (The Queen, we learn, attracted all eyes in a superb riding-habit from Paris which the polite enemy allowed to pass through their lines). Philip prophesied that French soldiers would refuse to fight against the legitimate heir to the throne of France; and it was certainly a very mild and bloodless campaign. But he was very vexed with Alberoni for having placed him in such a painful position.

The Cardinal's last hope was a new fleet which was to convey 5,000 soldiers and arms for 30,000 more to western Scotland and act as focus for a Jacobite rising. But this Armada did not even get as far as that of 1588—it was shattered by a gale in the Bay of Biscay.

This was the last straw for the King and Queen: they threw in their hands and made enquiries about peace-terms; and when they learned that England and France regarded Alberoni as the chief obstacle to a settlement they dismissed him. If ever a clever man could complain of his luck, Alberoni could. His work for the rejuvenation of Spain had scarcely started, but his four years of power had made a mark on European history if only from the fact that he had led Elizabeth Farnese into ambitions which had a lasting effect on the development of Italy. He went back there and lived on, an interested spectator of affairs, to the age of ninety-one.

Philip now accepted the Scheme. He and Charles VI acknowledged each other's titles, and he recognized both Orleans as heir-apparent in France and George I as King of England. In return Queen Elizabeth's title to both the Italian duchies was guaranteed by all the Powers. Victor Amadeus exchanged the kingdom of Sicily for that of Sardinia, and Stanhope's triumph was complete.

There was one interesting sequel. Philip had assumed that Stanhope's former offer of Gibraltar still held good. The British Government attached little importance to the fortress; it was expensive to garrison (it cost £100,000 a year) and Port Mahon, in Minorca, with a much better natural harbour, was all the naval base that Britain needed in the Mediterranean. But the nation and the House of Commons would not hear of its retrocession, so Stanhope had to declare that his offer had been conditional on immediate acceptance. Orleans (now competing with Britain for Spanish-American trade, and anxious to placate French sympathies for the Bourbon King Philip) continued to urge the claim on his British ally; but all that he could extort was a promise from King George that he would consider the matter later, "with the consent of my Parliament" i.e., at the Greek Kalends. The incident suggests that the instincts of the uninstructed multitude may sometimes give clearer political vision than the wisdom of experienced statesmen.

PEACE IN THE NORTH. The death of Charles XII closed an epoch in the history of the Baltic region. Geographical fact will always make it impossible for Sweden to support a large population; but for a century it had been stimulated by a series of warrior-kings to play a rôle in European affairs that was beyond its strength. The national spirit had been strained to breaking point, and now that the last of its imperious masters was dead it was ready to win peace at almost any price from the enemies which his reckless ambitions had raised up against it. This was implied by the Diet when it chose as his successor his younger sister Ulrica Eleanora and her husband Prince Frederic of Hesse-Cassel, rather than the young Duke of Holstein, the son of his deceased elder sister. For Ulrica and her spouse were nominees of the nobles whom Charles XII had pushed into the background. But when it came to making an all-round peace with the states which had been chipping off parts of the Swedish Empire, a critical situation arose. For these enemies had now fallen into two opposing groups, one dominated by Peter of Russia, the other by George of Hanover-Britain. To accept the demands of the one would be a challenge to the other. For Peter was ready to let Sweden keep her German conquests (Pomerania, Stettin and Stralsund) provided he could annex her east Baltic provinces, Estonia and Livonia; whereas George wanted as Elector to keep the

Swedes out of Germany and as King to keep Peter away from Britain's Baltic sources of ship-building materials. On this issue Stanhope could get little support from France, for it was a traditional French policy to keep Sweden established in Germany as a thorn in the side of the Emperor. And what was worse, Prussia was likely to be actively hostile, since Frederick William had recently fallen out with his father-in-law, and had entered into close relations with Peter.

But Stanhope was not easily discouraged. Ignoring the Hanoverian ministers who were influencing the King against Prussia, he sent an able minister, Sir Charles Whitworth, to win Frederick William over to a settlement with Sweden by which Prussia was to get Pomerania and Hanover to get Bremen and Verden; while to Stockholm he sent the brilliant young Lord Carteret (not yet thirty) to induce the new government there to accept these sacrifices in return for British naval and financial support against Russia. Carteret was almost immediately successful, but Whitworth had more trouble with the slow-witted Frederick William, and Peter tried to intimidate the Swedes by landing troops to ravage their coastal districts. However, the appearance of a British squadron made the Russians beat a hasty retreat to the rocks and shallows of the gulf of Finland, and this demonstration of British sea-power was enough to impel the Swedes to make sure (as they thought) of its support through a series of treaties by which they sacrificed Bremen and Verden to Hanover, Pomerania to Prussia and Schleswig to Denmark.

This was the pinnacle to Stanhope's achievements. Coming on top of the Quadruple Alliance and the Peace of Passarowitz it seemed to make him and his master the arbiters of Europe. But there was still one coping-stone wanting to the edifice—the consent of Russia. Nothing but force would expel Peter from Estonia and Livonia, and nobody was prepared to exercise it. He quickly found a weak spot in the situation of the Swedish government—the existence of young Frederick of Holstein who had a better claim to the throne than Ulrica and her husband. Peter now took up this prince's cause and betrothed him to his daughter Anna. Ulrica Eleanora appealed to Britain, whose friendship she had bought at such a price. But by this time the "South Sea Bubble" (p. 201) had changed the face of the British Government. Stanhope was dead, and his successor had neither the means nor the ambition for adventures so far afield. So the Swedes had to make what terms they could with Peter. By the Treaty of Nystad (September 1721) the Tsar gave them back Finland but retained all his other conquests.

Thus ended a chapter of history which had overlapped from the previous era. Sweden retired for good from the false position into which she had been forced by the House of Vasa. Henceforth she was a satellite of France or of Russia. All real power was in the hands of a Secret Committee dominated by nobles. For the next twenty years "safety first" ruled in the person of Count Horn, whose drowsy supporters were nick-named " Night-caps" in contrast to the fashionable tricorne "Hats" which typified the more enterprising spirit of the opposing group.

And another chapter opened, for Russia was now established as a Great Power. Peter proclaimed himself "Emperor of All the Russias." It was his *nunc dimittis*, for in January 1725, he died, worn out at the age of fifty-two by gigantic labours and debaucheries. He had had his heir Alexius flogged to death in 1718, and his immediate successors (his widow Catherine to 1727 and then to 1730 his grandson Peter II) could not wield effectively the tremendous power he had built up. The country remained far behind western standards in political, social and economic development; but henceforth it had always to be reckoned with in the affairs of Europe.

CHAPTER TWENTY-ONE

THE DYNASTS

1 7 2 0 – 1 7 3 1

WRANGLING between Hapsburg and Bourbon continued almost throughout the 1720's, chiefly over the determination of Elizabeth Farnese to provide for her offspring from the Italian provinces of the House of Austria. That there was little actual fighting was mainly due to the fact that the ministers ruling France and Britain were still co-operating to maintain peace. It would hardly be worth while to disturb the dust that has long settled on these affairs but for the light they throw on the working of a régime in which kings and queens regarded their realms as personal possessions.

The decade opened with financial crises in France and Britain which were evidence of failure to cope with the problems raised by developing capitalism.

THE MISSISSIPPI AND THE SOUTH SEAS. Industry and international trade were now growing at a rate which entailed a corresponding growth of credit; for the amount of gold and silver in circulation was falling far behind the need for exchange-tokens. The Bank of Amsterdam (founded 1608) had given the Dutch a long start, which the Bank of England (founded 1694) was now making up. But in such matters, which are in the main concerned with beliefs and ideas rather than with physical facts, man has to learn by the painful process of trial and error. France and Britain were both shaken by experiences of this sort in the year 1720.

It all began with John Law, the son of an Edinburgh goldsmith. (Before the development of banking, goldsmiths were traditional financiers—i.e., money-lenders). He was a man of ample fortune, great gifts, good looks and compelling personality. A thorough cosmopolitan, he enjoyed life, and made money at the gaming tables, in half the capitals of Europe before settling in Paris. At Amsterdam he conceived bold and original ideas on currency and credit, which soon became an obsession. For years he sought in vain a government that would let him put these ideas into practice—he applied in Scotland, England, Italy and France. But after the death of Louis XIV the fiscal position of France was so desperate that the Regent was ready to try almost anything once. At first all that Law asked was monopoly-rights for a discount-bank (i.e., an institution to buy merchants' bills for cash).

199

The business prospered, and Law was able to gain the Regent's ear for his great idea: that what the country needed was more currency, to be provided by his bank with Government support. If the bank could issue notes, which the Government would accept in payment of taxes and use to buy goods and services, the wheels of commerce would move much faster than while the very limited stocks of the precious metals were the sole means of exchange.[1] There was much opposition among Treasury officials, but once again the immediate effects were all that Law prophesied.

But even this was only part of his "System." He took over "The Company of the West and of the Mississippi" which had been formed to exploit the recently acquired colony of Louisiana.[2] Then he bought up the monopolies already possessed by the French East India Company, Africa Company, and China Company, raising the necessary capital by selling the share-certificates of his new Company, in blocks of 500, whereof 350 could be paid in bank-bills.

The idea of getting rich from trade without engaging in it oneself was an alluring novelty. The public imagination took fire. There were wild stories of mountains of solid gold and rocks of ruby in Louisiana. Everybody scrambled to buy shares—seats in the coaches to Paris were booked up months in advance. Law cleverly linked his Companies together by "long-firm" methods which have been developed since his time by shady financiers. As always in such cases, investment gave place to speculation: people bought scrip not to enjoy its revenue but to re-sell. The business went so strongly that at the end of 1718 Law was made Controller-General of Finances. He carried out what would now be called a conversion, floating a loan of 1,600 million livres in the name of his Companies to buy up the national debt. Henceforth the State was to owe to the Companies, and to pay them only half the interest it had paid to the public. The credit of the Companies was so raised by this evidence of their solidity that the price of their shares rose forty-fold.

But of course people who bought at that price found that even a dividend of 40 per cent. was worth only 1 per cent. to them. They began to ask questions, to sell their certificates, and to cash their notes at the bank. The trickle of sales became a stream, and the stream a flood, until the dam burst. Law, so brilliant in devising and launching the

[1] Students of economics will note that Law anticipated to some extent the modern "Douglas Credit Plan"—he wanted to base the issue of paper money not on precious metals but on the whole wealth, in goods and credit, of the community.

[2] Louisiana, named after Louis XIV, at that time comprised the whole Mississippi valley; its capital (founded 1718) was named after the Regent.

scheme had not known when to say "no." The Bank had put out 3,000 millions of notes, and the whole of the coin in the country did not amount to half a million. It was in vain that the Government ordered people to accept notes at their face-value. By the end of 1720 Law's notes had depreciated by 90 per cent. A few people who sold out in time made fortunes (the Duke of Bourbon had to bring three coaches to carry away his gold). But thousands were ruined, the Companies collapsed; and Law fled the country and died a pauper in Venice.

The Regency Government staggered under the blow, but no alternative was at hand, and gradually the fact emerged that, whatever the effect on individuals, the country had as much real wealth and as much specie as before the crash, and its economic life returned to its unpleasant normal.

What happened in England was a meaner and more sordid replica. The South Sea Company consisted of subscribers to a war-loan of 1701, who were promised exclusive privileges in the trade with Spanish America which was expected to result from the Spanish Succession War. As we have seen, the Treaty of Utrecht did not fulfil these expectations. The Company languished until in 1717 some of its Directors decided to imitate Law. The Stanhope-Sunderland Ministry was delighted at the prospect of paying a reduced interest to the Company, especially when the Company offered them £7,000,000 into the bargain. People thought that concessions bought at such a price must be of enormous value, and the price of shares rushed up to ten times the value of its assets. In such circumstances a crash was bound to come as in France, bringing ruin to thousands, fortunes to a few. The outcry against the Government for its criminal folly in entering upon the scheme was terrific; and there is no doubt that some ministers had actually taken bribes from the Directors of the Company.

It was now that the "Whig Schism" came in useful. Lord Townshend and Robert Walpole, who had proved his financial acumen by warning the Government against the scheme and then making £50,000 for himself out of it by timely buying and selling, were called in to clear up the wreckage and carry on the traditions of Whiggery.

FAMILY AFFAIRS. Spain having joined the Quadruple Alliance on the basis of Stanhope's Scheme, a conference met at Cambrai to clear up outstanding differences—the handing over of the Duchies, the question of Gibraltar, and so on. And now that Philip V had abandoned

7*

his claims to the throne of France, Orleans wanted to please the French people by a Bourbon family alliance. He therefore proposed a triple marriage project. Don Luis, heir to the Spanish throne, was to marry his daughter Mademoiselle de Montpensier; while Louis XV was to be betrothed to the Infanta Marie Anne (Philip's only daughter), and Don Carlos to another Orleans princess, Mademoiselle de Beaujolais. King Philip's intense family feeling made him welcome this proposal, and the Princesses were exchanged with much ceremonial across the Bidassoa—the Infanta to be brought up in France as its future Queen.[1] This was the crown of Dubois' career. He may, as French historians complain, have made French policy subservient to Britain's, but he had warded off war, and had anticipated the Family Compact which became a dominating feature of European affairs for nearly a century. He gained the traditional reward of clerical politicians, becoming Archbishop and Cardinal.[2] When the Regency was wound up, on the King coming of age at his fourteenth birthday, Dubois became the official Prime Minister. He saw himself another Richelieu, but died before he could prove it (August 1723). He was succeeded by Orleans, but he, too, was struck down, worn out by debauchery, bored with life and with himself, at the age of forty-nine. The position then fell to the only one of the Royal Dukes who was not absolutely impossible, the Duc de Bourbon. He had a feud with the Orleans branch of the family, and the mainspring of his policy was dread that the King would die childless and be succeeded by the son of the late Regent.

Meanwhile the Congress at Cambrai was doing little except make itself ridiculous. For two whole years the envoys disputed, with elaborate urbanity and much dining and wining, upon questions of precedence and procedure—questions which to them and their royal masters were infinitely more momentous than the welfare and happiness of nations. And even when, in 1724, they at last got down to business, their progress towards a settlement was imperceptible.

Elizabeth of Spain became impatient. The "placid Italian girl who would give trouble to nobody" had grown into a high-spirited dominating woman who gave trouble to everybody—"The Termagant of Spain." Her mind was set on the advancement of her two sons, and she regarded as enemies of God and man all who were not equally enthusiastic in

---

[1] The wedding of Don Luis was celebrated by a grand auto-da-fé. The activities of the Inquisition had by no means ceased with the passing of the danger to the Church; and the mass-burning of heretics had become as much part of Spanish national life as bull-fights.

[2] He had to be ordained priest the day before he was consecrated archbishop, having hitherto been only in minor Orders.

that cause. In 1724 she lived through a very trying experience. Philip V, a confirmed hypochondriac, got it into his head that he was about to die—he believed that the sun had struck through his back and withered his vital organs. He therefore determined to abdicate and prepare for the next world. For once in a way he would not heed his wife; and in January 1724 the royal pair retired (with a numerous retinue and vast impedimenta) to the monastery of San Ildefonso, leaving the throne to Don Luis. Luis, an obstreperous and irresponsible youth, refused to take his duties seriously, and his Orleans Queen (aged seventeen) abandoned herself to the wildest freaks of fancy. When Philip failed to die at Ildefonso and the boy-king exhausted the patience even of Spanish courtiers at Madrid, the situation became difficult. It was relieved by the death of Luis of small-pox after a reign of eight months.

THE BOURBON KINGS OF SPAIN

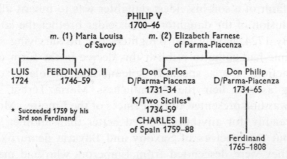

Philip returned to the throne, and Elizabeth determined to lose no more time in getting her boys settled in life. She decided to short-circuit the interminable arguments at Cambrai by a secret negotiation, direct with the Emperor. For this mission she chose Ripperda, a clever young Dutchman who had come to Madrid in an embassy from The Hague, had found employment under Alberoni, and had latterly qualified for a ministerial appointment by turning Catholic. His instructions on setting out for Vienna were to secure from the Emperor immediate admission of Spanish garrisons into the Italian duchies, and to test the possibilities of a close alliance with the Hapsburg family by the betrothal of the two Spanish princes to the two Austrian archduchesses. In view of the century-old Bourbon-Hapsburg feud which had led to two great wars, this proposal showed daring imagination, if nothing else.

"A KAISER CHASING SHADOWS." Elaborate precautions were taken to preserve Ripperda's incognito. He took obscure lodgings in the suburbs of Vienna, and only communicated with the Emperor by circuitous channels. He had a tricky game to play, for Charles VI, though high-souled, dignified and kindly of disposition, had a head full of crotchets. The first, which had distracted his policy ever since he became Emperor, was his claim to the whole heritage of Spain. Though he had twice publicly renounced it in solemn treaties, he still felt deep down in his conscience that these acts had been sacrilege— that this crown was his by a sacred right which no mere human arrangement could cancel. Equally sacrosanct were the Italian properties which Elizabeth of Spain had bullied him into surrendering. He evaded their occupation by Spanish troops in the hope that something would turn up to save him from the sacrifice, and the Chanceries were always on tenterhooks that this situation would lead to another general war.

The second crotchet was over the succession to his Hapsburg heritage. As long ago as 1713 he had informed to his Privy Council that in default of a son his eldest daughter was to inherit all his lands, to the exclusion of the daughters of his elder brother the late Emperor Joseph. By 1724, having two daughters but no surviving son, he felt that the time had come to publish this decree in the form of a "Pragmatic Sanction" (= a specially solemn and inviolable ordinance), appointing as sole heir the Archduchess Maria Teresa, now aged seven. It was first presented to the Princes of the Empire. Most of them assented readily, for anything seemed better than another succession-dispute; but the Electors of Saxony and Bavaria demurred, pointing out that they were descended from Emperors who had made similar decrees quite as valid as this one, and that the rights transmitted to them by their wives (the two daughters of Joseph I) were inalienable. Charles then laid siege to the other potentates of Europe with batteries of argument and persuasion, to induce them to promise to support the rights of the little archduchess. Prince Eugene, now the doyen of the Imperial Council, warned him that the only real guarantees would be a big army and a full treasury. But such solid assets were much harder to come by than promises.

His third will o' the wisp was the "Ostend East India Company." He saw how wealth was brought to Britain and Holland by privileged associations of traders, and how Spain, with far greater overseas possessions, had fallen into poverty for lack of one; and he asked himself why his Netherlands (up to now more trouble than they were worth to him) should not also trade with Asia—why Bruges and Ypres and Liége should not find overseas substitutes for their former markets in central Europe. The River Scheldt had been closed to navigation by a clause which the Dutch had forced into the Treaty of Westphalia to prevent Antwerp becoming a rival to their own ports; so the Emperor decided to make Ostend the headquarters of his Company, and began to build docks there. But the Sea Powers expostulated, declaring that the project was contrary to the spirit, if not to the letter, of Westphalia and Utrecht; and the Dutch added that they would feel themselves reluctantly obliged to take, sink or burn any Ostend merchantmen that should intrude in their commercial preserves. But Charles persisted, and widened his design by trying to develop the port of Trieste for commerce with the Levant, so as to re-open the old trade-routes and revive the prosperity of Imperial cities where grass was now growing in the market-places. His Company had not got as far as sending out any ships—it existed only on paper; but it was a subject of hot dispute—at the Congress of Cambrai, for instance.

Against these baffling shadows Ripperda contended in vain through the winter of 1724-5. He was about to abandon his mission and return to Spain, when in April 1725 success came suddenly through an utterly unexpected event.

THE FIRST VIENNA TREATY. A chill which Louis XV caught while out hunting in November 1724 intensified Bourbon's determination to provide for the succession without delay. The King was nearly sixteen, but his fiancée, the little Infanta, would not reach marriageable age for another ten years. Louis must be married as soon as possible to a woman old enough to bear children. The Secretary of State was instructed to make a catalogue of eligible princesses. Out of ninety "possibles" a short list of seventeen was selected. Confidential overtures followed in several directions, e.g., for the daughters of Frederick William of Prussia, of George Prince of Wales, and of Tsar Peter, but they all broke down—largely over the difference of religion. On the whole the strongest candidate seemed to be Marie Leschinska, daughter of ex-King Stanislas of Poland. True, her birth was royal only by courtesy. Her father had been a mere Polish noble until Charles XII had got him elected King by the Diet in 1704; and since Peter had driven him out in favour of Augustus of Saxony he had been living in obscurity on a French pension at Wissembourg. But her humble position would make her subservient to those who had placed her on the throne of France; she was a devout Catholic; and the fact that she was six years older than the King was, in the circumstances, a disparity in the right direction. So in March 1725 the betrothal was announced, and the Infanta was sent back to her parents.

Bourbon had expected trouble from Madrid, but the storm that burst there exceeded all imagination. Family pride was a dominant trait in King Philip; and it was the mainspring of Queen Elizabeth's existence. Almost inarticulate with fury, she goaded her husband to violent reprisals. The two Orleans princesses—one of them dowager Queen of Spain—were hustled back across the Pyrenees. (Philip made the only joke recorded of him by pretending to go back to France himself in submission to his wife's anathema on everything French.) The Spanish delegates were brought away from Cambrai. Above all, Ripperda was instructed to agree to all the Emperor's demands without further argument.

When, a few weeks later, the Treaty of Vienna (April 1725) was announced Europe was amazed. It made a close alliance between two courts whose antagonism had embroiled the continent for a quarter of a century. The Emperor merely renewed his Quadruple undertakings—to renounce Spain and give the reversion of the Duchies to Don Carlos, but Spain gave up the demand to garrison the Duchies, confirmed Austrian rights in Sicily, Naples and Sardinia, withdrew all claim to the Netherlands, and guaranteed the Pragmatic Sanction. It was so unlike the Termagant to make such wholesale concessions that people felt there must be something more behind the published terms. As a matter of fact some secret clauses were added a little later, but they scarcely redressed the balance: the Emperor undertook to urge his British ally to restore Gibraltar, in return for which King Philip acknowledged the legality of the Ostend Company, giving it "most favoured nation" rights to trade with the Spanish colonies—a concession which was bound to make trouble for him with England and Holland. Thus the Congress of Cambrai, which had for five years been trying to reconcile Austrian and Spanish claims, suddenly had the floor pulled from under it.

News of the Treaty reached George I and Townshend in Hanover, followed by rumours that Spain was to gain a direct interest in the Pragmatic Sanction by a marriage between Maria Teresa and Don Carlos, and that the signatories were going to recover Gibraltar by force and restore the Stuarts in Britain. It appears that these further reports had no firmer foundation than the boastful talk of Ripperda; but they seemed to be confirmed by a peremptory demand for the Rock from Madrid. King George was in a dilemma between loyalty to the Emperor and to the British constitution. He sent a special envoy to explain to the Spanish Government that British possessions could not be given away without the consent of Parliament; but Queen

Elizabeth was not impressed, and threatened an embargo on British trade with the Spanish colonies.

So the only response open to King George was a counter-alliance. The rest of Europe was so alarmed by the Austro-Spanish rapprochement that his League of Hanover (formed September 1725 by Britain, France and Prussia) was soon joined by the Dutch (who wanted support against the Ostend Company) and by Sweden, Denmark and Hesse-Cassel (who hoped for British subsidies). But Frederick William soon began to hedge. He had joined the League mainly because Britain promised to put pressure on Charles VI to give him Jülich and Berg; but at heart he revered his Emperor and hated his father-in-law, and Charles soon won him over by promising to persuade the other claimant to the Duchies (the Elector Palatine) to forego his rights; and in return for this promise Frederick William accepted the Pragmatic Sanction. But alas, Charles had just made a similar promise, for a similar *quid pro quo*, to the Elector Palatine. To such lengths did dynasticism lead an Emperor who in all else was the soul of honour. (However, Frederick William's own standards were no higher: he never told the other members of the League of his withdrawal.)

Thus Europe had split into two hostile groups, and the situation was more dangerous than ever. There was another sputtering of actual war, as in 1718. Parliament voted three squadrons—one to watch Russia in the Baltic, another to defend Gibraltar, and a third to blockade the Spanish treasure-fleet at Portobello. Ripperda returned in triumph to Spain, boasting that he had won the Emperor over to giving both the archduchesses to the sons of Philip and Elizabeth, and to sending money to refurbish the Spanish army. His stories were denied by an Imperial ambassador, Count Konigsegg, who arrived some months later at Madrid. (As a matter of fact the Imperial exchequer was empty, and the archduchesses were at this moment being secretly affianced to the sons of the Duke of Lorraine.) Ripperda, a few weeks after being made a Duke and a Grandee of Spain, was dismissed in disgrace. But even the fall of the chief author of the Treaty did not relax the tensions which it had created, for Konigsegg contrived to take his place as confidential adviser to the King and Queen, and to draw the two courts closer together than ever.

THE SECOND VIENNA TREATY. What really saved the situation was the fall of Bourbon and the death of George I. For French affairs now came under the direction of mild, timid, cunning old Fleury, while the accession of George II enabled the pacific Walpole to oust the

militant Townshend from the control of British policy. For George II
was prejudiced against Townshend by the mere fact that George I
had approved of him, whereas Walpole had won the support of Queen
Caroline, who ruled her consequential little husband by controls none
the less effective for being concealed and indirect. Walpole and Fleury,
personally as unlike as two men could well be, both felt their own
unfitness to ride the whirlwinds of war, and both wanted peace and
quiet to build up national resources. Thus they worked together to
dispel the threatening clouds.

As matters turned out they had no great difficulty in keeping the
allies of the Vienna Treaty from making trouble, For it was an un-
natural combination: the aims of Charles VI and Elizabeth Farnese
remained utterly incompatible. Neither had the resources to wage
effective war without the support of the other, but neither was really
willing to make the sacrifices called for by the Treaty. When Spain
attacked Gibraltar the Austrian forces did nothing in particular.
Spanish guns continued to fire at the Rock intermittently for six
months; then Elizabeth sulkily agreed to the Convention of Pardo
(March 1728), details being left to a congress which met at Soissons
three months later.

The main items on the agenda there were the Ostend Company, the
Pragmatic Sanction, and Gibraltar. The British Government was once
more prevented from surrendering the Rock by public opinion. Townshend (still Secretary of State, though fast losing ground) wrote to
William Stanhope, British envoy at Soissons:

What you propose about Gibraltar is exactly conformable to the
opinion I have always entertained. . . . But you cannot but be sensible
of the almost superstitious zeal which has of late prevailed among all
parties whatever. And I am afraid that the bare mention of a proposal
which bore the most distant appearance of England ever parting with
that place would put the whole nation in a flame.

So Stanhope had no option but to hold out against Spanish accusations
of bad faith. Another disturbing element at the Congress was Chauvelin, the French Foreign Minister, who stood by the tradition of
hostility to the Sea Powers, and was feeling his way towards a close
alliance between the two branches of the House of Bourbon.

And now it dawned on Queen Elizabeth that Charles VI had no real
intention of carrying out his pledges. In November (1728) she learned
of his trickery over the marriages, and with blazing impetuosity turned
back to France and Britain. The birth of a Dauphin had ended a main
cause of dissension with France by removing all chance of Philip's
accession there; her new minister, the able and energetic Patiño, was

anxious to end the influence of Konigsegg at Madrid; and Walpole wanted to make it impossible for the Opposition to force on an Anglo-Spanish war about colonial trade. So in November 1729 Spain, France and Britain made the Treaty of Seville. Spain revoked the privileges granted to the Ostend Company, renewed and extended the *Asiento*, and renounced Gibraltar and Minorca; in return for which the others guaranteed the succession of Don Carlos in the Italian duchies. Thus the Congress of Soissons faded out like its predecessor at Cambrai, leaving the unfortunate Emperor still clutching at his shadows.

The hostile groups were thus safely liquidated: the danger now was that the Austro-Spanish ex-allies would come to blows. The Emperor collected an army in the Milanese; and if Spanish troops had landed in Italy to occupy the Duchies public feeling would have impelled France to join Spain and Britain to join Austria; France would inevitably have invaded the Austrian Netherlands, which Britain would as inevitably have defended, and it would have been the old story over again. The situation came to a head in January 1731 with the death of the old Duke of Parma. Charles at once sent in his troops, on the pretext of occupying the Duchy in trust for a son who might yet be born to the widowed Duchess; and Spain appealed for support under the Treaty of Seville.

Walpole was cornered; but his resources for peace-keeping were not yet exhausted. To avoid having to support Spain with fleets and armies he bought off her enemy by accepting the Pragmatic Sanction. There was scarcely anything that Charles VI would not do to get Britain and Hanover on his side over that. It was on this issue that Walpole finally broke with Townshend, who resigned from the Government and devoted the rest of his life to the rotation of crops and the production of winter feed for cattle on his Norfolk estate.

By this Second Treaty of Vienna (1731) Emperor Charles for the sake of a scrap of Sanction-paper agreed to withdraw his troops from the Duchies, to suspend the Ostend Company indefinitely (thus sacrificing the natural rights of his Belgian subjects to his family interests), and to invest George II with Bremen and Verden (the bribe by which Walpole induced his master to consent to the Sanction). In December 1731 Don Carlos, with a Spanish army escorted by a British fleet, landed in Italy and took possession of the appanage which his fond mother had won for him by such prolonged and furious energy.

It was Walpole's masterpiece in foreign policy. He had turned aside a current that was leading to war, and had satisfied the Queen of Spain (at any rate temporarily) without sacrifice of the traditional Whig alliance with Austria.

CHAPTER TWENTY-TWO

THE POLISH SUCCESSION

1731–1734

DURING the 1720's Europe had been continually threatened with wars of succession; but it was not until the 1730's, just when these dynastic disputes seemed settled, that they burst into armed conflict.

SHADOWS BEFORE. The Second Vienna Treaty (1731) appeared to assure lasting peace. The Emperor was too keen on his Sanction to make trouble with anybody. In Spain a great constructive minister, Patiño, (a native Spaniard, for once in a way) was holding the Queen's family ambitions in check while he got on with his programme for national revival. In England Robert Walpole wanted to placate the Tory squires with a low Land Tax and gratify the Whig merchants with foreign trade—aims incompatible with war. In France Cardinal Fleury had equally little taste for adventure; he once said he did not want his régime to be famous in history. Like Walpole, he was absorbed in administration. He was no reformer—social evils continued almost unabated; but he alone of Louis XV's ministers contrived to bring expenditure and revenue into some sort of relationship. For this he needed a continuance of peace; and he was glad of support to that end from England, personified by Robert Walpole's clever brother Horace, ambassador at Paris.

But there were several forces threatening trouble. The ambitions of the Termagant were only quiescent: she had a second son to provide for in Italy; and on the other hand Emperor Charles could not reconcile himself to having even one Spanish Dukedom separating his northern and southern possessions in that peninsula.

And it was becoming doubtful how much longer England would be able to keep out of war. The peace-preserving Walpole was faced with a parliamentary opposition that grew in numbers and intensity every year. He was too greedy of power to share it; every discarded colleague became an opponent; and every political aspirant found opposition the only career open to him. And an effective line of attack was the undeclared war raging off the coasts of Spanish America. For although Spain, in her economic decay, could not supply her colonists with manufactured goods, she would not let foreign traders do so. With

Jamaica as headquarters British commercial freebooters did a pro-fitable trade with these colonists and took back great wealth to London and Bristol. In reprisal the Spanish governors licensed privateer coast-guard vessels. Their crews often exercised their right of search with brutal violence; but British seamen have seldom been backward in taking care of themselves, and often gave as good as they got. In Parliament the opposition charged Walpole with criminal weakness because he did not give them the protection of the Navy. He turned a deaf ear; but it was obvious that this exchange of outrage and counter-outrage would sooner or later lead to open war with Spain.

And in France old Fleury, as bent on peace as Walpole, also had to face an influential and vociferous war-party. Many of the nobles, headed by Marshal Villars and Count Chauvelin, clamoured for a return to the glorious days of Louis XIV—co-operation with Spain against British trade and colonies, or an alliance with German princes against the Emperor, or both at once. And the King, now in his early twenties, having been brought up to regard his great-grandfather as a model of kingly might and majesty, wanted to gain a little glory on his own account if it would not entail too much trouble and exertion. And there was one question now impending on which he felt strongly; the succession to the throne of Poland. Augustus II was growing old. His son would succeed him as Elector of Saxony, but there was no certainty that this son would be elected King of Poland. Louis and his court had always felt it a humiliation that the father of the Queen of France should be a mere ex-King; and this seemed a heaven-sent chance to restore him to his throne. At a meeting of the Royal Council in November 1732 King Louis announced his intention of doing so whenever Augustus II died.

This project was bound to meet strenuous opposition from Vienna. It would establish French power on both sides of the Empire; and weak as was the Emperor's position in general, on this particular issue he was strong. For in 1726 he had made a treaty with Russia by which the parties agreed to act in concert in all that concerned the future of Poland. Each had similar interests not only in preventing Poland from becoming an outpost of France, but also in thrusting the Turks back to Asia.

Thus the death of Augustus II would start a train of events of which no one could see the end.

THE POLISH ELECTION. On February 1st 1733 it happened, and the crisis began. Fleury would have been ready to support Stanislas if diplomacy would have sufficed; but it was obvious that fleets and armies would be required. Chauvelin as Foreign Minister eagerly pushed forward plans for war with the Empire, and the Cardinal could do no more than minimize the dangers which it might entail to France. He vetoed a proposal to attack the Austrian Netherlands, so as to avoid drawing the Sea Powers into the conflict; and reinsured against this by a Treaty of Neutrality with the Dutch. Walpole was vexed, pointing out to the States General that by joint action with Britain they might have prevented the war altogether—a much more statesmanlike course than merely contracting out of it. But, as Fleury had foreseen, that Franco-Dutch Treaty strengthened Walpole's case for keeping Britain out of the conflict, too; for it was obvious that if Britain went to war alone the Dutch would poach all the Spanish American trade. He was having great difficulty in holding back King George—always a loyal member of the Empire, and always eager for the tented field. But Queen Caroline (though she too felt primarily as a German on this issue), was too intelligent not to see the force of Walpole's arguments, and used her influence to damp down the bellicose fire of her strutting, fuming little husband, especially by pointing out the danger to Hanover.

Besides this negative contribution to the strength of France in the threatened war, Fleury made alliances with Sardinia and Spain. Victor Amadeus, having by astute combination of war and intrigue procured the title of King, devoted the next twelve years to internal reforms, and then (1730) abdicated in favour of his son Charles Emmanuel, whose reign took a similar pattern. By the treaty he now made with France he was to join in driving the Austrians out of Italy and receive as guerdon the Duchy of Milan. And a month later France and Spain made the secret Treaty of the Escurial, better known as the "First Family Compact" (November 1733). It was a much wider agreement than that with Sardinia. The signatories were to combine not only for the expulsion of the Austrians from Italy, but to curb British overseas trade and colonization, special mention being made of Gibraltar.

Such secrets seldom remained secret long in that heyday of espionage. When the Emperor learnt what was afoot he was shocked at the burglarious plot. Clearly the Polish election was a mere pretext— he had done nothing overt in that matter except to allow a Saxon force to enter Poland across the narrow neck of Silesia. And the Sea Powers, who had guaranteed his dominions in the Second Vienna Treaty, were saying that his interference in Poland made him an aggressor and thereby excused them from fulfilling their obligations. Who would have believed that human nature could be so depraved?

France overcame the difficulty of getting Stanislas into Poland by the expedient of embarking a "double" with much publicity at Brest while the real one made his way across Europe disguised as a commercial traveller. Once Stanislas was in Warsaw it was not difficult to get him elected. The "liberties" that the Polish nobles made so much of amounted to little more than the right to persecute Protestant Dissidents and to ill-treat serfs. Apart from a few great landed families like the Czartoyrskis and the Radzivills, most of them were ragged "Schlachta" (= squireens), glad to sell their votes for a few crowns and a bottle of schnaps. They complained that elections did not come often enough. The last, in 1697, had been a rare feast for them, with eighteen candidates. Now, with only three they did not fare so well. Russia and Austria at first nominated a Portuguese prince, but when this proved too much even for the Polish Diet to swallow they transferred their support to Augustus of Saxony, who promised the Duchy of Courland to the one and acceptance of the Pragmatic to the other. But while they were vainly trying to draw Prussia to their party, the Diet, 60,000 strong, assembled on the banks of the Vistula outside Warsaw, and finding a French envoy already on the spot with a couple of million francs to distribute, elected Stanislas by acclamation. "Rather a gipsy than a German!" was the election catchword. But a fortnight later Russian and Saxon armies invaded Poland "to protect the freedom of election" and 2,000 voters were scraped together from highways and byways to elect Augustus III behind a hedge of bayonets. With no Polish army in existence, no means of collecting one, and France a thousand miles off on the far side of Germany, Stanislas had to choose between capture and flight. After a second reign which had lasted only a few weeks he escaped to Danzig, a fortified German city owing allegiance to the Polish crown.

THE SIEGE OF DANZIG. Here Stanislas was beleaguered by a Russian army under Marshal Munnich. France could do little for him: a relief force would either have to march through Germany, where it would be exposed to attack by the Emperor, or to go by sea through the Baltic where it would arouse the hostility of the Sea Powers. The only support that she could give him was by stirring up her old clients, Sweden, Prussia and Turkey, against his enemies. Of these, the first two were useless. Sweden was torn by internal dissensions; and

Frederick William had a predatory eye on a bit of Poland for himself, to bridge the gap between Prussia and Brandenburg.

The prospects of intervention by Turkey, however, were more hopeful. The Russian and Austrian emperors had agreed to co-operate against the Sultan, and he had every reason for joining France in maintaining Poland as a check to their designs. But the Grand Vizier refused to move without a treaty binding France not to leave Turkey in the lurch; while France, though anxious for Turkish help, felt that it was beneath the dignity of the Most Christian King to make such a treaty with infidels. So the negotiations hung fire.

The Danzigers showed great courage and determination in defence of their suzerain, in the course of a siege which lasted from October 1733 to June 1734. Had the Turks attacked southern Russia during those eight months Munnich would have been drawn away. But Fleury continued to stand on his dignity; and when at last he brought himself to pen a few lines about France not making terms until assured of the security of the Ottoman Empire it was too late. Stanislas escaped disguised as a sailor, but his cause was now hopeless.

THE THIRD TREATY OF VIENNA. This siege was the only Polish part of the war. Most of it consisted of the Emperor's vain efforts to defend his Italian duchies and the Rhine frontier of the Empire against France. At the outset old Prince Eugene went on a special mission to The Hague and London, where in former days he had enjoyed such influence and honour. He argued that the Sea Powers could not afford to let Austria, their old ally, go under; and that France was really the aggressor in the Polish war. But both the States General and Walpole were set on keeping out of the conflict, and the Prince went empty away.

Everything went wrong for the Emperor. By the end of 1733 one French army under old Marshal Berwick had occupied Lorraine; another, under the still more aged Marshal Villars[1] was operating in northern Italy in conjunction with the King of Sardinia; and a Spanish army under Count Montemar had landed at Genoa to take possession of Tuscany. The Franco-Piedmontese force had little trouble in over-running the Milanese and investing Mantua. On the Rhine the French captured Kehl and besieged Philippsburg; and though Eugene brought up an Imperial army (joined later by 16,000 Russian troops, the first ever

---

[1] These honoured relics of *Le Grand Siècle* both died in the course of the War, Villars at the age of eighty-two, Berwick at sixty-four. Their old opponent Eugene followed them in 1736, in his seventy-third year.

seen in western Europe) it was too variegated to be able to do anything effective to relieve the place, which fell to the French in July 1734. Some of the oddities of eighteenth-century neutrality were to be observed in this Imperial army. The King of England refused to aid the House of Austria, but the Elector of Hanover sent a well-found contingent to support the Emperor; the Empress of Russia was at peace with France, but as auxiliary to Austria sent 16,000 of her soldiers to kill Frenchmen under the treaty of 1726; the King of Prussia had refused to let Munnich cross East Prussia to Danzig, but the Elector of Brandenburg, sent not only his quota to the *Reichsarmee* but his Crown Prince "to learn under Prince Eugene how laurels are won." (There were few laurels going in this campaign, however, and the chief lesson that Prince Frederick learned from it was the weakness of the Imperial forces.)

The campaign in northern Italy halted after the conquest of the Milanese; for Charles Emmanuel, having laid hold of the booty that he coveted for himself, saw no point in fighting to re-establish Spain in place of Austria as the paramount Power in Italy, and old Villars indignantly threw up his command rather than continue to act with such an obstructive ally. But in the south the Spaniards carried all before them. Marching down from Tuscany they conquered Naples and Sicily from the Austrians "with a piece of chalk," to the delight of the inhabitants; and in May 1735 Don Carlos was crowned "King of the Two Sicilies," thereby founding a monarchy which was to outlast that of France.

By the beginning of 1735 the Emperor was at the end of his tether. His Italian possessions were almost all in enemy hands; so was Lorraine; and in default of support from the Sea Powers he could have no hope of recovering them. Eugene persuaded him to cut his losses. After all, Lorraine was only an Imperial fief, and the Italian provinces were so hostile to Austrian rule as to be a liability rather than an asset. The Archduchess would have a much better chance of keeping together the rest of the patrimony without these outlying sources of trouble.

Soon each of the three anti-Imperial "allies" was trying to steal a march on the others by secret negotiations at Vienna: Elizabeth was renewing her efforts to get Maria Teresa as a bride for Don Carlos; Charles Emmanuel was scheming to gain the cession of the Milanese before Spain could claim it; Fleury was demanding Lorraine. Of course, France was the predominant partner in the alliance, and the war-party headed by Chauvelin was still ramping at Versailles; but the war had become a bore to the King, and Fleury saw a chance to cut the ground from under his colleague's feet. His representative at Vienna had the active support of the British ambassador there. One great problem was to find a substitute kingdom for Stanislas, so as to preserve the royal status of the Queen of France. A second difficulty was the betrothal of the Archduchess Maria Teresa to Duke Francis of Lorraine. It was odd that French territory should enclose a Province of the Empire; to have a personal possession of the Hapsburg family in that position would be quite impossible. But in the end the second problem suggested a solution for the first, and became the cornerstone of the Third Treaty of Vienna. Stanislas was to renounce the throne of Poland for ever, and to obtain in lieu thereof the Duchies of Lorraine and Bar as soon as the death of the old Grand Duke of Tuscany enabled that province to be given to Duke Francis by way of substitute. Stanislas was to retain the title of King, and on his death Lorraine and Bar were to revert to France as a sort of belated *dot* for the Queen of France. Don Carlos, who had been promised the reversion of Tuscany, would have to be satisfied with becoming King of the Two Sicilies. His Duchies of Parma-Piacenza were to revert to the Emperor, who was also to recover the Milanese, apart from some scraps for Charles Emmanuel. And finally—a concession which the Emperor valued far more than the Milanese—France acknowledged the Pragmatic Sanction.

When these terms were announced, in October 1735, Elizabeth and Charles Emmanuel were highly indignant; especially when the Austrian forces, now freed from the Rhenish campaign, marched into Italy and recovered the Milanese. Charles Emmanuel shrugged his shoulders and decided to make the best of a bad bargain that had been made behind his back; but it was long before Elizabeth of Spain could reconcile herself to giving up Parma, which she wanted for her younger son Don Philip. By the time the treaty was actually signed and sealed (November 1738) the situation which it contemplated had actually arisen; Maria Teresa had married Francis of Lorraine, and Gian Gaston, Grand Duke of Tuscany had died.

Lorraine was a big loss to the Holy Roman Empire; for it was German through and through. Charles VI had once more bartered the interests of the Empire for those of his family; but he had evaded the threat of a pro-French Poland on his eastern flank, and had gained in Augustus III another guarantor for his Sanction. Yet France, too, had done well out of the war, having consolidated her own eastern frontier; while Spain, for all the expostulations of its Queen, had established a royal offshoot of its reigning house in Italy. As for Britain, Walpole

could boast to Queen Caroline that of the 30,000 soldiers killed in
Europe during 1734 there was not one Englishman; and he was able
to go on building up the country's economic strength for another six
years. (All the same, it is arguable that if Britain had given active
support to Austria in 1734 there would have been no Austrian Succession War.)

SEQUEL IN THE NEAR EAST. The Polish War found on the throne
of Russia the Empress Anne. When Peter II died in 1730 the direct
Romanov line died out, except for his aunts Anne Duchess of Holstein
and Elizabeth. The nobles of the Privy Council thought this a

THE EARLY ROMANOVS

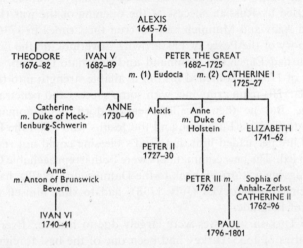

good chance to sell the throne to a nominee of their own, at the price
of a Constitution which would give them control. For this purpose
they picked on Anne Duchess of Courland, the daughter of Peter the
Great's half-brother Ivan, and made her declare that she would do
nothing without their consent. But this aroused much indignation, for
it seemed to threaten Russia with the anarchy which was paralysing
Sweden and Poland. With the support of a band of malcontents headed
by the clergy Anne overthrew the constitution and restored the autocracy. As a safeguard against any revival of the Constitution she employed foreigners in key positions—Biren, a Courlander, was her chief
minister, Ostermann, a Rhinelander, was in charge of foreign relations,
while Munnich, a Saxon, and Lacey, an Irishman, were her Generals.
Her first care was to ensure, in conjunction with Austria, that Poland

should not become an outpost of France. Then she turned back to the anti-Turkish designs of Peter the Great. As soon as Danzig had fallen she declared war on the Sultan, alleging that his troops had violated her southern frontier, and called on the Emperor for support under an agreement made in 1726, in return for the army which she had just sent to the Rhine.

Charles VI responded with zest, hoping to gain compensation for his loss of territory and prestige in Italy. If old Prince Eugene had been alive he would have made the Emperor face the facts of the situation— the emptiness of the treasury, the demoralization of the army, and the difficulties of the Balkan country in which the war would be fought. But the Imperial Council were now men of inferior calibre, who confirmed the Emperor's tendency to see only what he wanted to see. He was dazzled by Russian success at the opening of the war (Lacey had captured Azov and Munnich had overrun the Crimea in 1736), and by the memory of the Peace of Passarowitz—overlooking the fact that he had then had Eugene to command and negotiate for him. So in the summer of 1737 he launched his full available strength into the Balkan peninsula. His main army met with some success and penetrated as far as Nish. But he then recalled Senckendorff, its commander; for Senckendorff was a Lutheran, and the Jesuits who ruled the Emperor's spiritual life persuaded him that God's blessing could not remain with forces so led. The new commanders were both irreproachable Catholics; but Konigsegg was driven back to the Danube, and Wallis, having been overwhelmed at Crocyka (July 1738), had to shut himself up in the fortress of Belgrade.

These Turkish successes were largely due to France. Ever since the Capitularies of 1535 Turkey had been one of the best foreign markets for French goods—Marseilles had grown great on the trade; and of course the Turks provided the most effective of counter-irritants to distract the Hapsburgs. So the French ambassador at Constantinople had encouraged the Sultan to reject the demands of Russia and Austria and to use his forces to the best advantage. And France had another good card to play against Russia. At the Swedish Diet of 1738 the "Hats" under Gyllenborg, with the aid of French bribes, threw out the "Caps"; and the new régime was supported by a French subsidy to be spent in rehabilitating the armed forces.

Still, the regeneration of Sweden would take time, and the inherent weaknesses of the Turkish army were too great to be repaired by French diplomacy. Munnich had pulverized them at Khoten, and with their primitive siege apparatus there could be little prospect of their reducing the mighty fortress of Belgrade. But the Emperor, most feckless and luckless of rulers, contrived to muddle away all the advantages which he might have gained from the victories of his allies and the impregnability of his fortress. He sent different instructions about treating with the Turks to General Niepperg and to General Wallis, and kept them in ignorance of this. Each made separate contact with the Grand Vizier, who, with ambassador Villeneuve at his elbow, was quick to take advantage of the situation. The result was the Treaty of Belgrade (September 1739), by which the Turks recovered all that they had lost in the last war, including the fortress which dominated the whole area. And the defection of Austria, coupled with the growing threat from Sweden, compelled Tsarina Anne to sacrifice the fruits of victory gained at the cost of millions of roubles and a hundred thousand lives. All that she gained was a strip between the Bug and the Dniester. As for poor Emperor Charles he never smiled again, and in half a year he was dead.

This Treaty of Belgrade restored France for the moment to a supremacy in the affairs of Europe almost as unquestioned as she had enjoyed under Louis XIV. It was indeed a diplomatic masterpiece. The Sultan, secure for another generation, rewarded his benefactor with fresh commercial privileges; a Francophile party was in the saddle in Sweden; and at Moscow Munnich, the hero of the war, advocated a French alliance in place of the Austrian connection which had cost Russia so dear.

CHAPTER TWENTY-THREE

A YEAR OF CRISIS

1740

ECONOMIC forces now brought Great Britain into open conflict with France and Spain; while the deaths during 1740 of King Frederick William I of Prussia and of Emperor Charles VI of Austria put to the proof the value of the Pragmatic Sanction, and opened a dynastic conflict which persisted off and on till the Battle of Sadowa in 1866.

JENKINS' EAR. The Treaty of Belgrade freed France from the need for England's support in maintaining peace, and by 1740 the *entente* was practically dead. Walpole's régime of quiescent stability had released British energies for immense activity in overseas trade; that activity had led to an unofficial Anglo-Spanish war in the West Indies and along the Main. Whenever open war ensued between the two governments, it was obvious that France would be drawn in on the side of Spain, by economic forces as well as by the dynastic connection embodied in the Family Compact. There was already militant rivalry between British and French settlers in America and between British and French trading companies in India.

Walpole the pacificator was nearing the end of his political tether. An abortive Excise Bill had done permanent injury to his prestige; the Prince of Wales, at daggers drawn with the King, threw all his political and social influence against his Prime Minister; and the death of Queen Caroline deprived that minister of his private line to the King's ear. This wasting of Walpole's assets encouraged the Opposition in their efforts to hound him from office; and of all their lines of attack the most effective was to denounce him for struggling to preserve a peace which was not only ignominious to British pride but injurious to British commerce, and involved neglecting the wrongs of fellow-countrymen. Parliamentary orators drew harrowing pictures of British sailors languishing in foul Spanish gaols and maltreated by ruffianly Spanish *guarda costas*; and the agitation reached a lurid climax when (1738) they brought along a Captain Jenkins to produce from a cardboard box an ear, which he declared had been cut off by a Spanish cutlass, with the threat that the like would be done to King George himself, should he intrude into Spanish waters. Walpole

warned his opponents that war with Spain would mean war with France
—the recent marriage of Don Philip to a daughter of Louis XV showed
how the two branches of the Bourbon family were drawing together;
and that such a war would give an opening for another Jacobite rebellion. But the Opposition scouted all this: nothing, they declared,
could be worse for Britain than a continuance of the despicable Walpole-
Fleury combination, under cover of which France's trade was being
built up at Britain's expense; and as for Jacobitism, the minister himself
was undermining the Hanoverian dynasty by clinging to office in the
face of public execration. Petitions for the protection of the merchant
marine poured in from centres of foreign trade—London, Bristol,
Liverpool, Dundee, Southampton; the foundations of Whiggery were
crumbling beneath him. His opponents' evocation of patriotism-cum-
profit recalled the Elizabethan sea-dogs, and anticipated nineteenth-
century imperialism.

Walpole might have held out if he had had a united cabinet behind
him; but some of his most influential colleagues fell away, including the
Duke of Newcastle with his solid block of clients in the Commons;
and at last he was driven to a declaration of war (October 1739).
Nowadays a minister would resign rather than become responsible for
a policy in which he did not believe; but such niceties of constitutional
practice were not yet developed, and the King begged Walpole not to
leave him at the mercy of the Opposition.

If ever a war could be considered inevitable it was this clash between
the Latin and Anglo-Saxon races for world-trade; but it was inviting
disaster for Britain to embark on it under a minister who had no
heart in it and was painfully conscious of his own incompetence to
direct it.

And before any important action had been fought the situation was
complicated by the opening of another elemental struggle—this time
in central Europe.

THE SERGEANT-MAJOR KING. The Great Elector (reigned 1640–
1688) had made Brandenburg a leading state in the Empire; his son
Frederick I (1688–1713) made it a kingdom; but the reign in which the
Prussia of modern times began to take shape was that of Frederick
William I (1713–1740). We shall not expect to find its creator full of
airs and graces. It was as odd that such a gruff boor should have been
the son of the courtly Frederick I as that he should have been the father
of the enlightened Frederick II. Yet his reign was complementary to
theirs; for an era of retrenchment was necessary between a king with

an extravagant taste for ceremonial and a king with an extravagant taste for war.

Frederick William had the power which comes of singleness of aim. The purpose of his existence was to make Prussia strong, and in existing conditions this required a large army and a full treasury. To these ends he sacrificed everything and everybody around him. He was industrious, pious, loyal and honest; but his outlook was blinkered. Irresponsible autocracy was the only political conception he could really understand: "No arguing—the man is my subject!" People— even his own daughters—who dared to have ideas not in full accord with his own were in danger of his stick. Incapable of any under-standing of arts and sciences, he regarded interest in such trivialities as sloppy and degenerate. Travellers recorded the bleak and numbing air that hung over the country during his reign. His only recreation was hunting; his nearest approach to intellectual exercise was his "Tobacco Parliament," where of an evening he would sit gossiping with cronies as uncouth as himself, drinking small beer and smoking churchwarden pipes. Sometimes members of this very informal cabinet were bribed or cajoled into misleading him in matters of policy. For, grossly ignorant of history, and priding himself on his contempt for brains, he was easily gulled.

He certainly deserved the credit due to a zealous regimental sergeant-major, spending the best part of every day on parades, inspec-tions, and the consideration of details of uniform, organization and equipment. He made his standing army of 60,000 men the best-drilled and best-armed force in Europe. It was the first charge on his revenue —in fact he begrudged every thaler spent on anything else. It was recruited mainly from the peasantry, officered by nobles and gentry; the function of townsfolk was to provide the cost. And Prussia alone among the states of Europe had a nobility of military service, in which authority was not bought and sold by officers.

The civil service was as regimented as the army. "Ich stabilire die Gouverainté wie ein Rocher von Bronce!" he declared in his barbarous lingo. He was the most vigilant of stewards, with his eye (followed by his cane) everywhere. His ministers were mere clerks; they were paid as such and earned their pay hard. His regulations left no loophole for slackness or indiscipline, and he treated dishonesty in administration as equivalent to desertion from the army. "The gentlemen will say that what we order is impossible; but they must put their heads to it, and we hereby command them peremptorily not to argue but to make it practicable."

CROWN PRINCE FREDERICK. Frederick William's worst deed, from the point of view of posterity, was his warping of the personality of his son. Crown Prince Frederick, a keenly intelligent youngster, with a taste for philosophy, literature and music, was condemned to grow up in the atmosphere of a barrack. He found sympathy in his mother and sister, who had to spend three months of every year in the dullest and most provincial capital in Europe, and the rest at Wester-hausen, where cabbages grew up to the palace windows. The family had no home life. Any sign of cultural interests threw the omnipotent head of the household into transports of rage and disgust; an heir-apparent who wrote French verses and played the flute filled him with alarm for the future of Prussia.

In 1730, when the Prince was eighteen years of age, there came a crisis. He and the Queen and Princess Wilhelmina had long cherished a plan for a double marriage with the related House of Hanover: Frederick was to wed the second daughter of George II, and Wilhelmina was to become Princess of Wales. The King did not at first oppose the idea, but kept postponing a final decision owing to political differences with King George. For one thing, George was on bad terms with the Emperor, to whom Frederick William was devotedly loyal. The Emperor sent a carefully chosen envoy to Berlin to get into the Tobacco Parliament and draw the King away from his English relatives; and finally won his heart with the promise of Jülich-Berg. So Frederick William put his foot down on the double marriage and gave Wilhelmina to an impoverished and unattractive relative, the Margrave of Baireuth.

The Prince was worked up to a desperate resolve. While on a tour with his father round the western German courts he plotted with his friend Lieutenant Katte to escape into France and thence across to England. What he thought would happen next is not clear; but matters never got so far. The plan was betrayed to the King before the Prince could even mount his horse. Frederick William's fury nearly caused his death by apoplexy. This was a combination of the crimes he most abhorred—resistance to his authority and desertion from his army. When a Court Martial declared the Prince outside its jurisdiction and merely sentenced Katte to imprisonment, he raged and stormed and issued a decree by which Katte was to be beheaded and the Prince to watch the execution. For a time he seems to have thought of executing Frederick too, but protests from the other sovereigns of Europe, especially the Emperor, prevented him from going quite so far. After a period of solitary confinement Frederick was suffered to grovel at his father's feet and promise utter submission to his will. His education was begun afresh, under a committee of military governors who were to occupy him exclusively with religion, law, estate-management, and soldiering.

What Frederick had learned from this searing experience was not what his father thought: it had taught him that hypocrisy was both profitable and easy. Two years later he purchased a modicum of freedom at an even more soul-destroying price—by a political marriage at his father's behest to a princess who never had a place in his heart or mind. This necessitated a separate establishment, the castle of Rheinsberg. Henceforth by acting with tact and discretion, attending tedious religious services on Sundays and even more tedious parades all the rest of the week, he could spend his leisure as he pleased—in correspondence with Voltaire, in chamber-music and in literary composition. He wrote (in French of course) an *Anti-Machiavel*, refuting by lofty moral arguments the theory that for rulers the end justifies the means. All Europe looked forward with intense interest to the accession of such high-toned enlightenment to absolute power.

THE CRISIS. When, in April 1740, excessive eating, drinking and raging carried off the King at the age of fifty-one, Frederick was twenty-eight. He soon showed one characteristic trait: intense jealousy for his authority. The least attempt to curb his complete freedom of action always made him furious. This was seen during the first weeks of his reign by his chilling snubs to people who might suppose they had claims on him—the mother and sister who had stood by him in the trials of his youth; the aged Prince of Anhalt-Dessau, creator of the Army; and General von Schulemberg who had braved his father's wrath over the Court Martial.

What he was going to do with the power he grasped so eagerly he did not as yet know himself. Meanwhile he delighted in the concern felt on the subject by the governments of Europe. He instructed his ambassadors to remind them

that it is the way of youth to be adventurous, and that the alluring visions of fame may disturb the peace of countless nations in the world.

His eye, unclouded by animosities or loyalties, ranged round the continent during that summer of 1740, as he turned over in his mind whether he take a plunge for military glory or wait for circumstances to unfold. It was obvious that a new chapter was about to open in European affairs. Another contest between Britain and the Bourbons was pending—not, this time, to restrain France from dominating

Europe but for the lead in overseas settlement and trade. Now that the King of England was also Elector of Hanover, this conflict was bound to spread to western Germany; and when that happened Frederick, with his powerful army, would be able to put his support up to auction. If, on the other hand, he decided for immediate action, should he strike east or west? His father had been tricked by the Emperor over Jülich-Berg; but it was arguable that the immediate interests of the kingdom lay to the east, especially in acquiring the Polish provinces which separated East Prussia from the Mark of Brandenburg. For such a design Silesia, part of the Hapsburg heritage, would be an invaluable starting-place. This province, which forms the upper basin of the Oder (whose lower course ran through his own Brandenburg), was fertile, well-watered, well-populated—altogether a very eligible property. He had learnt all about it nine years before when a prisoner at Küstrin. And his family had dormant claims to part, at least, of it.

Then in October a crisis was precipitated by the death of Charles VI. He had laboured for a decade to assure the succession of his daughter to the family possessions; and although the Imperial throne was not hereditary—and in any case a woman was ineligible for it—he had extorted promises from the Electors to vote for her husband, the Duke of Lorraine. The central authority over those family possessions was weak and ineffective. They fell into three disparate groups (Austria with Carniola and Slovenia, Bohemia with Silesia and Moravia, Hungary with Transylvania and Croatia), each with its own institutions and forms of government. The only political union was a conference of ministers; the administration was chaotic, the revenue inadequate. Ancient tradition required costly court ceremonial, while essential services were neglected for lack of funds. The army was a babel of tongues, its equipment and training out of date, and its spirit de-moralized by defeat in the recent Turkish war. The death of Eugene had left no statesman of the calibre needed to cope with the situation. Maria Teresa, who now became "Queen of Hungary," had beauty, piety, courage, and goodness of heart. These qualities would assure the personal devotion which was the strongest bond of the monarchy; but how far would they avail against foreign bullets and bayonets? Fortunately it seemed that this question would not be put to the proof, for practically all the guarantors of the Sanction sent the young Queen assurances of good faith—none being more eloquent than the new King of Prussia.

But half-a-dozen of these potentates secretly cherished claims to all

8

or part of her heritage. Of the daughters of the Emperor Joseph, her father's elder brother, one had married Augustus III of Saxony-Poland, while the other was the wife of Charles Albert, Elector of Bavaria— who, moreover, had claims of his own dating from the sixteenth century. Charles Albert's special objectives were the Kingdom of Bohemia and the Imperial crown (the Wittelsbachs had always been jealous of the Hapsburgs about the latter); what Augustus particularly wanted was Moravia and Silesia, acquisitions which would connect Saxony and Poland into a solid block of territory. Elizabeth Farnese, seeking an Italian appanage for her second son Philip, egged on her husband Philip V to claim that in default of a male heir to the Austrian Hapsburgs he himself, as successor to the Spanish branch of the family, was their lawful heir. Lastly, Charles Emmanuel of Sardinia also trumped up claims to the Italian possessions, especially to the Milanese, long coveted by his family.

If one pretender took the initiative the others would be likely to rush in and stake out their claims; but these were incompatible with each other, and could not be effectively prosecuted unless some major Power stepped in to co-ordinate them. And of the other major Powers Great Britain and the Dutch Republic were old allies of Austria, and Russia was still bound by the alliance of 1726. There remained France, the hereditary rival of the Hapsburgs; but France, it seemed, could scarcely repudiate a guarantee only five years old, given in return for Lorraine. Moreover old Fleury had always pursued a policy of peace and goodwill, especially towards Austria.

For a week Frederick considered whether he should take advantage of the situation to enforce his Silesian claim. He did not want to give Augustus time to anticipate him by seizing the province. Of the other guarantors the Sea Powers could not intervene effectively and were both under pacific ministers. Fleury could be relied on to keep France from actively maintaining the Sanction. There was a certain danger from Russia; but the Empress Anne was known to be at death's door, and there was a prospect of a disputed succession. So Frederick prepared to strike.

There has been much argument as to whether he was justified in so doing. It is not our business here to sit in judgment on him, but this much may be said: whatever claim he had to Silesia was surely cancelled by the passage of time, being nearly two centuries old; but on the other hand Charles VI had as surely cancelled Frederick William's acceptance of the Sanction by failing to deliver the *quid pro quo*, the duchies of Jülich-Berg.

However, Frederick himself scarcely pretended to concern himself with questions of right and wrong. When his minister Podewils asked what excuse was to be made to Europe for the proceeding, he replied:

The question of right (*droit*) is one for ministers, and you had better take it up without delay, for the troops already have their marching orders.

In his Memoirs, written thirty years later, he admitted that

to these arguments must be added the possession of an army ready to march, a full treasury, and perhaps a desire to make a name for himself. All these were motives impelling the King to war against Maria Teresa.

And he added that the death of the Empress Anne in November was worth more to him than a thousand title-deeds.

In December, as soon as his preparations were complete, he sent a special embassy to Vienna, setting forth Hohenzollern claims dating from the sixteenth century, to certain parts of Silesia, and promising that if they were admitted he would defend the rest of the Austrian patrimony against all other claimants, and would give his vote and interest for Duke Francis as Emperor. Otherwise he would reluctantly be obliged to regard the enemies of the House of Hapsburg as his friends. Meanwhile he had sent his troops to take possession of his property. He flattered himself that the Queen would readily enter into his views in the matter.

At Vienna the high-spirited young Queen brushed aside faint-hearted counsels of despair, hurled defiance at the invader, mobilized her forces, and called on her guarantors to fulfil their obligations.

CHAPTER TWENTY-FOUR

THE AUSTRIAN SUCCESSION WAR

1740–1748

FREDERICK's invasion of Silesia began a confused struggle of which Carlyle declared that "Not Dismal Swamp under a coverlid of London fog could be uglier." The motive that started it was Prussia's hitherto latent desire to rival Austria in Germany; but to this were soon added the older rivalry between Austria and France, and the efforts of greedy rulers to get something for themselves in the general confusion. And there gradually emerged a deeper and more significant contest—between Great Britain and the Bourbon Powers for trade and dominion overseas.

THE FIRST SILESIAN WAR. Wars seldom go according to the plans of those who embark on them. Austrian mobilization was so cumbrous that Frederick had four months' start in Silesia; but when at last he was attacked by an Austrian army about equal in numbers to his own he was lucky to avoid defeat. He was swept from the snowy field of Mollwitz (April 1741) with his routed cavalry, and rode thirty miles without drawing rein. Only next morning did he learn that his rocklike infantry had saved the situation. It was a victory not for him but for old Dessauer's drill-book. Even now the invasion hung fire, for the Austrians remained secure in the fortress of Neisse for the rest of the summer.

But in one way Mollwitz was one of the decisive battles of the century, for it encouraged other claimants to come forward, and it led to a change in French policy. Fleury had been for appeasement with Austria, and if this line had been continued a little longer France would have been able to concentrate on the struggle now opening with Britain for world-trade. But the bellicose courtiers at Versailles who longed to renew the glories and opportunities afforded them by European War—the same people who had recently, led by Chauvelin, pushed France into the Polish Succession War—now found an effective spokesman in the handsome, vigorous, impassioned Count de Belleisle. What Belleisle advocated, in essence, was a return to the policy of Richelieu—to abase the Hapsburgs, to dominate Germany by keeping it divided, and to press forward French frontiers to the Rhine. News of Mollwitz made this policy prevail. A month or so later he set out with a magnificent retinue for a diplomatic tour of Germany, to raise a coalition of the Princes who had hitherto, with various degrees of good-will, acquiesced in the accession of Maria Teresa; and he particularly aimed at securing the votes of the Electors for Charles Albert of Bavaria, head of the Wittelsbach family which France had long been trying to play off against the Hapsburgs. France's excuse for this disregard of the Sanction, accepted with such formalities only two years before in return for Lorraine, was that such guarantees were always given "saving the rights of third parties"—a limitation which of course made them practically worthless. But the argument sufficed, especially now that Mollwitz had revealed Austria's vulnerability. Only a month after the battle Belleisle mediated at Charles Albert's castle of Nymphenburg an agreement by which Spain and Bavaria recognized each other's claims against the House of Austria; and the syndicate was soon joined by Saxony, Sardinia and Prussia (May–June, 1741). France for her part promised to send an army across the Rhine to support the Bavarians, and to induce Sweden to occupy the attention of Austria's ally Russia.

By the autumn the Marshal had done his work so well that of the twelve rulers who had signed the Sanction (mostly for substantial considerations) only one stood by it. That was gallant little George II, who prided himself on being a man of his word; and in this, if in little else, he had Parliament and the nation at his back. All the old anti-French passions, damped down since the great days of Marlborough, surged up, partly from sentimental sympathies for Maria Teresa, partly because of the connection between France and Spain, with whom the country was already fighting a commercial and colonial war. Parliament spontaneously voted £300,000 for the succour of her Hungarian Majesty. But there was another clash between British and Hanoverian interests. The King's generous impulses were checked by his fears for Hanover, exposed to attack both from Prussia and from a second French army which had just entered the Austrian Netherlands; and he was eventually driven to buy immunity for his Electorate by promising France to vote for Charles Albert as Emperor. His English ministers assured Maria Teresa that in this he was acting merely as Elector—that as King he was as firm as ever in support of her rights. But this was not much use to her, for as King he could do nothing to rescue Silesia or to procure the election of her husband Francis.

In September 1741 the outlook for Austria was grim. Six states were banded against her, and of the three potential allies left to her, George II dared not risk Hanover, the Dutch were clogged by their constitution, and Russia was paralysed by a disputed succession and a threat from Sweden. General Neipperg and the only available Austrian army had to remain in Silesia watching Frederick while Charles Albert with a Franco-Bavarian force of 80,000 men was marching down the Danube towards Vienna. It was in these circumstances that she made her famous speech to the half-rebellious Hungarian Diet at Pesth,

presenting to them her five-months-old son Joseph. The chivalrous Magyars may have brandished their swords with cries of *moriamur pro rege nostro*, as we are told; but they haggled over their rights and privileges before proclaiming their *Insurrectio* (= general mobilization), and by that time the Queen had been obliged to accept British mediation and make the very secret Convention of Klein-Schellendorf (October 1741), by which Neisse was to be surrendered after a mock siege, and all Lower Silesia was ceded to Frederick.

But there was no real bond of union to hold the anti-Austrian coalition together; the members were all jealous and mistrustful of each other, and their claims were incompatible. How could Augustus want Frederick to seize the province that divided Saxony from Poland? Could Frederick let Augustus encircle it by getting possession of Moravia? In Italy the Queen of Spain and Charles Emmanuel of Sardinia both wanted the Milanese. And what German ruler could want to see French influence dominating the Holy Roman Empire? The first symptom of this spirit was seen when Charles Albert, having captured Linz, remained there for a fortnight within three days' march of defenceless Vienna, and then turned off, marched into Bohemia, and took Prague instead. He may have made this move under pressure from Belleisle, who feared that the conquest of Austria would make Bavaria too powerful; or it may have been to forestall an invasion of Bohemia by Frederick. Whatever the reason it was fatal to the Elector's fortunes. He was proclaimed King of Bohemia, and in January 1742 was elected Emperor—the first break in a Hapsburg tradition of 300 years. But from that moment the tide turned in Maria Teresa's favour. A fresh army had now been collected from Italy and Hungary, and under Khevenhuller it destroyed the weak garrison which Charles Albert had left behind in Bavaria. The whole Electorate was laid waste, and on the very day that he was crowned Emperor at Frankfurt (February 1742) his capital, Munich, capitulated to avoid pillage.

That month also saw the fall of Walpole. It was manifestly dangerous to have a minister conducting a war in which he had no heart. The election of November 1741 reduced his majority almost to vanishing-point. He clung on for a few months longer in the face of a terrific barrage of opposition, but in February he had to make way for counsellors more in tune with the times. Control of foreign relations fell again (after nearly twenty years) to the dashing Lord Carteret. A more enterprising support for Maria Teresa was the keynote of his policy. He induced the King of Sardinia to change sides (already a familiar practice with the House of Savoy) and to declare war on Spain, with the promise of another strip of the Milanese; and the British fleet compelled King Carlos of the Two Sicilies to refrain from active support of his mother's designs in northern Italy.

Frederick felt that if this went on Maria Teresa would be in a position to demand Silesia back, so he denounced Klein-Schellendorf and invaded Moravia at the head of a combined army of Prussians and Saxons. But he got bogged in difficult country with his disjointed command, and had to concentrate on a siege of Brünn. When Prince

Charles of Lorraine (brother of Duke Francis) marched to relieve the place Frederick managed to drive him off by the battle of Chotusitz (May 1742). As a military action it was hardly more decisive than Mollwitz, but it lent force to British mediation at Vienna, where Carteret was trying to persuade Maria Teresa to make peace with Prussia in order to concentrate against (England's enemy) France. Once again she was induced, sorely against her will, to sacrifice Silesia—this time the whole of it (Treaty of Berlin, July 1742).

BETWEEN THE SILESIAN WARS. Belleisle's vision had faded. True, Maria Teresa had lost Silesia (at any rate for the time being), and the Wittelsbach was Emperor (at any rate in name). But Frederick had broken up the anti-Hapsburg union, the new Emperor's Electorate was ravaged, the French army trapped in Prague only fought its way to safety by a heroic but ruinous winter-march (December 1742), and in Russia the new Empress, Elizabeth Petrovna, had swung back to the Russo-Austrian alliance of 1726. Worst of all (from France's point of view) Maria Teresa had passed from the defensive to the offensive, with a scheme to annex Bavaria as compensation for Silesia, and to conquer Alsace-Lorraine from France as a substitute for Charles Albert.

This design came from the fertile mind of Carteret. The continuous thread running through all his policy was antagonism to France. Had he seen that it was the colonial sphere that really mattered he would have ranked as a far-sighted statesman; but (like his opposite number Fleury) his horizon was limited to Europe, and his method was to renew the Grand Alliance in some up-to-date form. The Austrian subsidy was doubled, and a force of 16,000 men (all that was left of the British army after twenty years of Walpole's cheeseparing) was sent over to the Netherlands, where it was to be joined by Hanoverian and Dutch contingents to form a "Pragmatic Army" which was to strike into Germany on behalf of Maria Teresa. The Hanoverians appeared, but not the Dutch. The States General passively resisted all Carteret's prodding, and the incomplete force remained eating (and drinking) its head off in the Austrian Netherlands all through the winter of 1742–3. The parliamentary Opposition, now led by William Pitt, attacked the Government for using British taxpayers' money to support a polyglot army defending Hanover, and demanded that support to the Queen of Hungary should be indirect, by attacks on French and Spanish possessions overseas.

At length the Pragmatic Army got under way. King George, always spoiling for a fight, took command of it as soon as he could get away from England. But its long delay had been fatal to success. Along the River Main, where it was shut in between river and forest, the French barred its advance and cut off its retreat, and only a tactical error by a subordinate French commander enabled it to fight its way back to safety. Dettingen (June 1743) was at first hailed in England as a great victory, and Handel hymned it in a famous *Te Deum*; but later information chilled this enthusiasm, especially when it became known that the King had worn a Hanoverian uniform. And it encouraged him and Carteret to develop their Continental line of policy instead of pursuing the interests of Britain.

They spent the rest of 1743 in Germany, giving free rein to their pro-Pragmatism, and promising subsidies right and left, regardless of the Parliament that would have to foot the bill. In August they had a fright: Charles Emmanuel, King of Sardinia, threatened to turn his coat again unless they increased his share of the Milanese. At first Maria Teresa refused to submit to this blackmail; but Carteret succeeded in persuading her to agree to the Treaty of Worms (August 1743)—an Austro-Sardinian agreement for the total expulsion of the Bourbons from Italy, cemented by £200,000 a year from London.

This provoked a sharp counter-stroke from France. Fleury had died early in 1743, and Louis XV announced that he would henceforth be his own Prime Minister. He was at this juncture under the influence of public-spirited Madame de Chateauroux, who tried to breathe into him an ambition to revive the glories of the *Grand Siècle*. This was not easy, for the King, though only in his early thirties, was already far gone in moral degeneration: but for the moment he caught the anti-British war-spirit rampant all around him at Versailles. The result was the Treaty of Fontainebleau (September 1743) which replied to Worms by a new and lop-sided version of the Family Compact. France undertook to declare war on England and Austria,[1] and to continue it until the two Spanish princes were firmly established in Italy and Gibraltar was recovered for Spain. Thus France enlisted in the service of Spain without fee or reward, or even running expenses. It was the Termagant's culminating triumph.

The first point of attack for France against England was always the Netherlands, and three months after the declaration of war a first-class French army crossed the frontier. It was nominally under the command of the King (complete with his court, his kitchens, his theatre and his Madame Chateauroux), but the real director of operations was Maurice de Saxe, an illegitimate son of Augustus II, who had taken service with

[1] Hitherto France's participation had been unofficial.

8*

France and was now to prove one of the greatest generals of the age. Austria did nothing to defend her province, assured that self-interest would compel the Sea Powers to do so. The Barrier proved useless, as usual. One after another the famous fortresses fell before the systematic advance of the French: Courtrai in May, Menin and Ypres in June, Furnes in July. But then came startling news. An Austrian army under Prince Charles of Lorraine had crossed the Rhine near Mainz and was sweeping into Alsace. Leaving Saxe with half the army in the Netherlands, King Louis hurried southwards with the rest. But at Metz the march was held up by an alarming illness of the King. And during the week that he lay between life and death Europe had yet another shock: the King of Prussia had struck into the war again!

THE SECOND SILESIAN WAR. Since the Peace of Berlin Frederick had brought his army up to strength and had organized his Silesian conquests; but the improved prospects of Maria Teresa made him fear that she would soon be in a position to demand restitution. So in June (1744) he made a secret treaty with France by which he was to invade Bohemia, while France (besides keeping up the attack on the Netherlands) was to send an army down the Danube to take Austria in the rear. When he learned that Prince Charles had taken the initiative he marched into Bohemia without further delay. As in 1740 he sent a polite explanation to Maria Teresa: he had no personal grievance, but was merely upholding the Emperor (his and her suzerain) on whose kingdom (Bohemia) and Electorate (Bavaria) she had laid unlawful hands. Three of the four invading columns with which he advanced on Prague passed through Saxony; but he assumed that the Elector would not object to this, as he was acting in the service of their common overlord. Augustus, away in Warsaw, was furious but (for the moment) helpless.

The Prussian movements went like clockwork, and Prague was captured without a hitch. But then Frederick made an error of judgment: he advanced on Austria up the Moldau Valley through the Bohemian mountains to the south-west. Here he was brought to a stand in mountainous wooded country, surrounded by wild Magyar horsemen who cut off his supplies. His only chance of extricating himself was for the French to keep Prince Charles occupied on the Rhine. But the illness of King Louis paralysed the French forces there, and the French Government did not worry itself unduly about the fate of the ally who had left it so badly in the lurch two years before. The Austrian army crossed Germany unmolested, and reinforced by Saxons and Magyars, forced Frederick to choose between fighting at a crushing disadvantage and retreating into Silesia. He chose the latter alternative, pushed back step by step by masterly movements (and equally masterly inactivities) devised by Marshal Traun, Prince Charles's Chief-of-Staff. It was a sharp blow both to Frederick's strength and to his pride; but he had a rare gift for looking unpleasant facts in the face and learning from them. In his Memoirs he admitted that

No general ever committed more faults than did the King in this campaign. . . . The conduct of M. de Traun was a model which every soldier who loves his profession ought to study. . . . But bad is often better for princes than good, for it renders them circumspect and modest.

Meanwhile Carteret after his delightful summer of 1743 had to face a parliamentary revolt. The Treasury begrudged the subsidies he had promised in the Treaty of Worms; that Treaty had provoked a formidable Franco-Prussian counter-alliance; a French army was in possession of the Austrian Netherlands, there were threats of a Jacobite invasion covered by a French fleet. The King had had to appoint Henry Pelham, brother of the Duke of Newcastle, as First Lord to ensure parliamentary support for the Government; and the brothers, brought up in the Walpole tradition, had no taste for adventurous policies. In November they compelled the King to dismiss Carteret.

Then early in 1745 the situation in Germany was changed by the death of the Emperor Charles VII. Nothing had gone right for that unhappy prince since his election, and his seventeen-years-old heir Max Joseph was glad to buy Bavaria back from Maria Teresa by undertaking to support her husband as the next Emperor. She followed up her advantage by a secret agreement with Augustus (Treaty of Warsaw, May 1745) for co-operation in reducing Prussia to the dimensions of the old Electorate of Brandenburg. France still pursued the primrose path in the Netherlands instead of coming to Frederick's aid; and although the allied army there, now under the Duke of Cumberland, was defeated at Fontenoy, that famous victory for French arms did no good for France's ally. As Frederick himself said, it might have been fought on the banks of the Scamander for all the use it was to him. When the Warsaw agreement took effect in an invasion of Silesia, he was in a very awkward position. However, he had learned his lesson from Traun, and that old master in the art of war was no longer at the elbow of Prince Charles. By skilful alternation of inaction and withdrawal the King enticed his adversary to advance on Breslau. Then, using a double-crossing spy to mislead the Prince as to his intentions, he suddenly smote him with devastating effect at Hohenfriedberg (June 1745).

Frederick was not the man to be unduly puffed up by winning a battle. He was badly in need of peace, having spent all his available cash and lacking the financial machinery to make war on credit. His problem now was how to bring Maria Teresa to agree to peace-terms that would leave him in possession of Silesia. Fortunately for him George II was in grave difficulties too. The imminence of the Jacobite invasion compelled him to withdraw the British regiments from the Netherlands; and to save Hanover he made a convention by which he and Frederick guaranteed each other's possessions. Frederick also promised support for Francis at the forthcoming election, and George undertook to induce Maria Teresa to accept this compromise within six weeks.

But Maria Teresa took a deal of persuading. She was extremely vexed with King George for abandoning her cause; and every instinct of family pride, of injured virtue, and of religion, forbade her to relinquish Catholic Silesia to a faithless aggressor who was nominally a Protestant and actually a scoffer at all religion. Even when in September the Election at Frankfort brought the Imperial Crown back into her family she was not mollified. The war was renewed with an Austro-Saxon invasion of Brandenburg; but in November Frederick threw back Prince Charles at Hennersdorf, while his henchman the old Dessauer annihilated the Saxons at Kesselsdorf. Saxony was knocked out of the war, and a Prussian army entered Dresden.

Frederick was all smiles and amiability—he wanted a quick peace. He made no demands against Saxony, and from Austria he asked for nothing but Silesia. The British Government, with the Pretender established in Scotland, urged more strongly than ever upon the Empress that she would never recover Silesia the way she was going. The advice was extremely unpalatable; but the downfall of Saxony was a convincing argument, and so was the situation in Italy, where her very unreliable ally Charles Emmanuel was becoming very restive at being left to fight single-handed against French and Spaniards because of her obsession about Silesia. He was not likely to be faithful to the alliance of Worms an hour longer than his own interests dictated, and his defection would result in Austria losing the Milanese as well as Silesia. So by the Treaty of Dresden (signed on Christmas Day 1745) she confirmed the cession of Silesia to Frederick—with bitter wrath and grief, and a silent vow that somewhen and somehow the iniquity should be undone.

THE LAST STAGE. The conflicts over Silesia and the Imperial Crown were now liquidated; but fighting went on for another two years for other parts of the heritage. The Peace of Dresden came at a critical moment in the Italian war. Maria Teresa's suspicions of Charles Emmanuel were justified: he was secretly considering a scheme brought forward by D'Argenson, the new French Foreign Minister, to expel both Austrians and Spaniards from Italy and federalize the peninsula under native rulers, including the House of Savoy. This scheme was an interesting anticipation of history; but Charles Emmanuel hung back because he saw that in its present form it aimed at French domination. When he heard of the Dresden negotiations he kept D'Argenson in play until a fresh Austrian army arrived in Lombardy; then he joined these Austrians in a vigorous campaign which threw the French and Spanish armies right out of northern Italy. D'Argenson was dismissed, and France practically abandoned the Spanish cause in Italy—to the indignant astonishment of Elizabeth Farnese, who could not understand why others did not share her passionate desire to establish her son Philip in Parma. But in July 1746 her political career ended abruptly with the death of her husband Philip V. For the heir to the throne was Philip's second son by his first wife, and this King Ferdinand VI was ruled by his wife Barbara, who as a Portuguese princess was by tradition pro-British. Ferdinand did not abandon the Bourbon interests in Italy, but had none of his step-mother's fervour for it.

The contest in the Austrian Netherlands continued to go in favour of France. In 1746 Marshal Saxe captured Brussels, Antwerp, Mons, Charleroi and Namur. Cumberland, having crushed the Jacobites at Culloden, returned with the English army, and for this campaign he replaced Charles of Lorraine as generalissimo. But the fortunes of war were not to be reversed by the mere substitution of one young prince for another. It seemed that Saxe's next move would be an invasion of the Dutch Republic; and there ensued a pale repetition of the events of 1672 (p. 61). The frightened States General sent a special embassy to Versailles to ask on what terms they could buy immunity, and when negotiations broke down a popular rising led to the revival of the Stadtholderate, which had been abolished on the death of William III in 1702. But there was no John de Witt to be lynched this time, and no William of Orange to connive at the deed—the Republic no longer possessed men of that calibre. The heir to the Orange tradition, who now became hereditary Stadtholder, Admiral, and Captain-General, was William Frisco, great-grand-nephew of William III and son-in-law of George II. He did his best, but his best was not good enough to have much effect on the situation. When Cumberland, reinforced by an Austrian contingent from Italy, tried to protect

Maastricht from Marshal Saxe, the battle of Laufeldt (July 1747) drove him back across the Maas. Maastricht was the gateway to Holland, and the Dutch were ready to pay almost any price for a quick peace. However Saxe had suffered considerable losses in the battle, and could not raise enough troops to invest the place in what was left of the campaigning season of that year. And by the spring of 1748 none of the combatants had enough war-spirit left to renew the fighting. Louis XV, in particular, had slaked his very limited thirst for military glory; the spirited Madame de Châteauroux was dead, and his new mistress, Madame de Pompadour, wanted to keep him and the Government under her control. He was easily persuaded, therefore, to round off Marshal Saxe's victories by offering magnani-mous terms which the allies were very glad to accept.

The peace conference which met at Aix-la-Chapelle in the spring of 1748 finally recognized the acquisition of Silesia by Prussia; Charles Emmanuel got his new strip of the Milanese, and Don Philip was set up in Parma-Piacenza, while France restored the Netherlands to Austria and the Barrier to the Dutch. Maria Teresa, Charles Emmanuel and Dowager Queen Elizabeth were dissatisfied with their respective shares of northern Italy, but they could not go on fighting without financial help which neither France nor Britain were willing to give them. The treaty was signed in October.

INDIA AND AMERICA. A clause of the treaty which passed almost unnoticed was the exchange by France and Britain of the non-European booty which they had taken from each other in the course of the war. "In order that he might rob a neighbour he had promised to defend, black men fought on the coast of Coromandel and red men scalped each other on the shores of the Great Lakes," as auxiliaries of French and British. But Frederick's aggression was not really so responsible for these distant struggles as Macaulay's epigram suggests. Underground forces had long been throwing Britain and France irresistibly into con-flict in those regions, and continued to do so long after the Silesian wars.

In India the rivalry was focussed by two chartered syndicates of traders. These East India Companies tried to outbid each other in obtaining privileges from Indian rulers; and as each maintained "sepoy" forces to protect its depots ("factories") there was always danger of armed conflict. In Bengal the English Company had its headquarters at Calcutta, the French at Chandernagore; on the Coromandel coast the English were at Madras, the French at Pondicherry. When France declared war on England in 1744 the French Company had just obtained a man of first-rate capacity as Governor—François Dupleix (1697–1763). It was he who first saw that a European state might succeed the Mogul Empire (now falling into decay) as paramount power, by intervening in succession disputes among the princes. His capture of Madras (September 1746) seemed the beginning of the end for the English Company, at any rate so far as south-east India was concerned; and its restitution at the Treaty of Aix did little to restore British prestige in Indian eyes.

In America the conflict was even deeper-seated. The thirteen British colonies had grown up spontaneously along a thousand miles of coast, and they differed in climate and soil as much as Norway differs from Morocco. They had Governors and officials appointed by the Home Government, but for all essential purposes ruled themselves by elected assemblies. Miles of trackless wilderness separated them from each other, and they never thought of themselves as "Americans." There was no tie between them save allegiance to the Crown.

The French colonists on the other hand, were all "Canadians," hand-picked by the King's Government for the life of backwoodsmen. Mostly trappers and fur-traders, they dwelt in isolated settlements along the St. Lawrence and the Lakes, dependent on the King's bounty for weapons, implements and for much of their food. The Royal Government was represented at Quebec by an aristocratic Governor-General and a bureaucratic Intendant, who between them regulated everything and were responsible for everything. The St. Lawrence gave the Canadians a highway into the interior, whereas nothing invited the British colonists to penetrate their difficult hinterland. Thus it was the French who explored the Lake country and sailed down the Illinois River to the Mississippi; and in the conflict now arising the advantage of the British in numbers (something like 2,000,000 to 50,000) was offset by the facts that the French were under centralized direction and were individually better suited to irregular warfare.

Up to the Austrian Succession War, and during it, neither Government realized how great a prize was at stake in those regions. Louisburg, a naval base built by the French on Cape Breton Island to guard the St. Lawrence when they lost Acadia at Utrecht, was captured in 1745 by volunteers from Massachusetts. Its position made it vitally important to the whole area, for it commanded the communications of Canada with France. But the British Government, which had contributed nothing to its capture save the loan of a few warships from the West Indian squadron, nonchalantly restored it to the French in the Treaty of Aix.

CHAPTER TWENTY-FIVE

THE EIGHT YEARS' TRUCE

1748–1756

NEITHER the Anglo-French nor the Austro-Prussian quarrels was really settled by the Treaty of Aix, and the years that followed were an uneasy and watchful truce while the contestants recovered from exhaustion. When the two-fold struggle reopened they had changed partners.

"THE GRAND INTELLIGENCE." Frederick of Prussia had two years' start in preparing for the next war. He was no lover of fighting for its own sake, but he knew that Maria Teresa would never be happy till she got back Silesia. He would not tempt fortune as long as he was left alone, but had no intention of giving up his winnings. He knew, too, that success was the only justification for his recent conduct; the very people who lauded him as a hero-king would throng to despoil him as a shameless aggressor if he showed any signs of weakness. To prevent such a catastrophe became the underlying purpose of all his activities. He sought to remain on good terms with Austria's traditional enemy France, and to keep her separated from her traditional allies the Sea Powers and Russia. He built up Prussia's economic resources by developing industry and commerce, by making canals and roads, by encouraging and regulating immigration. He augmented his army by a third with special attention to cavalry and horse artillery, reformed the Kadettenhaus where young officers were trained, and developed training in the light of experience gained in the late war. Above all, he took in hand his own military education, knowing that whatever can be improvised in time of war, the brain of the commander cannot be.

He was the supreme exponent of kingship as estate-management, pursuing with far better brains the labour begun by his father. By the incalculable processes of racial chemistry, conquering Teuton and subjugated Slav combined on the dreary wastes of northern Germany to form a tough, tenacious, laborious people imbued with the morality of the ant-hill which subordinates the good of the individual to that of the community; and this material his father and he hammered into a military shape. The army consumed four-fifths of the national income —the income produced by the rest of the nation toiling from dawn to dark from the cradle to the grave. Most of his subjects were little better than serfs. Frederick, whose enlightenment did not embrace economic or social studies, was content to leave them in that condition, but took care, in the interests of the State, that they should be kept in health and strength. As to the nobles, there was no Court for them to idle in; they spent their best years as officers in the army, and the rest in managing their estates. There was no calling, no aspect of the national life, into which the King's coldly critical eye did not penetrate. Everywhere peasants and burghers, officers and civilians saw the little man in his shabby snuff-stained blue coat, often to suffer the cutting contempt of his displeasure, occasionally rewarded by a dry word of approval. And he kept his own counsel; he once said that if he thought his shirt or his skin knew his thoughts he would tear it off. His ministers were overworked, underpaid clerks, forming a machine-tool powered and controlled by its master. And he claimed that he himself was the first servant of the State. The pomps of kingship had no attraction for him; he had no family, lived apart from his wife, and had only men about him, spending most of his time in a bungalow of his own design called *Sans Souci*, near Potsdam.

For recreation he read military history and wrote bad verses and the *Memoirs of the House of Brandenburg* (in French, of course—"German is for soldiers and horses"). He liked music—played his flute of an evening, and appreciated a visit from "old Bach." He enjoyed converse with intelligent foreigners, especially the cleverest of them all, Voltaire. The contact of these two typical products of their age is worth recalling. Frederick had long tried to induce the famous Frenchman to seek at *Sans Souci* refuge from the annoyances to which he was subject in France, and when at last he came, provided him with accommodation and a pension. At first all went well; Voltaire wrote his *Siècle de Louis XIV*, and touched up his host's French compositions. "Three steps from my cabinet," he boasted to an envious correspondent in Paris, "take me to supper with a man of intellect, charm and fancy, whose sole misfortune it is to be a great prince," But after a time he began to presume on his situation—he quarrelled with other French exiles, and even tried to intrigue with foreign envoys. That touched Frederick on the raw. Throughout his reign the least sign of outside interference in affairs of state exasperated him to frenzy—he insulted even his sister Wilhelmina, the one creature for whom he felt anything approaching love, when he thought she was trying to influence his policy. So Voltaire was told that he must change his ways or go, and eventually (1753) he went. The King characteristically sent after him

for the return of orders he had given him, and of a presentation copy
(one of the only twelve printed) of the royal poems. And as Voltaire's
books were delayed in transit he was detained at Frankfort for several
weeks until restitution could be made. *Tantaene animis caelestibus
irae?*

AUSTRIA LOOKS TO THE DAY. Maria Teresa once said she could
never see a Silesian without weeping. The loss was far more than that of
a valuable possession: it upset the balance between Teutonic, Slavonic
and Magyar elements in the Hapsburg lands, and afforded a dangerous
entry up the Oder into the heart of them. It made the Hohenzollern
a potential rival for the hegemony of central Europe; and as a devout
Catholic the Empress was horrified to see the province come under
Protestant Prussia. She was sure that it could not be God's will that
such a state of things should continue; and the ink was scarcely dry
on the Treaty of Aix before she was planning to help Him to right the
wrong.

In March 1749 she invited her Councillors to submit in writing their
views on the future policy of the Monarchy. All but one of them,
including her good-hearted but wooden-headed husband Emperor
Francis, were for continuing the old alliance. To be sure, England and
Holland had forsaken her over Silesia; but they remained her only
possible allies. But Anton von Kaunitz (1711–94) the youngest member
of the Council, presented a memorandum which made history. Agreeing that Silesia must be recovered, he considered the old allies useless
for the purpose. England was more and more absorbed in overseas
trade, and George II would never risk Hanover by fighting Prussia.
As for the Dutch, they had ceased to matter. So why not cut away
these clogging traditions and make friends with France? The Franco-
Prussian alliance was still nominally in force, but the actual relationship was far from cordial. And the Empress could buy French support
with the Netherlands, which had always been useless to Austria but
had been coveted by France for centuries. France would need help
when her struggle with England was renewed, and would at the very
least hold back her Turkish allies from attacking Hungary.

The Emperor was pained by the thought of partnership with the
Power which had robbed him of Lorraine, and crusted Councillors of
the old school were aghast at such a breach with tradition. But the
high-spirited Empress listened eagerly to advice which seemed to offer
the best hope of reaching her heart's desire. Kaunitz became, and
continued till her death, her most trusted minister. He has been

likened to Disraeli, with his studied eccentricities and hypochondria, his sagacity, political courage and dexterity, and the devotion which he inspired in his Empress-Queen.

In 1750 he went to Versailles as ambassador to test the ground. He attracted much attention with his exquisite lace cravats and embroidered coats, his dread of fresh air and inability to eat anything but boiled chicken; and he found plenty of people, including the King himself, ready to listen to his hints and suggestions. But the Court and the Government were not yet ripe for so bold an innovation in foreign policy; and when in 1753 Kaunitz was recalled to Vienna to become Chancellor he seemed to have failed.

Another indispensable preliminary to the reconquest of Silesia was a thorough overhaul of the administration. Something had to be done to turn the sprawling agglomeration of fiefs into a coherent state. France, and latterly Prussia, had shown what strength a country gained from centralized personal rule; and in the Hapsburg Monarchy there was the more need for this as the sovereign was the sole bond among peoples of half-a-dozen distinct races. The recent war had shown up the dangers of disunity. The troops of each province were raised and maintained by the Provincial Estates, variable annual grants fixed the numbers available, supplies were largely in kind; one province would look on unconcernedly while another was overrun by the enemy. Though Maria Teresa's possessions were far greater and richer than Frederick's, she could hardly put 20,000 men into the field against his 60,000 in 1740, and after 1742 her continuance in the war was dependent on British subsidies. Now that the struggle was suspended she turned to internal reforms to enable her to renew it more successfully. Her first Chancellor, Prince George of Haugwitz, set them going. The powers of the Provincial Estates were cut down, the feudal authority of the nobles was pared away; an attempt was made to unify legal procedure; a universal graduated income tax was introduced; the political power of the Church was restricted and its greed curbed by a Statute of Mortmain, with the full approval of the Pope; the government of Bohemia was united to that of Austria. Above all a regular army of 108,000 men was henceforth to be kept in being, its morale raised by better pay and conditions of service, its drill remodelled on Prussian lines, and its training adapted specifically for war against King Frederick.

THE POMPADOUR'S FRANCE. After the death of Madame de Châteauroux Louis XV took a permanent mistress, who kept a hold over his mind and will long after his amorous fancy had turned else-where. It was this Marquise de Pompadour (grass widow of a M. d'Étioles of the civil service) who had urged him to make the Treaty of Aix, restoring nearly all that had been gained by the hard-won victories of Marshal Saxe. The Court was again able to give undivided attention to the seven deadly sins, but the Peace made it the butt of the nation. Lampoons ridiculing the King and execrating his Scarlet Woman poured from the Press.

The Pompadour was not without good qualities. Though she gave herself great airs (at her receptions hers was the only chair in the room) she was charming and gracious to all. She opposed the extravagant claims of the clergy; she was a discriminating patron of the arts; she encouraged Montesquieu, Diderot and Rousseau; and after her death Voltaire said of her *"Après tout, elle était des nôtres"*—praise indeed from such a quarter. But her influence on the King was wholly bad. He had once had redeeming qualities of head and heart, but these were rotted by degrading vices which she encouraged in order to keep his spirit in thrall to herself. Her efforts to keep him amused were a terribly wearing task. The Court had to be constantly moving from palace to palace, to the disruption of governmental business ; and money had to be recklessly squandered at a time when the exchequer was already insolvent and taxation was ruining trade.

For some years an enlightened Controller-general, Machault, tried to bring the finances into order by combining economy with a 5 per cent. income tax on all classes, privileged and unprivileged alike. This, along with his efforts to prevent property from accumulating in the untaxable hands of the Church, and a scheme for internal free trade, might have saved the monarchy from disaster. Louis and the Pompa-dour, neither of them devoid of common sense, at first encouraged him; but the outcry was tremendous. The Parlements were furious at the threat to their tax-exemption, the hall-mark of their gentility; and the clergy reminded Louis of what happened to Henry II of England when he tried to diminish the privileges of Holy Church. In the end the King gave way and dismissed Machault—with assurances of un-diminished confidence in his policy. He realized that the Monarchy was on the road to ruin, but consoled himself with the thought that after all it would last out his time.

To add to the general discord, the Jansenist controversy cropped up again. The Archbishop of Paris ordered that the sacraments should be refused to all who could not produce their confessor's certificate that they accepted the Bull Unigenitus (p. 173). There were harrowing stories of people dying in spiritual anguish for lack of Extreme Unction. The hierarchy became more unpopular than ever. The Parlement of Paris condemned the ticket system and punished priests who imposed it. The King, haunted by terror as to the fate of his soul, exiled the Parlement to the provinces. In Paris and a dozen provincial capitals there were riots which had to be quelled by troops. Eventually, in December 1756 the King held a *lit de justice* to compel the registration of edicts imposing the Bull and removing the judicial authority of the Parlements over the clergy. The clamour died away; but it was significant that the Parlements, though bitterly hostile to reforms that threatened their pockets and privileges, should have won popularity by opposing the will of the sovereign. They were the only check on a government which ignored its duties and neglected its responsibilities.

The protest of the nation against the monarchy which had once been its pride took visible and tangible shape when in January 1757 the half-crazy Damiens wounded Louis with a dagger. He declared that he had not intended to kill him—merely to draw attention to his shortcomings as a king. He was put to death with horrible tortures, but the truth that he was trying to enforce could not be so easily obliterated.

THE STRUGGLE OVERSEAS. Anglo-French rivalry in India and America, though the home governments took little part in it, was too fundamental to be ended, or even greatly affected, by the settlement of Aix. Very shortly thereafter Dupleix achieved his masterpiece by making a nominee of his own Nawab of the Carnatic. But Robert Clive, a young clerk in the East India Company's service at Madras, volunteered to attack the Nawab's capital at Arcot, with a few hundred European and Indian troops. His success changed the history of India. Dupleix was a statesman, not a soldier, whereas Clive was a "heaven-sent genius" in war as in administration. Before long the situation had been reversed: the pro-French Nawab was replaced by a pro-British rival, Dupleix was recalled in disgrace, and the princes of southern India became convinced that the British were the side to back. But neither of the Companies had any vision of the future. What they wanted was not dominion, but dividends. In 1754 they agreed at a conference in London to drop all political and military schemes and not to let any future European war affect their relations. But the tide of events was too strong for these pacific resolutions; and within a couple of years they were locked in a deadly struggle which ended in expulsion for the one and monopoly for the other.

In America the struggle was ceaseless. The capture and restitution of

Louisburg convinced both sides of its value. The French strengthened its fortifications, and the British built Halifax to keep it in check. And as the boundaries of the Acadia ceded at Utrecht had never been defined, ill-feeling became so acute in the peninsula that a French missionary at Beau-Séjour paid Indians a bounty on British scalps, while the British deported a thousand French families to New England. But the most critical area was the Ohio valley. As in India, vision and vigour were on the French rather than the British side. The Marquis du Quesne, Governor of Canada, dreamed of a vast empire linking the Canadian settlements with those made along the Mississippi from New Orleans. He sent a party down the Illinois River to put up tin plates claiming the country for King Louis; but the Ohio would afford a much shorter line of communication between St. Lawrence and Mississippi valleys. On the other hand, pioneers from the British colonies were now finding their way through the Alleghenies, and their governments were beginning to realize that if the French were allowed to make good their claims all possibility of expansion for Virginia, Pennsylvania and New York would be gone for ever. Some Virginian pioneers were engaged in building a fort at the most important strategic point in the district, where the Monongahela enters the Ohio, when they were attacked and driven off by a force of Canadians, who completed the fort, and named it after their Governor. A body of militiamen, sent under a young officer named Washington to re-capture the place, was cut to pieces; and for the time being the French were undisputed masters of all the lands behind the British colonies.

At the instance of the Board of Trade and Colonies in London, delegates from seven of the colonies met at Albany, N.Y. to see if they could agree on a scheme for pooling their resources for the defence of British America as a whole; but the colonial legislatures one and all declined to surrender any of their sovereign independence to a central body, and the idea fell through. When the French Government prepared to send a fresh army of 6,000 men to Quebec, the very existence of the British colonies was threatened. The Newcastle Government was in terrible straits, for the last thing it wanted was a war with France. Eventually it sent Admiral Boscawen to cruise off Louisburg with the half-hearted instruction that if he fell in with French ships he was "to do his best to make himself master of them." He missed the main fleet in a Newfoundland fog, but came upon three stragglers, and as they refused to surrender he sank one and captured the others. It was "an untoward incident." The admiral had done too much or too little: he had incurred the odium of breaking the peace, but had not made his blow decisive. And his action lit the train that led to another Anglo-French war.

CHANGING PARTNERS. Everybody expected it to break out at once; but France was nearly as unprepared for war as Britain, and needed to make sure that she would not have to face a new Grand Alliance. So there was an interval of anxious military and diplomatic preparation on both sides.

The first thought of George II and his Newcastle Ministry was for Hanover, exposed to attack from France on one side and from France's ally Prussia on the other. They naturally turned for support to the old Alliance. Little was to be hoped from the Dutch, who no longer had either the money or the heart for a spirited foreign policy; but they were shocked to get what amounted to a refusal from Vienna. For Kaunitz and the Empress were still hoping for a French alliance against Prussia.

With France preparing actively to invade Great Britain, King George and his ministers were terrified at the prospect of isolation. All that Newcastle could think of was a plan to keep Frederick from attacking Hanover by an understanding with Elizabeth of Russia. She controlled a vast reservoir of inexpensive man-power, and detested Frederick for his sarcasms about her private life, while her minister Bestuchev regarded him as the chief obstacle to Russian expansion along the Baltic. So in September 1755 handsome young Sir Charles Hanbury Williams was sent on a special mission to wheedle the susceptible Tsarina and bribe the covetous minister into an alliance. Within a month Russia had agreed to keep 50,000 men at Britain's disposal on the frontiers of East Prussia, in return for a subsidy of £100,000 in peace and £500,000 in war, both parties promising to make no separate terms with "the common enemy."

Now it was Frederick's turn to be startled. He knew that the two Empresses hated him and had renewed in 1746 the alliance originally made in 1726, and that Kaunitz and Bestuchev had recently discussed joint action with Count Brühl of Saxony; but he had comforted himself with the reflection that Russia could not go to war without money, which she certainly could not procure from Austria. That deficiency had now been made good. And to his enquiries at Versailles as to what support he could expect from his old ally he received evasive replies.

Where else could he look for help? Only to London. Unfortunately he had always been on bad terms with his uncle George II, and since the Peace of Aix he had wrangled with the British Government over half

a dozen subjects. He had compensated himself for the depredations of
English privateers during the war out of the interest due to English
subscribers to his Silesian loans. He had annexed East Friesland,
which King George claimed for Hanover. He had ridiculed a plan by
which George and Newcastle had hoped to bribe the Electors to
nominate Maria Teresa's son, Archduke Joseph, "King of the Romans"
(i.e., heir presumptive to the Empire).

But necessity makes strange bed-fellows. George was anxious about
Hanover, Frederick about East Prussia and Silesia. The remedy was
obvious : a defensive alliance. The upshot was the Convention of
Westminster (January 1756) by which they agreed to maintain peace in
Germany by joint resistance to any incursion by foreign armies.
Hanover would be shielded by Frederick's hold over his ally France,
and Prussian territory would be shielded by George's hold over his
ally Russia.

That Convention had results quite unexpected by its signatories.
France, too, had been looking round for support. Frederick was too
anxious about Silesia to start trouble in the Empire by attacking
Hanover. Spain's overseas possessions gave her a common interest,
as well as a family connection, with France; but enquiries at Madrid
showed that nothing was to be expected from easy-going Ferdinand
and his Anglophile Queen. But just at that critical moment Prince
Starhemberg arrived at Versailles from Vienna. There had been signs
that the seeds sown by Kaunitz six years before were now germinating,
and Starhemberg was sent to nurse them into life. He brought a letter
from the Empress to the Pompadour addressing her as "Madame ma
Soeur"; and this condescension, contrasted with Frederick's bitter
allusions to her position,[1] broke down the last resistance in that influential quarter. The Council still included crusted old characters who
held by traditional policies, but the King had long amused himself
by keeping agents of his own in foreign capitals—*le Secret du Roi*,
people called it. He and the Pompadour called in the Abbé Bernis, a
clerical politician of the Dubois type, to conduct the French end of the
discussions with Starhemberg. At first all that was proposed was an
end of the age-old hostility between the two courts—nothing was said
about France picking a quarrel with Prussia. In fact King Louis had
announced that he was sending to Berlin a semi-Royal Duke to renew
the fifteen-year agreement of 1741, when news came of the Convention

---

[1] When, on arriving at Potsdam in 1750, Voltaire had delivered her greetings,
Frederick had replied *Je ne la connais pas*. These bitter words now cost him as dear
as his epithet for Elizabeth of Russia, *la Catin du Nord*.

of Westminster. There was nothing expressly anti-French in that engagement. True, it warned all and sundry to keep out of Germany, but Frederick always maintained that it was to France's own interest to concentrate on the naval and colonial struggle with Britain. But the French Government was disgusted to see its supposed ally shaking hands with its mortal enemy; and from that moment its negotiations with Austria took a new impetus.

Preparations for war became more hectic than ever. Newcastle, in a frenzy of apprehension, imported 12,000 Hessians to defend Britain from invasion; but the first blow fell elsewhere. Admiral Byng had been sent to forestall an attack on Minorca; but by the time he reached the island he found that the French had already landed there in strength. After an indecisive brush with the enemy's fleet he returned to Gibraltar, whence he was sent home, court-martialled and shot "to encourage the others." The brilliant, dissolute young Duc de Richelieu captured Port Mahon by a dashing *coup de main*, and Britain had lost the key to the western Mediterranean before the war was well begun.

France declared war in April 1756, and on May 1st made the first Treaty of Versailles with Austria. But Louis and his Pompadour would not go as far as Maria Teresa wanted. They were annoyed with Frederick for making a pact with England, but they saw no reason why they should endanger victory over their own enemy by fighting Austria's. So they merely undertook to pay Maria Teresa an annual subsidy, and to keep out of her Netherlands, provided that she would refrain from supporting England or Hanover. Only if Prussia actually attacked Austria would France send an army into Germany, and then only 24,000 men. It was but a half-hearted agreement, but any pact between France and Austria was a startling breach with tradition.

Earlier in the year another envoy with an historic Austrian name had set out from Vienna. Prince Esterhazy came to St. Petersburg to find out how the recent Anglo-Russian treaty affected the Austro-Russian alliance. But Kaunitz need not have been anxious. Hatred of Frederick was the mainspring of Elizabeth's existence. Her pact with England had no other object than to give her the means to attack him; and when, soon after Esterhazy's arrival, she learned of the Westminster Convention, she felt like a tigress baulked of her prey. Without as yet denouncing the Hanbury Williams' treaty (for she badly needed the money) she continued to prepare for war against Frederick; and she assured Esterhazy that there was nothing that she would like better than to join Austria in an immediate attack on him, with or without the full support of France. But this was going a little too fast for Austria.

Troops and stores had to be moved to Bohemia, and negotiations had to be completed with Augustus of Saxony-Poland, who had never forgiven Frederick for his cavalier treatment of Saxony in the last war, and hated him as much as was possible for such a mild and flaccid person; and with the Government of Sweden, where another minor revolution had brought the Francophile militarist "Hats" back into power with designs for the recovery of Further Pomerania.

The British Government had an anxious time all through that summer of 1756. They had lost the opening phase of the war, not only in the Mediterranean but in America, where the French captured Fort Oswego, the only British outpost from which land operations against Canada might have been launched. The one reassuring thought for George II and his ministers was that Frederick was pledged to action against any disturber of the peace in Germany. Hanover was secure, at any rate.

Then in August came a thunderbolt. Frederick himself precipitated a European war by invading Saxony en route for Bohemia, thereby exposing Hanover to instant attack and making it impossible for him to defend it.

CHAPTER TWENTY-SIX

THE SEVEN YEARS' WAR (PART I)
1756–1758

THE Seven Years' War was the first World War: it was fought in three continents. An attempt by Russia, Austria and France to "encircle" Prussia was combined with an Anglo-French struggle in India, where the issue was decided in 1757, and in America, where it continued two years longer.

FREDERICK MISCALCULATES. Frederick had precipitated a European War for the second time because he had discovered that Austria and Russia were turning their pact of 1726 (p. 211) into a military partnership to crush him. Of course he had always known that Maria Teresa was intent on getting back Silesia, and that Elizabeth hated him for his bitter tongue; he was aware, too, that the military cliques at St. Petersburg and Vienna were eager to strike him down before his army grew any stronger. But not till 1753 did he learn through his Secret Service (a polite term for the bribery of foreign officials) of the aggressive coalition being knit together by Count Brühl, general factotum to Augustus of Saxony-Poland. Brühl was not a real statesman. He wanted to push Saxony into Prussia's leadership of northern Germany without the expense of building up its resources to win the position. The first charge on the revenue was the cost of keeping the self-indulgent Elector in a good humour, and the second was his own princely income. His design was to get others to do the actual fighting while Saxony got a full share of the spoils. He had now made a compact with Kaunitz by which, when Prussia was overcome, Austria was to recover Silesia, Russia to annex East Prussia, and Saxony to acquire Magdeburg and Halberstadt.

When Frederick learned of these negotiations and of renewed Franco-Austrian discussions, he felt he must act without delay, especially as 150,000 Russians were already quartered on the frontier of East Prussia. A well-aimed, unexpected blow might paralyse Austria before Russian support could become effective. This would make France draw back—she was still nominally his ally, and had everything to gain by concentrating on her war with England. So he sent Maria Teresa what amounted to an ultimatum. He had learned, he said, that she and the Tsarina designed to attack him. Unless she could assure him that this plan had been abandoned he must consider himself at war with her —it was for her to decide. The Empress and Kaunitz were disconcerted. Saxony was defenceless; the value of the Russian army was doubtful; their own preparations were far from complete. But Maria Teresa was furious at the tone of Frederick's missive: she intimated to him that she was too angry to reply to it. Whereupon the Prussian army crossed the frontier into Saxony (August 1756).

It is usually assumed by historians that the Diplomatic Revolution had already made war inevitable and that Frederick was wise to get his blow in first. But it is arguable that his action turned a mere possibility into a certainty. Whatever discussions had gone on, there was as yet no hard-and-fast agreement between his enemies; and Austria could not attack him without forfeiting the very limited support promised by France in the recent Treaty of Versailles. But his invasion of Saxony changed the whole position, for as King of Poland Augustus was the nominee of Elizabeth, and his daughter was the Dauphine. Furthermore his threat to the dominions of Austria brought the Treaty of Versailles into full effect, and at the same time forfeited his own claims to British support under the Convention of Westminster.

The fact was that he had made two serious miscalculations. He thought that his new associate England would be able to restrain Russia through Hanbury Williams' subsidy-treaty, and he thought that France would see that it was to her advantage to keep out of Germany. These errors were now to bring his kingdom to the verge of extinction.

It was only to be expected that he should prelude his attack on Austria by an occupation of Saxony; for his experience in 1744 had taught him the danger of having a hostile Saxony on his flank and rear. Moreover the Electorate was very accessible from Brandenburg and covered the passes through the Erzgebirge into Bohemia, and he knew that Brühl could not improvise forces capable of resisting the Prussian army. In mid-August he sent the King-Elector polite regrets that stern necessity compelled him to attack the Austrian dominions by way of Saxony, coupled with a promise to hand back the Electorate safe and sound, *after the war*. While Augustus was protesting the Prussians quietly marched in and took possession. Within a fortnight Frederick was in Dresden and Augustus had fled to join his little army, now holding the Elbe gap between the fortresses of Pirna and Konigstein. At Dresden Frederick ransacked the archives (to the great scandal of the rulers of Europe) and found confirmation of the "encirclement-plot" by which he justified his aggression. He took over the government of Saxony for the duration of the war, turning to his own use four-fifths of its revenue and taking great credit to himself that he did not take it all. But when he set out to force the Pirna pass he met with unexpectedly tough opposition. Augustus had only 15,000 ill-clad, ill-armed men, but in a strong position in this "Saxon Switzerland" they obstructed the 60,000 Prussians for an all-important month. Here was another of Frederick's miscalculations—he had forgotten that worms sometimes turn. When he beat back at Lobositz an Austrian relief-force under General Browne, the Saxons had to capitulate and Augustus fled to Poland; but by this time it was too late in the year to embark on the invasion of Bohemia. So Frederick went into winter-quarters in Saxony with the uncomfortable knowledge that by his precipitancy he had given his enemies full notice of his plan of campaign.

Another unexpected result of his move—this time highly favourable to his cause—was the emergence of William Pitt as a British war-minister. Newcastle, having made the Westminster Convention for the security of Hanover, kept beseeching Frederick all through the summer to do nothing rash. England's war with France had opened disastrously at Minorca and Oswego, but so long as Prussia did not start a war in Germany Hanover, at any rate, would be safe. When Frederick, ignoring these pleas, plunged into a sea of trouble, dragging England in with him, Newcastle's colleagues fled the wrath to come; and the King found himself obliged to send for William Pitt, the man to whom the nation instinctively looked to stop the rot.

At once a new spirit began to blow through Whitehall. The King's Speech at the opening of Parliament took the nation into the Government's confidence over foreign affairs, a subject which had hitherto been treated as a high monarchical mystery. A Militia Bill was rushed through to replace the imported Hessians with a Home Guard. Fifteen new regiments were raised, some from the Highland clans which had lately been in rebellion. Tremendous activity broke out in Portsmouth and Chatham dockyards. The colonies were addressed in terms of reassurance and encouragement. Admiral Watson was instructed to help the East India Company to restore the situation in Bengal. Arrangements were made for a Hanoverian-Hessian "Army of Observation" to defend Hanover and Brandenburg from the French.

PRUSSIA SENTENCED TO DEATH. The immediate outcome of Frederick's assault on Saxony was a coalition for the express purpose of tearing his kingdom to pieces.

In January the Imperial Diet placed him under its ban. To be sure its bark was worse than its bite, but its action focussed the jealousy of the lesser German states.

In February Elizabeth of Russia became a party to the Treaty of Versailles (1756), Maria Teresa agreeing to pay her £100,000 a year to keep 120,000 men in the field until Prussia was reduced to the status of Würtemberg or Hesse.

In March Sweden joined the alliance. An attempt to overthrow the oligarchy in favour of King Adolphus Frederick and Queen Ulrica Eleanore (sister of Frederick the Great and a chip of the same block) had broken down, the ringleaders had been executed, and the "Hat" party resumed the tradition of taking French money to pursue a French policy. War was declared on Prussia and an army mobilized at Stralsund to invade Prussian Pomerania.

In May Austria, now secure of Russian support, clinched her alliance with France. They had no enemy in common: Austria wanted to attack Prussia, and France wanted to fight Britain; but the French Government could not deny that Frederick's invasion of Saxony brought the Treaty of Versailles (1756) into play. The country had not yet recovered from the last war; and to plunge into another would ruin the work of Machault, the ablest finance minister of the reign. But the destinies of France were in the hands of a woman whose political ideas were infantile. Madame de Pompadour was wax in the hands of expert statesmen like Kaunitz and adroit diplomatists like Starhemberg. The result was a Second Treaty of Versailles signed on the anniversary of the First (May 1st 1757). This was surely the most sacrificial agreement ever made by a great Power of its own free will. France was to provide 120,000 men and pay Austria a million sterling a year until specified cessions had been secured from Prussia: Silesia for Maria Teresa, Magdeburg and Halberstadt for Augustus, East Prussia for Elizabeth, Pomerania for Sweden. And for France? Merely a part of the Austrian Netherlands as an appanage for King Louis' son-in-law Philip in exchange for Parma—which was to revert to Austria! France was to throw herself heart and soul into a struggle for Austrian objectives, while her own real interest—the overseas contest with Britain—was not even mentioned. It looked like a masterpiece of foreign policy on Kaunitz' part; but in the long run it proved as harmful to Austria as to France.

Still its immediate effect was to close the ring of foes gathering round Frederick. Nobody could suppose that a little kingdom of five million inhabitants could cope for long with the three greatest Powers in Europe, whose combined populations were at least ten times as great. And the first half of the campaign of 1757 seemed to bear out the general expectation of his ruin. Frederick started with a daring four-pronged drive into Bohemia to sweep up the magazines Austria had collected for

THE SEVEN YEARS' WAR 1756-1763

Battlefields..........✗
Fortresses..........★
Sovereign
    States...SAXONY
Provinces....Lusatia

an invasion of Silesia. The Austrian commander-in-chief was our old acquaintance Prince Charles of Lorraine. If he had been able to learn from defeat he should have been a wise general by now, and his brother the Emperor drew up a treatise for him on these lines. But Frederick seldom acted twice alike. Having seized valuable stores, he re-united

his dangerously scattered forces and marched on Prague, where Prince
Charles awaited him in a strong position outside the city, with General
Daun coming up with reinforcements. "The Battle of Prague" (May
1757) has become a synonym for the noisy confusion of war. In mur-
derous, head-on, close-order fighting the Austrians lost 9,000 and the
Prussians 14,000 out of approximately 60,000 on each side; but it was
the Austrians who had to retire, and Frederick was able to proceed
with his siege. He intended after taking Prague to destroy Daun's
force and then march through Moravia and dictate peace at the gates
of Vienna. But Prague held out, defying bombardment and blockade.
A force had to be detached to hold off Daun, and when it failed
Frederick went to do the job himself. The result was Kolin (June
1757) the first disaster of his career. Partly by the errors of his generals
and partly by the inexactness of his orders to them, he lost half his
precious infantry, including 400 officers—the flower of the Prussian
nobility. Luckily for him the Austrians were too busy celebrating the
victory (the Order of Teresa was founded in honour of it) to press it
home, and he was able to get back into Saxony. But he could do nothing
more until he had called up reserves and reconstructed his battalions;
and all the time his enemies were gathering strength.

Throughout the summer Job's tidings kept pouring into his headquarters. The Swedes got across the Piene into Pomerania. The
Imperial Diet was encouraged by Kolin to form an "Army of Execution" against him, and France was sending 30,000 men to join it, and
draw him into central Germany while the Austrians were conquering
Silesia. The Russians invaded East Prussia and destroyed at Gross-
Jägerndorf the weak force which was all that he could spare, thus clearing their road to Berlin. And England, his only ally, lost Pitt, the one
man who could make her support worth having. For the Duke of Cumberland, appointed General of the Army of Observation, refused to go
overseas while Pitt (the rival of his crony Henry Fox) was Secretary of
State; and the old King, taking advantage of a fall in the minister's
popularity due to his failure to improvise victories in three months,
dismissed him. And Cumberland failed to justify his dictatorial
attitude by success. When he came to grips with the French army
under D'Estrées he found himself at a grave disadvantage not only
in numbers but in military capacity. Step by step he was driven back
through Westphalia and across the Weser into Hanover; and when he
tried to make a stand at Hastenbeck he was heavily defeated. D'Estrées
was now superseded, as a result of shabby intrigues at Versailles, by the
Duc de Richelieu. Cumberland continued to retire until, having

reached the Elbe estuary at Stade, he could retire no further. King George, trembling for Hanover, sent his son secret powers to make terms, and Cumberland lost no time in acting on them. By the Convention of Klosterseven (September 1757) he agreed to break up his army, sending the Hessians home while the Hanoverians remained at Stade. The Kingdom of Prussia was thus exposed to attack from the west as well as from the east. There were moments when Frederick gave way to despair. "Oh my brother" he wrote to Prince Henry, "how happy are the dead!"

THE CLASSIC VICTORIES. But he and Prussia were not dead yet. A promise of better things came with the reinstatement of Pitt. For six weeks (with a war on!) the King had vainly sought a combination of Whig grandees that would command the support of Parliament. At last Pitt, knowing that he alone could save England from disaster, made a bargain with Newcastle by which "the Duke gave everything and Mr. Pitt did everything." It was not a very elevated system, but it worked, to the great detriment of England's enemies. Klosterseven was a great shock to Pitt, who only heard of the King's letter to Cumberland a week after it had been sent. He at once protested against it as a breach of faith with Frederick—Richelieu was already sending a dozen regiments to strengthen the French army which was now joining the Imperial forces at Erfurt—and as ruinous to British interests overseas, for if Frederick was overcome the French would be able to concentrate on the struggle in America. He insisted that the Convention be disavowed and the defence of Hanover (covering Brandenburg) resumed. He told Frederick that, as the French Government also disapproved of the terms of the Convention, and had in fact broken them, the Army of Observation would be re-formed if a competent general could be found to command it. Frederick nominated his cousin Ferdinand of Brunswick, a well-trained, capable and staunch officer, who quickly won the confidence of all concerned.

The northern sky began to lighten, too. The Swedes, lacking united and energetic direction, marched across and around their corner of Pomerania without venturing outside it. And the Russians returned to their own side of the Niemen of their own accord. The Tsarina was in poor health, and her heir, the Grand Duke Peter, was a fanatical admirer of Frederick. General Apraxin, the victor of Gross-Jägerndorf, was in no mind to offend the future Tsar; so he retired into Latvia with the excuse that there was nothing for his army to live on in East Prussia.

Meanwhile Frederick was getting his forces into shape for another

9

burst of activity. His enemies outnumbered him by three or four to one, but he had the great advantage of unity in aim and method: he carried the whole policy of Prussia, military and political, under his own shabby three-cornered hat. The Austrians were invading Silesia, but they moved slowly, and he decided he must first bring to battle the Combined Army in central Germany. It was a very mixed affair, three-fifths being French troops under the Prince de Soubise (the Pompadour's latest fancy as a general) while the rest was made up of contingents from a dozen South German Duchies, Bishoprics and Free Cities, commanded by Duke Frederick Joseph of Saxe-Hildburghausen. The discipline of the French suffered from association with such a moth-eaten survival of feudalism, and although Soubise knew that his function was to distract Frederick's attention he was surrounded by aristocratic young officers who were spoiling for a fight. Thus, when the Combined Army made contact with the Prussians near Rossbach in Thuringia, the two generals were argued into marching past them to cut them off from their base. It was a hazardous operation; still, the allied forces were at least double Frederick's, and the movement was screened by a line of low hills. But those hills screened his movements too. When the allied vanguard rounded them they were met with devastating fire from well-placed batteries followed by a sudden cavalry charge. Before the main body of the allied infantry could get into line of battle it was thrown into a helpless jam of men, horses, guns and waggons. Within half an hour of the first cannon-shot the Combined Army was a fugitive rabble (November 1757).

Tremendous was the sensation in Europe. The glory of France had been overthrown by a petty kingdom which had until lately been proud to be her client. It was the first victory of a purely German army over the French—people disregarded the fact that the defeated host was itself largely German. A death-blow by delayed action had been struck at the French monarchy. England was delirious with joy. "The King of Prussia" and "The Protestant Hero" became favourite inn-signs. George Whitefield in his new Tabernacle in the Tottenham Court Road acclaimed the triumph of the true faith over Papist powers of darkness. Parliament doubled Frederick's subsidy.

But Frederick was not out of the wood: he had yet to deal with the Austrians in Silesia. Forty thousand of them were besieging Schweidenitz, one of the chief fortresses of the province, while another 60,000 under Prince Charles were acting as a covering force. And on the way thither the King learned that General Bevern, whom he had sent ahead to keep the enemy engaged, had hesitated so long that Schweidenitz had fallen and the united Austrian armies were now making for Breslau. Bevern managed to get his force into safety across the Oder, but this left the capital defenceless, and despite the King's stern orders it capitulated almost at once. Prince Charles represented himself as releasing faithful Austrian subjects from bondage, and almost all the garrison joined him —only its Prussian officers marched out on the terms of the surrender.

Frederick pressed on, grim and dogged, to hurl himself and his weary army for the second time in a month against an enemy of more than double his strength. Charles and Daun had strung their forces out to cover Breslau and Schweidenitz, and Frederick knew that without a decisive victory Silesia was as good as lost. The night that he came within reach of the Austrian position at Leuthen (December 1757) he relaxed his usual taciturnity, went along the bivouacs chatting to the troops in colloquial German, and smiled when they greeted him as "Old Fred" (*alte Fritz*). It was a well-timed gesture, and on the morrow he and his army excelled themselves because of their confidence in each other. The Austrians were drawn up in orthodox line of battle, but he declined to play the game according to their rules. The high precision of movement made possible by the Prussian drill-book enabled him to take tactical liberties impossible to half-trained troops who needed time to arrange themselves. He marched up to within a couple of miles of their centre, but then, making vigorous feint to his left moved to the right behind some rising ground to re-appear on his enemy's flank, with his guns wheeling into a position from which they could enfilade the Austrian ranks. The Austrian commanders tried to re-form line in the new direction, but their ranks were already overcrowded, and this manœuvre, attempted under fire, merely turned them into a flock of bewildered, panic-stricken sheep. This battle of Leuthen was the one perfect example of Frederick's famous "oblique attack"—the engagement of one of the enemy's wings to the exclusion of the other.

Thus the year which had begun with Prussia in danger of extinction ended with Prussian territory cleared of the enemy, and its King secure of a place among the great captains of history.

FREDERICK HOLDS ON. Frederick half hoped that his victories would win him peace with Austria. He had never aimed at more than holding his own, including Silesia; and after Leuthen the Empress was further from recovering her lost province than ever, while of her allies the French army was demoralized by Rossbach and the Russian Government paralysed by intrigue. But Maria Teresa was as resolute in adversity as Frederick himself. Though the French Government was

too corrupt to wage war successfully, subsidies could still be extorted
from French tax-payers to set a fresh Austrian army in the field.
And Elizabeth of Russia soon showed that she was by no means
done with; she rose from her sick-bed, replaced the appeaser Apraxin
by the Prussophobe Fermor, and made Grand Duke Peter understand
that he must keep himself and his German wife out of politics. So
Frederick had to prepare for a third campaign.

But this time he was relieved of two of his former anxieties. Firstly,
his western approaches were now covered. Pitt had resuscitated the
Army of Observation, and by taking Hanoverians as well as Hessians
into British pay (thereby evading the terms of Klosterseven) he gained
control over the whole force. Never again would King George be able
to work behind his back, or the Hanoverian tail wag the British dog.
And Ferdinand of Brunswick quickly proved his mettle. Within a
month of taking command at Stade he had driven Richelieu back to
the Weser; by April (1758) Richelieu's successor Contades was glad
to retire with his army across the Rhine; and in June the French were
soundly beaten at Crefeld. Secondly, Frederick was now sure of
financial support, for Pitt had promised him a subsidy fixed for the
current year at £650,000. It seemed inconsistent for Pitt, who had made
his name by castigating ministers for hiring German troops to defend
the King's "beggarly electorate," to do that very thing on a larger scale
than ever; but he found, like many in his position, that office alters
opposition's point of view. He could now argue that it was to Britain's
own interest to prevent France from conquering Prussia and so freeing
her hands for the struggle in America—he was "winning Canada on
the plains of Germany," he said; and he kept France mindful of the
need for home defence by "commando raids" on her coast.

Frederick knew that he must expect a Russian invasion in the
summer, but he dared not go to meet it in Poland, where he would be
at the end of a long supply line. So he decided meanwhile to invade
Moravia and take its chief fortress Olmütz, to keep the Austrians busy
trying to recover it while he was fighting their allies. But this plan
went badly adrift. Siege technique had never been his strong point—
his temperament leant to daring strokes and the clash of battle. His
sappers were slow in preparing the lines round Olmütz, Daun was
manœuvring with a fresh army in dangerous proximity, and in June a
great convoy of waggons bringing up food and munitions was cut up
by Croat light infantry and Magyar horsemen at Domstädtl. Frederick
had to raise the siege and return to Bohemia; and by the time he
got there he learned that Fermor was invading Brandenburg leaving a

trail of destruction and desecration behind him, and was now besieging the old fortress-town of Küstrin (of gloomy memories for Frederick). As the Prussian army approached, Fermor drew off his army and took up a position near Zorndorf, where his front was covered by a little river and his flanks by woods. Frederick could not wait: Daun was on the march towards him. So he crossed the Oder and attacked Fermor from the rear. The Prussians, burning to avenge Muscovite atrocities, hurled themselves against a semi-savage enemy with his back to the wall, and the losses in the death-grapple were fearful (August 1758). After it the Russians withdrew into Poland, and Frederick was glad to let them go.

For he had now to re-organize his shattered army and try to relieve Neisse, the key to upper Silesia, which was beleaguered by the Austrians. Daun barred his way thither in an impregnable mountain position near Hochkirch, and for a month Austrians and Prussians remained in a stale-mate. Then old Daun, with unwonted initiative, marched round Frederick's position by night and swept down upon his sleeping camp. The Prussians were badly mauled, and Te Deums were again sung in Vienna. But Daun failed to follow up his success, and Frederick contrived to slip past him and relieve Neisse after all.

When he went into winter quarters in Saxony he could claim that after manifold dangers and difficulties he still held all his own territory (except East Prussia, which he had abandoned for the moment as too distant to defend) and Saxony as well. But his losses in men and material were almost as disastrous in a so-called victory like Zorndorf as in a so-called defeat like Hochkirch. He had no reservoir of reserves to call on, and his tactical methods demanded years of barrack-square drill. Moreover his losses included irreplaceable senior officers like Schwerin and Keith. His depression was further deepened by the death of his favourite sister and correspondent, Wilhelmina of Baireuth. In writing to his brother Henry he expressed a sense of frustration:

There is nothing left but to mingle our tears for our losses. Nothing is come of our campaign, on the one side or the other, but the loss of a great many worthy people and the misery of many poor soldiers crippled for life, the ruin of provinces and the burning down of flourishing towns. . . . Sad fruits of the wickedness and ambition of certain people in power!

But he did not go on to name these ambitious "people in power"; and he secretly instructed his army surgeons not to save the lives of badly wounded soldiers who would have to be supported as pensioners from his Treasury.

THE BEGINNING OF THE END OVERSEAS. The 1758 campaign, which produced only negative results in Europe, cleared the way in North America for the supremacy of the Anglo-Saxon race. The war had opened with gloomy prospects for the colonies. In 1756 neglect of the navy forfeited British mastery at sea; the loss of Oswego had driven British interests from the Lake country; and the Indians of the Five Nations who inhabited all that area became the firm allies of the French. Even in 1757 Pitt's control had been intermittent, and he had not yet learned the lessons of experience in planning a war of outposts in trackless forest. And the new French Governor of Canada, the able and high-spirited Marquis de Montcalm, captured Fort William Henry, which had hitherto protected the backblocks of New England from the Canadians and their Indian allies.

But for the campaign of 1758 Pitt was able to plan with a bolder, freer hand. The King's Speech to Parliament at the beginning of the year was in effect William Pitt's Speech to the Nation, and it contained a significant pronouncement: "The main business of the war is the succour and preservation of America." For such a design control of the sea was essential, and the start which England had made in expansion the previous year was decisive. Already in 1758 Pitt was able to send troops and supplies to America at his pleasure, and to cut the French off from their water-highway into Canada.

Quebec was the key to Canada and Louisburg the key to Quebec. Others before Pitt had seen this, but he was the first with the will and the power to act upon the perception. He sent 20,000 troops—enough, Lord Chesterfield wrote to his son, to eat up all the French in Canada —and they arrived in plenty of time for a full-length campaign. Pitt had the veteran commander, Abercrombie, supported by three youthful officers of high promise—Jeffrey Amherst, Lord Howe, and James Wolfe. The naval side of the operations was in the hands of Boscawen, an authentic member of the line of great British Admirals, who was as familiar with the approaches to the St. Lawrence as with those of the English Channel. Louisburg was duly taken, but the French beat off Abercrombie's frontal assault on Fort Ticonderoga with such heavy losses that any further advance upon Quebec became impossible for that year. Elsewhere the land-forces made valuable gains: Colonel Bradstreet took Fort Frontenac, built by the French nearly a century before to guard the upper St. Lawrence; and General Forbes, having been given the task of clearing up the Ohio situation, set out with 5,000 men from Philadelphia, and fought his way by an unexplored route, carrying all his stores, to Fort Duquesne—only to find that the French, hearing of his approach in such strength, had already evacuated it. He rebuilt and garrisoned it, and renamed it "Fort Pitt" (the present-day Pittsburg) because, as he wrote to the minister, "It was the being animated by your spirit that now makes us masters of the place."

Thus, although Abercrombie's failure had postponed the assault on Quebec, two important and permanent stages had been reached in the conflict. Firstly, Louisburg was not only taken but dismantled. Halifax was henceforth without a rival, and the whole of the maritime provinces became definitely British. Secondly, the Ohio question was answered once and for all. The British colonies were to be free to expand to the limit of their will and capacity.

Events in India were equally prophetic. Even while the rival Companies were agreeing not to allow any war between their respective Governments to affect their amicable competition (p. 245), a new field of conflict was arising, this time in Bengal. The Nawab of that Province, Suraj-ud-daula, at the instigation of the French at Chandernagore, destroyed the English factory at Calcutta and caused the death of 120 civilian survivors in the Black Hole (June 1756). When news of this reached Madras, Clive, just back from his first visit home, decided that the recovery of Calcutta must be the Company's first care; otherwise its position would not be secure even at Madras. The naval squadron under Admiral Watson was the Home Government's only contribution to the operation, but it was a very important one, for it enabled Clive and his little force to sail up the coast unmolested. Having intimidated the Nawab into restoring Calcutta and promising amends for his misdeeds, Clive clinched his advantage by destroying the French station at Chandernagore; and then, feeling that Suraj-ud-daula was too entangled with the French to be trustworthy, he entered into a plot to overthrow him in favour of one of his nobles, who promised vast bribes to the Company and to Clive himself. Clive played Indian politics by Indian rules—with corruption, treachery and falsehood; but he won what he wanted more than a reputation for fair play— domination of north-eastern India. At Plassey (June 1757) Suraj-ud-daula's 50,000 (including some French) fled in such panic from Clive's 3,000 (including some British) that there were very few casualties on either side; yet this was one of the decisive battles of modern history, for it settled that Britain and not France should one day become paramount Power in India. And the spoils of India contributed largely to the capital with which Britain carried through the Industrial Revolution.

CHAPTER TWENTY-SEVEN

THE SEVEN YEARS' WAR (PART II)

1759–1763

THE outstanding features of the second half of the war were Frederick's dogged courage in withstanding the assaults of enemies whose strength must have crushed him if it had ever been co-ordinated; and the founding of the British Empire by sea-power and the genius of William Pitt.

PITT's *ANNUS MIRABILIS*. During the close season between the campaigns of 1758 and 1759 there was a vital change in the French war-direction. It was high time. The country's fortunes had never fallen so low since the Hundred Years' War. Her troops had been worsted in Germany, in America and in India; her overseas trade was destroyed, and her treasury was empty. The Abbé Bernis, who as Foreign Minister had the general direction of affairs, was appalled at the effects of the policy he had undertaken. He now urged the King and the Pompadour to leave Prussia to be dealt with by Austria and Russia, and to concentrate on the war with England. But though Louis had the sense to see the wisdom of this course he lacked the energy of will to impose it on the Marquise, who was still under the spell of Maria Teresa's flattery. So, complaining that his head was in a whirl, Bernis got leave to retire with a cardinal's hat. His successor, the Duc de Choiseul, had been ambassador at Vienna, where he had just clinched the Austrian alliance by the betrothal of the heir to the throne to the little archduchess Marie Antoinette. The governmental system of the French monarchy no longer produced great statesmen, and Choiseul was probably as good a choice as could have been made, for he was an intelligent little man, abounding with ideas and self-confidence and energy. Though a keen supporter of the Austrian alliance, he saw that the obligations which France had undertaken in the second Treaty of Versailles severely handicapped her in the vital struggle with England. Her best hope in that conflict would be a renewal of the Family Compact with Spain, the only other Power with a navy. There was no hope of this in the lifetime of King Ferdinand, but that did not seem likely to last much longer; and meanwhile Choiseul induced the Empress to agree to a Third Treaty of Versailles (March 1759) which halved her subsidy, cancelled the undertaking to send a French army to

264

central Germany, and dropped all mention of the partitioning of Prussia. The money thus saved Choiseul proposed to spend on a great scheme—nothing less than an invasion of Britain. The French navy, instead of vainly trying to cope with the British all over the world, was to be concentrated in home waters. Armies—50,000 for England and 15,000 for Scotland—were mobilized near the north-eastern ports. Flat-bottomed invasion-barges were built at Dunkirk, Le Havre and Rochefort.

What Pitt meant to England was abundantly shown by the response to this threat. He sent one squadron under Hawke to blockade Brest, another to Gibraltar to prevent the Toulon squadron's egress into the Altantic. But not a ship or a regiment would he withdraw from the operations already planned in Germany and America; and the fruits of his prescient intrepidity were reaped in one field after another in the course of the year.

The harvest began on August 1st, when at Minden Ferdinand shattered a formidable French thrust against Hanover, thereby making that Electorate and Frederick's western flank secure for the rest of the war. A fortnight later Boscawen destroyed the Toulon squadron in a running fight which ended with the beaching of the last four surviving ships near Lagos, where they were captured or destroyed without regard for Portugal's theoretical neutrality. This compelled Choiseul to drop the English part of his invasion scheme; and the Scottish part was now ruined by the fact that though he was permitted to make plans the choice of instruments to execute them lay with the King's mistress. It was characteristic of the régime that Conflans, whom she nominated to command the fleet, was made a Marshal of France because naval rank was beneath his aristocratic dignity; and that the Duc d'Aiguillon, commander of the troops, refused to take them from Morbihan to embark at Brest, where he would be subordinate to Conflans. This brought ruin on the whole scheme. For while sailing to Morbihan Conflans had the misfortune to encounter heavy weather—and Admiral Hawke. He took refuge in rockbound Quiberon Bay, never supposing that his enemy would hazard his ships by sailing in after him before a westerly gale. He little knew Hawke, or the spirit breathed into the services by Pitt. The destruction of the French fleet was complete. Invasion was henceforth out of the question; Quiberon (November 1759) was the Trafalgar of the Seven Years' War.

Meanwhile the British Government and nation had just been relieved of anxiety about the campaign in Canada. Pitt had planned a three-fold attack on Quebec, the headquarters of the French Government in

9*

America. Twenty ships of the line were to escort 10,000 troops under Wolfe from Louisburg up the St. Lawrence; 12,000 New England militiamen with a stiffening of regulars were to approach the fortress via Lake Champlain under Amherst; and a mixed force of British and Redskins (convinced by the events of 1758 that the British were going to win after all) was to take Niagara and join the others by way of Montreal. British superiority was overwhelming, both in men and munitions. In April Montcalm had appealed to his Government for reinforcements, but Choiseul was entirely taken up with his invasion project—perhaps he reckoned that even if Canada were lost he would recover it by the conquest of England. In any case, British sea-power made it probable that any help he sent would be intercepted. But the weight of the odds against the French could not be appreciated in England. Quebec seemed impregnable; the ancillary forces were held up, and for months it seemed that Wolfe was baffled. Then came the thrilling story of the scramble up the cliffs, the battle on the Plains, and the Happy Warrior's death in the hour of victory. More difficulties lay ahead, but the instinct of the British people told them truly that this engagement, though a mere skirmish in respect of numbers, made one of the great decisions of modern history. It made a fitting climax to the exciting four months from August to December 1759, when as Horace Walpole said, the bells in the steeples were worn out with ringing for British victories.

A BLACK DAY FOR THE PRUSSIAN ARMY. The one discordant note in the rejoicing was the calamitous situation of our ally. Each year Frederick had to face his mighty antagonists with forces reduced both in quantity and quality. Of the peerless army with which he had marched into Saxony in August 1756, not a quarter remained. The ranks were filled with half-trained recruits, of whom a large proportion were not his own subjects, but had been crimped by his press-gangs in Mecklenburg, Pomerania and Saxony; and even with these he could raise only 100,000 to meet 120,000 Austrians, 140,000 Russians and a new *Reichsarmee* of 40,000 men. He had opened each of the earlier campaigns with a bold attack, but he was now forced back on to an uncongenial defensive. He wrote to his brother from his grim winter-quarters in Breslau:

Flashes of my old spirit appear from time to time, but the sparks are quickly douted because there is no longer the fire which used to keep them alight. If you saw me you would see hardly a trace of what I used to be—you would see an old man, his hair turning grey, half his teeth gone, and all his old fire and animation. . . . My great difficulty is that whereas in former years our enemies have never worked together, and I was able to strike them down one after another; this year they are going to attack at the same time. Small miracles will not save us—we must have angels of death to destroy armies, fire from heaven to wipe out hordes of barbarians. The months of August and September will be critical.

His forecast proved right. For three months the Austrians in Silesia eluded all his attempts to bring them to battle before the return of the Russians. In June the latter under their new general Soltikov invaded Brandenburg again and captured Frankfurt-on-Oder. Frederick strove to prevent an Austrian force under Loudoun from joining him; but after marches which he himself described as "dreadful and cruel" in torrid heat, he failed. The Allies, with nearly double his numbers, took up a strong position at Kunersdorf (August 1759), just outside Frankfurt. He could not await a better opportunity of attacking them— Daun and the main Austrian army was marching north as if against Berlin. His assault, carried through with the cast-iron persistence of Prussian discipline, became the bloodiest massacre of modern war. After six hours of it half the Prussian army lay dead or wounded on the field, and a well-timed cavalry charge shattered the survivors. The King made frantic efforts to stem the rout—"My children, will you desert your father?" "Dogs, would you live for ever?" "Will no cursed bullet hit me?" When at the end of the day he rode from the field, dazed by disaster, not 5,000 troops remained under his orders. Turning over the command to his only surviving general, he made his way to a castle in the neighbourhood, where he gave himself up to despair. His armies had been defeated before, but at Kolin and Hochkirch their discipline had preserved them from demoralization. There was now nothing to shield Prussia from the spoliation and dismemberment which he always said he would not live to see.

But the Russians and Austrians had no common aim, and no plan to exploit their victory. The moment it was won they went their different ways. Frederick began to realize that all was not lost after all. The remnants of his army were already rallying round their colours, and soon he was in a position to march against the Russians who were now trying to establish themselves in Silesia. Soltikov, a mere courtier-general, was in no mood to fight another Kunersdorf to win the province for Austria, and moved back into Poland. And when Frederick turned to drive the Austrians out of Saxony, he found Daun equally unwilling to face the music. The French ambassador pointed out to the Austrian

Government that it was useless to overrun Frederick's lands or take his fortresses—his strength did not consist in these but in himself and the spirit which he breathed into his soldiers. Only by destroying him and them could Silesia be recovered. But such was the respect he inspired, even with a crippled army, that when Daun held a council of war at Dresden all the twenty-two officers present were for avoiding battle, and if necessary evacuating Saxony.

The survival of Prussia after Kunersdorf was, as Frederick wrote to his brother, the Miracle of the House of Hohenzollern. He suffered another set-back when a force which he sent ahead to press the Austrian retirement from Saxony was surrounded and cut to pieces at Maxen. But even then Daun did not feel safe until he was back in Bohemia; and the campaign ended with Frederick still in possession of Saxony.

NEW KINGS AND NEW POLICIES. The campaign of 1760 was a rather dull tailpiece to the excitements of 1759. The capture of Montreal completed the subjection of the French in Canada; the battle of Wandewash and the fall of Pondicherry completed their discomfiture in India. In Europe Frederick had more difficulty than ever to keep his footing in the swirling tide of adversity. He had to debase both money and man-power still further, melting down the annual bullion from England with its own weight of copper, and forcibly enlisting everything within reach that looked like a man. After Maxen, when 15,000 laid down their arms without firing a shot, people said that the morale of the Prussian army was broken, and that Frederick's enemies had him beaten at last. But they were wrong. He had not been present at Maxen: wherever he went he animated the most unlikely human material with his own unquenchable courage. Patriotism could not be expected in such a mixed array, but it was replaced by the spell of the Great Captain evoking the fighting-spirit latent in human nature. It was seen in two more carnages during 1760. When the Austrians attacked him on the march near Liegnitz, much as he had attacked the Franco-Imperial army at Rossbach, they were bloodily repulsed; but his most desperate efforts in marching and fighting failed to expel them and the Russians from Silesia, or to prevent a detached force of them from raiding Berlin and exacting a ransom of two million thalers— nearly half the amount of his English subsidy for the year. Yet once again he contrived to restore the equilibrium before the end of the year. Daun tried to settle down for the winter on the Elbe, between him and his home bases; but he fell on them at Torgau (November 1760). By an ill-advised variation of the oblique approach he divided his outnumbered forces to attack in front and rear simultaneously. He and Ziethen failed to synchronize their movements, and he was only saved from disaster because Daun was too afraid of him to emerge from the defensive. A third of the Prussians were killed, but they had made the Austrians glad to shut themselves up at Dresden, leaving all the rest of Saxony still in Frederick's hands. Thus the situation at the end of 1760 was, in a military sense, scarcely changed from that at the end of 1759.

In the political sphere, however, the year 1760 marked the beginning of the end of the war. The death of Ferdinand VI, in October 1759, caused a revolution in the foreign policy of Spain. For the past decade that country had stood outside European affairs, Ferdinand having no mind for anything but his Italian Opera[1] and his Portuguese queen. But he was now succeeded by his half-brother the "Baby Carlos" who had been established first in Parma, then in Naples by his mother the Termagant. Carlos left his Neapolitan throne to his third son, taking his second with him to Spain as heir to that kingdom. (The eldest was an imbecile.) He also brought with him a resentment against England that had been fermenting ever since an English admiral had bullied him into desertnig family interests in Italy during the Austrian Succession War (p. 231).

His accession was a great stroke of luck for Choiseul. The Austrian alliance had become a sore embarrassment for France. Russia and Austria had hopes of Prussian spoils—they had just renewed their alliance for another twenty-five years with the proviso that if Austria recovered Silesia, Russia was to have East Prussia, to be exchanged with Poland for the Ukraine. But France stood to gain nothing in Europe and to lose everything overseas. Choiseul now had his hoped-for chance to balance the Versailles Treaty with Austria by renewing the Family Compact with Spain. One of the first acts of the new King was to take up long-standing Spanish grievances against England—the depredations of her privateers in the Caribbean, and the encroachments of her traders along the Main. Pitt, sensing that France and Spain were drawing together, replied with suave assurances, but he was not in the least intimidated. On the contrary. Since Lagos and Quiberon Bay the British fleet had been more than a match for the French and Spanish combined; and though France had no more overseas possessions to lose, Spain had plenty.

But in October (1760) events were given another new turn by the

---

[1] Under the management of the famous male soprano Farinelli, who sang the same four songs to the King every evening for ten years.

death of old George II; for the twenty-three-years-old grandson who succeeded him was a complete contrast to him. George III was pious and
of highly respectable private life; he spoke no German, never went to
Hanover, and "gloried in the name of Britain." Under the guidance of
his mother, the daughter of a minor German prince, and of his tutor, a
narrow-minded Scottish laird who now became Earl of Bute, he had
imbibed the Toryism expounded in Bolingbroke's "Patriot King."[1]
According to this famous pamphlet, published in 1749, all the evils of
the British state were due to the system which enabled a faction to
monopolize power by bartering Government favours for votes. The
only remedy was a restoration of the Royal power to its position before
the accession of George I. There was much to be said for this point of
view; Pitt himself had always condemned the borough-mongering and
the manipulation of "patronage" by which people like the Pelhams and
the Russells ruled the country. But to end the system the young King
would have to get rid of Pitt. A ministry forced on the Crown by
ignorant public passion was as incompatible with Patriot Kingship as
one nominated by corrupt parliamentary faction. But nobody except
Pitt could run the war; so the logical conclusion was that it must be
wound up as soon as possible, despite the fact that it was carrying the
country to new heights of greatness. At his very first Council the King
spoke of the war as "bloody and expensive," and when he made Bute
Pitt's colleague as Secretary of State it was obvious that a struggle for
mastery of the Government was in progress, and that with this mastery
was bound up Britain's continuance of the war.

THE FALL OF PITT. For a time Pitt held his own. When Choiseul
threw out peace feelers in the spring of 1761 he kept control of the
negotiations, and continued to prosecute the war with the utmost
vigour, launching attacks on Belle-Isle (off Quiberon) and Martinique.
The Belle-Isle affair was no smash-and-grab raid; 10,000 picked troops
and fourteen ships of the line were employed; and when the island had
been mastered sea-power enabled the British forces to hold it for the rest
of the war, as something to barter for Minorca. In the peace-talks Pitt
demanded the whole of Canada, half the West Indies, a monopoly of
the Newfoundland fisheries, and the restoration to Frederick of his
Rhenish duchies. Choiseul demurred over the fisheries and over the
Duchies (which he had promised to Austria), but Pitt was adamant over

---

[1] That George III was actually brought up on it as a text-book is a legend without
historical foundation. It certainly would have been quite outside the comprehension
of the Princess; and there is no evidence that she ever actually exhorted her son to
"Be a King."

both. The fisheries were of greater economic value (about half-a-million sterling yearly) than all Canada, and were an invaluable training-ground for seamen; and he scorned to buy good terms for England at the expense of her hard-pressed ally. Pitt became convinced that Choiseul was playing for time while he renewed the Family Compact; and as a matter of fact it was signed the very day that he broke off the negotiations over a demand of Choiseul's for concessions to Spain (August 1761).

The Franco-Spanish connection became one of the dominating factors in European affairs for the next half-century. In this form, it guaranteed the possessions of all branches of the Bourbon family (in France, Spain, Naples and Parma), and pledged the Kings of France and Spain to stand together in war and peace. The King of Spain was to declare war on England on or before May 1st, 1762; both parties were to put pressure on Portugal not to allow England to use her ports to their detriment. Only existing possessions were guaranteed—Spain did not bind herself to fight for the recovery of those which France had already lost.

Pitt knew all this—his secret service was always highly efficient; and he realized that Spain was only delaying a declaration of war until her annual treasure-fleet arrived from Panama to finance France's next campaign as well as her own. He laid his information before the cabinet, saying that he proposed to anticipate matters by seizing the galleons and attacking Havana and Manila, Spain's chief centres in West and East Indies respectively. He pointed out that the navy was eating its head off, now that France no longer threatened invasion and Canada was won. Immense gains were in prospect both in trade and in bargaining assets, and all possible rivalry to Britain as a world-power would be eliminated. But to his amazement the other members of the cabinet demurred. They had long chafed at his haughty demeanour in taking the whole conduct of the war upon himself. Now at last the covert opposition of the King, expressed in the cabinet by Bute, nerved them to make a stand. They argued that war with Spain was not inevitable, and that the country could not stand any more expensive adventures. For three days the issue was in doubt. The other ministers dreaded to part with the greatest war-minister Britain ever had with the war still on; and Pitt longed to be able to round it off with a triumphant peace on his own terms. But at last a complete deadlock was reached, and Pitt resigned (October 1761).

Events quickly justified the line he had taken. The moment the silver-fleet touched Cadiz Spain broke off relations, and in January 1762

Bute (now chief minister) had to declare war on him. Pitt's war-plans were now put into operation three months late, but they were so well laid that success was quick and complete. Havana and Manila both fell, and so did four more of the French West Indian islands.

But Britain had nothing to gain by continuing the war. She had won all she could win, and the only obstacle to peace was our ally's refusal, despite his hopeless prospects, to sacrifice an inch of territory. His grip on Saxony was shaken by the loss of Dresden; the Russians were in occupation of East Prussia; the Swedes were in Prussian Pomerania; Silesia was slipping from his grasp—its chief fortress, Schweidenitz, was taken in October (1761). His material resources were at an end, his country stripped bare of men, money, animals, food-stuffs—there was scarcely seed-corn left for 1762. Although the campaign of 1761 brought no great battles, it wore his army down to 30,000 bedraggled and exhausted men and boys. But that army still had its vital spark— the haggard, grim little King. Each campaign seemed to put five years on his age, he was often crippled by gout, and he treasured the precious phial which could release him from the burden of life if the very worst came to the very worst; but always he forced heart and nerve to carry him through when, as the poet says, there was nothing left except the will which says "Hold on." At the end of 1761 he reached the nadir of his fortunes. His only hope of raising a force to keep off annihilation when the fighting began in 1762 lay in the British subsidy, and now even this failed him.

For Bute saw in this subsidy his one means of compelling Frederick to "be reasonable"; and whatever may be said in favour of his peace-policy, his method of pursuing it left a stain on Britain's reputation for good faith which has hardly been wiped out to this day.[1] When, in November 1761, Frederick authorized his ambassador to sign the annual subsidy-treaty, Bute demanded the deletion of the clause which forbade the parties to negotiate for peace. Frederick growled an assent, provided that Bute insisted on the return of his Rhenish provinces. But then Bute (having by this time a Spanish war on his hands) refused to renew the treaty at all, proposing in lieu thereof a mere parliamentary grant; and meanwhile asked for information about Frederick's plans for 1762 and about his terms for peace with Russia and Austria. We are not surprised to learn that Mitchell, the British ambassador at Berlin, was taken with an illness which prevented him from delivering this message in person.

---

[1] Much play is made with it in German text-books. Bismarck, William II and Hitler all threw it up against Britain.

Thus the indirect result of the deaths of King Ferdinand VI and King George II was to bring Frederick face to face with utter and irretrievable ruin.

STRANGE EVENTS IN RUSSIA. From this prospect he was saved as by a miracle—the death on January 5th, 1762, of Elizabeth, Empress of Russia. There was nothing miraculous about this event in itself: she was only fifty-two, but a life of unbridled self-indulgence had long since wrecked her health. The miracle was that it should have befallen just at this moment. For her nephew Peter of Holstein, who now became Tsar, was a fanatical admirer of the King of Prussia. Within a few hours of his accession he sent off couriers ordering his armies to cease fire, and informing Maria Teresa of his withdrawal from the war. Frederick declared that the news made him twenty years younger. He sent an envoy to St. Petersburg to congratulate the new Tsar on his accession, with full authority to treat for peace. Peter at once agreed to evacuate Prussia, and, after some hesitation, to guarantee the recovery of Silesia —an undertaking which implied war with Austria.

All this was another worry for Bute, since it made Frederick less disposed than ever to make concessions. So he hinted to Galitzin, the Russian ambassador, that if his new master really wanted to hasten peace he would do well to join in putting pressure on Frederick to restore at least part of Silesia to Maria Teresa. This was of course an act of treachery towards an ally who had for five years struggled heroically against odds while England was building up a world-empire. But it was worse than a crime, it was a blunder. For Peter's adoration of Frederick was known to all; it was inevitable that he should pass the communication on to Berlin. Frederick, now no longer in such desperate need of English money, put no restraint on his anger and disgust. The Anglo-Prussian alliance turned to an estrangement which cost England dear in her own hour of need, fifteen years later. And the deed did not delay by an hour the conclusion of a Russo-Prussian peace (May 1762), followed by a military alliance.

Bute showed the same lack of information, tact, and common honesty in a similar proposal at Vienna. Disregarding his negotiations with France, he suggested that Austria should renew the old alliance and join in throwing the Bourbons out of Italy. Kaunitz, suspecting a trap, acidly replied that as he did not understand these proposals he could not reply to them.

Sweden soon followed Russia's example. The "Hats" had joined the chase in 1756 hoping for a bit of the skin as soon as the three great hunters had slain the bear. But, like everybody else, they thought it would be over quickly. Their French subvention was quite insufficient to keep them going for a long war, and they were practically bankrupt; and now it appeared that the bear was not going to be killed after all. Queen Ulrica had the pleasure of seeing her insolent opponents come begging her to intercede for them with her illustrious brother. Frederick consented for her sake to grant terms based on the *status quo ante bellum* (May 1762, at Hamburg).

Peter III had a short reign. Though a man of thirty-four he had the mind of a self-willed child—a result perhaps of repression under his formidable aunt; and within a few weeks he had affronted all the chief elements of his people. He gave offence to the military by substituting Holsteiners for the Imperial Guards, and by introducing Prussian discipline; to the clergy by confiscating Church lands—rushing in where even Peter the Great had feared to tread; and to the whole nation by his pro-Prussianism. And he had a wife. Sophie of Anhalt-Zerbst (she took the name Catherine on admission to the Orthodox Church) was one of the most remarkable women that ever lived. Brought from a poverty-stricken little German court, an uneducated, unsophisticated girl of fifteen, to marry the heir to the greatest empire in the world, she developed a keen intelligence and a lust for power born of innate consciousness of the capacity to use it. Fortune had now placed within her grasp a unique opportunity for domination. She had given her husband ample cause for jealousy; and now that he was Tsar he was talking of divorcing her and marrying his ugly and stupid mistress. Catherine saw a prospect of being immured for life in a convent, or perhaps packed off to Siberia, unless she got her blow in first. She had always made a parade of Orthodox piety and Russian patriotism, and this pose now stood her in good stead. She entered into a conspiracy with a group of officers and courtiers led by her latest lover, Gregory Orlov, to dethrone her husband in favour of her infant son, with herself as Regent. But she soon contrived to change this design in favour of her own direct succession. The Tsar brought his offences to a climax by insisting on a war against Denmark to avenge wrongs done to his father. On the very day that he was to set out with his army, Catherine drove out from the Peterhof before daybreak and went to the Cathedral, where the archbishop proclaimed her Empress in her own right. The Council and the leading officials did homage to her, and she published a manifesto declaring that her purpose was to protect the Church from Lutheranism and the State from alliance with Russia's hereditary foe. Peter made no resistance, but meekly abdicated on a promise of fair treatment. He was hustled off to a lonely castle where a fortnight later he died—of a sudden colic, it was announced. There was no inquest.

The anti-German sentiments of Catherine's manifesto were mere window-dressing. She was by nature an opportunist, unaffected by irrational impulses for or against anybody or anything. Having nothing to gain by going on with the war, she withdrew from it. Her troops continued to evacuate Pomerania and East Prussia as Peter had promised; those which he had sent to Silesia to fight for Frederick were withdrawn again into Poland.

Frederick was disappointed, but he had much to be thankful for. He could now concentrate on recovering Schweidenitz. At Reichenbach he defeated the Austrians' last attempt to hold him off, and before the end of the campaign the fortress was back in his hands. His brother Henry was equally successful in Franconia, inflicting a defeat on the reconstructed Imperial Army at Freiberg which compelled the Diet to withdraw from the war. And Ferdinand of Brunswick rounded off his achievements in the west by capturing Cassel.

THE PEACE OF PARIS. Meanwhile Bute was pressing on towards peace. He had been head of the Government since May, when the unfortunate Duke of Newcastle was edged out of the position to which he had devoted a long life and a large fortune. He had stood up as bravely as he dared for fair play to Frederick, but all that was over now, and the King's favourite controlled the patronage which was the main source of political power. Bute and Choiseul were equally eager for a quick settlement, and for similar reasons: the dread lest public feeling should push Pitt back into office. (Choiseul said he would rather be a galley-slave than conduct any more negotiations with Pitt.) Spain demurred at first, having hopes of conquering Portugal and no first-hand experience of the British navy. But a stiffening of British troops (under Colonel Burgoyne, whom we shall meet later in less happy circumstances) helped Portugal to put up an unexpectedly stout resistance; and engagements in the East and West Indies made the Spanish Government sadder but wiser as to the capacity of the British fleet. And so in November (1762) a settlement was pencilled at Fontainebleau. Britain was to annex Canada, all the disputed lands east of the Mississippi, and half the West Indies, France retaining only some other West Indian islands, together with fishing rights off Newfoundland which caused disputes right down to the *Entente Cordiale* of 1905. In Africa the little island of Goree was restored to France, but Britain retained Senegal, the chief entrepot for the slave-trade. In India France got back her "factories," but was to keep no military establishments; and she exchanged Minorca for Belle-Isle. Spain ceded Florida to recover Havana, and got back Manila in return for a promise (never fulfilled) of a ransom of half a million sterling. She also received from France "Louisiana," the land beyond the Mississippi, as compensation for having to abandon the hope of recovering Gibraltar. France and Britain withdrew their troops from Germany, Bute making no stipulation about Frederick's Rhenish provinces.

Fortunately for Frederick, Austria was as exhausted as Prussia. France and Russia had deserted Maria Teresa; the action of France in making terms with England was particularly galling after the Empress had so high-mindedly rejected Bute's advances. The withdrawal of French subsidies had already compelled her to demobilize part of her forces, and now the *Reichsarmee* had been disbanded. It was an agonizing grief to have to renounce Silesia for the third time; but there was nothing else for it. Negotiations at Hubertusburg ended in a treaty signed a few days after that of Paris. It consisted of 157 Articles which really amounted to a restoration of the pre-war position.

It certainly could not be said of this war as of the last that it settled nothing. In the first place, England came out of it indisputably *the* world Power and *the* naval Power; and although France, sore and resentful, succeeded in shaking Britain's position fifteen years later she could not reverse the verdict. Pitt had founded the Empire cheaply, both in blood and wealth. India had cost eighteen British lives at Plassey, 180 at Wandewash. Some thousands died in the winning of Canada; but the total was not a tithe of the casualties suffered by Prussia, or Austria, or Russia, in any one of their numerous engagements. And though the National Debt was doubled, the effect of this was negligible compared with the terrible privations which the war imposed on all the continental belligerents. For Britain's navy had swept her trade rivals from the oceans and ports of the world, and made London the centre of world-trade.[1] On the debit side, the desertion of Frederick confirmed the legend of "Perfidious Albion." Three times in fifty years[2] we had

---

[1] One great reason for this supremacy in world-commerce was the circumstance that in Britain the seat of Government was a great port, and the hub of the nation's trade, whereas France was ruled from Versailles, 100 miles from the sea. Even the water for its fountains—little was required for any other purpose—had to be brought ten miles; the coarse voices of colonists, traders and merchants were never allowed to penetrate such elegant purlieus, and there was no public body in which they could make themselves heard.

[2] In 1711–13, in 1733–4; and in 1761–3.

left an ally in the lurch, and each time we had to pay the penalty of diplomatic isolation.

Secondly, the war established Prussia as a north German Protestant rival to south German Catholic Austria. The age-old Holy Roman Empire, already covered with little cracks, now had a fissure which was to widen until the fabric disintegrated. And Hapsburg prestige suffered a corresponding diminution. Maria Teresa, despite powerful allies, had been unable to tear Silesia from the upstart, and had been excluded from the Peace of Paris.

Thirdly, the war had set the French Monarchy moving fast down the road to ruin. France's entry into it had been senseless, and she came out of it with her trade ruined, her empire lost, her army discredited, her navy destroyed, and her expenditure for debt-service alone greater than her revenue. The writing was on the wall!

CHAPTER TWENTY-EIGHT

REASON AND ROMANCE

WE have now to hold up the narration of events to consider how the influx of new ideas released aspirations to liberty, equality and brotherhood which, just after the end of our period, disrupted the Old Régime altogether. We shall see this new spirit permeating the arts and sciences as well as political and social ideas.

THE SOVEREIGNTY OF REASON. The influence of the English Revolution of 1688, confirmed by the Hanoverian Succession in 1714, was now felt by educated people all over Europe. A political revolution, carried through without bloodshed or violence, and safeguarding parliamentary rule, religious toleration, freedom of speech and equality before the Law, aroused general astonishment and admiration. And it drew attention to the writings of its oracle, John Locke. The quintessence of eighteenth-century "Enlightenment" is to be found in his three famous books: the theory that ideas do not arise spontaneously in our minds, but result from the report of our senses (set forth in the *Essay on the Human Understanding*), the notion that government derives its authority from the consent of the governed (in the *Treatise on Civil Government*), and the view that religious belief is a matter for the individual soul (in the *Letters on Toleration*). And underlying all this is a belief that human Reason is sufficient, if applied resolutely and dispassionately, to sweep away all the decaying lumber left behind by the defunct civilization of the Middle Ages, leaving the ground clear for a new, higher and happier future.

France being the centre of European culture and French its universal language, the most famous apostles of the new spirit were nearly all Frenchmen. But they got most of their ideas, directly or indirectly, from England. Montesquieu, Voltaire, Rousseau, Diderot, Turgot, Buffon, Quesnay, the Rolands, Helvétius, Lafayette, Mirabeau, all crossed the Channel to see the political and social liberty in its home.

Of these visitors the first to make a mark on educated Europe were Montesquieu (1689–1755) and Voltaire (1694–1778). Montesquieu's *Lettres Persanes* (1721), purporting to be correspondence between Persians sojourning in Paris and their friends in Tehran, were a satire on French manners and institutions—a type of literature common in England, but a startling novelty on the Continent. Then, after a quarter of a century of unremitting study, enquiry, travel and thought, appeared his *L'Esprit des Lois* (1748), which purports to show the connection of each country's laws with its climate, its forms of government, its religion and its commerce. A notable feature was its eulogy of England's separation of government into three independent factors—the legislative, the executive, and the judicial. This separation, he argues, is the surest guarantee of liberty—and in France the three functions were under the direct control of the Crown. Montesquieu misinterpreted what he saw in England. Whatever Parliament, Ministry and Bench may be in theory, they were not, and are not, independent of each other in actual fact. But the book made a widespread, profound and lasting impression on thinking people all over Europe. Twenty-four editions of it were sold in two years, and it continued to be read and discussed, despite the ban of Church and Parlement, right down to the Revolution.

Even more influential, because more varied in its attack on the ideas of the Old Régime, was the writing of François Marie Arouet, better known by his pen-name Voltaire. Indeed, he has been called "the most puissant man of letters that ever lived." And he owed even more to England than did Montesquieu, for he drew from it the ideas which inspired his life's work. The circumstances in which he came to this country, a fugitive from the régime which it was his destiny to shake, are illuminating. The son of a lawyer, he caught the attention of Regency society by clever talking and versifying and playwriting. But when a dissipated young nobleman made public jest of his adopting a pseudonym he replied that he would rather invent a new name than tarnish an old one. A few nights later, while dining with the Duc de Sully, he was summoned to the front door, where he was dragged into the street and thrashed by three hired bullies, whose employer directed operations from a coach-window, admonishing them not to hit his head, as something good might yet come out of it. (This considerateness, we learn, drew warm approval from the bystanders.) What shocked Voltaire even more than the outrage itself was that his aristocratic patrons merely laughed at the notion that a person of humble origin could nurse a grievance against a person of their own class. And when, having taken fencing-lessons, he challenged his assailant, the latter obtained a *lettre de cachet* consigning him for some months to the Bastille.

Thus he came to England predisposed to admire a free country. He learned to appreciate English literature, not only the contemporary

Augustans, Pope, Swift and Addison, but Milton and even Shakespeare —though the latter seemed uncouth to one brought up on the traditions of Corneille and Racine. He was astonished to see persons of his own social status becoming ministers and ambassadors, and Sir Isaac Newton buried in Westminster Abbey. Above all he absorbed through every pore the ideas of John Locke. When he went back to France his *Lettres sur les Anglais* (1734) portrayed to his astonished compatriots (who had supposed that "everyone not French went on all fours and ate hay") a land where everyone was allowed to get to heaven his own way, where all men were legally equal, where no one was exempt from taxation except the poor; where "the peasant's feet are not tortured by sabots, he eats white bread, he is warmly clad, and is not afraid to re-roof his house lest his taxes be raised."

The *Lettres* were publicly burned, and Voltaire had to flee again; but he had begun a craze for all things English. He was already on bad terms with the Catholic Church owing to his biting sarcasm over its treatment of Adrienne Lecouvreur, who, dying at the height of her beauty and fame, was buried in quicklime in waste-ground because she was an actress. This incident heated his hatred of ignorance, fanaticism, tyranny and cruelty into burning passion. *Ecrasez l'infâme* became his watchword, and for the rest of his long life hardly a day passed but he fought clericalism with his deadly pen. Besides his purely literary work —twenty-eight tragedies, seventeen comedies, the *Henriade* (an epic with Henri IV as hero), books on Charles XII and Louis XIV which set new standards in historical writing—he published thousands of pamphlets, leaflets, pasquinades, epigrams, cautionary tales, open letters. When Calas, an ailing elderly Protestant, was condemned by Church courts for hanging his strong and vigorous son to prevent his turning Catholic, and was broken on the wheel (1762), Voltaire agitated incessantly for two-and-a-half years until he compelled the authorities to reverse the verdict and restore the family to their property. And this was only one of several such cases.

Voltaire was no constructive thinker, being merely, as he himself said *un grand démolisseur*. But demolition was a necessary preliminary to construction. His ridicule acted on the Old Régime like the fresh air that crumbles a mummy to dust when its case is opened. Bitterly as he attacked the Church he was no atheist; but God, in his view, had put into the heart of man a sense of right and wrong by which he could grow towards the light. He did not want to destroy the Church of eighteenth-century France, or even to disestablish it—merely to make it like the Church of England, dominant but not exclusive. Again, ardently as he opposed caste-privileges, serfdom, and arbitrary punishments, he was no republican. The monarchy would do well enough as it stood, if it would but make good laws and keep them.

These views made him an object of hatred and fear to those who battened on the existing evils in Church, State and Society; but no literary man ever enjoyed greater fame in his lifetime. After the Berlin episode (p. 241) he settled at Ferney, where he could slip over into Switzerland whenever his enemies became threatening. There for twenty years of active-minded old age, he poured forth a glittering stream of invective against obscurantism and oppression, and kept up a wise and witty correspondence with the keenest intelligences of Europe—kings, poets, philosophers and savants. And when just before his death he paid a last visit to Paris, the whole fashionable and intellectual world crowded to do him homage.

ENCYCLOPEDIA AND SOCIAL CONTRACT. Up to the middle of the century the new spirit was incubating; Voltaire was known as an anti-clerical satirist, Montesquieu had just brought out his *Esprit des Lois*: that was all. But thereafter there began to gather a loosely-knit band of thinkers and writers collectively known as *Les philosophes*: Helvétius, Holbach, Condorcet, D'Alembert, Diderot. Some were deists, others atheists, and they were divided by all sorts of personal interests and jealousies, but all alike believed in the power of Reason, they all worshipped Nature, they all had faith in the essential goodness of Humanity, they all looked to a new era when men would unite as brothers to realize this goodness, and believed in the capacity of wise government to create this millenium. ("It is the wise legislator that makes the good citizen" wrote Helvétius.) Diderot, the standard-bearer of the movement called upon

Nature, Sovereign of all beings, and you her adorable daughters, Virtue, Reason, Truth to be for ever our only divinities! It is to you that the incense and homage of the earth are due. Show us what man must do to win the happiness that you make him long for. Inspire him with courage, give him energy, let him esteem his dignity, let him cherish his equals. That he may himself enjoy, let him make others enjoy.

Diderot (1713–84) was editor-in-chief of the famous *Encyclopédie des Arts et Sciences*, designed as a compendium of human knowledge—political, social, physical, biological and technical. It was a manifesto of nature-worship and of faith in human perfectibility. In the course of the twenty years that the undertaking was in hand (1751–72) there was a constant coming and going of collaborators—D'Alembert, Marmontel,

Rousseau, Voltaire, Buffon, Turgot, Quesnay; for they all fell out, sooner or later, with the editor's uncompromising atheism, or became alarmed at the persecution of the work by the Church. But Diderot stuck to his guns, and by the time the last volumes appeared there were thousands of subscribers.

A notable product of the humanitarian spirit of the age was Beccaria's *Dei Delitti e delle Pene* (On Crimes and Punishments). The author (1735–93), an enlightened Italian aristocrat, produced this little book as a diversion from mathematical and economic studies, without in the least foreseeing its far-reaching effects. It set forth sensible, scientific principles as to the purpose and nature of punishments, deprecating unnecessary severities, especially torture. It was translated into half the tongues of Europe and was the starting-point of prison-reform in Germany, France, Russia—and even, later on, in England.

The Encyclopedists were none of them democrats: they looked for their golden age to the advent of some beneficent, all-powerful, all-wise, Solon. The first French apostle of the sovereignty of the people was Jean Jacques Rousseau (1712–78). Like the others he worshipped Nature, and like them he got many of his ideas from England—the only country, he said, where men could think for themselves. But unlike them he was no respectable bourgeois, but an irresponsible shiftless neurasthenic, who, at any rate towards the end of his life, was un-doubtedly a little mad. But he set forth in matchless French prose a point of view which has profoundly influenced the modern world. He created a love of wild life and simple pleasures in an age when it was assumed that beauty could only be found in trim gardens and smiling cornfields, and when "country-bred" was a term of contempt. He gave a new twist to the doctrine of the Fall of Man by looking back to an imagined time when men lived pure, good and happy lives before civilization depraved them and made them miserable.

He contributed to the first uprising of the religion of Nature in the middle of the century with a *Discourse on Sciences and Arts*, written as a prize essay, in which he took the paradoxical view that these activities had done more harm than good. This essay aroused immense interest and made its author famous. But the most fruitful years of his life were between 1760 and 1763, which he spent as the guest of the Duke of Luxembourg, living in a secluded garden-house, thinking, walking, communing with nature, and producing three epoch-making books.

The first, *Julie, ou la Nouvelle Éloise*, a long-drawn-out love-story, told in letters (an idea which he got from Samuel Richardson). To our taste it seems mawkishly sentimental, but it did more than any other book to create a taste for Romance, and for the beauties of woodland, cloud and stream as background for it; and it created a taste for novel-reading in fashionable circles.

Then came *Émile, ou L'Éducation*. That optimistic era, with its faith in human nature, was naturally interested in Youth, the raw material of the golden age to come. *Émile*, though cast in the form of a narrative, describes an education designed to bring out latent goodness, instead of flogging out the Old Adam. This was a startling notion to people who had always assumed that sparing the rod would spoil the child. Rousseau had no practical experience of bringing up children (he left his own on the doorstep of a foundling hospital), and the book contains some unsound and unpractical ideas. But at the back of it lie truths which placed education on a new footing; and every boy and girl who to-day enjoys school life instead of hating it owes a great debt to half-crazy Jean Jacques.

Within a few weeks of *Émile* appeared the book with which its author's name is chiefly associated. *Le Contrat Social* is quite short—scarcely more than a pamphlet, but it is a miracle of lucid and concise exposition; and the theory of democracy which it set forth changed human destiny, for it became the bible of the Jacobins. Its famous opening sentence "Man is born free, but everywhere he is in chains" warns us that we are in for sentimental declamation rather than reasoning based on observation. It declares that society results from a bargain by which men gained security at the price of their individual liberty, placing themselves and all that they have at the disposal of the General Will, which is the only true sovereign. Rousseau's debt to Locke is obvious; but he knew little history, apart from some isolated scraps about the Greek and Roman Republics; and much as he admired England he never realized the power of organic constitutional growth. But we can see the working of his spirit all around us to-day—for instance, the patriotism arising from the conception that the State consists of the whole body of citizens. And that very word "citizen" began to take on a new and electrifying significance.

THE BIRTH OF FREE TRADE. The liberating impulse was applied to economics by two other Frenchmen: Gourlay (1712–59) and Quesnay (1694–1774). Gourlay, indeed, was the first person ever to be known as an "economist." France, which Louis XIV's Colbert had made a model of regulated industry and commerce, now became the scene of reaction against it. Colbertism had been pushed to such lengths that the artificer had to gain the approval of government officials for the purchase of his raw material, for every stage of manufacture, and for the quality and quantity of the finished goods. There were hordes of inspectors to protect the consumer—e.g., to see that no stockings for men weighed less than 5 ounces, or for women less than 3 ounces. Particular branches of trade were restricted to particular markets or ports—e.g., the East India trade to L'Orient, the Levant trade to Marseilles. Gourlay, himself an official, visited England and Holland, where he saw the advantages of greater elasticity; and when he became Royal Intendant of Commerce in 1751 he did all he could to soften the regulations. In particular he allowed Indian fabrics to compete with French, thus compelling French manufacturers to improve their wares to their own ultimate advantage. He summed up his doctrine in a phrase which became the watchword of British economists in the next century: *Laissez faire, laissez passer.* His reforms were neither radical nor lasting, but they were a sign of the times.

So was the teaching of Quesnay, surgeon to the King and protégé of Madame de Pompadour. He made a hobby of such studies, wrote the articles on *Fermiers* and *Grains* for the Encyclopedia, and in 1760 published *Maximes générales du Gouvernement économique d'un Royaume agricole.* Like nearly all other enlightened Frenchmen of the day, he drew many of his ideas from Locke; but he developed them along a line of his own. He argued that agriculture is the only true source of wealth, the only really productive activity. Industry consumes more than it produces; and government should not make regulations to ensure large profits to manufacturers. Let all production and labour and prices be freed from control; then competition will lower the profits of industry,[1] the "productive class" will gain the recompense it deserves, and the natural flow of economic currents will produce a stable and just equilibrium. Above all, let there be an end of raising revenue from customs dues levied on the movement of corn between the provinces of France, for this causes famines in some parts and gluts in others, thereby reducing taxable values as a whole. Quesnay and his disciples were known as "physiocrats" because of their belief in the power of nature.

But in economic evolution as in political, Britain led the way. To be sure, Navigation Laws encouraged British sea-faring, the trade of the colonies was restricted to the mother country, and commerce was

---

[1] This of course would affect the labouring classes, who were still tied down by medieval guild rules which, with the cheapening of money operated strongly in favour of employers. Industrial wages were in many parts of France as low as 5 sous a day. Even the highly-skilled tapestry-workers of Gobelins were only paid the equivalent of a shilling a day.

regulated with an eye to a favourable balance in money.[1] Still, this "Mercantile Theory" was never so hidebound in Britain as in continental countries, and Adam Smith's *Wealth of Nations* (1776) opened his countrymen's eyes to its fallacies. Smith developed the arguments of the French economists and physiocrats with compelling gusto. He brought a wealth of illustrations to show that the individual is more likely to discover his own best interests than any government, and that what is best for the aggregate of individuals must be best for the State. One of his first disciples was the younger Pitt, who brought in proposals for free trade with Ireland and a commercial treaty with France (1786). The prejudices of English manufacturers (led by Josiah Wedgwood, most famous of British potters) compelled Pitt to abandon the former measure, and the effect of the second was cut short by the opening of the great war with France in 1793; but Free Trade was by this time in the air, and in the next century it enabled the Industrial Revolution to give Great Britain a lead in the economic transformation of the world.

ROMANCE AND *AUFKLÄRUNG*. The new religion of Enlightenment had two deities: Reason and Romance; and of these the former was the elder. The birth of romance is usually dated from the appearance of *Julie*, in which heart prevails over head, sentiment over intelligence, emotion over common sense. But Rousseau was not quite the first in this field. As usual, the pioneers were English. Samuel Richardson's *Pamela; or Virtue Rewarded* (1740) and *Clarissa; or the History of a Young Lady* (1747-8—in 7 volumes) are insufferably long-winded tales with plots like those of the modern novelette; while the "naturalist" aspect of the new movement was first expressed in Thomson's *Seasons*, which appeared twenty years earlier. But it was Jean Jacques who, writing in the *lingua franca* of European culture, set the movement going on the Continent.

He could not have done so had not the educated classes everywhere been ripe for it. In England we see the new spirit working in Gray's *Elegy* (1751); in Goldsmith's *Vicar of Wakefield* (1766) and *The Deserted Village* (1770); in William Cowper's exposition of tea-pots and sofa-cushions; in the love of the mysterious and shadowy exemplified by Macpherson's *Ossian* (1765); in the revival of ballad and folk-song begun by Percy's *Reliques of Ancient English Poetry* (1765); and soon it

[1] E.g. the export of woollen goods to Portugal was specially encouraged under the Methuen Treaty (1703) because it brought (besides the oceans of port which gave our eighteenth-century ancestors gout) an annual £50,000 worth of Brazilian gold into the country.

began to inspire the lyric mood-pictures of Wordsworth and Coleridge, who were still very young men when our period closed.

The German word for Enlightenment is *Aufklärung*, and this term is especially connected with the birth of German Literature, which proclaimed the spiritual unity of the German people long before they had any prospect of political unity. Politically there was as yet no German fatherland; only a congeries of jealous little states, a vague sense of a great past, and an inarticulate hope of a great future. But German national feeling came to life when the German language, towards the end of our period, came into use as a literary medium. It was Prussia that was destined, a century later, to create a united Germany, albeit by debasing the German spirit; and it is noteworthy that the golden era of German literature began when Prussia rose to greatness under Frederick II. Not that the leaders of the movement were Prussians, or that Frederick himself took the smallest interest in it. But his deeds in the Seven Years' War kindled the national imagination. Although the most persistent of his foes was German-speaking Austria, his success in beating off the three greatest military Powers of Europe stirred even the south Germans who had joined in the attempt to crush him. And it was this heart-raising emotion, as Goethe said, which in making Germans proud of their Germanity set them in revolt against the French influences which had hitherto been accepted in educated circles without question.

German critics consider that Klopstock began it with his *Messias*, a lofty (but to us unreadable) epic of the *Paradise Lost* type, which was completed in 1773 through the patronage of the King of Denmark, at a time when no German ruler recognized German as a literary language at all. Then came Lessing (1729–81) whose *Hamburgische Dramaturgie* disparaged French classical drama, with its formal correctitude, and substituted Shakespeare's rough-hewn energy as the appropriate model for German playwrights; while Herder (1744–1803) bade Germans develop their own national traditions, instead of imitating foreign models, and was the first collector of folk-songs.

Then appeared a German writer who ranks with the greatest in the history of mankind. Wolfgang von Goethe embodied all the tendencies of the age. Born in 1749, his first literary effort was a French tragedy; but when he went to Strassburg to perfect his French he fell in with disciples of Herder, and discovered the possibilities of his mother tongue. There followed a marvellous outpouring of lyrics, not decked out with artificial tropes and classical allusions, but springing from the heart of Man in Nature. And his romantic drama *Götz von Berlichingen* (1773) which depicts the later Middle Ages with an unrestrained vitality that threw overboard Racinesque decorum and good manners, opened to German youth new vistas of art and of life. Then came *The Sorrows of Young Werther* (1774), the story of a young man who shoots himself for love, which, maudlin as it seems to modern taste, was the first German "best-seller."[1] Translated into all European and some Asiatic languages, it made the world aware for the first time of German literature.

Goethe afterwards turned to classical restraint; but these literary wild oats started a fashion of "Storm and Stress" (*Stürm und Drang*) which treated passions and instincts as the highest attributes of man's nature. As examples of this we need but mention the early works of Schiller (1759–1805), whose *Robbers* (1781) and *Fiesco* (1783) display with crude violence the spirit which in *Don Carlos* (1787) the poet transmuted to altruism, humanitarianism, the brotherhood of man and the love of liberty.

Thus the swelling flood of German literature was part of the tide which during the latter half of our period was sweeping Europe towards the cataract of the French Revolution.

ARTS AND SCIENCES. The social and political tendencies of an age may be reflected in its art as faithfully as in its literature. This was particularly the case with the Rococo art which, arising in France, spread to Germany and Italy in the time of Louis XV. Like the society it was designed to please, it pushed artificiality to the point of genius. It replaced the grandiloquence of seventeenth-century Baroque by delicate and finicking charm. The age of Louis XIV, like that Grand Monarque himself, loved to stalk through stately rooms, walled by vast canvases depicting noble deeds and great occasions; the tired and disillusioned age of Louis XV preferred intimacy, privacy and elegance; its pictures were exquisite little representations of *fêtes galantes*, and *divertissements champêtres*.[2] The first artist of this genre was Watteau (1684–1721), and the last was Fragonard (1732–1806) who combined it with

---

[1] Thackeray ridiculed its sentimental "simplicity" in his parody of the story in English verse:

> Charlotte, having seen the body,
> Borne before her on a shutter
> Like a well-conducted person
> Went on cutting bread-and-butter.

But Thackeray lived two generations later ; the young Goethe's own contemporaries did not laugh at it. Napoleon slept with it under his pillow.

[2] The Rococo outlook on art is well exemplified by the warning given to Fragonard by his master when he set out for Italy: "If you take Michael Angelo and Raphael seriously, it is all up with you (*tu es fichu*)!"

the taste for rustic simplicity which had been made fashionable by Jean
Jacques (see, for instance, "The Slipper" in the Wallace Collection).
And after the middle of the century the new spirit in literature had a
direct counterpart in Chardin, the first of the realists, with his bourgeois
domesticities. All these painters were French, for French taste still
ruled the polite world by which painters lived. Foreign rulers such as
Frederick and Catherine collected French pictures (some of the best
Watteaus are in Berlin and Potsdam to this day) and tried to collect
the painters themselves. But towards the end of the period painters of
high rank were produced by Great Britain, which had imported its
artists from Holbein to Canaletto. The two most famous of them
represent the two tendencies which we have already seen at work.
Sir Joshua Reynolds (1723–92) stood for the traditional, academic view
that only idealized aspects of nature, and dignified mythological and
historical subjects, were worthy of the artist's brush; and that anything
personal or typical was vulgar. Reynolds painted some noble portraits
in the grand manner; only his studies of children, such as the famous
"Age of Innocence" (National Gallery) suggest the new outlook. His
rival Gainsborough (1727–88), on the other hand, was never held back
by classical restraints. His portraits have an unaffected intimacy which
fully accords with the change in public taste. And it was highly characteristic of the age that what he really liked painting was landscape.
Ever since the middle ages the artist had assumed that Man, standing
in a special relation to God, was all that really mattered in the universe;
but Rationalism and Nature-worship was shifting his point of view.
The landscape which had been mere background for human figures
became the main interest, with humanity incidental. When Gainsborough tells us that

there was not a tree of any beauty, no, nor a hedgerow, stone or post
around my native town that I did not treasure in my memory from my
earliest year.

he is speaking (quite unconsciously, for a less self-conscious artist never
lived) for a new age in the history of art.

Music is not so easily integrated with political and social history as
the literary and plastic arts; for its swift development during the past
few centuries has telescoped it into unaccountable shapes; and such
figures as Johann Sebastian Bach (1685–1750) belong to no age or time.
We can see external influences more clearly in Handel (1685–1759), the
professional entertainer who lived and worked in close touch with his
audiences, catering for them at first with the artificialities of Italian

opera (Julius Cæsar singing soprano in a full-bottomed wig), but towards the end of his life with the oratorios, which appeal to the spirit of the evangelical revival. Another sign of the times was Gluck, who in the last twenty years of our period reformed opera in the direction of simplicity and truth. Above all he can see it in Mozart (1756–91). Born when Rococo was still flourishing, he spent his twenties (the middle years of his life, alas!) in producing exquisite "entertainment music" (*Galanteriekunst*, the Germans call it) for refined society. But about his thirtieth year something happened in his soul, and there followed that amazing outburst of truth and beauty which gave us the three great operas, the three great symphonies, the last great chamber-music. It is noteworthy that the new element which he brought to opera was the musical delineation of humanity; but an aspect of the romantic age conspicuously lacking in his work was rusticity: it has never a breath of the open air. That breath, and the influence of folk-music, was provided by Haydn (1732–1809), despite the fact that most of his work was done as wage-paid service to a great aristocrat.

The later decades of our period were, as we should expect, full of research into the working of nature; but it would be beyond our scope to do more than mention a few examples of it. Lavoisier (1743–94) gave modern chemistry some of its most fruitful methods, especially the use of the balance, and led the way with experiments in the composition of water and air. Benjamin Franklin (1706–90), dabbling in science as a side-line in a long life of political and literary activity, enquired experimentally into the nature of electricity and turned his discoveries to practical use by inventing the lightning-conductor. Linnæus (1707–78) was a Swedish botanist whose *Fundamenta botanica* established a universal system of classification for the vegetable world. And Buffon (1707–88), distinguished writer as well as savant, produced with the aid of collaborators in the manner of the *Encyclopédie*, an *Histoire Naturelle* in 40 quarto volumes, designed as a conspectus of Nature, vegetable, animal and mineral.

CHAPTER TWENTY-NINE

THE ENLIGHTENED DESPOTS

1763–1773

DURING the last twenty-five years of the Old Régime the rulers dominating European politics all prided themselves on putting into practice the teachings of "Enlightenment," of "Reason," of "Philosophy"; and at this stage we shall do well to examine just what these claims amounted to.

FREDERICK RESTORES PRUSSIA. Frederick the Great was the supreme example of Enlightened Despotism; and in re-building Prussia after the Seven Years' War he had unlimited scope. He described in his Memoirs the situation that faced him in 1763.

To form a conception of the general ruin which had befallen the country, the despondency and spiritlessness to which the people were reduced, one must picture a devastation which left hardly a trace of human habitation over whole districts; some towns lying in rubble and ruin, others half-destroyed by fire; no seed-corn set aside, no horses for tillage, a reduction of half a million in a population of 4½ millions. Nobles and peasantry alike were so beggared and plundered that only a few wretched rags were left to cover their nakedness. No credit was to be had, even for daily sustenance; there was no police in the towns; the spirit of reason and discipline was replaced by selfish and lawless greed.

The moment peace was secure he set agriculture going again by releasing stores collected for the unfought campaign of 1763—horses for the plough, unthreshed grain for seed, officers to supervise operations.

After this most pressing need had been met, he turned to the provision of national schools. Prussia was a century ahead of England in this respect. Even before peace was signed he wrote from Hubertusburg to inform his Minister of the Interior that he had engaged eight Saxon school-inspectors to raise the standard of village schools throughout Brandenburg and Pomerania; and a few months later he issued a General School Regulation, setting up a system of compulsory and universal schooling between the ages of five and fourteen, in reading, writing, and the essentials of Christianity. It is noteworthy that he looked to education to increase the worth of his subjects to the State. But it would scarcely have occurred to him that any of them, of whatever rank, had any claim to a share in the responsibilities of government, local or national.

As to economic policy, he was a cast-iron "mercantilist." He expounded the theory in his Memoirs.

When a country has few products and relies on the industries of its neighbours, the balance of trade must go against it; and if this continues it must in the long run lose all its gold. There is no remedy for this but an increase of manufactures. The working-up of the country's own raw material is all gain; the working-up of imported material provides at least the profit of the labour so expended.

The consumption of imported luxuries, such as spices, sugar and coffee, he severely repressed, lest it should cause a leakage of the specie received for Prussia's own exports of wool, linen and timber.

Monopolies, loans and exemption from excise were all employed to encourage nascent industries, such as tobacco and porcelain. But when they were established the privileges were withdrawn, and open competition was revived in order to stimulate efficiency. School grounds and churchyards had to be planted with mulberry-trees, and the families of school-masters and clergymen were to occupy themselves "for their own profit and that of the State" in preparing silk thread. Many of his decrees prefigured National Socialism: people were forbidden to take money out of the country; marriage-licences were only issued on production of certificates that the household china had been bought at a Berlin factory; every family had to buy a fixed minimum of salt, the supply of which was a Government monopoly.

MOTHER AND SON. The strain of the Seven Years' War had greatly aged Maria Teresa, as it had her enemy Frederick; the radiant health, beauty and vitality of her younger days had gone. But she still retained her queenly presence, her frank and kind demeanour, her devout Christian faith, and above all her loyalty to old friends and servants. She had stood by Daun long after he had proved himself unable to cope with Frederick; and when he had to be superseded she contrived a fictional command for him. She never wavered in her wifely devotion to her husband, Emperor Francis, even when she realized, sadly, that he lacked the capacity to be helpful in dealing with the problems of government. And it was the same with Kaunitz. His foppery and vanity increased with age, and his alliance with France and Russia had turned out very badly; but she recognized his loyalty to her House and to herself; and perhaps she realized that his cynical sharp-sightedness was a valuable corrective to her own impulsive warmth.

Archduke Joseph, to whom she fondly and proudly looked to carry on the Hapsburg tradition both as Emperor and as ruler of the Austrian heritage, was carefully brought up for his future position. From the age of twenty he attended meetings of the Council and discussions between his mother and the Chancellor. He was a highly enlightened and intelligent young man, but moody and temperamental. He was, indeed, incubating ideas of his own about the Austrian domains. The invigorating effects of central control could be seen working in Prussia. If ever there was a government that needed such a master-mind it was Austria, and Joseph determined that when his time came he would supply the want. The death of his charming young wife, in November 1763, cast on his life a shadow which never lifted. He agreed, for reasons of State, to marry Princess Josepha of Bavaria; but try as the unfortunate young woman would to win his heart, he could not bear the sight of her; and when she too died (May 1767) he remained celibate for the rest of his life.

The underlying aim of Kaunitz in these years was to restore the prestige of the House by recovering Silesia (or an equivalent), and by marriages with Bourbons. One archduchess was married to the young Duke of Parma, another to King Ferdinand of Naples, the youngest, Marie Antoinette, to the future King of France; and the Archduke Leopold, to whom Joseph assigned the succession to their father's Duchy of Tuscany, was now wedded to the Infanta Louisa, daughter of Carlos III. The wedding festivities at Innsbruck in August 1765 were interrupted by the sudden death of the Emperor Francis. This was a terrible blow to Maria Teresa. She forsook all worldly pleasures, cut off her hair, gave away most of her wardrobe, and insisted that Joseph (who was duly elected Emperor) should also share her sovereignty over the Hapsburg heritage, and take from her shoulders the burden of its actual government.

Joseph's pent-up spirit was now released. He busied himself from morning to night in sweeping reforms. He cleared out the old gang at the War Office, replacing the aged Daun by his friend Lacy; he confiscated much of the property of the Church; he sold his father's vast hunting apparatus, and turned the Prater (hitherto an Imperial deer-forest) into a public park. All this deeply grieved Maria Teresa, and as soon as she recovered from her prostration she began to intervene. But these Hapsburgs were a devoted family,[1] and the tactful mediation

[1] Maria Teresa nursed the young Empress Josepha when she died of small-pox. In doing so she herself contracted the dread fever, in a particularly virulent form; whereupon Joseph scarcely left her side until against all expectation she recovered. Experience during this epidemic converted them to the new prophylactic inoculation, and they founded a hospital to apply it.

of Kaunitz contrived a working compromise between the old and the new.

"THE SEMIRAMIS OF THE NORTH." Second only to Frederick in reputation as an enlightened despot was Catherine II. Coming to Russia half educated, and with no assets but courage, intelligence and vitality, she had assiduously prepared herself for the opportunity which in 1762 opened before her. She learned not only to speak Russian but to understand Russia, and set herself to become a great Empress by being a great Russian. Apart from this she was a supreme opportunist, being fond of quoting the view of her "master" Voltaire that systems and theories lead to intolerance, infatuation and persecution. "Politics," she said, "are compounded of circumstances, conjectures and conjunctions." Her Russianism went so deep that at one time she thought of undoing Peter the Great's westernizing of fashions at her court, and reverting to the flowing robes and beards of the Russian Middle Ages. And, her subjects being the most religious people in Europe, she—by nature a sceptic, like Frederick and Joseph—never appeared before the populace without the double cross of the Orthodox Church between her clasped hands, and stood hour after hour through its services, consisting largely of chanting which tormented her tone-deaf ears.

The foundation of her foreign policy was what she called "The Greek Project"—a dream that Russia should revive the Byzantine Empire, release the Balkan peoples—mainly Slavs by race and Orthodox by religion like the Russians—from subjection to the Sultan, and replace the Crescent by the Cross on the summit of St. Sophia at Constantinople. She hoped to begin with a kingdom of Dacia based on what is now Rumania, for her younger grandson Constantine; and she imported a Greek nurse, and a Greek cadet-corps for him to play soldiers with.

As for her "enlightenment," it did not go very deep. She corresponded in French more fluent than correct with Voltaire and Diderot, and gave them presents and pensions.[1] They repaid her with gross flattery, even suggesting that the private life of such an exalted being was beyond the decencies expected of ordinary folk. But after a few tentative experiments in liberal reform she found that Russia was not ripe for it, and she was too practical-minded to try to force the pace. She was confronted with this backwardness when, early in her reign, she tried to institute an up-to-date code of laws. The details were to be

---

[1] She was particularly generous to Diderot relieving him from poverty by buying his library and then asking him to keep the books until she needed them, and to act as librarian at a salary.

worked out by a commission of notables who would represent the nation and bring forward its needs and wishes; and in 1767 she drew up —with her own hand, for she loved writing—her famous "Instruction" (*Nakas*) to guide its labours. But this was little more than a string of generalizations, drawn from Montaigne and Beccaria, reflecting the sentimental optimism of the age, such as "The rich ought not to oppress the poor," and "We should distinguish between moral and political offences"; and it scarcely touched on the vital question of serfdom. The commission met at St. Petersburg, but no form of procedure had been laid down for it, it had no experience of getting business done in committees, and Catherine was relieved when the Turkish war gave her an excuse to suspend its sittings. Nothing more was heard of "The Great Russian Code."

Her attitude to serfdom was characteristic. She was not by nature hard or cruel; she adored children; she was (nearly always) good-natured and forbearing, even to servants; when she intervened in the course of justice it was (nearly always) on the side of mercy. But though serfdom was little more than a century old she saw that to disturb it would cause a damaging upheaval in Russian society. So she left it alone, and the knout and strappado without which it could not be maintained. When a visitor drew her attention to the degraded filth of some serfs by the roadside she replied "How can you expect them to take care of bodies which do not belong to them?"—which showed that she penetrated to the heart of an evil which she did nothing to alleviate. And her general good-humour did not extend to any word or deed that seemed to curtail her sovereign power, for this power was in her eyes that of Russia itself; and in some ways she was right.

In the matter of finance, for instance. How did she raise from her impoverished people and her primitive machinery of government the millions which she spent in reckless profusion on her favourites and palaces, her armies and fleets? The answer is simple. The expenditure was almost wholly internal, and could be met with paper money. She had some notion that reckless use of this would in any western country bring bankruptcy and ruin; but when the cost of the Turkish war compelled her to try it she made a surprising discovery. The value of currency depended largely on the confidence inspired by the sovereign whose image and superscription it bore, and in Catherine's Russia there was absolutely no limit to this confidence. Right up to the end of the war her rouble-notes retained their face value. Elsewhere rulers could only command their subjects' actions—she could command their faith. By building up on the foundations laid by Peter I this legend of imperial omnipotence she imposed herself on Russia and Russia on Europe.

STRUENSEE IN DENMARK. In Frederick V (1746–66) Denmark had a king who cultivated enlightenment with some success, being the patron of Klopstock (the father of German literature), Basedow (a pioneer in education) and Holberg (the Danish national poet); and his minister Bernstorff steered the country safely through the perils of the Seven Years' War—albeit he owed something to fortune when Tsar Peter II (formerly of Holstein) was dethroned just when setting out to avenge his father's grievance against Denmark.

But Frederick was succeeded by a seventeen-years-old son, Christian VII, who was almost incapable of mental exertion; and an early marriage to a young sister of George III of England seemed to do him more harm than good. In 1768 he was sent on a tour which took him to England, France and Germany, and from Hamburg he brought back to Copenhagen a clever young doctor named Struensee. Struensee had been brought up by rigidly pious parents, but when he grew up he had gone to the other extreme—turning atheist under the influence of the encyclopedists, and taking to wildly licentious living. The King and Queen of Denmark were greatly taken with him. He became Court Physician, then a member of the Council of State. As the King's mental derangement developed he had long periods of complete torpor; and Struensee gained complete control over the Government, abolished the Council, and set about making the country into a model state by a combination of Prussian absolutism and French culture. He established the most up-to-date medical service in Europe: he abolished torture and reduced the number of capital offences; he prevented the nobles from systematically evading payment of their debts to tradesmen; he restricted the forced labour which made slaves of the peasantry; he reduced the hordes of government officials, and put a stop to the corruption of those that kept their posts. But his head was turned by the immense power which had fallen to him. He treated the Danes with lofty contempt, and ridiculed the idea that it might be worth his while to learn their language. Reforms which might have been acceptable if spread over a decade gave offence when driven through in a few months. He made enemies recklessly—the nobles by withdrawing their privileges, the official class by dismissals, the Lutheran clerics by the scandal of his relations with the Queen.

Pride went before a fall—and not very far before it. In January 1772 after Struensee had been in power for less than a year, a band of

officers and courtiers concerted a *coup d'état*. He and his chief henchman (who had acted as the King's keeper and pummelled him if he
protested against Struensee's innovations), were arrested, tried for
treason, and beheaded. The Queen was banished to Celle where her
foolish young life ended (possibly to the relief of her highly respectable
brother George) a few years later.

For the time being Struensee's work was undone; but when Crown
Prince Frederick became old enough to be Regent for his father (now
certifiably insane) he brought some of these reforms into permanent
shape. For instance serfdom was abolished in Denmark in 1787—
two years ahead of France and twenty years ahead of Prussia.

CHAPTER THIRTY

THE BOURBONS AND THE JESUITS

1750–1770

ENLIGHTENED Despotism in the Latin countries was directed largely against the Society of Jesus; for which by its concentrated and worldly-wise zeal it had gained power, influence and wealth which drew on it intense hostility, not only in Protestant countries but among devout Catholics, and even at Rome itself.

THE JESUITS EXPELLED FROM PORTUGAL. The war on the Jesuits opened in Portugal. Though a small country, its geographical position had thrust it into the vanguard of fifteenth-century exploration. Its seamen rounded the Cape and opened a route to Asia which brought it fabulous wealth. But the importation of gold raised prices, and as in Spain led to a disinclination for industrial and agricultural enterprise. Then a devout king introduced from Spain the Holy Inquisition and the Society of Jesus to set up a heresy-hunt against Jews and Moors. The Jesuit fathers gained control of education, especially at Coimbra, the university where the nobles were educated. King Sebastian (1557–78) took clerical vows, and when he perished in a crusade against the Moors the royal House became extinct. For sixty years Portugal was absorbed in Spain, and this enabled the Dutch, now in their golden age, to monopolize the trade which the Portuguese had set up with the East Indies. In 1640 a convulsive effort regained Portuguese independence under the House of Braganza; but although the discovery of gold and diamonds in Brazil in the 1690's made the monarchy independent of the Cortes (=assembly), the nation became poorer than ever. The Methuen Treaties (1703), made Portugal a commercial and therefore a political satellite of Great Britain. Viticulture was so stimulated that all other activities wilted, and the country became dependent on Britain even for its food and clothes. Worst of all a syndicate of British wine-merchats created a monopoly and beat down prices until the growers were on the point of starvation. Royal piety won for the kings the papal title of Fidelissimus,[1] but cost the country vast sums for churches and convents and for a futile crusade

---

[1] Corresponding to the "Most Christian" Kings of France, and the "Most Catholic" Kings of Spain.

against the Turks. By the death of John IV (1706–50) a tenth of the population were living in religious houses; trade, industry, army and navy were reduced to shadows; the internal administration was run by the Jesuits in the interests of their Society; and foreign relations were directed from London.

But the next king, Joseph (1750–77), though a poor creature both as a ruler and as a man, opened his reign with one notable deed, at any rate: he appointed, first as Foreign Minister and then as Prime Minister, Sebastian José de Carvalho de Mello, Marquis de Pombal. Pombal's ascendancy was greatly increased by the courage and wisdom with which he organized rescue and relief after the famous Lisbon earthquake (1755), when 30,000 people were killed in the twinkling of an eye. "Bury the dead and feed the living" was his watchword in preventing after-effects which might have been worse than the disaster itself.

He used this ascendancy to do very much what Strafford a century before had tried to do in Ireland and England—to build up by high-handed methods the royal power which sustained him. He undid the worst effects of the Methuen Treaties by encouraging the manufacture of silk, sugar, wool, paper, and glass; he founded the sardine fisheries which have meant so much to Portugal ever since; and he established a rival wine-company to break the English monopoly. He reconstructed the army with the aid of officers imported from Germany. The Portuguese army was never in the same class as the Prussian, or even the Austrian, of course; but it sufficed, with British aid, to check the Spaniards in the last year of the Seven Years' War (p. 275).

These activities brought Pombal into conflict with the Jesuits. The extent and success of their overseas missions had led them to embark on commercial enterprises; and the great wealth which they thus accumulated led to all manner of evils. In Paraguay they exploited the docility of the natives to set up a sort of theocracy—a Jesuit state, governed despotically by Mission Fathers, to the great financial profit of the Society. When in 1750 Spain ceded Paraguay to Portugal in exchange for territory at Sacramento, the Jesuits encouraged their subjects to resist the transfer. To Pombal it was insufferable that any organization should set itself against the King's Government directed by himself. He had already gained control of the Inquisition;[1] the Society he determined to extirpate from Portugal altogether. He accused it of illicit trade, and of plotting against the State, and made the Inquisition close its schools. When the King was attacked at night

---

[1] The Portuguese Inquisition had never been quite so stern as the Spanish. After 1728 it even allowed accused persons to be confronted with the witnesses against them.

in the streets by nobles whose family pride he had outraged by his amorous intrigues, Pombal charged the Jesuits with complicity in the attempted regicide—which he was suspected of having organized for this very purpose. He demanded from Pope Clement XIII authority for the degradation and execution of the accused Fathers. The Pope hesitated, for Rome was full of Jesuits, being the headquarters of the organization. Pombal, losing patience, had all the Jesuits in Portugal put aboard ship and landed at Civita Vecchia, the chief port of the Papal Domains (September 1760). Then he outlawed the Society and confiscated its property.

Pombal was no "liberal." He enforced the strictest censorship in Europe, and his secret police kept the prisons crowded with persons suspected of disaffection towards his régime. But he made the government of Portugal more efficient and economical than it had ever been before, and he spent the sequestered Jesuit wealth in establishing a complete system of primary and secondary education, by the founding of 800 schools. Naturally he made many enemies, especially among the aristocracy and the higher clergy; and when King Joseph died (1777) their pent-up hatred found vent. The timid, pious Queen Maria (she died a religious maniac) was egged on by a strong-minded step-mother to dismiss Pombal, and further proceedings were only stopped by his death shortly afterwards at the age of eighty-three. Little of his work survived, but his career was a notable example of the governmental spirit of the age.

THE JESUITS EXPELLED FROM FRANCE. The next country to get rid of the Jesuits was France. Here their enemies were many and varied. The Pompadour had once been well-disposed towards them; but they were hand-in-glove with the Dauphin, whose somewhat ostentatious piety was a protest against her influence at his father's court; and when, later on, they made a bid for her favour, she had already taken sides against them. Secondly, there were the Jansenists, who in spite of persecution by triumphant Jesuits in the last days of Louis XIV, still had a great hold over devout French people. Indeed, nothing had done the Society more harm with the general public than the ruthless measures which had culminated in the Bull Unigenitus. Thirdly, they had supported the Monarchy in its quarrels with the Parlements, and this had brought on them the vindictive hatred of the whole legal profession. Fourthly, the Encyclopedists and *philosophes* regarded them as the embattled and disciplined foes of liberal and humanitarian ideas.

But in France as in Portugal, it was their secular interests that led directly to their downfall. Père Lavalette, Superior-General of the Society in the French West Indies, ignoring the orders of the Government that he should confine his energies to his religious duties, had turned his headquarters on Martinique into a great banking and trading centre. But in 1755 goods which he sent to cover bills of exchange on his Marseilles correspondents were captured or destroyed by British commerce-raiders. The law-courts ordered him to pay 1½ million francs to his creditors; whereupon he declared himself bankrupt. The question then arose whether the Society as a whole could be made responsible for the debt: was it one and indivisible, or a federation of independent establishments? The General of the Order, Ricci, maintained the latter view, despite the unified organization on which the Society had always prided itself. The lower Courts having found in favour of the creditors and called on the Society to pay, it appealed to the Parlement of Paris. To bring its cause before a body so hostile was a daring move; but the Dauphin was trying to get rid of Pompadour and Choiseul, and the Jesuits hoped for powerful allies. But everything went wrong for them. The Parlement demanded to see the Society's Constitution, and on the strength of that document pronounced a verdict against it. It then went on to enquire whether this Constitution was compatible with the laws of the realm. In April 1762 the King, under the influence of Pompadour and Choiseul, decreed the abolition of the French branch of the Society, upon charges of trying to make itself independent of the Royal authority, and of withdrawing the King's subjects from their natural allegiance to that of a foreign potentate. Further decrees secularized its members and sequestrated its property.

THE JESUITS EXPELLED FROM SPAIN. The next scene of the discomfiture of the Society was the Most Catholic Kingdom of Spain.

Charles III—the "Baby Carlos" who had been set up first as Duke of Parma-Piacenza and then as King of The Two Sicilies by his fond mother the Termagant, and had succeeded his half-brother as King of Spain in 1759—had a good eye for a statesman. Bernardo Tanucci, who helped him make a success at Parma, was an ex-professor of Constitutional Law. A monarchist through and through, he crushed the pretensions of nobles and clergy, and made the dual Duchies a small-scale model of benevolent despotism. Carlos, on being promoted to Naples (1734) took Tanucci with him to tackle the problem presented there by clerical domination. For a population about half that of modern London there were 22 archbishops and 120 bishops, and the Church owned two-thirds of the landed property—all of it tax-free and giving sanctuary to fugitives from justice. Tanucci made a concordat with the Pope by which ecclesiastical property paid half the ordinary taxes, and the right of sanctuary was limited to actual church-buildings. Then, as at Parma, he turned the aristocracy into courtiers, drawing them away from the estates on which they had exercised feudal independence.

When Carlos became King of Spain he had to leave Tanucci behind to guide the young son who succeeded him in Naples; but having spent twenty-nine of his forty-three years in Italy he was more of an Italian than a Spaniard, and he took with him two Italians, Grimaldi and Squillacci as ministers. Grimaldi, being concerned mainly with foreign affairs, did not come into conflict with the Spanish people; but Squillacci roused a hornets' nest by domestic reforms which ignored old Spanish customs. He was very severe on brigands, whom the populace hardly regarded as criminals at all; he lit the streets of Madrid with oil-lamps, and banned the sombreros and capes which made it difficult to identify footpads. When the public ignored these edicts his police went their rounds armed with shears to abbreviate offending garments. This was too much for Spanish patience. On Palm Sunday 1766 there was a riot in the streets of the capital. The mob, sweeping aside the police, smashed the street-lamps, looted Squillacci's house, and as they could not lay hands on his person, burnt him in effigy. Next day they assembled before the palace, led by a monk with a crucifix, demanding his head. The King swallowed his pride and sent the ministers back to Naples; but the humiliation bit deep. He called to office a distinguished and intelligent nobleman, Count d'Aranda, to undertake the special task of finding out what underlay the disturbances and who had organized them. Aranda set to work in the deepest secrecy with the aid of two capable lawyers, Campomanes and Monino. He reported that the real culprits were the Jesuits, who in their pride at the purity of Spanish Catholicism, resented the intrusion of a "Voltairean" from Naples. The King was a devout Catholic, but already in Naples he had strongly resisted interference even from the Pope—he certainly would not tolerate a religious Order which compelled him to dismiss a confidential minister; and he readily agreed to Aranda's proposal to root it out of the country. Once again the Minister made his arrangements effective by keeping them profoundly secret until the moment for action. Sealed orders were sent to the Governors of all provinces, at home and overseas, to be opened on April 2nd, 1767. They directed that all Jesuits were to be arrested forthwith, taken to the nearest seaport, and embarked on ships which were to deposit them (since they acted as the Pope's subjects) on Papal territory. When the date came the King issued a Pragmatic Edict of expulsion, and expressly forbade any discussion of the measure, even favourable, inasmuch as "it does not belong to subjects to judge or interpret the will of the Sovereign." Six thousand members of the Society arrived off Civita Vecchia; but the Governor of that place, having no instructions from the Pope, refused to receive them. Conditions on board became pestilential, and many of the passengers died. At last the Pope allowed them to be disembarked, on King Carlos promising to provide for their sustenance at the rate of a shilling a day a head.

Aranda was another Iberian Strafford, bent on making the monarchy absolute; and when his very aggressive personality made him insufferable the King fell back on his subordinates, Monino (a lawyer's son who after organizing the reconquest of Florida was made Count of Floridablanca), and Campomanes, a practical economist. Between them, these two developed an adequate banking system, fostered textile industries, reconstructed the fleet, swept away internal customs-barriers, made thousands of miles of road and hundreds of miles of canal, and gave the people the rudiments of a system of education.

THE SOCIETY DISSOLVED. Europe now beheld the astonishing spectacle of the Bourbons making a special "Family Compact" for the complete destruction of these spear-head troops of militant Catholicism. The fact was that the Divine Right of Kingship mattered much more to them than that of the Papacy. They had more than once maintained their authority against that of Popes, in the same spirit as our own Henry II and Henry VIII. The Society was closely connected with the Papacy, and by destroying it they were depriving the Holy See of one of the most potent instruments by which its authority was carried into different countries and maintained there against that of Kingship.

In January 1769 the Kings of France, Spain and Naples jointly presented Clement with a formal demand for the suppression of the Society; but the old Pope, overwhelmed with distress and anxiety at the dilemma in which he was placed, died in the night before the Consistory at which the issue was to have been decided (February 1769). At the Conclave for the election of the new Pope there was a bitter struggle between pro-Jesuit and anti-Jesuit factions among the Cardinals; and as usual in such cases the result was a compromise. The sensible, moderate Cardinal Ganganelli, who became Clement XIV, postponed action on one pretext after another; but at last the pressure of the

Bourbons became too strong for him, and he issued the famous Bull *Dominus ac Redemptor* (April 1773), which, after reciting the Society's misdemeanours at length—their meddling in politics contrary to their own Constitution, their quarrels with parish clergy, their admission of heathen converts far too easily to the sacraments—declared it abolished, giving its priests the option of joining some other Order or becoming secular clergy under the authority of bishops.

The Society, ignoring its own vow of obedience, refused to die. It took refuge in Prussia and Russia under a succession of Polish "Generals," arguing that Papal Bulls are not binding within the territory of any sovereign who does not authorize their publication. The Papacy did not lift the ban until the turn of the century.

FALL OF CHOISEUL. There had been one juncture in this long conflict when the Jesuits had reason to hope that the Bourbon coalition against them would fall to pieces. That was when in 1770 Choiseul had fallen from power.

Choiseul had done wonderful service to France. He had pulled her together after the disasters of the Seven Years' War, and had put her on the road to recover the leadership in world-power which she had then lost to England. He had set on foot the reform of the army and the reconstruction of the navy, in spite of financial embarrassments which could not be remedied without a change of heart in the ruling classes. As to his own particular department of foreign affairs, it is true that he had let slip a valuable opportunity over Poland; but he had acquired Lorraine and Corsica. Lorraine had merely been incorporated in the kingdom on the death of King Stanislas (February 1765) in accordance with an existing treaty (p. 216); but the acquisition of Corsica was entirely due to Choiseul's enterprise. The island belonged to the Republic of Genoa, which twice had to call on France to suppress revolts there. On the second occasion the Corsicans under their patriot-hero General Paoli had given so much trouble that Genoa was glad to accept an offer from Choiseul for the purchase of the island. A considerable French army was needed to master it, but the task was accomplished in 1769—just in time to make an infant born to the Buonaparte family of Ajaccio, and christened Napoleone, a French subject.

But by this time Choiseul's position was undermined. His ally the Pompadour had died in 1764. Death had also removed some of his opponents—the Dauphin in 1766, the Dauphine in 1767, the Queen Marie Leszczinska in 1768; but the minister could not, or would not, adapt himself to the changed position which now arose at Court. The King, oddly enough, was much upset by the death of the wife he had so wronged and neglected, and for a time the "Devout Party" at Court hoped that at last, at the age of sixty-five, he had turned over a new leaf. But old vices were ingrained, and before long he was ensnared by a young woman of good looks but ill repute named Jeanne du Barry. Choiseul protested indignantly against this fresh degradation of the Crown; and Madame du Barry joined the Devotees (who hated him for the part he had taken against the Jesuits) in a concerted effort to drive him from office. This may seem a strange alliance, but as a matter of fact the Devotees had degenerated in moral rectitude after the death of the Dauphin. Their new leader, the Duc d'Aiguillon, was a far from exemplary character, and it was over his misdeeds as Governor of Britanny that the contest at Court came to a head. The Parlement of Rennes found a true bill against him for abuse of authority. The King ordered the case to be transferred to Paris—the Parlement of Paris was even more hostile to the Duke—the King summarily closed its proceedings—the Parlement declared the Duke suspended from his privileges as a Peer—the King annulled the suspension at a *lit de justice*—whereupon the Parlement went on strike, closing all law-courts within its jurisdiction. D'Aiguillon, supported on the Council by two allies Maupeou and Terray, now urged upon the King that if he wanted to prevent another Fronde he must deal firmly with this defiance of his sovereign power. As a preliminary measure they demanded the dismissal of Choiseul, who had long been hand-in-glove with the Parlement; and in this they were supported by the influence of Madame du Barry.

For a time Louis held out. He knew that Choiseul, whatever his errors of judgment, was by far the most capable minister of his reign, and chief author of the two main lines of policy which France was still pursuing—the Austrian alliance and the Family Compact. But the minister's enemies urged that he was fomenting the Anglo-Spanish quarrel so as to lead France into war and enhance his own importance. Louis XV was determined that the tranquil pursuit of vice at Versailles should not again be upset by war. A royal order of December 24th, 1770, dismissed him from office and banished him to his estate. D'Aiguillon took over foreign affairs, Maupeou became Chancellor and the Abbé Terray became Controller General of Finance. For a moment the Jesuits hoped that the change of ministry would entail a relaxation of the measures against them; but this would have flouted public feeling and would have strained the bond with Spain.

Then it was the turn of the Parlement of Paris to feel the heavy hand of the ruling clique. During the night of January 20th, 1771, the members were all aroused by gendarmes and required to state then and there that they would resume their sittings. Of the 200 only 40 acquiesced, and even these retracted their consent next day. They were all dismissed and banished to various parts of France. The Government then took the momentous step of abolishing Parlements altogether, replacing them by six local *Conseils Supérieures*, with a central Court of Appeal in Paris. To commend the innovation justice was henceforth to be gratuitous and speedy.

The new tribunals were certainly an improvement on the old, but their creation was a dangerous step. Frenchmen had long been complaining of the Government's inefficiency and of the injustice of the social system; and they now began to ask why, if old institutions can be swept away so easily, the broom should stop at the Jesuits and the Parlements.

The evil old King saw the trouble ahead, but he only shrugged his shoulders. The régime would last out his time; his successor must shift for himself.

CHAPTER THIRTY-ONE

POLAND DISMEMBERED

1764-1772

THE partition of Poland stood out as a cynical piece of international knavery even in the eighteenth century. It came about through the "circumstances, conjectures and conjunctions" which Catherine said were the stuff of politics—notably a Russo-Turkish war which led to the first phase of "The Eastern Question." But Sweden, threatened with a similar fate to Poland's, escaped it by a return, in the nick of time, to a real working monarchy.

A RUSSO-PRUSSIAN ALLIANCE. After the Seven Years' War Russia and Prussia were drawn together by common interests. Catherine needed an ally behind her before she could launch into her "Greek Project"; and where could she look for such support? To England? But with the Treaty of Paris England had withdrawn from European affairs; and recent events did not encourage reliance on a country whose policy was the sport of party manœuvres. To France? But France, enfeebled by the war and, under Choiseul, preparing to renew the colonial struggle with England, had no attention to spare for issues in eastern Europe. To Austria? But Russian expansion at the expense of the Turk was bound to arouse hostility at Vienna, especially if directed against the lower Danube. That left only Frederick of Prussia, the warrior-king who had promoted the marriage which had been the start of Catherine's fortunes.

And Frederick was glad to take the hand she offered. He was on bad terms with every other Power in Europe. Everybody admired him but nobody trusted him. Maria Teresa would never be happy till she got back Silesia or an equivalent; the Bourbon-Hapsburg alliance made Austria's enemies France's; as for England, the thought of her treachery bit into Frederick's soul like acid into iron. But in Catherine he recognized a kindred spirit with kindred aims in at least two directions.

In the first place they both wanted to keep Poland chaotic and helpless. Catherine was, both by instinct and policy, ultra-Russian; and millions of people Russian by race, speech and religion, lived inside the Polish frontier. Moreover, control of Poland would greatly aid her designs against Turkey. Frederick, for his part, had always had his eye on Polish Prussia, to "sew up" (*recoudre*), as he put it in a memorandum written when Crown Prince, East Prussia to Brandenburg; and to get hold of it he would need a friendly understanding with Russia. And he shared her fear that on the death of Augustus III, now imminent, France would again try to put a candidate of her own at Warsaw, and build up Poland to act in French interests; whereas Prussia and Russia wanted Poland kept weak by the *liberum veto* and religious dissensions. (The latter were a new source of trouble. Poland's subject populations included Lutherans on the west and Orthodox on the east. In 1563 these minorities had been given equal civil rights with the Catholic majority; but under Jesuit influence these rights had been reduced, and "Dissidents" had recently been formally excluded from all public offices.)

Prussia and Russia had similar interests in Sweden also. There, too, they wanted to prevent the re-erection of a strong monarchy, lest they should be compelled to disgorge the parts of the former Swedish Empire which they had acquired in the Northern War fifty years before (p. 197). The eclipse of the Swedish monarchy in 1721 had been largely due to the ruin brought upon the country by the military ambitions of Charles XI and Charles XII, and the disputed succession had enabled the nobles to impose a constitution which gave all power to the Diet; worst of all, these nobles were mostly poor, and hungry for foreign bribes. Since then faction and corruption had demoralized the Government and had prevented Sweden from making trouble for her neighbours; and Russia and Prussia naturally wanted this immunity to continue.

Frederick and Catherine were still picking up the threads broken by the death of Peter III when the death of Augustus III forced them to come to an understanding without delay. The result was a treaty (April 1764) by which the parties guaranteed each other's possessions, and agreed to promote the candidature of Stanislas Poniatovski ("*de longtemps connu à l'impératrice et dont la personne lui était agréable*" as Frederick wrote with ironical euphemism in his Memoirs), and to prevent any interference with Polish "liberties." In a secret article they noted that in Sweden "ill-disposed persons wanted to upset the established form of government and thus jeopardize the true interests of the country"; and they therefore agreed "to maintain the said form of government in order to preserve the general tranquillity of the North"—i.e., they would for their own ends forcibly perpetuate anarchic misrule. They expressly undertook to prevent the King of Sweden being granted power to make laws, to raise taxes, to convoke the Diet or appoint ministers and officials. As they monopolized those rights in their own governments, it is interesting to note the considerations which in Frederick's mind affected the situation:

Their Swedish Majesties, not being at the head of an army fit to fight, ought to bend before the circumstances of the actual position, and not brave almost certain destruction by imprudence.

In writing to his sister the Queen of Sweden he sugared this might-is-right pill with family affection:

You will conceive, my dear sister, how it would touch my heart and your own, for you to be some day reduced to come to Berlin with all your family, through having failed to follow the counsels dictated by my tender regard for you and yours.

The Polish election came on in September 1764. The Poles liked the novel prospect of having one of themselves as King, but not an ex-lover and dependant of an Empress of Russia; so they put up a candidate of their own, a General Branicki. The French also had an iron in the fire—in fact several. Three envoys arrived from Paris, one from the Government, two others in the *Secret du Roi*, none knowing the instructions of the others. Too many cooks spoiled the French broth, and the contest was eventually limited to the two Poles. Had France and Austria actively supported Branicki Poland might have been saved from her impending fate; but the presence of a Russian army round the election-meadow outside Warsaw ensured the election of Poniatovski, and in November he was crowned "King Stanislas Augustus" at Cracow.

And then the excitement began.

A POLISH REVOLUTION. Poniatovski belonged to a group of patriotic magnates who, seeing that Poland's neighbours designed to take advantage of her weakness, sought to abolish the veto, and make the monarchy hereditary. Of this group the most powerful were the Czartoryskis of Lithuania, commonly called "The Family." Stanislas Poniatovski belonged to a junior branch of it and had married a Czartoryska; and his advancement, however questionable its origin, seemed a heaven-sent chance to promote their reforms. He was, superficially at any rate, an attractive person, had visited Paris, London and Vienna and had imbibed the enlightenment of the age together with its easy-going morals. Ambitious to make a career, he had been glad to be taken by Hanbury Williams to St. Petersburg (p. 247)—ostensibly as "Polish Secretary," actually as a lure for the Empress Elizabeth, who had a weakness for good-looking young men. Whatever his success with her he had certainly made a hit at "The Young Court" : the Archduchess Catherine had become infatuated with him. She was a generous mistress, and she now, as Empress, procured his election to the throne of his native country. She knew that "The Family" had designs incompatible with her own, but she counted on Poniatovski's loyalty and dependence on her support.

But the situation got out of hand. Before the election the patriots contrived to carry some of their reforms in the Diet, including the abolition of the Veto and a renewed ban on Dissidents. Stanislas, knowing that this would bring down on him Catherine's displeasure, tried to get promises of support from France and Austria—which of course angered her still more. After two years of bickering she put her foot down. Her ambassador at Warsaw, Repnin by name, who had all along acted as if Poland was a Russian dependency, now organized a "Convention" at Radom (November 1767) under the protection of Russian troops. "With arguments furnished with cannons and bayonets," as Frederick wrote to Voltaire, Repnin extorted full civil rights for Dissidents and a formal request to the Empress Catherine "to take the integrity and Constitution of Poland under her protection." This was, and was intended to be, a guarantee of chaos. No country in Europe was as yet fit for religious equality : it was certainly not to be found in Catherine's Russia, or even in countries that boasted of democratic liberty like Britain and Holland. No one, therefore, could seriously suppose that Poland, one of the most backward of European peoples, was ripe for it. There was much opposition to this heavy-handed intervention by a foreign ruler; but Repnin had a short way with protesters. The Bishop of Cracow (the religious capital of Poland) and half-a-dozen other prominent clerics were seized by Russian soldiers and carried off to prison at Smolensk.

This was bending the bow too far. At the little town of Bar in Podolia, an independent Confederation met and raised a rebellion "*Pro Libertate et Religione*" (February 1768), calling for the renewal of religious exclusion and the dethronement of Stanislas Augustus. This latter demand shows how confused the issues had become, for Poniatovski was in Catherine's bad books for supporting Polish nationalism against her. But the patriot leaders could not forget that he was her nominee, and had weakly accepted Repnin's demands at Radom; and they (quite unjustly) suspected him of having connived at the kidnapping of the bishops.

But, the sword once drawn, the time for argument and explanation was past. Bands of Catholic patriots went about slaughtering Dissidents and burning down their villages; and this gave Catherine an excuse to send in troops "to restore order." A horrible Jacquerie raged over southern Poland for months, the Poles butchering in the name of the Catholic Faith and the Russians in that of Toleration.

Frederick was privately vexed with Catherine for provoking the trouble. "Why," he asked his brother, "could she not content herself with ruling Russians, without interfering in Poland where she has no authority at all? The question of the Dissidents has spoiled everything." What perturbed him most was to see that this religious war in Poland was leading to complications which were likely to involve himself. For France was now intervening again in the affairs of eastern Europe.

A RUSSO-TURKISH WAR. French influence in Poland had been a tradition ever since a Valois prince became its first elected king in 1573; not only was Louis XV's Queen a Pole but the late Dauphine had been a daughter of Augustus III. The latest developments convinced Choiseul (not yet fallen from power as narrated in Chapter XXIX) that he had been remiss over the recent election, and by way of substitute he stirred up trouble for Russia at Constantinople. France had ruined her former prestige there when she formed an alliance in the Seven Years' War with Turkey's two enemies, Russia and Austria; but Vergennes, now ambassador to the Porte, had learned his business from men of the golden age of French diplomacy. And he had something to build on, for the Sultan already had three grievances against Russia. Catherine had broken Russia's undertaking in the Treaty of the Pruth (1711) not to intervene in Polish affairs without Turkish concurrence; she had, in preparation for her Greek Project, been fomenting discontents among the Sultan's Balkan subjects; and Russian troops, chasing Confederate Poles into Rumania, had destroyed villages on Turkish territory. Vergennes harped on these strings with such skill that in September 1768 Turkey declared war on Russia—virtually in support of the exclusive privileges of Polish Catholics!

Catherine called on her new ally to fulfil the terms of their agreement. That was just what Frederick had dreaded. Searing experience had taught him that nothing is so unpredictable as the fortunes of war, and that (as he wrote to his brother) those who are least active make the fewest mistakes. The rulers of Austria felt much the same. If Prussia joined Russia against Turkey, France would be almost bound to support her protégé, and would drag her ally Austria into a general war, of which Maria Teresa had had enough to last a lifetime. So Kaunitz devised a plan to draw Frederick away from Catherine by an Austro-Prussian pact. It was a daring conception, but not more daring than the Franco-Austrian alliance which he had created twelve years earlier. And there was just a chance that Frederick might be induced to return Silesia if he could be indemnified elsewhere—say by taking West Prussia from Poland.

Emperor Joseph gladly undertook to open negotiations by a personal interview with Frederick, being (like everybody else) eager to meet the most talked-of man in the world. His mother was reluctant to let her precious boy come under the spell of this Satanic personage; but at last the meeting took place at Neisse, in August 1769. Frederick could be a delightful companion and was an adept at winning hearts by subtle flattery. He agreed that the peace of the world depended on their friendship. "You and I are Germans. What is it to us if France fights England over Newfoundland codfish, or Turks seize Russians by the hair on the Euxine?" Joseph was not altogether taken in. He reported to his mother that the King was a wonderful talker, "but everything he said showed him a rascal" (*fourbe*). Still, the interview was followed by letters agreeing to keep out of the war.

Meanwhile the Turkish and Russian forces had at last overcome the difficulties of mobilization. Neither party had the men, munitions or money for effective war—as Frederick remarked in his caustic way, it was a contest between a blind man and a one-eyed man. Catherine, in the latter rôle, had the advantage. One of her armies took Azov and the Crimea; another penetrated the Rumanian provinces to Bucharest.[1] Her fleet sailed from the Baltic, calling at Chatham to take on stores and Admiral Elphinstone to act as adviser to the commanding officer Count Orlov, who, though a very terrific personage and Catherine's latest lover, had never been to sea before. The Turkish fleet, lacking an Elphinstone, was defeated at Chesmé off Chios and destroyed by fire-ships. Catherine received Orlov as a conquering hero; and when Elphinstone (whose indispensable contribution to victory she patriotically ignored) remarked to her that the Russian fleet was only one degree more efficient than the Turkish, she replied with characteristic penetration, "Yes; but the ignorance of the Russians is that of youth; the weakness of Turkey is that of imbecile old age." (But the dotard was to be an unconscionable time dying!)

---

[1] "Rumania" was not yet a state, but the term was already coming into use for the two Turkish provinces (Moldavia and Wallachia) along the lower course of the Danube. Their inhabitants claim to be of Latin race.

"THINGS BAD BEGUN . . ." These Russian victories, by threatening Joseph's long-cherished hope to advance the Hapsburg frontier to the Black Sea, were one of the determining causes of the Partition of Poland. The other seemed equally irrelevant.

Joseph had met Frederick at Neisse to agree about keeping out of the Russo-Turkish war; in June 1770 Frederick returned the visit to see what could be done to bring that conflict to an end. They met at Neustadt, where the Austrian army was engaged in manœuvres. The King laid on flattery with a trowel, appearing in Austrian uniform and announcing that he and his staff had come as recruits to join the Emperor's "Sons of Mars." But this time Kaunitz was present, and did most of the talking. While the conversations were in progress couriers arrived from the Sultan asking both Emperor and King to intercede with Russia. The meeting broke up with Frederick undertaking to induce "his" Empress to be moderate in her demands; and he brought away a conviction, which he intended to impress on Catherine, that Joseph would go to any length rather than let Russia become established on the Lower Danube.

The Tsarina had been perturbed to hear of the interview, for she could not afford to lose her only friend. So in order to give a personal touch (always her strong point) to the discussions she invited Prince Henry of Prussia, now visiting his sister at Stockholm, to look in at St. Petersburg on his way home. He came, and stayed four months (October 1770–January 1771) acting as Frederick's mouthpiece. But when she produced her sketch of peace-terms they made Frederick's hair stand on end, for they included demands for the cession of Rumania as well as the Crimea. He told Henry to tell her that this amounted to a declaration of war on Austria. And his concern at the possibility of another general war brought back into his mind the notion of reconciling the conflicting claims of Russia and Austria, and adding West Prussia to his own kingdom, all at the expense of Poland. The idea was not new. It had been in the air for a century. Frederick William had talked of it; Augustus II had offered parts of Poland to buy the consent of his neighbours to his becoming hereditary king. In the present circumstances the plan had fresh attractions. It would obviously be to the advantage of the two Empresses to take different bits of Poland rather than fight about the same bit of Turkey; and whereas Frederick had everything to lose if obliged to join Russia in fighting a combination of Austria, France and Turkey, he had everything to gain by a partition of Poland. So he sent his brother to St. Petersburg with a tentative suggestion. Catherine eagerly took it up, for her funds and supplies were exhausted and her regiments at a tenth of their paper strength—and she strongly suspected that in any case Frederick would evade his obligation to support her in the field.

But when Frederick dropped similar hints at Vienna the scheme met with an obstacle. Austria was on the point of making an agreement with the Sultan to declare war on Russia in return for a subsidy of £750,000 and the province of Little Wallachia. Austria had not ratified the pact, but the mere proposal enabled the Empress and Kaunitz to take a high moral line and decline to sanction the partition of Poland.

". . . MAKE STRONG THEMSELVES BY ILL." Nevertheless Maria Teresa was in great distress. Nothing could now prevent Catherine and Frederick from acquiring parts of Poland and whatever her personal feelings she felt it her duty to get some equivalent for Austria, either at the expense of Poland (e.g. Galicia) or of Turkey (e.g. Rumania). But she was under great obligations to Turkey; for the Sultan had magnanimously refrained from taking advantage of her difficulties in the Seven Years' War, and she had just made a pact with him which he had honoured by paying the first instalment of the subsidy without waiting for her to fulfil her part of the bargain. And as to the Poles, she had always upheld them as fellow-Catholics, and hated the thought of joining Protestant and Orthodox "monsters" in robbing them. Joseph was prolific with alternatives. Why should Austria not take out her compensation in Germany, by recovering Silesia, or by getting hold of Anspach and Baireuth? True, Frederick had conquered the one and had reversionary claims to the other; but he would surely be willing to make concessions, when he was getting something for nothing in Poland. And this arrangement would leave all the discredit of the partition to him and Catherine.

This seemed the best way out of the dilemma; so Van Swieten, the Austrian ambassador at Berlin, was instructed to lay the proposal before Frederick. The King was all smiles to learn that Austria had decided to take part in a general settlement; but when the ambassador went on to mention the proposed conditions, he leapt from his chair. "Do you think I have gout in my head? It is only in my foot! We are here to discuss the disposal of Poland, not of Prussia!" Van Swieten hastily mentioned that Austria might consider taking Bosnia and Belgrade from the Turks instead. The old King answered that he had no personal objection to this, though it seemed a shabby thing to do in view of Austria's obligations to the Sultan. And when early in 1772 news reached Vienna that Frederick and Catherine had actually signed

FIRST PARTITION OF POLAND 1772

Frontier before Partition
Acquisitions of Prussia
Acquisitions of Russia
Acquisitions of Austria

an agreement sketching out the portions of Poland that each was going to take, Joseph and Kaunitz convinced the Empress that it was Poland or nothing. After long hesitations and many "jeremiads" (as she herself called them), torn by remorse and ashamed to show herself in public, she at last resigned herself to her fate—or rather, to Poland's. "The crime cries to Heaven!" she exclaimed. "What an example we are setting to posterity, prostituting our honour for a wretched bit of Poland!" This last phrase implied that her honour was a question of price; and when it came to fixing the Austrian share of the booty, she haggled with great determination. Like Alice's carpenter over the oysters, "With sobs and sighs she sorted out Those of the largest size."

The final division was signed at St. Petersburg in August 1772, "In the Name of the Most Sacred Trinity," for the pious purpose of "preventing the disruption of the Polish State." The "rightful claims"[1] of the signatories were set forth in detail. Catherine took White Russia with a population of two millions; Frederick got Polish Prussia minus Danzig and Thorn, with about three-quarters of a million; the Austrian share was Zips and Galicia, with three millions. No wonder the sarcastic Frederick remarked that she had not a dainty appetite after all, since she devoured nearly as much as Catherine and himself put together. And whereas Catherine's new subjects were nearly all of Russian blood, speech and religion, and Frederick's were mostly German and Lutheran, Maria Teresa brought into her polyglot patchwork of peoples yet another discordant element, who, living on the far side of the Carpathians, weakened still further the strategic unity of the Monarchy.

The next business was to get the consent of the Polish King and Diet; but the attention of all concerned was now drawn off to events in Sweden which demonstrated by contrast the cause of Poland's misfortunes.

SWEDEN AVOIDS POLAND'S FATE. In Sweden as in Poland the "liberties" of the nobles had made monarchy a sham. In a sketch of the constitution drawn up in 1746 for the instruction of Crown Prince Adolf Frederick it was expressly stated that Kings of Sweden were too wise to strive after sovereignty; and at his accession a few years later he had taken oath "to abhor unlimited power, and to regard all who opposed

---

[1] It was characteristic of Maria Teresa's innate honesty that she insisted on the deletion of the word "rightful" in the draft; and of her weakness as she grew older that she let it be put back in the final document. And it was equally typical of Frederick to mark the event by a blasphemous jest: "This will unite three religions. We communicate in the Eucharistic Body of Poland; and if this is not for the good of our souls, it is for the good of our countries."

the existing constitution as traitors." The dominant Hat party had a metal stamp of his signature made, so that they need not make even a pretence of obtaining his approval for their decrees.

For years France had used their venality to keep the country subservient, but times were changing. French bribes were now outbidden by the purchasing-power of British merchants. So in 1769 Choiseul came to the conclusion that France was on the wrong tack. "Hereafter," he told the French Minister at Stockholm, "the King commands you to use your knowledge and talents to re-erect monarchical power in Sweden." He could of course be sure of the support of the King and Queen for this change of policy, but he relied even more on the disposition of the Crown Prince Gustavus (born 1746). A high-spirited, intelligent, volatile, egotistic young man, he spoke French as a second mother-tongue, had a pretty taste in French literature, and corresponded with the Encyclopedists. It was disturbing rumours of his dynamic character that had made Frederick and Catherine add the secret annex to their treaty of 1764.

Towards the end of 1770 Gustavus went on a visit to Paris, where for three months he was the lion of French society. In March 1771 news reached him (at the Opera) of the death of his father; and he set off home next morning with a secret treaty of alliance and a substantial instalment of the subsidy which France had formerly paid to the Hats. On the way he visited his redoubtable uncle at Berlin, who dilated to him upon the dangers to himself and to Sweden of any attempt to violate the constitution. Gustavus seems to have succeeded where many failed, for Frederick reported to his partner Catherine that he was quite harmless.

He found Stockholm a battlefield of intrigue, the three subordinate Orders hoping to overthrow the haughty Hats, and French diplomacy (now conducted by the resourceful Vergennes) pitted against the Russian and the British. The eyes of all were on what was happening to Poland through the impotence of its monarchy; pamphlets poured from the Press expressing alarm for the future of Sweden and praying for another Gustavus Adolphus to pull the nation together. Gustavus III did not appear likely to fill the need, after all. He played the part of an affable, accessible young King (the first for fifty years who could speak Swedish), too taken up with frivolities, especially theatricals, to bother about politics, though good-humouredly anxious to pour oil on the troubled waters of the Diet. But behind the scenes he was concocting a military *coup d'état* with his brothers and a group of officers. On August 19th, 1772, just when the guard was being changed at the

Palace, he appeared in the courtyard, and called on the troops to support him in ending a régime of corrupt, cowardly, quarrelsome chat-
terers. The soldiers responded with enthusiasm; and so did the
populace when, a few hours later, he rode through the streets to the
Chamber. The ministry and the nobles could not resist the pressure of
public feeling. They accepted without demur his new constitution, and
the bloodless revolution was complete. The Diet was to remain the
legislative and fiscal authority, but could only deal with matters
proposed to it by the King. He needed its consent to make war or peace,
but alone appointed to all high offices in State and Army.

This raised uncomfortable questions for Frederick and Catherine.
They were under treaty obligation to each other to take arms against
just such an event, but they were now at a critical stage in the partition
of Poland. Catherine urged Frederick to do something about it. He
wrote reproachful letters to his sister and nephew:

If your happiness were solid I should be the first to felicitate you; but
the facts are very much the reverse. I enclose a copy of my guarantee
signed at St. Petersburg. If I cannot find expedients to smoothe over the
crisis I shall have to fulfil the treaty; for one does not undertake such
obligations for nothing.

But he was too practised a player to take his eye off the ball—and the
ball just now was Polish Prussia. And so Gustavus III, with the moral
and financial support of France, was able to establish his new régime
undisturbed.

Thus the Partition of Poland saved not only Turkey but Sweden from
a like fate; and offered one more proof that monarchy was the only form
of government that could give security and independence to peoples
lacking the political education which circumstances had afforded to
the British.

KUTCHUK-KAINARDJI. Sweden settled, the attention of the Powers
reverted to Poland and Turkey. When Stanislas Augustus refused to
acquiesce in the spoliation of his kingdom, the three burglarious sovereigns summoned what is known in Polish history as "The Relegation
Diet." But it, too, resisted persuasion, threats and bribery, until Russian, Prussian and Austrian troops advanced on Warsaw. By the treaty
signed September 1773 Poland had not only to agree to the partition,
but to promise not to alter the constitution which had made it possible.
It was easy to read the intention behind this clause.

It now only remained to wind up the Turkish War. Catherine was
hampered by an insurrection in the south, headed by a Don Cossack

named Pugatchev. The peasants had been falling in status for centuries, but they could not reconcile themselves to being their landlords' chattels. Peter III in his very short reign had excused the nobles from compulsory state-service, and the peasants hoped for a corresponding emancipation from forced labour. When this was not forthcoming they declared that Peter's orders had been withheld, and that Pugatchev was Peter himself, come to liberate them. Wherever the movement spread he hanged the landlords and divided the land among the people. The Tsarina had no little difficulty in raising forces to suppress the rebellion; but Pugatchev was eventually captured and put to death in Moscow with the refinements of cruelty on which eighteenth-century Russia prided itself.

All this gave the Turks time to gather strength. Twice Russian armies plunged into Bulgaria, only to outrun their supplies and find themselves in danger of destruction. Catherine, her inefficient governmental machine and impoverished people exhausted by the long-drawn-out war, called on Austria to make the Turks come to terms. Sultan Mustafa was in January 1774 succeeded by Abdul Hamid, who after a defeat in Silistria agreed to the famous Treaty of Kutchuk-Kainardji (July 1774). Territorially Russia acquired only a few places at the base of the Crimea; the concessions she demanded all looked to the future: the right to use the Black Sea and to "protect" the Rumanian Principalities. The Sultan promised to tolerate Christian worship, and to "take into consideration" representations by Russia in favour of his Balkan peoples who belonged to the Greek Orthodox Church. These stipulations were so scattered about the treaty as to escape notice; but taken together they could be interpreted as giving Russia the right to interfere in the internal affairs of the Ottoman Empire whenever she considered the rights of its Christian subjects contravened. And that interpretation became one of the most disturbing factors in European politics for over a century.

When the rulers of Austria heard the terms of this treaty they made further demands against the Turks, claiming to have saved them from worse sacrifices. Joseph had long had his eye on the Bukovina, which, though really part of Rumania, might be regarded as an extension of Galicia. His mother did not like this demand; but the Maria Teresa who had in her young days carried all before her with her high spirit and proud uprightness of conduct, was nowadays a pathetic figure, swept along by her impetuous son in spite of scruples and misgivings. As Frederick caustically put it, *"elle pleurait et prenait toujours."* So the helpless Turk had to sign away the Bukovina (May 1775), and the acquisitions of Austria became far greater than those made by either of her partners in crime, though she had not fired a shot nor moved a soldier.

"Poland had been sacrificed to maintain peace between the three monarchs," wrote Frederick in his Memoirs; but the next passage exposes his sophism while displaying his prophetic vision.

The partition, so far from ending the jealousy between the Powers, gave it something to feed on. Russia wanted to expand towards Europe, Prussia to consolidate, Austria to swell out so as not to be stifled. The "civilizing" mission of Russia, the "historical" mission of Austria, the "political" mission of Prussia, all led to annexation and conquest. The decadence of Turkey and the anarchy of Poland opened a boundless field for them. They liked bargaining better than fighting, and their rivalry led to alliance; but the alliance did not remove the causes of the rivalry. On the contrary, it gave them fresh nourishment. If it had been possible to stop at the treaty of 1772, partition would have been not only lucrative but clever and politic; but history does not stand still.

This was written nearly twenty years before the final partitions which he did not live to see.

CHAPTER THIRTY-TWO

AMERICAN INDEPENDENCE

1773-1783

WE are now to see how a war between Britain and her American colonies developed into another stage of her long struggle with France for world-power. A temporary lapse in British mastery of the sea assured the Thirteen Colonies of their independence; but Britain emerged with her sea-power restored, her hold on India and Canada strengthened, and the French monarchy hurtling towards the abyss of the Revolution.

THE LAST CHANCE OF THE FRENCH MONARCHY. In May 1774 Louis XV died, full of years and dishonour. Carlyle has made famous the stampede of courtiers "with a sound like thunder" from the fœtid death-chamber to acclaim the new King and Queen. Optimism is generally in the air at a change of kings; on this occasion there was every sign that the new reign would be a complete contrast to the old —and who could ask for more?

Louis XVI and Marie Antoinette are said to have fallen to their knees praying for Divine aid because they were "too young to reign." They remained so all their lives. Both were totally ignorant of the world outside palaces, and neither of them had the receptive mind or penetrative vision that might have made up for faulty education. Louis had inherited from his father (who had led the "devout" reaction against the vices of the old King's court) a horror of dissipation. But his moral stature and mental equipment were quite inadequate for the absolute rule of twenty-five million people in such critical times. Pious and benevolent, he was painfully anxious to do something for the welfare of his people, if only he knew how. This dumb consciousness of his own inadequacy made him gauche and taciturn—he was the only Bourbon who lacked kingly grace on public occasions. His sole escape from a distracting and puzzling world was in physical activity—hunting and smithery—in which brawn could replace brain, and which gave him appetite for vast meals; and these caused premature obesity, digestive troubles, and further mental obfuscation.

The Queen was a very different order of being—lively, frivolous, capricious, avid of pleasure and admiration. Her position in France had from the first suffered from the fact that she embodied the Austrian alliance which had brought such misfortunes on the country. But she did not trouble herself much about this or anything else in these early days. She had inherited none of her mother's powers of reflection and application—only her beauty and charm.

The King's first act, after taking counsel with his maiden aunts, was to send for Maurepas, now well on in his seventies. The old man had spent the last twenty-five years in retirement, but to the middle-aged princesses he represented their father's policy before he let it slip into the hands of designing mistresses and careerist ministers. He was vain and frivolous, but was neither fool nor rogue. He refused to do more than act as unpaid general adviser, and most of his appointments turned out well.

Of the "barricade of good men" which Maurepas built up round the King, we need here mention only two. The new Secretary for Foreign Affairs was Vergennes, who, having proved a capable diplomatist at Constantinople and at Stockholm, was now to show equal ability in a wider field. But the most significant and hopeful of the appointments was that of Turgot (1727–81) as Controller-General. For Turgot was the most enlightened disciple of the most enlightened Physiocrats. Coming of the official class, he imbibed in a precocious boyhood all the teachings of the *philosophes* and the *économistes* except their atheism, and while still in his 'teens contributed to the Encyclopedia. He studied economic problems not only from books but from practical observations abroad, particularly in England. His passionate devotion to the public weal, his tireless industry, and his resource in applying principles to practice, had found scope when at the early age of thirty-four he became Intendant at Limoges. During the next fourteen years he turned Limoges from one of the most miserable to one of the most prosperous provinces of France. He twice refused promotion in order to carry on his work there; but the post now offered him put him in control of the whole financial and economic policy of the country. The fiscal situation of the Government was desperate. Terray had never hoped to do more than stave off for a while the ruin that seemed to be inevitable; but Turgot undertook at the outset that there should be no bankruptcy, no more loans, no new taxes. He would rely on two simple but drastic remedies. The first was *economy*, reducing expenditure below revenue—Mr. Micawber's infallible prescription for human peace of mind. The second was *reform*—agricultural, industrial, commercial and administrative—to broaden the basis of taxation. He knew that these operations would make him the best-hated man in France; and on taking office he made the King realize for the first time that

11

wealth lavished on court and courtiers was wrung from the tears and sweat of poverty-stricken men and women. Louis, deeply touched, promised to support him through thick and thin; but this high resolution did not endure more than twenty months, which did not give Turgot much time to carry through his programme.

Among his minor measures were a drastic reduction of the Household, the restriction of the tax-farmers to their legitimate profits, and a reorganization of public diligences which halved the time taken for transport. But three of his reforms were of transcendant importance. Firstly, he established internal free trade in corn, removing customs-barriers which caused famines in some provinces and gluts in others, and robbed the peasant of all motive to improve his methods of farming. Secondly, he swept away the *jurandes*, the moss-grown relics of the medieval guilds, which hampered production and paralysed initiative in industry. Thirdly, he abolished the *corvée royale*—the obligation upon the peasantry to maintain the highways, taking them, often for days at a time, from the tillage by which they lived. In future labour on the roads was to be paid for out of a *subvention territoriale*, payable by all classes—even by those who could best afford it!

And that was as far as Turgot had time to go. His reforms were immensely popular, but each of them struck at the privileges of at least one section of the community. The Queen took up the cause of the disgruntled courtiers and the cashiered officers; Maurepas was offended at being elbowed aside, the King by patronizing references to his lack of experience. The Parlement refused to register the last of his edicts, declaring that

any system which under an appearance of benevolence tends to establish equality among men . . . would lead to the overturn of all ordered society. What would not be the dangers of a project which would confound the orders of society by imposing a uniform taxation?

The King enforced the registration by a *lit de justice*, but the complaints of the Queen, his brothers, his aunts, and his household were sapping his resolution; and, well-meaning as he was, he was shocked at ideas which seemed to threaten the social pyramid of which he was the apex.

A few days after the abolition of the *corvée* Turgot appeared with a memorandum longer, more intricate and more revolutionary than ever. It proposed to set up elective parish councils, which were to send delegates to district councils, which were to elect provincial councils, which were to elect a national council. These councils were to control such local concerns as the repair of roads and bridges, the relief of the poor, the maintenance of the police, and the assessment of taxation. This system, coupled with the establishment of Normal Schools for the training of teachers, with special emphasis on the teaching of civics, would create a new sense of citizenship and national unity. In ten years it would provide an instructed, virtuous, patriotic nation, which would look up to its King with admiration and affection, and would make him envied by all other sovereigns in the world.

But these proposals frightened King Louis out of his wits. What seemed to Turgot a buttress for the monarchy seemed to him a danger to it; for in his eyes a king restrained by any sort of elected assembly was no king at all. A few weeks later a disagreement among ministers gave him a pretext for sending Turgot a brief note of dismissal. Great was the rejoicing at Versailles. Before the year was out the *corvée* was reimposed, the provincial customs-barriers were re-erected, the *jurandes* re-established. But the nation had caught a vision of a promised land.

THE AMERICAN REBELLION. Meanwhile exciting events were taking place across the Atlantic. George III and his ministers had been trying to make Britain's thirteen American colonies contribute to the cost of governing and defending them; and in 1774 they had sent delegates to a "Continental Congress" at Philadelphia to concert measures to defeat this inroad on the sacred British principle of "No Taxation without Representation."

This is no place to weigh the rights and wrongs of the quarrel, or to follow the course of the campaigns; our sole concern with it is its effect upon European affairs. One of the most important of these influences, in the long run, was the wording of the Declaration of Independence by which the leaders of the Congress (more particularly Thomas Jefferson of Virginia) defined their natural rights as human beings.

It consisted of three parts: a statement of the principles of democracy, an indictment of George III, and a renunciation of allegiance. The last is merely a sentence, and the second a distorted account of recent events. But the opening exordium expressed with matchless clarity the theory of democracy:

We hold these truths to be self-evident: that all men are created equal; that they are endowed by their Creator with certain inalienable rights; that among these are life, liberty and the pursuit of happiness; that to secure these rights governments are instituted among men, deriving their just powers from the consent of the governed; that whenever any form of government becomes destructive of those ends it is the right of the people to alter or abolish it.

We may wonder what the claim to "human equality" can have meant to a slave-owning community; but the phrase "endowed with inalienable rights" cut away the roots of kingship by the Grace of God; and the claim that governments, having been instituted by man for his own convenience, can be unmade by him with the same purpose, is the inmost spirit of revolution. Such ideas had been deduced by the abstract reasoning of Locke and Rousseau: they now ceased to be Philosophy and became Law. And the Contract theory seemed less of a fiction in a primitive country than in the Old World.

The first two campaigns went on the whole in favour of the King's forces and very many of the colonists rejoiced in their success. But in October 1777 an army under General Burgoyne was cut off and compelled to surrender at Saratoga Springs; and this proved the turning-point of the war, for it brought to the rebels an alliance with France.

FRANCE AND THE AMERICANS. One of the worst results of the fall of Turgot was that it removed the chief obstacle to France becoming involved in the American War. The King dimly realized that the country could not afford another war just then, but without Turgot he quickly succumbed to the forces that were pushing the Government into it. Of course, the temptation to take advantage of Britain's extremity was very strong. Vergennes had declared on taking office that the ascendancy given to England by the Peace of Paris (1763) must arouse the indignation of every patriotic Frenchman. The partition of Poland, carried through without France's consent, had demonstrated to all the world how her prestige had dwindled. But there was much to be said against as well as for intervention in the American War. Some years more of preparation for the forces and of recuperation for the treasury would be required before France could wage war on an adequate scale; and it was always dangerous to encourage rebellion. But on the other hand French commerce had everything to gain by ending the British monopoly of American markets; and could France let Britain suppress the rebellion and then turn her troops against Spanish possessions and so gain the whole of North America?

At first Vergennes decided to let England exhaust herself while he built up his resources, and meanwhile to keep the rebels going by underhand support. The means and the instrument for this lay ready to hand. Caron Beaumarchais (afterwards famous as the author of *Figaro* and *The Barber of Seville*) developed a scheme to supply the Americans with munitions. The Congress had already sent Silas Deane to make purchases of war-material, and Beaumarchais gained the secret and unofficial approval of Vergennes for a bogus commercial House, "Roderigue et Cie," to trade in artillery, small arms, ammunition and uniforms. The firm was founded on loans from the French and Spanish Governments, and made large purchases from French arsenals; but the British Government dared not complain for fear of precipitating a war which would compel it to fight on two or three fronts.

Congress had neither cash nor goods to send in payment, and Beaumarchais had to pledge his own credit and that of the "Friends of America." There were plenty of these. The intellectual world was deeply touched by the spectacle of republicanism, seen at the safe distance of 3,000 miles. Voltaire (now a very old man) acclaimed the religious equality which he thought was to be found there; to Rousseau the Red Man (who really had nothing to do with the case) was a noble Child of Nature; to men nurtured on the classics Washington and Jefferson seemed to have stepped out of the pages of Plutarch. Benjamin Franklin, who came to join Deane in the autumn of 1777, became the darling of French society. With his unpowdered hair falling on his shoulders, his literary and scientific fame, his coat of russet homespun and his broad-toed shoes, he seemed the embodiment of republican virtues and of homely wisdom, the spokesman of a people rightly struggling to be free.

Beaumarchais sent over not only material but men—professional German officers like Kalb and Struben, who turned American militiamen into soldiers, and young French aristocrats like the Marquis de Lafayette, who volunteered to serve under Washington, "the American Cincinnatus." Lafayette, the type of all that was romantic and chivalrous in France, wrote home glowing accounts of a land where Liberty was no mere philosophical abstraction, but a way of life and government . . . "a land seen hitherto only in my dreams, where only good-will, patriotism and freedom dwell, and all men are brothers."

It was now that Frederick of Prussia took his revenge on Britain for leaving him in the lurch in 1763. If he had made the least sign of supporting his former ally the French Government would not have dared to send its troops and supplies across the Atlantic; but he made it clear that he had no such intention.

Vergennes held back until Saratoga showed that the Americans had a real chance of success. Then, fearing that King George would make concessions and turn re-united forces against the possessions of France and Spain, he came to terms with Deane and Franklin. He found them stiff bargainers; for many members of Congress were reluctant to see the infant Republic entangle itself with European alliances, and had an instinctive distrust of Papist Frenchmen.

Vergennes was not far wrong in fearing an Anglo-American reconciliation. Saratoga made King George ready for almost any concession that would leave the colonies nominally under his sceptre. Lord North introduced a Bill in November (1777) appointing a commission to go over and offer a treaty renouncing parliamentary taxation, and offering the colonies what we now call "Dominion Status." There is little doubt that if the offer had been made promptly Congress would have accepted it; for the British forces still held New York and Philadelphia, and Washington's "Continental Army" had shrunk to 4,000 ragged half-starved men. But the Bill was hung up over the Christmas recess, and by the time it was re-introduced (February 1778) the Americans had made a military alliance with France.

The war was to be jointly prosecuted until the freedom, sovereignty and unconditional independence of the United States was recognized; and "whatever the issue" neither side was to make any claim for compensation against the other. King George's response was an immediate declaration of war on France. North made frantic efforts to escape the responsibility of office. The nation looked to Pitt, now Lord Chatham, feeling that the Americans might draw back if he were head of the Government; and that if the war had to go on he was the man to conduct it. But Chatham could not work with the main body of the Whigs, who openly supported the rebels, and called for an immediate recognition of American independence and the concentration of the British war-effort against France. It was to oppose this resolution that Chatham made his famous last appearance in the Lords. With his passing passed all hope of a last-minute Anglo-American reconciliation. Henceforth the King had the wretched North in a cleft stick—there was no alternative to his carrying on a policy which he did not believe in, and a war he knew himself incompetent to manage.

BRITANNIA CONTRA MUNDUM. The effect of France's intervention was not felt at once. All depended on sea-power. So long as Britannia ruled the waves France could not fight a war in America. But if the French navy could wrest away the trident even for a time there might be a different story to tell; and a struggle for it went on in every quarter of the globe for five years. The French fleet had been overhauled since 1763 and was now at a higher pitch of efficiency and morale than ever before; whereas the British, with Lord Sandwich as First Lord, was honeycombed with corruption and mismanagement.[1] But the début of the French in American waters was not auspicious. A squadron under Comte d'Estaing appeared off Sandy Hook, but lacking the nerve to force its way into New York harbour retired to Boston. There the officers duelled and the crews brawled with their supposed allies until the spring of 1779, when they made off to capture West Indian islands for King Louis.

After two more years of diplomatic labour Vergennes brought in Spain (1779). The Spaniards were not interested in sentimental talk about "liberty," and had too many colonies of their own to be supporters of rebellion. It was only when Vergennes agreed that an immediate objective should be the re-capture of Gibraltar that King Carlos implemented the Family Compact. The blockade of the Rock began in July 1779, but Rodney interrupted it long enough to reinforce and revictual the fortress for a prolonged resistance.

During the next two years practically every other state in Europe followed, actively or passively, the lead of the Bourbon Powers. They had all suffered from British arrogance towards neutral shipping in wartime—the stopping of vessels and the confiscation of all goods that could possibly aid her enemies, and they now joined to enforce "The Freedom of the Seas."

Vergennes won the support of the Dutch, Danish and Swedish Governments for a general statement of international law on the subject: (1) a neutral flag protects all merchandise other than contraband of war, even when it belongs to belligerent subjects; (2) nothing can be treated as contraband of war save arms and munitions; and (3) a belligerent cannot merely proclaim a port to be in a state of blockade and then seize on the high seas any ship plying to it: the blockade must be an actual fact. Britain naturally refused to admit these restrictions on the use of her sea-supremacy; but it was a grave embarrassment to her when Catherine of Russia (anxious to safeguard her growing overseas commerce, and to make a return to France for support in the recent Turkish war) promulgated a Declaration of Armed Neutrality (March 1780), and made conventions with Denmark, Sweden, Prussia, Austria, Naples and Portugal (*et tu Brute!*) to implement it.

And this was not the worst. The Dutch, being the neutral State with the most developed overseas trade, were making vast profits from supplying the Colonies with munitions of war. They used St. Eustatius as the chief entrepôt for this trade, and in two years this barren West Indian islet

[1] The loss of the *Royal George* (August 1782), dirged by Cowper, was due to dockyard "graft."

became the richest spot in the world. In December 1780 papers taken on an American ship showed that the Dutch Republic was about to enter into an open alliance with the American Congress; whereupon the British Government declared war on it, feeling that an open enemy was less dangerous than a deceitful friend; and Dutch overseas possessions including St. Eustatius with its immense booty, became the prey of British naval power.

Nevertheless, Britain's enemies now included the second, third and fourth naval Powers, and every man's hand was against her, not only in Europe and America but in Asia. For Vergennes made a strong bid to recover French supremacy in India, by stirring up the Nizam of Hyderabad and the Sultan of Mysore to join the Mahratta rulers of Central India in a great confederation to destroy the East India Company; and the British Government had its hands too full to be able to spare troops or stores or ships for such a distant theatre of war.

King George's spirit was not a whit shaken by all this; and as a matter of fact he seemed more than once on the verge of complete success. It was long before Franco-Spanish support began to make itself felt in America. Both parties were intent on their own interests —France in the West Indies and Spain at Gibraltar. And the British, learning the lesson of Saratoga, abandoned their heavy-footed European soldiering in favour of light-armed "bush-whacking," often conducted by American "loyalists." This proved particularly successful in the south. Savannah was occupied, and it was found that Georgia had no heart in the war. Then, as soon as D'Estaing had cleared off to the West Indies, General Clinton (who had succeeded Howe after Saratoga) brought 7,000 men by sea and captured Charleston. By the end of 1780 South Carolina seemed settled down under British rule again. In the north Washington was having great trouble in keeping his famishing and neglected force in being. The States were flooded with currency which came to be worth little more than the paper the notes were printed on. Business came to a standstill; and supplies for want of which the American army was starving poured into British camps, where they were paid for in hard cash.

YORKTOWN. The Americans did not fail to apprise Vergennes of their disappointment at the lack of practical support from France; but in 1781 the alliance suddenly turned imminent defeat into decisive victory.

This change of fortune was an object-lesson in the importance of sea-power. Lord Sandwich, though not such a rascal as Whig historians make out, lacked the character and the brains to direct a broad scheme of naval strategy. Instead of following Pitt's famous maxim and keeping the enemy's ships shut up in their harbours, he dissipated the navy's strength by trying to convoy merchantmen, defend the West Indies, raise the siege of Gibraltar, and hunt separate enemy squadrons, all at the same time. Certainly, Britain had the good fortune to have at hand one of her traditional line of sea-dogs, Sir George Rodney;[1] but he was not allowed to concentrate on the one thing needful—the destruction of the enemy's main fleet. This cost Britain her American colonies.

Clinton had returned to New York leaving Cornwallis in command at Charleston with instructions to reduce North Carolina and Virginia by the methods which had been so successful in South Carolina and Georgia, and then join in the destruction of Washington's ragged remnants. But Cornwallis was now faced by Greene, ablest of the American generals, and guerrilla began again in South Carolina. So he gambled on a swift march into Virginia, hoping that Clinton would be able to reinforce him there.

But Clinton had himself been thrown onto the defensive. Lafayette had gone home in the winter of 1779, and had convinced the Government that if France did not strike in vigorously the rebels would be worn down into submission, when the British would be able to concentrate against France. So in the following summer a well-equipped French army was sent to Newport under Rochambeau. It had been lucky to evade the British fleet, and for nearly a year it had to remain immoble in Rhode Island. But in the spring of 1781 a powerful squadron under Comte de Grasse arrived in the West Indies with instructions to take whatever action would best assist the Americans. Rochambeau and Washington decided for a concentrated attack on Cornwallis, who had fortified himself for the winter in the Yorktown peninsula at the entrance to Chesapeake Bay. He had chosen that spot in the expectation that British control of the sea would keep open his communications; but he was deceived. By a skilfully executed plan two French squadrons and two armies, one American and one French, converged on Yorktown at the right time and place. Everything went wrong for the British. Rodney had gone home on leave, taking four ships to refit, before the arrival of the French fleet was known. The frigate which should have warned his deputy, Graves, went aground, and when the British squadron arrived off Chesapeake Bay it had to

---

[1] We may note the difference in spirit between eighteenth century and twentieth century warfare in the fact that when war broke out Rodney was in Paris, prevented from leaving by his creditors—until his debts were paid by a French nobleman.

fight at a grave disadvantage. Thus the sails which Cornwallis saw coming in from the Atlantic were not British but French. Meanwhile Washington and Rochambeau had taken possession of the neck of the peninsula. Cornwallis was now in a hopeless situation, cut off from food and ammunition, and under concentrated fire from sea and land. By the middle of October (1781) he was obliged to surrender.

A few weeks later Rodney was back, and British naval strength was concentrated again; but that short lapse was fatal to Britain's hopes of retaining her Colonies.

ANGLO-AMERICAN PEACE-MAKING. It is said that when North heard of the surrender he threw up his hands, exclaiming "It's all over!" Why was it "all over"? Britain still had powerful armies in America; she held two of the three chief ports and three of the four chief towns; her economic resources were scarcely tapped; she had recovered command of the sea. But the situation was made hopeless by the spirit of the nation and of Parliament. There had always been strong opposition to the war. The Rockingham Whigs had adopted independence as their American policy as early as 1768; Fox and Barré had exulted over every British set-back and had exhausted the vocabulary of abuse against Lord North and his colleagues. At first all this had made little impression on the public, which supported the Government's determination to keep control over the Empire; but by this time the nation no longer had any heart in the struggle. They were angry at the increased taxation, at the mismanagement of the war, and at the losses inflicted by French privateers. For a year past North had been fighting a losing battle in the House, and after Yorktown his majority shrank to single figures. The King used every kind of argument and entreaty to induce him to hold on, but by March 1782 the situation had become quite impossible.

So the Opposition Whigs came into office again, with Rockingham as Prime Minister and Fox and Shelburne as Secretaries of State. They were a very varied assortment, agreed only on ending the war against the Americans. It was the bitterest of all the fruits of defeat to the King to have these men as his ministers; but by this time he had become expert at political wire-pulling. Of the two Secretaries of State he naturally preferred Shelburne, the disciple of Chatham, and by favouring him in every possible way at the expense of his colleagues he soon had the Cabinet at loggerheads.

The Government at once opened negotiations with the American delegates in Paris. The Americans missed their best chance by untimely stiffness. They objected that the credentials of the British envoy, Oswald, seemed to imply that the States were still dependant and while the document was being redrafted news came that Rodney had destroyed the French fleet off The Saints in the West Indies (April 1782), and that the last great assault on Gibraltar had been repulsed. These events greatly strengthened Shelburne's position, and it was further improved by a breach between the Americans and the French. Jay the chief American delegate discovered that Vergennes had been secretly proposing that Canada should be extended to the Ohio, and that the boundary between the United States and Spanish North America would run from Fort Cumberland to Alabama, cooping up the States between the Alleghenies and the sea. Vergennes was not really acting dishonourably: France was pledged to win American Independence, not to any specific frontiers. And he was in a difficult position. France badly needed a quick peace; but she had undertaken to help Spain to win back Gibraltar, and there was no longer any hope of success in that enterprise. Vergennes' only hope was that the United States would forgo part of the unexplored west to compensate Spain for a peace without the Rock; or, alternatively, that England would give the Rock back to Spain in return for an Ohio frontier for Canada. To counter this move, Jay sent a secret messenger to London to persuade Shelburne to make a separate peace. And as a whole year had passed since Yorktown, with the war in an expensive state of suspended animation, Shelburne agreed. A preliminary treaty was signed on November 30th, 1782, with the proviso that it was not to take effect until France and Spain had made peace with Britain too.

Americans sometimes say they have never lost a war or won a peace; but on this occasion they contrived to gain all they wanted, and more than was warranted by the actual military position. They frustrated King George's last faint hope that some formula would be found to save his pride; not a shadow of connection was left between the Thirteen States and the Mother Country. And the only concession that they made proved illusory. Shelburne dared not face Parliament without safeguards for the "loyalists" who had upheld the idea of a united Empire, and without an arrangement for the payment of the debts, amounting to millions sterling, owed by Americans to British firms. The Americans eventually bought evacuation of their soil by British troops (strongly placed at New York, Philadelphia and Charleston) at the price of very guarded phrases about "placing no impediment" in the way of debt-collecting, and "earnestly recommending" the several States to let bygones be bygones with their "tories." But as neither of these stipulations was carried out, they got something for nothing at all.[1] They also retained the fishing rights on the Newfoundland Banks which they had enjoyed as British subjects. Altogether Jay, Franklin, Adams and Deane could congratulate themselves on their skilful diplomacy.

ANGLO-FRENCH PEACE-MAKING. A state of war continued between Britain and the Bourbon Powers until the following spring; and the long-drawn-out negotiations gave time for Britain's naval recovery to bring her out of the struggle with smaller losses than at one time seemed inevitable. Rodney had saved Jamaica by the Battle of the Saints; Sir Eyre Coote saved India at Porto Novo, and Warren Hastings by a masterly disposition of military and naval forces made it impossible for Admiral Suffren to recover the lost ground. Sir George Elliott, after one of the stubbornest defences in the history of warfare, saved Gibraltar. Thus the Peace of Versailles (March 1783) left matters pretty much *in statu quo ante bellum* in the West Indies, India and Africa. France's greatest gain was Britain's retrocession of Minorca to Spain; for the British naval base at Port Mahon had always been a potential threat to Toulon. France also procured for Spain Florida and everything west of the Mississippi, by way of substitute for Gibraltar.

The Independence of the United States was greeted with delight all over the Continent—by reactionaries because it seemed to mark the decline of Britain as a World-Power,[2] and by liberals as a vindication of human brotherhood and the Rights of Man. A Danish writer has recorded the general emotion:

I still remember vividly the day when the victory of struggling liberty was celebrated in the harbour of Elsinore. It was a fair day; the harbour was full of merchant ships of all nations, dressed for the occasion, their mastheads adorned with long pennants. . . . This unusual decoration, the joyful people who swarmed on the decks, and the gun-salutes from the warships and from every merchantman that possessed a pair of cannon made the day festive for us all. Father had invited a few guests, and we boys were bidden to the table. Father explained the significance of the festival; our glasses, too, were filled with punch, and as toasts were drunk to the success of the new republic, Danish and North American flags were hoisted in our garden.

---

[1] Some 50,000 of these Loyalists, their property confiscated, and their homes destroyed, fled during the next few years to Nova Scotia and Ontario, where they were granted land by the British Government, and became one of the most characteristic elements in the Canadian nation of to-day.

[2] Frederick the Great cited the decadence and ruin of Britain as proof of the weakness of parliamentary government as compared with enlightened autocracy.

Things were not quite what they seemed. The French monarchy had doubled the debt which had threatened its existence even before it entered on its crusade; and many of the élite of the nation had come back from it full of a dangerous enthusiasm for liberty and equality. And Britain took a new lease of life, now that George-the-Thirdism was destroyed by the disaster it had brought on the country. The poor King could not himself see that he had been at fault. He wrote to Shelburne:

I should be miserable indeed if I did not feel that no blame on this account can be laid at my door, and did I not know that knavery seems to be so much a striking feature of the inhabitants of America that it may not in the end be an evil that they have become aliens to this kingdom.

But though he stuck together the broken pieces of his authority with patience, skill and pertinacity, he could never really restore it—even when he dished the Infamous Coalition of Fox and North which ousted Shelburne, and contrived to instal another nominee in the person of young Mr. Pitt, aged twenty-four (1784). For Pitt was no North, and the "King's Friends" in the Commons were never again the solid phalanx they had been before American Independence.

CHAPTER THIRTY-THREE

JOSEPH AND FREDERICK
1 7 7 8 – 1 7 8 6

THE Emperor Joseph II was full of restless ambitions which, sensible and well-meaning as most of them were, gave a great deal of trouble to himself and to others, and in the long run did nobody much good. One of his schemes impelled Frederick of Prussia to band together the other Princes of Germany against his interference.

BAVARIAN SUCCESSION. In December 1777, just after Saratoga had settled the issue of the War of Independence, the death of Elector Maximilian Joseph of Bavaria threatened to start another war in Europe. He had no near relatives, and Joseph II had long coveted a part of his Electorate to fill the awkward gap between the Tyrol and Bohemia. Joseph and Kaunitz had been bargaining with Charles Theodore, Elector Palatine, who as head of the other branch of the Wittelsbachs would inherit Bavaria. Charles Theodore, who had no Bavarian sympathies, readily agreed to barter a share of the Electorate in return for Austrian support in taking over the rest of it. Maria Teresa had never liked the bargain, and when the death of Max Joseph brought it into effect she pleaded with her son not to do anything rash; for any aggrandizement of Austria was bound to displease Frederick of Prussia. Frederick, growing cautious with years, would not be likely to rush into war; but when the late Elector's ministers, indignant that Bavaria should be carved up between a foreign heir and a greedy neighbour, appealed to him, he urged the Duke of Zweibrücken, who as next of kin had to approve the partition before it became valid, to refuse his consent. The Duke did so, and even returned the coveted Order of the Golden Fleece with which Joseph tried to bribe him.

This put Joseph in a quandary. Frederick backed up his diplomatic action by mobilizing an army, and Austria had to follow suit; yet France, still nominally Austria's ally, declared that a situation which had arisen through Austrian aggression did not call the alliance into play. In the negotiations which followed—and indeed in all Prusso-Austrian relations for the next ten years, it is odd to note how the situation has been reversed since 1740. Frederick of Prussia has become the guardian of public law against the egoistic aggression of the House of Austria! A kind of war began in 1778, but there was no serious fighting, and polite communications continued to pass between Frederick and Joseph. Frederick had lost all taste for war, knowing too well that when once it has begun there is no knowing where it will end; and Joseph, though he put on a bold air and stood his ground, was inwardly quaking to find himself pitted against the most renowned captain in the world. But when the armies went into winter quarters the issue was settled by diplomacy. Frederick made sure of Russian support by winning over Potemkin, Catherine's reigning favourite, while Joseph and Kaunitz redoubled their efforts to gain a counter-balancing support from France. Marie Antoinette acted as her mother's agent in trying to get Louis XVI and his ministers to renew the active partnership, but the only result was to draw on her the wrath of those who ascribed France's discomfiture in the Seven Years' War to that connection. Even when Joseph hinted a willingness to exchange the Netherlands for Bavaria, giving Flanders to France as the price of her acquiescence, Vergennes refused to renew the policy which had cost France so dear.

And now Catherine suddenly announced that if Austria did not come to terms with Frederick forthwith, she would feel obliged to intervene on his side. This message stirred up a whirlpool of discussion and dissension at the Hofburg, eventuating in letters to Versailles and St. Petersburg asking France and Russia to arrange a settlement (November 1778). France being tepid towards Austria and engaged in the American war, Catherine had matters all her own way at the conference which met at Teschen (March 1779). Scraps of territory were thrown to Austria to save her face, but Joseph had to renounce his Bavarian claim; and the settlement marked another stage in the rise of Prussian ascendancy in the affairs of Germany.

JOSEPH'S HOME REFORMS. Six months later Maria Teresa died (November 1780), her last days darkened and perplexed by a sense of undeserved failure, and by dread of the changes that her clever but enigmatical son would make when she was gone. Joseph, for all his devotion to her, could not repress a sense of relief. "Now I am no longer son," he said to Kaunitz. At last he would have a free hand for schemes of reform which were to make his dominions a better place to live in. Philosophy should reign supreme. He saw visions of Czech and Magyar, Pole and German fused into a unified state under an efficient and beneficent government. His Lorraine blood was a fresh element in the in-bred Hapsburg family, and he was determined to drag the monarchy out of medieval obscurity into the clear light of eighteenth-century Reason.

But he was one of those who rush in where angels fear to tread. Like an eager and intelligent child who has been spoiled by having his own way, he was furiously impatient of obstacles. Of course his mother had been in accord with his desire to make people happy, prosperous and good by the wise use of absolute power; but her instincts were too conservative to allow her to sweep away time-honoured traditions. Joseph had no such inhibitions. His restless activity and quick-wittedness made him attack one evil after another without waiting to carry any of them to a conclusion and to learn from his mistakes. The result was chaos. It seemed to him self-evident that anyone who opposed him must be either fool and knave or both not to see that he knew what was best for them.

It would not be worth our while to study in detail reforms which came to nothing; but the same general principles ran through all: uniformity, efficiency, the subordination of local and personal interests to the common good. The powers of the old provincial governments he pared away. Distinctions of race and speech he tried to smooth out—German was to be the official language for all public business. The main administrative centres were to be newly-created "circles." The seigneurial powers of landlords were to be replaced by local courts with trained magistrates, as the base of a judicial pyramid with its apex at Vienna. All citizens were to have equal civil rights; where serfdom lingered it was to be abolished; labour-rents due from peasants to landlords were to be rigidly limited.

But the men to work these admirably designed institutions could not be improvised. Sloth and incompetence and corruption were too ingrained in Austrian officialdom. "I can only hope that I have made the least bad appointments," he confessed to his brother in a moment of disillusionment. His attempts to punish shortcomings by salary-cuts merely added ill-feeling to the other evils; and so did his rough handling of the provincial assemblies. "This is my system," he told the Estates of Bohemia in 1784; "it is not for you to discuss whether it is desirable or not—merely to consider the best means for carrying it into effect."

Joseph was not a devout Christian, but on the other hand he was no enemy of the Catholic Church. What he disliked about it was the intrusive authority of the Papacy and of the foreign Heads of religious Orders. He discouraged pilgrimages and practices which to his philosophic mind smacked of idolatry. He claimed, in the interests of state-unity, to appoint bishops, and tried to make them dependent on state-paid stipends instead of their own episcopal endowments. He insisted on monastic Orders renouncing outside authority, and abolished contemplative Orders as of no practical use, devoting their revenues to public charities. By the end of his reign he had closed about 700 monasteries and nunneries; though as there were some 1,350 left it could not be said that his subjects were denied opportunities for the religious life. But what gave even greater offence to the ecclesiastical authorities was his Edict of Toleration. Non-Catholic sects were to be allowed to build their own places of worship, provided that these did not look like churches and had no steeples or bells. There were to be restrictions even on the persecution of the Jews.

Nevertheless he avoided any formal breach with Rome; and when Pope Pius VI came on a visit to Vienna to moderate his reforming ardour, he received him with all possible respect and honour. That visit was an unprecedented event in the history of the Papacy, and made a great sensation throughout Europe. Pope and Emperor engaged in theological discussions, using, as the latter afterwards admitted, long words which neither of them really understood; but Joseph succeeded in his main purpose—to convince the Pope of the orthodoxy of his religious views without committing himself to any reversal of his policy towards the Church.

JOSEPH AND CATHERINE. As if this multifarious domestic activity was not enough, Joseph also launched out on a line of his own in foreign policy. The humiliation of Teschen had brought home to him the uselessness of relying any longer on the French alliance which had been the mainspring of Hapsburg policy since 1755. The internal condition of France, and the tendency there to ascribe all the country's ills to the alliance, compelled Austria to look elsewhere for support; and what direction more obvious than Russia, the dictator of Teschen? Joseph had taken the first step just before his mother's death by a personal visit to St. Petersburg. Maria Teresa, who could not conceal her disgust at Catherine's morals, was very reluctant to authorize the contact, but it turned out a great success. Joseph charmed the charmer so successfully that he remained (*incognito*, as "Count Falkenstein") long beyond the ten days originally allotted to the visit. When Catherine confided to him her (revised) dream of a Byzantine Empire for her grandson Constantine and a kingdom of Dacia for her lover Potemkin, to be carved out of the Ottoman Empire, Joseph turned aside the subject with airy persiflage. But he had breached the wall; and Frederick tried in vain to counteract the effects. For Catherine felt that her Greek Project was now within reach of realization, especially as France and Britain, who each had reasons for defending the Sultan, were now cancelling each other out. And for the conquest of Turkey an alliance with Austria would be far more serviceable than her existing alliance with Prussia. Frederick, indeed, could never be party to a plan for the destruction of the Ottoman Empire—it was too useful to him as a check on Austria.

So as soon as Joseph was in sole control of Austrian policy he sent proposals to Catherine for a mutual guarantee, which she as promptly accepted. He promised to defend all the possessions of Russia in Europe, while she gave a similar undertaking about all Austrian possessions save those in Italy; and they agreed to maintain the existing régime in Poland. Further correspondence strengthened the understanding, and in 1782 Catherine felt it was strong enough to stand a strain. Having provoked disturbances among the Tatars of the Crimea she announced her intention of ousting the Turkish Government from that peninsula and the Kuban, and called on Joseph for support, assuring him that these provinces would be kept entirely separate from Russia. For Russia she wanted only Otchakov and a strip between the Bug and the Dniester, with perhaps an Ægean island or two as bases for her fleet. Joseph could take any Turkish province he had a fancy for, as his share of the spoils.

But the Emperor did not welcome the prospect. Was it likely that Frederick would look on with folded arms while Austria expanded at the expense of Turkey? If Austria was to engage in such a risky undertaking she must have in view substantial gains—part of Wallachia and of Servia (including Belgrade) together with the Morea and Cyprus to be exchanged with the Venetian Republic for Istria and Dalmatia (which would give Hungary access to the Adriatic). Catherine was taken aback at the demand for valuable parts of her projected Byzantine Empire, and her sharply-worded rejection stung Joseph into refusing more than "general support." However, this "general support" proved very useful, for he mobilized an army on his Hungarian frontier and drew off part of the Turkish forces in that direction. Constantinople was ravaged by plague and fire, and the Sultan's demoralization was completed by diplomatic pressure from his French ally. For Vergennes, realizing that the substitution of a Russian-controlled Byzantine Empire for Turkey-in-Europe would be very injurious to French interests, hurried on the Treaty of Versailles with Britain so as to have his hands free to support Turkey. It seemed at one time that France might join hands with Britain in giving this support, for British interests were equally threatened by Catherine's Greek Project. But

Fox, now Secretary of State, had designs for a league with Russia and Prussia directed against France.[1] Vergennes had therefore to content himself with a warning to Joseph that action against the Ottoman Empire would cost Austria the friendship of France, while the French ambassador at Constantinople adjured the Sultan to surrender to the inevitable before he was overtaken with total ruin. So by the Treaty of Constantinople (January 1784) Turkey formally ceded the Crimea and the Kuban to Russia.

JOSEPH AND THE BELGIANS. The "Eastern Question" thus laid aside for the time being, Joseph's quicksilver mind reverted to the acquisition of Bavaria, which was to him what the Greek Project was to Catherine. But this time he conducted the quest by a roundabout route.

On the tour through the Austrian dominions which he had taken after his mother's death he had paid a hurried visit to the Netherlands. The Dutch Republic, next door, was much weakened by having joined in the war against England, for overseas trade was its life-blood; and the prosperity of the Southern Netherlands, which the Sea Powers and united to suppress in the Treaty of Westphalia, was now reviving owing to their having fallen apart. Ostend had become a thriving port on the trade which had formerly gone to Amsterdam; and Antwerp, once the greatest port of northern Europe but ruined by the clause which closed the River Scheldt to shipping, naturally wanted to share in the boom. Other Belgian cities which would be enriched by its revival joined Antwerp in a petition to the Emperor for permission to ignore the restriction. When Joseph got back to Vienna he consulted Kaunitz on the subject. But Kaunitz said No; such a flagrant breach of the great Treaty which was the basis of the existing European system would bring disgrace on the House, would provoke a general war, and would break up the French alliance. But Joseph hated to let this revival of Belgian prosperity fade away—it was the only hope of making the provinces worth having—or bartering. And the closing of the Scheldt was not the only "restrictive treaty" from which it was suffering. There was also the Barrier Treaty made in 1715 as part of the settlement of Utrecht. Dutch garrisons had still to be maintained out of Belgian revenues, although the forts had fallen into decay, and in spite of the fact that, the Dutch and the French now being allies, Dutch defences against French aggression were an anachronism. So without more

---

[1] This was the birth of the anti-Turkish Liberal tradition of the nineteenth century.

ado the Emperor ordered their demolition. The Dutch Government withdrew its troops without demur, but a dispute arose over the possession of Maastricht, the greatest of the fortress-towns. Joseph cut the argument short (August 1784) by what he intended to be a compromise: if the Republic would agree to the opening of the Scheldt and make no further obstruction to Belgian trade with the East Indies, he would withdraw his claim to Maastricht. Assuming that the Dutch would acquiesce, he sent a "token-ship" to navigate the Scheldt in each direction, refusing to listen to Kaunitz, who warned him over a matter of such vital importance to them that the Dutch would resist. But the Chancellor was right. Dutch men-of-war stopped both the ships and turned them back. The Emperor could not possibly ignore such a public challenge, and both sides prepared for war. Everything depended on the line taken by France. Joseph hoped that his sister would be able to influence the French Government in his favour; but Vergennes dared not throw over the Dutch lest they should fall back into the arms of Britain, and the Sea Powers be re-united as the basis of a new anti-French coalition. So he declared that the Dutch were only defending their well-established rights, and that if France intervened it would have to be on their side.

But by this time Joseph did not greatly care, for he had dashed off at another tangent. Could he not combine the Scheldt question with another, of infinitely more direct concern to him: the consolidation of Austria by the exchange of the troublesome Netherlands for Bavaria? The Elector Karl Theodore, having no attachment to Bavaria and no direct heir, was quite ready to strike a bargain; but (as in 1778) the consent of the Duke of Zweibrücken would be required. And meanwhile Joseph had raised up another difficulty for himself. Enquiry showed that he would lose financially by giving up the Netherlands for Bavaria; so he decided that he must have Salzburg as well, compensating its Prince-Archbishop[1] by lopping Luxemburg and Limburg off the Netherlands for him. But he had left one or two factors out of his calculations. It had apparently never occurred to him that the Belgian people might object to being handed over as a going concern to Charles Theodore or that this prince might object to taking over a discontented state, stripped of two of its best provinces. Nor had he reckoned on Frederick of Prussia finding out about the negotiations and once more working up the Duke of Zweibrücken to refuse his consent. When the Duke declared that he "would rather be buried under the ruins of Bavaria than agree," Joseph remarked that his reply

---

[1] The employer, for a time, of Mozart, whom he treated as a menial.

"smacked of Potsdam." Probably he was right; but it vetoed the whole transaction.

THE LEAGUE OF PRINCES. And that was not the end of the troubles which the scheme brought upon its author. For centuries the princes of Germany had talked of forming an association that would give them the union that is strength, now that the Holy Roman Empire was no more than a name and a tradition; and the actions of Joseph II seemed to indicate that it was against the Hapsburg himself that this united strength was needed. He was continually interfering with them and claiming powers long in abeyance, in the interests of his personal dominions; and the ecclesiastical princes feared that he would force his Italian nephews into the sees of Cologne, Trier and Mainz, and thus gain a majority in the Electoral College which would enable him to make it a family preserve.

It did not take Frederick long to see in the feeling aroused by the Bavaria-Belgium project a situation to be exploited for the weakening of Austria and the strengthening of Prussia. Since Catherine, his last friend in Europe, had gone over to his enemy, he could look for support only to the lesser princes of Germany. They could not easily learn to look on the seizer of Silesia as the protector of their interests against Austria, and their spiny particularism made them very wary of any form of federalism. But Joseph's recent activities made them wonder whose turn it would be next to be cajoled or bullied by him. And this kind of aggression grows by what it feeds on: if at his next attempt Joseph got Bavaria he would become stronger and more off-hand than ever. His readiness to give away Luxemburg (which did not belong to him) showed how little he regarded imperial interests compared with those of his hereditary dominions. So Frederick was able to lay the foundations of a League of Princes (*Fürstenbund*) with the support of the Electors of Hanover, Saxony and Mainz (July 1785). Nearly all the other princes—even those of the Catholic south, most closely bound by tradition to the Hapsburgs—joined in the course of the next few months. Its avowed purpose was defensive—to maintain the constitution of the Empire as fixed at Westphalia, and to protect individual princes against undue interference from Vienna. Secret articles called specifically for united action to prevent exchanges of territory within the Empire.

The League was very short-lived. Its historical importance lay in the precedent it created for the princes of Germany looking to Prussia for support against Austria. It would be interesting if we could know how Frederick would have developed it; but he died in 1786 and it faded away. For the new King of Prussia was no empire-builder. His father, the late King's brother August Wilhelm, had died of a broken heart in the midst of the Seven Years' War because of harsh words from the King after a set-back. It would seem that he lacked the Hohenzollern toughness, and his son inherited the weakness. A completer contrast to Frederick can hardly be imagined than this Frederick William II—large, flabby, good-natured, ruled by favourites (male and female), given to self-indulgence and to spiritualist superstition. His uncle had made no attempt to fit him to carry on his work for Prussia; and indeed it was the great weakness of the Frederician system that nobody could work it but Frederick. His army—a third of it of foreign birth—was dependent on his personality for the vitality which gave it power; lacking this it degenerated into a mere façade, destined to be crashed into rubble by Napoleon at Jena. It was the same with the administration. Of late years he had relied a good deal on his chief minister Hertzberg; apart from him he left mere clerks instead of ministers, and machinery instead of a live governmental organism. Frederick William II was greeted with frantic delight by a nation which felt relieved to be rid of its iron-handed taskmaster; but it soon began to feel ashamed of a Court flaunting the evils which the Prussian monarchy had long eschewed—reckless extravagance on luxuries, the political influence of worthless courtiers, and the domination of a *maîtrese-en-titre*.

CHAPTER THIRTY-FOUR

JOSEPH COMES TO GRIEF
1 7 8 6 – 1 7 8 9

JOSEPH II in a moment of vision likened himself to a man who, impatient to enjoy the amenities of woodland round his country-house, plants fully-grown trees instead of saplings. It was "more haste less speed" with him, and his incessant activities and constant disappointments wore him out, body and soul, by the time he was fifty.

ANOTHER TRIPLE ALLIANCE. One result of the death of Frederick the Great was a renewal of Anglo-Prussian friendship after twenty-five years of estrangement. Ever since 1763 Frederick had been bent on winning France over to his side against Austria; whereas Britain was in the midst of a struggle with France which lasted off and on for a century and a quarter. And Frederick's resentment over the betrayal of 1762 had made him do all that he conveniently could to embarrass Great Britain in the American War. But times were changed. Frederick William was a mild and good-humoured person; and the younger Pitt, who became Prime Minister in 1783, was absorbed in a national revival, which would be ruined by another war; but a situation now arose which compelled Prussia and Britain to join in armed intervention.

The scene of it was the United Provinces. There in 1747 an invasion by Marshal Saxe in the course of the Austrian Succession War had provoked a revolution. As always, the extremity of the Dutch people was the opportunity of the House of Orange. The Stadtholderate, abolished on the death of William III in 1702, was revived and made hereditary in the person of William of Nassau, great-nephew of William III and son-in-law of George II. Hereditary monarchy is supposed to give strength to a state—that was the reason for its adoption in this case, and Poland is always cited to exemplify the negative of the proposition. But conditions in the United Provinces required something more—a leader of personality, and at this juncture the House could not supply the want. This William IV was muddle-headed and half-hearted, and when in 1751 he died, leaving his newly-gained position to a three-year-old child, sovereignty in the Republic became more confused, and party feuds ran higher, than ever. In the Regent-

343

Mother, "Anne of England," the connection of our royal family with the House of Orange, begun by the Stuarts, was continued under their Hanoverian supplanters. She showed herself active and clear-headed—which is not surprising when we remember that, if she had George II for father she had Caroline of Anspach for mother. But she died in 1759, and was succeeded as regent and guardian by the Duke of Brunswick-Wolfenbüttel; who gained such a hold over his ward that when in 1766 the latter came of age he prolonged his tutelage by an "Act of Consultation." Wilhelmina of Prussia, niece of Frederick II, married the Stadtholder in 1767, hoping to be able to egg him on to kingship. But he had not it in him to take such a line; and her uncle who, as we saw in Sweden (p. 317), never let family affections affect his politics, refused to be drawn into trouble on behalf of a nephew-by-marriage who had not the grit or the means to fend for himself. The merchant oligarchy maintained their traditional connection with France, while the Orange party continued to look for support to England. When the States General tried to profit by Britain's difficulties in America the effect was in the end disastrous for the Republic. This was a blow for the States General, but the Stadtholder failed to take advantage of it, and Vergennes contrived to keep French influence paramount at The Hague. When in 1787 he died, just after making a new treaty of alliance with the Republic, the "Patriots" were actively planning to abolish the Stadtholderate again.

This state of things was utterly contrary to British interests. From the time of Edward II to that of George VI, Britain has always feared to see a strong Power established in the lands of the Rhine-delta; and the strength of British governments throughout those centuries can be measured by the firmness with which they guarded against such threats. For a time Pitt looked the other way; peace was essential to his plans. He hoped that Frederick William's accession would bring Prussia to do something to check the Franco-Dutch connection, for the new King was far more susceptible of romantic ideas than his uncle, and it was his own sister whose position was at stake. But he and his court were too intent on enjoying themselves to want trouble with France, and Hertzberg, whose sober counsel he had inherited with the crown, felt that Prussia must not get entangled on the Rhine so long as there was a possibility that Russia and Austria might join forces against her. Thus the Francophile "Patriots" felt immune from outside interference; until in Jnue 1787 their over-confidence led to a false step. The Princess had left her refuge at Nymegen to stir up the Orange partisanship, when she was arrested, locked up at Gouda, and eventually compelled to return to Nymegen. Even now Frederick William feared to commit himself. He collected an army in his Rhine provinces, but did not venture on any firmer challenge than a request for satisfaction from the States General: to which the latter replied that they, a sovereign body, could not apologize to the wife of their subject the Stadtholder! But on September 7th came news which changed the whole situation: the Turks had declared war on Russia, and this war was bound to involve Austria. Frederick William's hands were now freed, and within a week his army had crossed the frontier into the Dutch Republic, under the command of his cousin the Duke of Brunswick. The Orange cause had always been supported by the populace; the Free Corps of the "Patriots" had made themselves very unpopular by their insolence, and the sight of the famous blue uniforms of the Prussian army excited a spontaneous rising. The Prince and Princess made their entry into The Hague amid rapturous enthusiasm, and the "Patriot" party was overthrown.

Thus Frederick William had pulled the chestnuts out of the fire for Britain. The natural outcome of the episode was a triple alliance of the Orangist Government with each of the Powers which had reinstated it (August 1788). Vergennes' successor Montmorin dared not, in view of the internal weakness of France, take up the challenge from the Prussian army and the British navy; and the outcome was a disastrous blow to the prestige of the French Monarchy. Napoleon mentions it as one of the events which led to the French Revolution.

ANOTHER TURKISH WAR. Even the Fürstenbund did not make Joseph give up all hope of the Bavarian exchange; but there was obviously no more to be done in that direction for the time being, so his thoughts reverted to the Near East. He had received a flattering invitation from Catherine to join her on a spectacular progress in the spring of 1787 through her new provinces on the Black Sea. She was about to embark on the second—she hoped the final—phase of her Project, and she needed his co-operation. To be sure, he had not been much use in her earlier venture, but there were now better prospects of keeping his attention on the matter in hand. A flotilla of gorgeous galleys bore her and her court and the diplomatic corps of St. Petersburg down the Dniester, to inspect the great arsenal at Kherson and the naval base at Sebastopol which had been prepared by Potemkin; and she invited Joseph to join her at Ekaterinburg and accompany her to Sebastopol where her grand new flagship was to be christened *Joseph II*. Joseph feared to risk himself again within the spells of the fascinating old harridan. He particularly did not want to be inveigled into another

Turkish war, just when trouble was brewing in Belgium and Hungary. He hoped to get what he wanted from the Sultan as a fee for interceding with Catherine; so he could not afford to offend her, and accepted her invitation. But his worst fears were realized. Two months later he returned to Vienna, practically pledged to co-operation in an attack on Turkey during the following summer.

However, a failure of the harvest in the Ukraine compelled Catherine to spend all her available funds on importing grain. She had to break up her army and postpone the campaign; but to save her face she instructed her ambassador at Constantinople to demand the cession of Georgia. Unfortunately for her, Sultan Abdul knew all about the famine and its effects on her army. His own forces were not fit for war, but if he struck now he would at any rate have better prospects than if he waited till his antagonist was ready. So his reply was to cast the Russian ambassador into the dungeon of the Seven Towers.

The Turks hoped that Austria would stand aloof as in 1784; but Joseph had been so carried away by his Crimean trip that he reverted with characteristic vehemence to his earlier policy of close co-operation with Russia. While his ambassador was cooing at Constantinople about mediation he gathered his forces along the Danube, and in February (1788) he launched a sudden attack on Belgrade. He thus proved, if proof were necessary, that where the advantage of the state was concerned his "enlightenment" was just as immoral as Frederick's. He could not deny that the Turks had set an example of good faith and even generosity when Austria had been in peril; but the cession of Belgrade had rankled ever since 1739, and its recovery seemed worth the loss of honour.

But he soon had cause to repent his misdeed. His supplies broke down, and his troops were stricken with typhus; all thought of besieging Belgrade had to be abandoned. The Grand Vizier, left free by Russian inaction, pressed him back across the Danube, and laid waste Temesvar. Joseph returned to Vienna broken in health and hopes. The re-organization of the army had been one of his hobbies, but he lacked the qualities of a good operational commander. He could not delegate responsibility, and his impatience for results and querulous fault-finding rubbed everybody up the wrong way. And he had no stomach for the horrors of war—it pained him beyond endurance to see prosperous lands turned into wilderness. This sensitiveness did him credit as a man but paralysed him as a general.

Nor did the Russians achieve anything in this 1788 campaign except at the very end of it, when, after a six months' siege they captured

Otchakov. Apart from the effects of the famine they were distracted by a threat from Sweden.

Gustavus III had always had his work cut out to hold the position he had won by his *coup d'état* of 1772; and latterly popular discontents, caused largely by a series of bad harvests, provided a fertile field for the intrigues of Catherine, who had never reconciled herself to a strong Swedish monarchy challenging her supremacy in the Baltic. She had recently made a compact with Denmark to overthrow it at the first opportunity; and Gustavus foresaw that this opportunity would come if she crushed the Turks. So he determined to silence opposition at home and anticipate the danger from abroad by a sudden swoop on St. Petersburg from Finland. But everything went wrong for him. A naval action by Catherine's Scottish Admiral Grieg, and a mutiny in the Swedish army, which (instigated by Catherine) refused to undertake operations not sanctioned by the Diet, placed him in a desperate position. From this he was rescued, oddly enough, by a Danish invasion of Sweden; for it aroused the patriotic spirit of his people. The Dalesmen of Dalecarlia rallied round him and checked the invaders; and this gave time for the newly-formed Triple Alliance to intervene. Britain, Prussia and Holland all had strong reasons for maintaining a balance of power in the Baltic. The Danes, threatened by a Prussian army and a British fleet, had to get out of Sweden and make their peace (October 1788). And Gustavus made the most of his new popularity to carry an Act of Unity and Security, confirming and enlarging the powers he had gained in 1772.

Thus throughout 1788 Catherine's forces and supplies had been divided; but in 1789 she was able to concentrate them in the south, and the Turks soon felt the difference. Her armies overran Moldavia and Bessarabia, won a victory at Ismail, and captured Bender; while the Austrians under Loudoun carried Belgrade by storm (October) and occupied Servia, and a subsidiary force took Bucharest and gained possession of the passes into Wallachia. It seemed that another campaign must lead to the partition of the Ottoman Empire.

From that fate it was saved by the results of Joseph's folly.

THE UNHAPPY ENDING. The rebellions which now broke out in Belgium and Hungary were noteworthy in that they did not aim at forcing changes on a conservative ruler, but at preserving institutions against a radical one. The idea of a federation, in which each of the nations under Austrian rule would keep its own traditions and government, linked together only by that sovereignty, never occurred to Joseph, and would never have satisfied his passion for homogeneity. (It was resisted by his successors until nothing could save the Hapsburg Empire from disruption.)

The Austrian Netherlands, like the Dutch Republic, consisted of a number of separate provinces. The sole bond of union was the Emperor's viceroy—at this critical period the husband of Maria Teresa's favourite daughter, Maria Christina. Each of them had kept its own constitution through the two centuries under Spain and the seventy years under Austria. But Joseph II had no patience with such cob-webbed local customs: to him they were mere "antediluvian rubbish," hindering him from setting up a just, efficient and sensible government. The religious edicts which he had imposed on the whole of his dominions had caused as much heart-burnings here as elsewhere, but it was not until in 1786 he began to devote special attention to reno-vating Belgian institutions that their discontent became audible. This happened first over a decree closing all clerical seminaries save one, to be carried on under Austrian supervision at Louvain. Hundreds of students, unable to gain admission to it, or unwilling to enter an Austrian institution, carried a spirit of anger and suspicion all over the provinces.

Then by two edicts in January 1787 he overturned the whole adminis-trative and judicial systems. One of the edicts re-divided the provinces into circles, each under an intendant appointed by Vienna, who was to hold nearly all the powers hitherto exercised by Estates and Town Councils. The other swept away all existing law-courts to make way for tribunals working on a uniform code, with two courts of appeal and a supreme Council of Revision at Brussels. This was far more economical of time and money than the old medley of powers and juris-dictions—in fact it was the prototype for the judicial system of modern Belgium. Introduced gradually, and with provision for the displaced functionaries, it might have been accepted, if not welcomed; but Joseph was too eager to be tactful.

These decrees aroused passionate opposition. The Estates of Brabant refused to vote the taxes, and had the temerity to draw the Viceroy's attention to the clause in its charter (the famous *Joyeuse Entrée*) which authorized insurrection against a sovereign who infringed it. Joseph indignantly suspended the constitution; whereupon the Brabanters enrolled armed bands called Serments, and their example was followed by the other provinces. All this happened while Joseph was far away in the Crimea. The Viceroy, alarmed at the demonstrations, suspended the edicts until the provinces could lay their case before the sovereign himself. When Joseph heard of this he hastened back to Vienna in haughty indignation. But though he took a high-and-mighty tone towards the deputations from the Low Countries, he could not shut his ears to the common sense of Kaunitz, who pointed out that with a Turkish war in prospect, with Prussia ready to pounce on him and France unable to help, he could not afford to provoke armed rebellion in this distant possession. So the Edicts of January were revoked in August.

But the Belgians' blood was up. The clergy, now assured of support from Estates and populace, insisted on the withdrawal of the ecclesiastical innovations as well. This made Joseph regret having made any concessions at all, and he determined to crush the spirit of revolt by main force. He transferred the Viceroy's powers to a military commander with orders to "purify the dark, incomprehensible and impracticable constitution" by force of arms. But the futile attempt of the inadequate garrison to impose his will only made the Belgians realize its impotence. Van der Noot, the leader of the national movement, intrigued at The Hague and Berlin for support, and organized a refugee army on Dutch soil. When this little force, without waiting longer for foreign aid, marched in, the Austrian General was driven into Luxemburg; and Joseph, with his army engaged in the Balkans, had to capitulate. He sent his Vice-chancellor Cobenzl to offer the restoration of the constitutions, the reinstatement of the old seminaries, and an unconditional amnesty. But it was too late. In December 1789 "The United States of Belgium" proclaimed his deposition and the foundation of an independent republic. What happened to it belongs to a later phase of history, for the Belgian revolution was swept into the mightier cataclysm which had begun six months earlier at Versailles.

The causes of offence in Hungary were religious and national as in Belgium. The Magyars acknowledged Joseph as their king, but regarded themselves as co-ordinate with the Austrians. His refusal to be crowned at Pesth seemed to show a desire to obliterate their separateness, and his announcement that the unity of the state required the use of the German language for all public business looked like an intention to rule Hungary with Austrian officials. That was not Joseph's purpose; but he set to work here, as elsewhere, to reconstruct the administration, with his circles and intendants and all the apparatus of centralization. And the Magyar aristocracy were particularly offended by his attack on their feudal powers, for the circles replaced "County Congregations" of nobles which had always been the main bulwark of their "national liberties"; the abolition of serfdom and of tax-exemption robbed them not only of their property but of their pride and prestige; and his uniform conscription ended the picturesque voluntary "insurrection" which had hitherto been their substitute for regular military service.

When the peasantry did not get all they had hoped from the abolition of serfdom they quarrelled with their former owners, appealed in vain to Joseph (who detested insubordination almost as much as he detested oppression), and broke into a savage *jacquerie*. And when he required troops and money for his Turkish war the Magyars demanded a restoration of the old institutions, including the national Diet at Pressburg. If the campaign of 1788 had been successful, and the Belgian affair had not gone so badly for the Government, Joseph might have browbeaten them, but his difficulties encouraged them to raise their demands. A party among them went so far as to send a secret mission to Berlin, asking Frederick William for "protection" and a new king. Thus at Pesth as at Brussels Joseph was forced to capitulate to the forces of conservatism. On February 4th, 1790, he withdrew every decree he had made since the death of his mother, with the single exception of the abolition of serfdom.

A week later he was dead. His health had never been robust, and work and worry had destroyed it. The asthmatical tendency which he had inherited from his mother developed rapidly towards the end, making it impossible for him to lie down or to snatch more than a few minutes' sleep at a time. Old Kaunitz, with his horror of sickness, refused to come to see him, and his labours were doubled by having to conduct the government by correspondence. And the condition of affairs was enough to weigh down the toughest spirit. He was still at war with Turkey, and was threatened by Prussia; his peoples had rejected the enlightened reforms by which he had hoped to inaugurate a golden age—Belgium had broken away altogether. The old régime, of which he was in many ways the finest flower, was dying in convulsions in France, rocking the throne of his sister. With a desolating sense of failure and impotence he turned his face to the wall.

EPILOGUE

FRANCE ON THE SLIPPERY SLOPE
1779–1789

THE story of France during the 1780's was really the prelude to the history of the Revolution; but the final push which disintegrated the Old Régime was given by the American War, and therefore forms a fitting epilogue to this book.

TURGOT was followed (1776) as Controller-General by Necker, a Swiss banker, rather too satisfied with his own financial skill, but an intelligent and honest man. The circumstances of his appointment made it almost inevitable that he should cancel all Turgot's reforms; but in any case all hope of retrenchment had faded when France embarked on the American war. Necker had to start with a loan, and in order to build up the Government's credit he issued a *Compte Rendu au Roi*, the first national balance-sheet in the history of France. Old-fashioned folk were shocked at the opening to the public gaze of this holy of holies of the Monarchy; while courtiers were embarrassed and taxpayers staggered at the disclosure of extravagant pensions to useless, worthless hangers-on at Versailles. Worse still, the document was utterly misleading, for Necker could only create a credit balance by omitting from the debit side the cost of the war.

Then he tried (taking a leaf out of Turgot's book) to spread a sense of responsibility throughout the nation by nominating local bodies to undertake tax-assessments, hitherto in the hands of royal Intendants. This innovation worried the King. "One can see things that exist," he complained, "but one can only form a mental image of what does not exist; and we ought not to rush into enterprises of which we cannot see the results." So the Controller could only try his scheme of local government on a very restricted scale; and it must be admitted that the result justified the King's apprehensions. For several of the assemblies passed resolutions which showed the spread of democratic ideas. They called for the replacement of the *corvée* by a general tax, and the appointment of local officials by elected bodies instead of by the Ministry. When it seemed that Necker might act on these demands, old Maurepas alarmed the King with prophecies of trouble with Parlement and ministers. So Necker had to go.

351

The next Controller was Calonne, an ex-Intendant, clever, tricky, and anxious to please his patrons. There were to be no more harsh economies, no more indecent disclosures of royal bounty. All was to be made right by borrowing. And just as a man who wants to borrow does well to establish his credit by appearing prosperous, so a state that wants to borrow must dazzle by expenditure. Versailles flowed with financial milk and honey: Calonne was the most "delicious" of ministers. One old marquis when rallied on his avidity replied "Well, everybody was holding out his hand, so I held out my hat." In three years a sum greater than the whole cost of the American War went down the drain of Versailles. Of course, borrowing to pay the interest on one's debts may be done once, perhaps twice, but not a third time; and in 1786 Calonne had to propose the substitution of a general tax for the corvée, and free trade in corn. "But this is pure Necker!" exclaimed the dismayed King—though it was really diluted Turgot. To put his projects into shape Calonne summoned a congress of "Notables," selected from nobles, clergy, lawyers and officials, trusting that they would be complacent towards proposals of the minister who nominated them. Calonne opened the proceedings with a specious address which gained approval for his reforms; but to the general surprise the assembly refused to consider the imposition of new taxes without knowing the exact financial position of the Crown, which Calonne would not—perhaps could not—disclose; and Lafayette was chief spokesman for a small but clamant group which demanded a meeting of the States General. This assembly, a sort of atrophied Witanagemot, had not met since 1614; its supercession had been symbolic of the rise of the autocratic Bourbon monarchy; and the idea of its revival was as appalling a thought as the Day of Judgment. The Queen and the Princes of the Blood worked on the King to get rid of the minister no longer delicious, who had embarked on levelling reforms and had called into being an assembly where such frightful words were uttered (April 1787).

It was an age of feverish impulses, irreconcilable with each other or with common sense. The liberal spirit took practical shape in an Anglo-French commercial treaty (1786) whereby Pitt and Vergennes laid old enmities to rest—as they fondly thought, for ever—with an agreement that the two countries should exchange and enjoy each other's staple products instead of wastefully trying to exclude them. Yet almost simultaneously the spirit of reaction was carried to fantastic lengths by an ordinance demanding four quarterings of nobility from candidates for commissions in the army, to exclude young men of the middle-classes—the most intelligent part of the nation, as became evident when the Revolution opened careers to talent.

Never had there been such a general interest in politics. "The whole nation has got into the habit of discussing public affairs," wrote Lafayette to his friend John Jay; this habit being largely due to the example of America. And Beaumarchais' famous comedy *The Marriage of Figaro* (1786) enabled the aristocracy to laugh at the absurdities of a social system on which they were a glittering scum.

The Monarchy's loss of prestige was shown in the unpopularity of the Queen. Blame for ill-fated foreign policy and for extravagant expenditure were implied by two of the commonest soubriquets by which she was assailed: "L'Autrichienne" and "Madame Deficit." This cruel prejudice appeared very strongly in the famous affair of "The Queen's Necklace." The very phrase was a slander. It was a story ready-made for Dumas or Eugene Sue, of an adventuress obtaining a diamond necklace by means of a forged letter, an impersonation of the Queen, and a midnight assignation in the park at Versailles. Marie Antoinette had nothing whatever to do with the plot, yet when Madame La Motte was publicly branded as a forger, the crowd sympathized with her and heaped baseless calumnies on Marie Antoinette.

On the fall of Calonne the Queen obtained his place for a candidate of her own, Loménie de Brienne, the free-thinking Archbishop of Toulouse. But he could not invent any expedients beyond those which Calonne had inherited from Necker and Necker from Turgot. His only original contribution was to call on the Parlement to register the proposals in the form of edicts. But the Parlement of Paris, like the Notables, demanded a fiscal statement, and when this was refused declared that the King could not create new taxes without the approval of the States General. Again that ominous name! The Parlement called for it merely to make itself popular and to save its own pockets from the threatened universal tax; for it assumed that the Privileged Orders of the States General would prevent any rash innovations. The King and Brienne tried to silence the Parlement by exiling it from Paris, but these tactics were now out of date. The members were acclaimed as martyrs, the cheers being mingled with abuse of the Queen. So they had to be recalled and the projects dropped.

And now Brienne brought forward a new proposal: Parlement was to authorize a huge loan, spread over the next five years, at the end of which (in 1792) the States General should be summoned. (A great many things might happen in five years!) The King forced acceptance at a *séance royale*, a sort of informal *lit de justice*, but as soon as his

12

back was turned the Parlement protested against the proceedings, and in face of its opposition the loan could not be floated. In Dauphiné opposition to the Government took the startling form of an unauthorized meeting of nobles, clergy and commons at Grenoble, which called on the other Provinces to join in refusing to pay any more taxes until the States General had been summoned.

The position of the Government was now desperate—there was no money in the Treasury even to meet current expenses. An appeal to the Clergy produced merely a reiterated demand for the States General. There was nothing for it but unconditional surrender, and the States were summoned for the following May. Brienne retired into obscurity with a Cardinal's hat; and, Necker being recalled, the bankers came to the rescue with a loan to enable the Treasury to carry on till the States should assemble.

All thoughts were now bent forward to that date. It was so long since the last States had met that many knotty problems came up. How were the delegates to be chosen, and how many? And how were they to sit and vote—in three separate Houses, or all together? Parlement pronounced that everything must be done as in 1614; but in 1614 the Estates, each of approximately the same numbers, had sat and voted separately, which meant a permanent two-to-one majority in favour of Privilege. The popular demand was now for the Third Estate to have as many delegates as the other two combined, and for the whole assembly to sit, debate and vote as one body. That appeared to give privileged and unprivileged equal voting power; but as a matter of fact some of the nobles and clergy were sure to support liberal reforms, whereas no member of the Third Estate would support conservatism. The Parlement's refusal to approve this arrangement showed that it regarded the States General as a bulwark against innovation; and this discovery aroused such agitation that Necker obtained the King's approval for double representation of the Third Estate, leaving undecided the question whether the Houses were to meet separately or as one body.

Thus the excited attention of the whole civilized world was centred on Versailles when at the beginning of May 1789 the deputies assembled there to create a new Heaven and a new Earth.

FOR this as for all other periods H. A. L. Fisher's *History of Europe* (Eyre and Spottiswoode) is the beginning of wisdom. An illuminating conspectus of it will be found in Volume II. (We are not putting cart before horse in using Fisher as "further" reading; it is when one is somewhat confused by detail that a highly-focused work like his can be most helpful.)

The relevant volumes of the *Cambridge Modern History* are of variegated value, for the specialists who wrote the various chapters had not all the same objects or the same type of reader in mind. This is not the occasion for detailed analysis; every student must develop a capacity to discriminate between what is useful for his purpose and what is not. Students who read French will find the *Histoire Générale* of Lavisse and Rambaud (Armand Colin) more homogeneous and better balanced; while the Alcan series *Peuples et Civilsations* (Tomes X and XI) are more recent, more condensed and more developed on cultural and economic matters than the Cambridge work. An extremely useful little book is the *Histoire Moderne* for Lycées published by Hachette. The French have different ideas from ours as to what a history text-book should aim at, and in some ways theirs are better. The annotated illustrations are particularly helpful.

Rivington's *Periods of European History* (Wakeman's *Ascendancy of France* and Hassall's *Balance of Power* are the volumes for our period) seem to modern tastes too crowded with political and military detail; but the effort needed to group apparently disparate facts is very valuable to the historical student. A more modern series is Methuen's *History of Medieval and Modern Europe*. W. F. Reddaway in the volume that covers 1715–1815 views the historical landscape through a wide-angle lens. For the first half of our period Ogg's *Europe in the Seventeenth Century* (Black) is a book of similar type.

All who want to know what happened in seventeenth-century England will still go to Ranke; but the volumes in the *Oxford History of England* (G. N. Clark's *Later Stuarts* and Basil Williams' *Whig Supremacy*) are more up to date, and easier reading (Ranke loses flavour in translation). The student should also try Seeley's *Growth of British Policy* (Cambridge). (It is one of the books which interested this writer, as a boy, in historical study.) There is grand reading for young and old in Macaulay, but he was not very interested in the European affairs which were so important for his hero and for us in a present study. For the Spanish Succession War we are in luck's way with Trevelyan's *Queen Anne* (Longmans, Green) and Churchill's *Marlborough* (Harrap). The latter would be precious if only for its portraits and maps for one cannot understand a historical personage without knowing what he looked like, or a campaign without a grasp of the terrain.

For France, A. J. Grant's *The French Monarchy*, 1483–1789 (Cambridge) is sound; our period coincides with its second volume. But France, as the hub of European culture at this time, needs special attention. In Lavisse's great *Histoire de France des Origines à la Révolution* (Hachette) (Volumes VII–X) the author enjoys the elbow-room the subject needs. On Louis XIV the indispensable beginning is Ogg's volume in the Home University Library; Hassall's classic in the *Heroes of the Nations* is more detailed but less entertaining. Incidentally, Voltaire is still worth reading on the subject, if only to see how even a cultured and enlightened Frenchman of the next generation was dazzled by the Great King. Of course, Voltaire was not a historian in the modern sense, but he could write. So can Hilaire Belloc, and his *Monarchy* (Cassell) contains much excellent matter, while the axes that he brings out to grind are too conspicuous to be dangerous even to the most unwary.

For central Europe Coxe's *House of Austria* (Bohn) still has something to offer those willing and able to brush off historical cobwebs; a modern view is presented with graphic vigour in A. J. P. Taylor's *Habsburg Monarchy*. Robertson and Marriott's *Evolution of Modern Prussia* provides groundwork for G. P. Gooch's *Frederick the Great* (Longmans, Green) which should be "required reading" for all students of the period. (People nowadays seem to lack the digestive capacity for Carlyle: that is their misfortune.) Of Martin Hume's many books on Spanish history, the best is his *Spain: its Greatness and Decay* (Cambridge). Nisbet Bain's *Scandinavia* and *Slavonic Europe* (in the same *Cambridge Historical Series*) plod sturdily but somewhat unobservantly through unfamiliar historical territory. On Russia Kluchevsky is the most modern authority, but his interests are mainly in social history, treated for specialists. Most of us will be satisfied with Bernard Pares, the standard one-volume modern work. Mahan's *Influence of Sea-power on History* (Sampson Low) has profoundly influenced historians as well as politicians since its appearance in 1890, and it is still worth while to catch the new light which it threw on the dynastic and national rivalries of the seventeenth and eighteenth centuries. Students interested in the Sea Affair—and it is a commendable interest for us British—should on no account miss Julian Corbett's *England in the Mediterranean* (Longmans, Green).

Serviceable short books on *Maria Theresa* and *Joseph II* were provided by J. F. Bright for Macmillan's "Foreign Statesmen." J. B. Bury did *Catherine II* in the same series, and all Bury's work is in the highest class for scholarship; but easier going will be found in *The Romance of an Empress* by Waliszewski (Heinemann)—a work by no means so meretricious as its English title suggests.

INDEX

Abdul Hamid, Sultan, 318, 346
Académie Française, 167
Acadia, 52, 156, 160, 239, 246, 332
Aiguillon, Duc d', 304
Aix-la-Chapelle, Treaty (1668), 53, 58
Aix-la-Chapelle, Treaty (1748), 238–9, 242
Alberoni, G., Cardinal, 175–6, 185, 191–4
Alembert, J. d', 281
Almanza, Battle of (1707), 147
Alsace, 7, 22, 89–90, 110, 232
Alt Ranstadt, 118–19
America, North, Colonies, 246, 250, 262, 275 ; War of Independence, 323–32
America, South, 125, 156, 201, 210–11, 298
Amherst, General Baron, 262
Amsterdam, 13, 109, 128, 199, 339
Anne of Austria (Queen of France), 17, 22
Anne (Queen of England), 132, 154–5
Anne (Tsarina), 217–18, 226–7
Antwerp, 128, 134, 144–5, 205, 237, 339
Apaffy, Count, 80, 84
Apraxin, Field-Marshal Count S., 257, 260
Aranda, Count P. de, 301–2
Architecture, 168
Argenson, R. E., Marquis d', 237
Armed Neutrality, Declaration of, 327
Asiento, The, 156, 161, 209
Athens, 85, 98
Augsburg, League of, 96
Augustus II (Poland), 110, 115–17, 119, 211, 233, 312
Augustus III (Poland), 213, 226, 231, 250–3, 303
Azov, 112–13, 120, 218, 311

Bach, J. S., 170, 241, 288
Baden, Ludwig Margrave of, 106, 130, 140–1, 144, 148
Balance of Power, 152
Baltic Sea, 27–35, 112, 114–15, 120, 160, 176, 187, 194–6, 247
Banking, 109, 154, 199
Bar, Confederation of, 309
Barcelona, 107, 109, 142, 146
Barrier Treaties, 110, 128, 145, 149, 153, 155, 160, 184, 234, 238, 339
Barry, Jeanne Marquise du, 304
Bart, Admiral Jean, 107

Bavaria, 4, 6, 56, 100, 123, 135, 140–1, 184, 204, 226, 229–32, 234–5, 334–5, 340
Beachy Head, Battle of (1690), 103
Beaumarchais, Caron de, 324–5, 353
Beccaria, Marquis de, 282, 294
Belgium, 338, 348–9 (*and see* Netherlands, Spanish and Austrian)
Belgrade, 191, 218, 346; Treaty of (1739), 219–20
Belleisle, Marquis de, 228–9, 231, 345
Belle Isle, 270, 276
Bender, 120, 347
Berlin, Treaty of (1742), 232
Bernis, Cardinal de, 248, 264
Bernstorff, A. G. von, 184, 187
Berwick, Duke of, 138–9, 146–8, 161, 214
Bestuchev, A., 247
Bevern, Duke of, 258–9
Biren, Duke of Courland, 217
Black Sea, 88, 112–13, 312, 318, 345
Blake, Admiral R., 15
Blenheim, Battle of (1704), 140–1
Bohemia, 4, 226, 231, 234, 250, 253, 256
Boileau, N., 168
Bolingbroke, *see* St. John
Boscawen, Admiral E., 246, 262, 265
Bothmer, Count H. von, 184, 188
Bouchain, Battle of (1711), 154
Boufflers, Marshal Duc de, 134, 148
Bourbon, Duc de, 201–2, 206–7
Boyle, R., 166
Boyne, Battle of the (1690), 103
Brabant, Lines of, 142
Brandenburg, 8, 29–33, 62, 64, 72, 178, 221, 307
Breda, Treaty of (1667), 51–2
Bremen-Verden, 7, 28, 73, 76, 184, 187, 191
Breslau, 259, 266
Brienne, Loménie de, 353–4
Brihuega, Battle of (1710), 152, 183
Bromsbrö, Treaty of (1645), 28
Brühl, Count H. von, 247, 251
Brunswick, 69, 86
Brunswick, Ferdinand Duke of, 257, 260, 265, 275
Brussels, 237, 348
Bubble, The South Sea, 203
Budziac, Treaty of (1672), 83
Budapest, 80
Buffon, Count G. L. de, 282, 289
Bukovina, 318

357

EUROPE
IN
1789

NORWAY

SCOTLAND

NORTH

IRELAND

SEA

DENMARK

ENGLAND

UNITED PROVINCES

Bremen H

Verden KIN

AUSTRIAN NETHERLANDS

SAXO

Seine

Rhine

LORRAINE

BO

Loire

ALSACE

BAVARIA

FRANCE

SWITZERLAND

TYROL

ES

PIEDMONT

M

VENETIAN REPUBLIC

P

Ebro

R

G

TUSCANY

PAPA
STATE

PORTUGAL

Tagus

S P A I N

CORSICA
(to France)

SARDINIA

M E D I T E R R

MILES 100 0 200 400 600 MILES